Florida A&M University, Tallahassee
Florida Atlantic University, Boca Raton
Florida Gulf Coast University, Ft. Myers
Florida International University, Miami
Florida State University, Tallahassee
University of Central Florida, Orlando
University of Florida, Gainesville
University of North Florida, Jacksonville
University of South Florida, Tampa
University of West Florida, Pensacola

The Social Transformation
of Eighteenth-Century Cuba

Sherry Johnson

University Press of Florida

Gainesville · Tallahassee · Tampa · Boca Raton

Pensacola · Orlando · Miami · Jacksonville · Ft. Myers

First cloth printing, 2001
First paperback printing, 2004

The maps on pages 131 and 133 are reproduced by express permission of
the Ministry of Education, Culture, and Sport, Archivo General de Indias,
Sevilla, Spain.

Library of Congress Cataloging-in-Publication Data
Johnson, Sherry, 1949–
The social transformation of Eighteenth-Century Cuba /
Sherry Johnson.
p. cm.
Includes bibliographical references and index.
ISBN 0-8130-2097-2 (c : acid-free paper); ISBN 0-8130-2800-0 (pbk.)
1. Cuba—Social conditions—18th century. 2. Spaniards—Cuba
—History—18th century. 3. Cuba—Foreign relations—Spain.
4. Spain—Foreign relations—Cuba. 5. Cuba—History—To 1810.
6. Spain—Armed forces—Reorganization. I. Title.
HN203 .J64 2001
306'.097291—dc21   2001048074

The University Press of Florida is the scholarly publishing agency
for the State University System of Florida, comprising Florida A&M
University, Florida Atlantic University, Florida Gulf Coast University,
Florida International University, Florida State University, University of
Central Florida, University of Florida, University of North Florida,
University of South Florida, and University of West Florida.

University Press of Florida
15 Northwest 15th Street
Gainesville, FL 32611–2079
http://www.upf.com

To Mom, Dad, and my girls

Contents

Figures

Acknowledgments

During the completion of this book, I have incurred many debts, both personal and professional. I gratefully acknowledge the financial support I received from several institutions, including the Andrew P. Mellon Foundation; the Lydia Cabrera Award Committee of the Conference on Latin American History; the Jay I. Kislak Foundation; the Social Sciences Research Council; the Department of Education Title VI Program; the Escuela de Estudios Hispanoaméricanos; the Department of History at the University of West Florida; and the Institute for Early Contact Period Studies, the Department of History, and the Center for Latin American Studies at the University of Florida; and likewise acknowledge the continuing support from the Department of History, the Latin American and Caribbean Center, the Cuban Research Institute, the College of Arts and Sciences, the Department of Sponsored Research, and the Florida International Foundation, at Florida International University.

I am also indebted to the various archival repositories and institutions and their professional staff members that made this book possible, including the Archivo General de Indias; the Archivo General de Simancas; the Archivo Histórico Nacional de España; the Biblioteca Nacional de España; the Archivo Nacional de Cuba; the Biblioteca Nacional de Cuba José Martí; the Archivo del Arzobispo de la Habana; the archives in S.M.I. Catedral, Iglesia Espíritu Santo, Iglesia Santo Angel Custodio, and Iglesia Santo Christo del Buen Viaje; the Library of Congress; Houghton Library, Harvard University; the National Archives; the Diocese of St. Augustine Catholic Center; Special Collections and Rare Books of the P. K. Yonge Library of Florida History and the Latin American Collection, both at the University of Florida; and the Special Collections of the Green Library at Florida International University.

I am particularly grateful to the many professionals who over the years have encouraged my interest in Cuba. In Spain, José Hernández Palomo, G.

Douglas Inglis, and Juan Marchena Fernández offered helpful advice. Scholars of Cuba who have generously provided guidance from the inception of this project include Allan J. Kuethe, Franklin W. Knight, Louis A. Pérez, Jr., Jean Stubbs, and K. Lynn Stoner. This work could not have been completed without the cooperation and friendship of many scholars in Cuba, including Jorge Ibarra, Fé Iglesias, Raquel Vinat, Sergia Martínez, Leandro S. Romero, Pedro M. Pruna, and René González. To all of these people, I extend my sincerest thanks.

Former colleagues at the University of Florida to whom I am indebted include Samuel Proctor, the late Darrett A. Rutman, Michael E. Moseley, Eldon R. Turner, the late George E. Pozzetta, John Ingram, Bruce Chappell, and James E. Cusick. Special thanks are extended to Latin Americanists Lyle N. McAlister, David A. Bushnell, Neill Macaulay, Jeffrey A. Needell, David P. Geggus, and John V. Lombardi, all of whom contributed their knowledge and advice. I owe a special debt to Murdo J. and Sheena Mac-Leod. My colleagues at Florida International University, Mark D. Szuchman, N. David Cook, William O. Walker III, Lisandro Pérez, Uva de Aragón, Anthony Maingot, and Damián Fernández, have been a continuous source of support and advice for the past six years, and I am privileged to have studied and worked with these scholars. Without the friendship and support of Bill Waller, Karen Waller, Ron Lewis, Gladys Marel García, Fidel Requiejo, and Karen Y. Morrison, life as an academic would have been difficult, if not impossible.

This book was written for my parents, Edgar W. and Marianne Shelly Johnson. Their love and respect for Cuba and the Cuban people were instilled in me as indelibly as if these sentiments had been genetically transmitted. My father and mother did not live to see this book's completion, so it is to their memory that it is dedicated.

1

Sin Azúcar, No Hay País

(Without Sugar, There Is No Country)

Jealousy, vindictiveness, and betrayal are hardly the celebratory adjectives upon which to craft a national history. Instead, historians responsible for creating national myths prefer to employ positive descriptors such as nationalism and patriotism, which translates into the Cuban variant "cubanidad." Of course, the presentation of one's history in such a way does much to stir the emotions but does little to explain events. Indeed, such rhetoric actually gets in the way in the face of evidence that the Cuban people (*el pueblo*), enshrined as "ever-faithful," became alienated from the royal administration long before they were awarded the dubious designation. The realization that two of the fundamental personalities of the eighteenth century, Luis de Las Casas and Francisco de Arango y Parreño, were directly responsible for that alienation and were not as beloved by their contemporaries as they are by subsequent generations of historians is but one instance where emotion impedes an unbiased evaluation of processes and events.

Passion and politics play a large part in the historiographical place of the island vis-à-vis other areas of the Americas. To date, Cuban history concentrates on political and economic issues. Numerous political narratives examine wars, rebellions, and uprisings and, within that context, are dedicated to celebrating the exploits of a few great men (and, less frequently, their women). Economic studies overwhelmingly concentrate on the spread of sugar cultivation and its impact domestically and internationally. Another problem is that processes in Cuban history are seen in isolation; rarely are external influences considered when evaluating the outcome of events on the island. If society is analyzed at all, it is subsumed by the transcendental importance of politics and the economy, and with few exceptions, Cuban historiography has been held hostage to studies of sugar, slavery, colonialism, and dependence.

This work will break with the standard approach and will explore the significance of a unique social dynamic that began as early as 1763. Most important it will look for relationships between and among the protagonists, for example, between Cuba and Spain, between Cuba and the rest of Spanish America, and between Cuba and the wider Atlantic world. It will further seek to uncover relationships on a personal level, for example, between man and society, between man and the state, and between man and his family. Gender relationships played an important part in forging the unique relationship between Crown and colony, as did the issues of race and class, of honor and fidelity, and of betrayal and vengeance. The most important organizational themes of this book are accommodation, acceptance, and alienation. While political and economic issues cannot be ignored, they will be relevant only insofar as how they influenced the social dynamic between and among groups in Cuban society.

Many of these fundamental social relationships may be explored by beginning with the enigmatic life history of the "man who taught Cuba to think," Félix Varela, one of the most influential intellectuals of the nineteenth century and one of the icons of Cuban history. Most of the 180–plus biographies of Varela and his writings acknowledge that Varela's father, Francisco de Varela, and his grandfather, Bartolomé de Morales, each attained a high rank in the Spanish army. Yet all failed to ask one crucial question: Why did a young man so thoroughly inculcated into the ideological foundations of the Spanish national character reject completely the family tradition of military service? Nationalist hagiography attributes young Varela's decision to enter the Seminary of San Carlos and pursue a religious calling to his religious fervor. No analysis considers that a crisis of epic proportions must have occurred for a youth to reject completely the honorable way of life that his grandfather, father, and uncles had pursued. The crisis that ultimately manifested itself in the life decisions of Varela grew out of processes set in motion in Cuba in the century before. This work will delve into the development of and success and crisis in Cuban society from the mid eighteenth century through the early nineteenth century to provide answers to the enigma.

To understand the likewise enigmatic colonial roots of Cuban identity is to recognize that Cuba's place in Atlantic history in the second half of the eighteenth century is remarkably different from what scholars have long believed. To begin with, a century and a half of viewing Cuban history through the refractive prism of sugar, slavery, and St. Domingue must be discarded. For Havana in particular, and for the island of Cuba in general, significant social and spatial change occurred between 1763 and 1800, not because of sugar, but rather from peninsular immigration to Cuba as a result of military reform after 1763. Census data combined with parish records demonstrating explosive population increase in and around the city uphold this hypothesis, and reports of military officials confirm that neither Havana nor Cuba was the same place in 1800 that it had been in 1762. Many questions arose: How and why had such change occurred? More important, to what extent did immigration affect Cuba's society? What was the significance of such social change in Cuba compared with other areas of Spanish America or Spain? What was the perception of Cuban Creole society within the wider imperial context? Finally, what were the nineteenth-century consequences of late-eighteenth-century processes and perceptions?

Existing historiography provided unsatisfactory or only partial answers to these questions. The argument in favor of population change being caused by the expansion of sugar fails because change began virtually immediately after the return of the city from British control and because population increase occurred in the European and free colored sectors, precisely the groups that would not work on the sugar plantations. Historians who have examined the influence of the military on reform in Cuba, such as Allan J. Kuethe, G. Douglas Inglis, Bibiano Torres Ramírez, Juan Marchena Fernández, and Carmen Gómez, did not place military reforms within two contexts, that of the Spanish empire as a whole and within a close analysis of Cuba's military society as it changed from 1763 through 1808. Simply put, the Cuban case was unique, and understanding its ramifications demanded rethinking dominant paradigms in tandem with relying upon existing works.

Jack P. Greene's *Pursuits of Happiness: The Social Development of Early Modern British Colonies and the Formation of American Culture* provides a theoretical framework to understanding changes in Cuba in comparative perspective. Except for borrowing the adjective "Creole" to describe British North Americans, Greene's work has nothing whatsoever to do with Cuba or Spanish America; nevertheless, it became one of the primary inspirations to understanding how the changes in Cuba might be contextualized within a wider scope of the Spanish Empire. Greene's book argues that, contrary to prevailing historiography, which has maintained that the New England experience should be the model for the development of the United States, it was the southern colonies that were the dominant forces in shaping British American culture and social development.[1] The issues raised regarding the North American colonial experience provoked similar questions about the nature of Cuban history and historiography within a Spanish American context. *Pursuits of Happiness* implicitly suggests how easily the Spanish mainland (New Spain or Peru) could be substituted for New England, how Cuba could be substituted for the Chesapeake, and how fruitful a similar line of inquiry could be if applied to the eighteenth-century Caribbean.

Greene posits four assumptions—products of post–Civil War historiography—that he feels have incorrectly shaped historical interpretations of British American colonial development. First, New England more closely resembled Old England than did the Chesapeake. Second, the "New England . . . experience was normative in Anglo-American development." Third, the New England experience represented a suitable model for the remainder of colonial development. And fourth, New England thought served as the model for a British American historical tradition.[2] Greene compares the colonization of the Chesapeake and New England and determines that it was the Chesapeake, not New England, that more closely resembled Old England. In a tripartite, sequential model for development, Greene proposes a third and final developmental stage that is represented by social replication, as locals, because of their increasing wealth and influence, sought to emulate British society.[3] Indeed, such mental unification created a "psychology of accommodation" between the Chesapeake and the mother country.[4] Greene challenges the assumption of the homogeneity of colonial British America and the unqualified acceptance of all things New English. Indeed, he argues that such acceptance has had a detrimental effect upon North American historiography. Greene feels that the New England colonies were the anomaly within the British colonial world and the Chesapeake and southern colonies more closely resembled Old England; thus, they were more closely tied to the mother country.

While not all of Greene's conclusions are applicable in their entirety, they still offer a comparative framework that may be applied to Cuba within the Spanish American colonial experience. Until recently, the history of Spanish America has been seen from the perspective of the mainland areas, primarily New Spain (Mexico) or Peru. Although some might contend that the mainland experience was normative in Spanish American colonial development and that it represents a suitable model for the remainder of colonial development, a growing body of literature testifies that the conquest-acculturation-assimilation model of development is fraught with contradictions and inconsistencies. Moreover, neither colonial Mexico nor colonial Peru resembled Spain, particularly not in the area of greatest concern to this research, social composition. Although Mexico City did develop as the intellectual center of Spanish America, dominated by a small number of peninsular and Creole families of the elite ranks, the masses of acculturated mestizos and semiacculturated indigenes had little in common with the small white Creole population or the even-smaller group of *peninsulares* sent from Spain to govern the overseas provinces. Moreover, only in the fortress cities of the Caribbean was the reconquest mind-set that glorified military experience and made heroes of those in military service even remotely applicable to the population in general. Greene's central hypothesis that New England was aberrant and the remainder of the British colonies represented the norm cannot be adapted in its entirety, for Cuba cannot be said to represent the normative model in Spanish American colonial development. Nevertheless, the intellectual model and methodological techniques of Greene's work are useful for this study.

The slowness in recognizing the uniqueness of the Caribbean experience stems from the state of the research. The difficulties in working in Cuba notwithstanding, Spanish America as an area of historical inquiry still lags behind the state of scholarship concerning North America and Europe. Even though the focus of much of the early historical research has concentrated upon mainland Spanish America, the work of many generations of historians has been valuable in establishing the institutional and governmental framework of the Spanish colonial system. However, aside from the institutional framework and the imperial context, the differences between the mainland and the Spanish Caribbean are more numerous than the similarities. Put another way, except for the commonalities of culture and governance, Cuba differed significantly from New Spain or Peru. The island's economic structure was different, its function within the imperial system was different, and most important, the structure of Cuba's society was very different from that of the mainland. Thus, in drawing an analogy to Greene's work, we find that Cuba, like the southern British colonies vis-à-vis their northern neighbors, was inherently different from New Spain and Peru. From this realization emerged the central hypotheses of this book: how relevant was the social structure of eighteenth-century Cuba in understanding the enigma of Cuba's loyalty to Spain, and how did changes in the 1790s in conjunction with social realities contribute to the alienation of certain sectors of Cuba's elite?

That Cuba as a whole was distinct from the remainder of Spanish

America has only recently been studied in any systematic way by scholars. A pioneer in such research, Allan J. Kuethe, has shown conclusively that the Cuban response to imperial dictates differed from the responses of the mainland. Particularly in the areas of military reforms and economic concessions, Cuba led the way in being the area where reforms were enacted earliest and with most success.[5] The uniqueness of the Cuban experience is central to the thesis of Jorge I. Domínguez, who maintains that a modernizing Cuban elite realized that their best hope for commercial success and political power was to remain part of the Spanish Empire. Domínguez argues that rather than seeking independence, Cuban Creoles sought to tie the island even more thoroughly to the metropolis to maintain the economic status quo.[6] Other analyses maintain that slavery was the driving force behind Cuba's loyalty and the bourgeois landowning class desired the presence of the Spanish army to protect against slave rebellions, particularly after a successful slave rebellion destroyed the sugar industry in the French colony of St. Domingue after 1791.[7] Such recent interpretations are valuable contributions to understanding the economic motivations for Cuban loyalty, but except for stressing Creole fears of an increasingly black population, no modern analysis examines the processes of social ordering, the instinctive way a community views itself and its hierarchy of people, as a factor in understanding Cuba's loyalty to Spain.

Establishing what contributed to social ordering is particularly pertinent because of issues raised by modernization theory and the transformation of the world economy as a result of the spread of capitalism through international commercial transactions.[8] Modernization and world systems theories are a bit shopworn from having hung in the historians' storefront a bit too long. Yet the position of Cuba within an expanding Atlantic economy is undeniable, and the impact of capitalism, and its economic incarnation, sugar production, on Cuba remains a highly controversial topic. Thus, even though the paradigm may have fallen from grace, it remains relevant insofar as it remains the dominant lens through which to view Cuban history. In spite of growing evidence to the contrary, many historians believe that with the spread of sugar cultivation, particularly after 1789, Cuba's economy—and by association, its society and its collective social values—easily fell prey to encroaching capitalist penetration by British and North American mercantile interests.[9] Along with the acceptance of capitalism as an economic system and integration into a world capitalistic system came the acceptance of the ideology of capitalism, specifically the ideals embodied in individualism and self-government.[10] One subset of modernization theory details the transformation of society from traditional to modern, that is, from one based upon status or prestige deriving from ascribed or inherited criteria to another based upon the importance of class, wherein prestige was inherent in the acquisition of wealth, property, or other forms of capital.[11] However, exposure to and involvement in the world capitalist economy did not necessarily entail the social acceptance of the ideology of capitalism. Regardless of how pervasive the products and purveyors of capitalism were in Cuba, it does not necessarily follow that merchants or a mercantile ideology came to dominate society. Quite the contrary. The purveyors of modern, enlightened ideals—Luis de Las Casas and Francisco de Arango y Parreño—were viewed as negative forces for the island by their contemporaries.

A recent field of inquiry, accommodation theory, helps to explain why the majority of Cuba's free population identified with Spain. Accommodation theory examines the mechanisms through which those in power are able to retain power. In a recent introduction to a collection of essays about identity and empire, Daniel Levine outlined five sets of issues relevant to the new questions being asked: "the meaning of human agency, the impact of capitalism, the nature of resistance, the capacity to form and maintain organizations, and, in methodological terms, concern with linkages and mediations."[12] Such a line of inquiry dovetails well with the "psychology of accommodation" proposed by Greene in evaluating the British North American experience.[13] Of the issues raised by Levine, linkages and mediations between the source of power and local interests, the role of human agency in forming such linkages, and the nature of resistance are germane to this research. Borrowing again from Levine, human agency may be defined as "the conscious efforts of social actors to understand and work on their situations." Human beings appear as active subjects, not as objects: "acting on, if not always prevailing in the situations in which they find themselves."[14]

Accommodation theory seeks answers within a social framework, and perhaps the hardest task for social historians is to see a past society as it saw itself. Central to the question is the issue of status and ethnicity, and understanding the composition of Cuba's population, expressed in many censuses, lies at the heart of the issue. Historical analyses of Cuba's population growth abound and share two characteristics: all reiterate the growth in population after 1774, the date of the first "official" census, and all begin and end their analysis within the conceptual framework of "sugar determinism," that is, in anticipation of the sugar boom.[15] Most historical analyses begin with the 1774 population figures, compiled before the boom and for a much different purpose; the preconceived ending lies sometime in the nineteenth century after unrestricted slave imports did alter the population composition significantly. Virtually all historical analyses fail to consider that in 1763—or 1792, or 1813 for that matter—Cuba's inhabitants, quite correctly, saw themselves as being predominantly European, therefore, phenotypically and/or "legally" white.[16] In this, Cuba was significantly different from other areas of Hispanic America and from other islands of the Caribbean. While Cubans were well aware of the danger of slave rebellions, even in 1792 the spectre of an independent Haiti was a decade in the future. Cubans had no way of knowing that the slave rebellion on the neighboring island would degenerate into a racial war and that multinational attempts to reconquer St. Domingue would prove unsuccessful. Additionally, it is anachronistic to suppose that Habaneros in 1763 anticipated the population changes associated with the sugar boom thirty years in the future or the even more remote increase in slave importations in the nineteenth century. Their frame of reference could only have been the "here and now" of the Spanish Empire in 1763. Unlike Mexico City or Lima, Havana was not "an island of white faces in a sea of brown."[17] The differences were obvious to royal officials, evidenced in a report sent from the intendant of Upper Peru, Francisco de Viedma, to minister of the Indies, José de Gálvez in 1784: "How can we possibly appoint to the office of subdelegate people who do not even know who their fathers are?"[18] When Habaneros asked themselves who were their equals in the Spanish Empire, they did not look toward the majority of mainland Spanish America's mestizo and Indian masses. Because of the Spanish Empire's hierarchical social structure, even the lowliest white *veguero* (tobacco farmer) on the island enjoyed elevated prestige over persons of color elsewhere in Spanish America.

Another fundamental concern of this book is evaluating whether and to what degree reform and accommodation extended to the population of color. This task was complicated in the light of a recent trend that emphasizes resistance and rebellion rather than accommodation. Many historians puzzled over why Cuba experienced relatively little unrest in the black population, especially since the uprising in neighboring St. Domingue in 1791 was so close and was felt so deeply on the island.[19] Several reasons immediately stand out. The first is demographic. Free coloreds constituted only a minority (15 percent) of Cuba's free population, and slaves, while numerous (30–40 percent), did not equal or surpass the free component until the mid-nineteenth century. A second reason was that Cuba was an almost totally militarized society, and the opportunity for a successful rebellion was therefore limited.[20] Yet the factors contributing to the lack of rebellion in Cuba weigh as heavily in favor of accommodation as they do in favor of repression. Just as the population of European descent occupied a privileged position within the Spanish Empire as a whole, so, too, Cuba's population of African descent were privileged, not just within the Spanish Empire but also within a wider Caribbean context. To begin with, plantation slavery in service to sugar production had not yet become widespread in Cuba, certainly not in comparison to St. Domingue or Jamaica, so most of Cuba's slaves were not subject to the dehumanizing experience of the *ingenio* (sugar plantation).[21] Instead, they were engaged in urban occupations or on smallholdings in the countryside. In addition, the majority of the island's free colored population lived in Havana, where most of the male heads of household served in the militia. Thus, when Cuba's free coloreds also asked themselves who were their peers, they did not look to people of African descent on other islands of the Caribbean or the mestizo masses in Latin America. They, too, thought of themselves as privileged because of the unique status they enjoyed.

It has become increasingly evident, therefore, that rebellion theories are only marginally applicable to race relations in Cuba even into the early nineteenth century. Rather than seeking rebellion and resistance where little to none existed, this study turns to a more traditional body of scholarship. Nearly a generation ago, Herbert S. Klein proposed that the circumstances of the population of color in Cuba were unique, especially with regard to their legal protection under Spanish law, their access to freedom, and their access to status via militia service.[22] Studies by Verena Martínez-Alier and by Kuethe demonstrate that the free colored population of Cuba distanced itself from the slave population, a conclusion that is buttressed by a literary tradition exemplified by Cirilo Villaverde's classic novel, *Cecilia Valdés*.[23] Pedro Deschamps Chapeaux elaborated upon many of the points raised by Klein in his work about nineteenth-century Havana.[24] Recent works support this established body of scholarship. Ann Twinam's work on status and illegitimacy throughout Spanish America makes clear that, depending upon time, place, and circumstances, the "stain" of being of mixed blood or illegitimate birth was not insurmountable.[25] The life histories of Cuba's free and freed colored community compare favorably to the positive interpretation offered by Jane G. Landers's study of Spanish Florida for the same period.[26] Finally, an important new book by Ada Ferrer establishes that the virulent racism among the races in Cuba did not evolve until the late nineteenth century, after both slavery and Spanish dominion had ended.[27]

Thus, rather than stressing differences, this book will view Cuba's free society as the sum of its parts rather than as individual pieces. It will address the complex interplay between metropolitan desires and the accommodation of the many groups representing varied Creole interests, all set within the temporal framework of the post-1763 military reforms. The evidence for human agency is inferred from the behavior on the part of those involved. Military retirees, when offered the choice of returning to Spain or remaining in Cuba, elected to remain on the island. Agency on the part of peninsular officers and soldiers is evident in their choice to transfer to the many regiments created in the 1770s and 1780s and to promote their sons into service on the island. Marriage is seen as a contractually defined obligation undertaken in the interest of advancing the family's well-being by rational human beings. The Crown spent much time and effort promulgating laws designed to mold society into what it thought should be the proper social order. Yet by its own acknowledgment, it implicitly sent the message to Cubans that they were worthy of being part of the new imperial hierarchy. Lastly, when agency and accommodation were no longer a goal of the royal government, the attitude of the people changed from acceptance to resistance and rebellion.

What, then, was the social, economic, and political reality of eighteenth-century Havana? During the British occupation, Havana's residents had enjoyed their ability to purchase coveted consumer goods from the British merchants that had descended upon the city. With the return of Spanish rule, the government had instituted a degree of *comercio libre,* or free trade, which, while not the economic freedom of unrestricted laissez-faire, was a vast improvement over the previous system. The rebuilding of Havana and its fortifications pumped enormous quantities of money into Havana's economy, creating an economic prosperity that was beneficial to almost all. While it appeared that many landholders close to the city would lose their land because of royal confiscations for rebuilding the city wall and the Campo de Marte, eventually many were compensated for their losses and thus were co-opted into the system. Other families profited from the growing economy by transforming their suburban garden tracts into rental lots to accommodate the growing population.

The social reality of Havana's free society after 1763 reflected the changes wrought by military reform. When war with Great Britain was imminent in the 1770s, Habaneros saw twelve battalions of troops sent from Spain garrisoned in their midst. At least a third of the eligible white civilian heads of household interacted with the permanent military establishment by becoming militia members, where they came in contact with many peninsular officers. What better way to gauge a man's worth than to serve with him in defending one's home? Two-thirds of the free colored heads of household enjoyed a measure of social prestige by similarly becoming militia members. The families of militia members were also co-opted into the military establishment by the extension of the *fuero militar,* or military privilege, to all militia members. Countless others who did not serve in the militia benefited from the military presence by enjoying the economic presence of several military regiments and naval squadrons in Havana. Havana's families encouraged their daughters to marry Spanish arrivals, because to do so would increase their family's prestige, not to mention ensure a daughter's future financial security if the newcomer happened to be a military member. Throughout the period in question, the social worth of no less than one-third of Havana's white population was validated and revalidated by continual intermarriage with Spanish-born newcomers. For their part, newly arrived Spanish men could be reasonably certain of the purity of lineage of their white, Creole brides, something that could be less certain in New Spain, New Granada, or Peru. Thus, when eighteenth-century Habaneros asked themselves who they were or with whom were they linked by kinship and *compadrazgo* (symbolic kinship ties), their response would have included tangible linkages to peninsulares and to Spain.

Proceeding within the working hypothesis that Cuba was inherently different from the mainland, and within the theoretical framework of accommodation theory, several additional historiographical traditions provide models for this research. The first and most important concerns the impact of the Bourbon reforms upon Cuba. The catalyst for a change in metropolitan thinking was the capitulation of Havana in 1762 as part of the crushing defeat suffered by Spain and her French cousins during the Seven Years' War. Considerable historical attention has been directed toward the siege and capture of the city and the subsequent reforms that were gradually implemented in Cuba and throughout Spanish America in the following decades.[28] Historians' opinions diverge, however, when evaluating the scope, efficacy, and particularly the consequences of reform measures instituted by the Spanish Bourbon monarchs, Charles III (1759–1788), and his son, Charles IV (1788–1808).[29] The Bourbon enlightened despots and their advisers sought to implement administrative, military, fiscal, and commercial reforms, usually at the expense of Creoles, a process that one historian has likened to a "second Conquest."[30] Such reforms were implemented earliest in Cuba, and the island became a "laboratory for reform," where new ideas were tried and were accepted or rejected before being extended to other areas.[31] Consequently the successful reorganization of Cuba's administration, fiscal policy, and military structure became a model for similar reforms in other areas. Cuba was unique, however, in the ability of the monarchy and Creole elite to reach an accommodation of interest in the fiscal, administrative, and military spheres.[32]

The most pertinent historiographical tradition within the body of Bourbon reforms literature argues that one reason why reforms were unsuccessful was that Spanish America lacked a military tradition. Accordingly, military reforms were superimposed upon a population unaccustomed to military service and were exacerbated by fiscal and administrative measures designed to extract greater amounts of revenue by an increasing number of incorruptible outsiders.[33] Studies of New Spain, New Granada, and Peru have found that military reforms were generally unsuccessful for a variety of reasons. One original contributor to the debate, Lyle N. McAlister, argues that reforms implemented in New Spain served to undermine the existing social order by breaking down the *sistema de castas* while simultaneously providing military training to large numbers of Creoles. The behavior of peninsular officers, moreover, alienated large segments of the Creole population and ultimately propelled the colony toward independence.[34] Several of McAlister's students have continued his tradition by examining the impact of military reform elsewhere in Spanish America. For example, studies of the armies of Peru and New Granada have found that military reforms were extremely difficult (if not impossible) to accomplish in those areas.[35] On the other hand, Christon A. Archer addressed the nature of the Spanish army within New Spain's society. Archer's argument maintained that regardless of the extension of privileges or the increased prestige military service brought to participants, Spanish armies were seen by the populace as unwelcome intruders. Popular distaste for peninsulars was reciprocated by the officials themselves, who viewed service in Mexico and everything Creole with equal disdain. To the populace in general, military service itself was to be avoided at all costs.[36] Jorge Domínguez's work documented the vast social and economic differences between Mexico, Chile, Venezuela, and Cuba. Domínguez concluded that in places where a large majority of the population did not benefit from an increased military presence, the Spanish army was viewed as an army of occupation sent to enforce unwelcome and unfair taxation. In such areas, Bourbon reform measures were actively resisted by Creoles at all social levels.[37]

Cuba, however, was the exception. As Kuethe argues, "Military reform was a success" and in Cuba represented the greatest success of all areas of Spanish America.[38] The accommodation process between metropolitan interests and the Creole elite, whom Kuethe defines as being mostly planters, worked in many complementary ways. The royal goals of transferring to Creoles the responsibility for the island's defense and the concomitant financial burden of such a defense were accomplished while, at the same time, elites were co-opted into the royal fold. By 1781, the competence of local militias allowed regular troops to take the offensive to lay siege to and capture Pensacola, while Cuban militia units remained on the island to protect against another British invasion. By late century, local elites were able to control the officer corps in both the regular and militia forces and, through such service and the payment of generous sums of money, were rewarded with titles and positions at court. While accepting a greater tax burden, members of the Cuban elite lobbied for and received special commercial privileges including comercio libre with select Spanish ports in 1765 and unrestricted slave imports in 1789 accompanied by the non-promulgation of a revised slave treatment code.[39] Moreover, many historians agree that military expenditures fueled the expansion of Cuba's economy that contributed to the sugar boom and ultimately made Cuba profitable for the Crown.[40] Although the island's elites diversified their economic bases, during the height of military activity Cuba's governors and treasury officials never refused the *situado* (subsidy) money sent from Mexico. Thus, although the military reforms enacted in Cuba were the most widespread and the most stringent, they did not lead to the alienation of the local population as they had in other areas of Spanish America. Moreover, the degree of militarization did not diminish in the wake of 1763; instead, even greater numbers of the civilian population became indoctrinated with military values of loyalty and fidelity, and in turn they enjoyed the social and economic benefits of having a garrison in their midst. Such militarization only fueled the Spanish mentality embodied in the cultural baggage of the Reconquest.

Proceeding from the important theoretical and historiographical traditions, several bodies of scholarly thought inform the individual chapters of this work. In chapter 2, I introduce one of the most important protagonists of this work, Bartolomé de Morales, and I use him and the course of his professional career and personal life to exemplify the social dimension of reform. Through Morales's life, this book argues that the basis for Cuba's population growth from 1763 through 1795 came from the immigration of significant numbers of peninsular men. The arrival of several battalions of troops and the expansion of the royal bureaucracy on the island were the reasons why so many Spanish males journeyed to Cuba. More important, between 1763 and 1792, not only did such immigrants become the reason for an increase in population numbers, their arrival explains why the population of Havana remained predominantly European (*español*) through 1796. Descriptive contemporary accounts of the island and a body of literature regarding immigration to Spanish America in general and to Cuba in particular forms the historiographical framework for chapter 2.[41]

Chapters 3 and 4 examine in detail the social changes that the arrival of large numbers of *peninsular* military units entailed. Chapter 3 introduces the thesis that the increase in population between 1763 and 1778 was attributable to the assignment of military units to the island and presents evidence that the resettlement of military retirees was part of a deliberate plan as part of Spain's reform package. Ordinary soldiers from the rank and file were intended to be transported and resettled in created communities close to major population centers as part of Bourbon reformers' resettlement schemes. Upon retirement or separation these men engaged in petty agricultural production for the city and the garrison rather than in sugar cultivation. In addition to ordinary men, many peninsular officers chose to remain in Cuba. Not only did the officer corps become permanently assigned to the island; more important, they saw remaining in Cuba as their best chance for social and professional advancement. That they arranged for their sons to follow in their footsteps and enter the military and remain in Cuba—as opposed to using their influence to have their sons assigned to Spain or Mexico—speaks volumes to the way such men viewed the opportunities in military service in different parts of Spanish America. Equally important was the realization that Caribbean service was equivalent to service in Spain. Without question, the disastrous failed invasion attempt of Algeria (Argel) in North Africa in 1775 altered radically how service in the Caribbean was viewed. Algeria precipitated the fall from power of Alejandro O'Reilly and his followers, especially Luis de Las Casas, and the concomitant ascendance of the Gálvez family. The period when the Gálvez family dominated Spanish imperial life (1775–88) marked the period in which Caribbean service was tanta-mount to acceptance and prestige throughout the Spanish Empire.

The permanent assignment and retirement of many soldiers form only part of the supporting evidence for the hypothesis that military reforms significantly affected Havana's society. The argument for a significant so-cial transformation is advanced in chapter 5 by an analysis of the patterns of intermarriage between *peninsulares* and Creoles. The historiographical tradition detailing the process of migration in search of a mate is compara-tively recent yet already well studied.[42] An extensive body of literature defines the juridical foundations of marriage and the contractual nature of choosing a mate,[43] and yet other studies identify the family as the corner-stone of patriarchal society.[44] The changes implemented by the promulga-tion of the Real Pragmática sobre Matrimonios of 1776 illuminate the de-sire of the Crown to interfere in colonial society. Beginning with the works of Richard Konetzke, many studies of how such legislation was imple-mented in other areas of Spanish America form a comparative framework to examine the processes and consequences of peninsular-Creole intermar-riage in Havana.[45] Yet the processes in Havana go far beyond interference in civil society. Since Havana was so thoroughly militarized, royal interfer-ence began at an earlier date than elsewhere and was more wide-reaching simply because so many segments of the city's society fell directly or indi-rectly under military scrutiny.

Chapters 6 and 7 examine the consequences of the period when the carefully crafted military society began to fall apart. Chapter 6 describes in detail the governorship of Luis de Las Casas (1790–96), "a son of the Span-ish Enlightenment and a lover of novelties. . . . the perfect governor [to promote] an economic bonanza."[46] While acknowledging that he fostered the development of a small and privileged group of commercial interests, this chapter delves deeper into Cuban society to understand how his favor-itism toward sugar planters and Basque merchants alienated the Cuban people. The increasing resistance on the part of smallholders in the coun-tryside to Las Casas's demands that they contribute to agricultural devel-opment by working on the roads and bridges led to open rebellion by 1794–95. By the end of his term, the opinion of "el pueblo" was that "the island had never had a worse governor than Las Casas."[47] More important, in the face of open rebellion in the countryside, the captain general was powerless to contain the discontent because he also had alienated the mili-tary, who served as the peacekeeping force on the island. Chapter 7 demon-strates that the members of Cuba's military society were hurt by Las

Casas's reforms, which amounted to a purge the magnitude to which Cuba had not experienced since the arrival of Alejandro O'Reilly thirty years previous. While Habaneros might have acknowledged that in 1763 they were guilty of failing to defend the island from enemy attack, no such claim could be sustained by 1794, especially in the context of the failure of reforms elsewhere in Spanish America and the military disasters in Africa and Europe. Las Casas's vindictive and arbitrary administration, whose venom was felt from the lowliest widows and orphans to the highest levels in the Cuban military establishment, nearly destroyed the accommodation between Crown and colony. Motivated by Bourbon parsimony and personal jealousy, Las Casas represented the worst example of the capriciousness and incompetence of Charles IV and Manuel de Godoy. Chapter 8 carries the consequences of the purge and the increasing alienation of Cuban society to their conclusion in the nineteenth century. It ties together the vindictiveness of Las Casas against the family of Bartolomé de Morales and others into the reformist ideology of the nineteenth century through the experiences of his grandson, Félix Varela. It revisits one of the enigmas in Cuban history, the failed attempt on the part of Francisco de Arango in 1808 to form a Junta Superior to govern the island. This chapter demonstrates how enmity born of the factionalism and vengeance in the 1790s replicated itself in resistance to the Arango faction in 1808. Lastly, the book concludes by demonstrating how social polarization transformed itself into the political ideology of the disciples of Félix Varela after the Spanish constitutional debacle of 1820–23.

In the wake of the military reform, virtually all segments of Cuba's free society understood the seriousness with which the Spanish Crown addressed the problems of the island. With perhaps the exception of slaves, almost all benefited from the increased military presence. Upper- and mid-level landowners profited from an economy that grew as military expenditures increased. Professional military members enjoyed the prestige of being peninsular in a Creole world and the potential for career advancement by remaining on the island. Ordinary soldiers served their tours of duty and were allowed to separate from service on the island, where, as artisans and tradesmen, they could capitalize upon the economic prosperity. Career enlisted men retired with their families and their pensions, thereby benefiting the government by being inculcated with the ethos of military life.

Immigration contributed to population increase and social change, but intermarriage sealed the social contract between the peninsular and Creole world. By allowing a significant degree of intermarriage between Creoles and peninsulars, the Spanish monarchy implicitly sent the message that Cuba's families were worthy—perhaps favored—citizens of the Spanish Empire. The admission was particularly gratifying in the wake of legislation that stated the opposite. For Creole families so favored, the visible statement of their social worthiness was an important factor in their acceptance of the Spanish regime. When that social contract broke down, Cuban Creoles entered the nineteenth century with deeply mixed feelings. On the one hand, they were bewildered and hurt by their having been betrayed by their monarch—a mark of his ineptness and ingratitude. On the other hand, the tradition of loyalty and military glorification was too strong to abandon, especially since the alternative—sugar cultivation and the importation of increasing numbers of African slaves—was equally unacceptable. Cuba's nineteenth-century intellectual movements and its increasingly alienated Creole population, thus, drew their legacy from the success and failure of Bourbon policies from the century before.

Wherever I May Serve His Majesty Best

On a pleasant December day in late 1764, a ship ending its transatlantic voyage approached Havana from the west following the north coast of the island. Many travelers journeying to Spanish America shared the rail, but few would impact the course of Cuban history as much as did one young lieutenant from the Regiment of Navarre, Bartolomé de Morales.[1] Born in Ciudad Algeciras on the southern coast of Spain, he had enlisted in military service in 1751 at age sixteen. Although he began his military career as an ordinary soldier, Morales had passed quickly from the enlisted ranks. Like many of his talented peers, he had been selected for commissioning as a lieutenant in 1763. At age twenty-nine, after serving in Ceuta and the Portuguese campaign, he transferred to Havana with the Regiment of Navarre as part of the *refuerzo* (reinforcement) troops.[2] Among the thousands of men who would come to Cuba all hoping "to make America,"[3] he would participate directly in implementing the reforms intended to create a loyal population on the island. Perhaps like none other, Morales's life course would epitomize the twin processes of militarization and social integration that transformed the island forever.

By 1764, the city of Havana that beckoned Lieutenant Morales already had celebrated its 250th year of existence. Originally established on the southern coast of the island in 1511, San Cristóbal de la Havana was relocated to its present location in 1519.[4] In 1634, the city had been granted the title "Key to the New World" because of its strategic position guarding the sea-lanes that exited the Caribbean. Taking advantage of its magnificent, bottle-shaped natural harbor, the prevailing winds, and the Gulf Stream, which flows through the Florida Straits, ships laden with treasure and sailing from such mainland ports as Portobelo in Panama and Vera Cruz in Mexico united and revictualed in Havana, and set out on their return journey to Spain. However, until its shocking fall to British forces, the city did not enjoy the royal attention lavished upon more prosperous cities, such as the mining centers of Mexico and Peru.[5] Once the island cycle of exploration, settlement, and exploitation of available mineral resources and Indian labor in the early sixteenth century had run its course, Cuba and the surrounding islands were almost abandoned. By mid-century, the indigenous population had been virtually eliminated by the combined effects of conquest, disease, and overwork, a demographic disaster from which it never recovered.[6] Because no other European nation rose to challenge Spain's dominance in the Caribbean, the city's defenses were left to ill-led and ill-paid local militias. Except for a poorly located fortification on the western side of the city, the town was virtually unguarded.[7]

Changes in European political alliances in the mid sixteenth century sent French, English, and Dutch "raiders, traders and invaders" to the Caribbean to challenge Spain's hegemony.[8] In 1555, French corsair Jacques Sores sacked Havana, prompting the Spanish Crown to institute the first series of reforms in its defense policy. From a policy of neglect, Spain transformed the Caribbean basin by erecting a string of fortifications designed to repel outsider challenges to her dominance, and Havana became the nexus of Spanish power.[9] The Spanish navy, the Armada de Barlovento, was assigned to the area to protect trade and treasure routes, and a royal order mandating a *flota* (convoy) was issued in 1561.[10] After expelling foreign interlopers from Spanish territories and establishing permanent settlements on the North American mainland at St. Augustine and Santa Elena to protect the homebound treasure fleet, Pedro Menéndez de Avilés was named royal governor of the island.[11] As part of a comprehensive defense plan, Menéndez ordered construction to begin on Havana's famed fortifications, efforts that accelerated in the 1590s under the direction of engineer Juan Bautista Antonelli. On the western perimeter construction began on impregnable walls designed to encircle the city, six feet thick and fourteen feet high, punctuated by gates at each end and near the center.[12] The most impressive structure by far, however, was the Castillo del Morro, which perched upon a promontory and guarded the entry to Havana's harbor from the east. After 1570, subsidies to pay for the increased defense spending arrived from Mexico. Although costly, such reforms were successful. The city was bypassed by English corsair Francis Drake in 1586 in favor of more easily attained prizes in Nombre de Dios and Cartagena de Indias, and for nearly two centuries afterward, Havana was considered to be impregnable by her enemies.[13] Thus, before ever setting foot on Cuban soil, Morales was confronted by topographic features that dominated the city's life: the sea, the wall, and the forts that symbolized the military orientation of Havana's government, economy, society, and culture.

Now only a half mile out, Lieutenant Morales saw the unmistakable outline of El Morro and the features of the coastline. To the west of the city, outside the impregnable walls, lay a friendly hinterland charged with providing provisions to the city. Small clusters of houses marked the location of adjacent barrios, Nuestra Señora de Guadalupe and Jesús, María, y José, or further in the distance even smaller hamlets such as San Miguel del Padrón, Santiago de las Vegas, and Wajay. Rising further to the west, beyond the Chorrera River, the Loma (hill) de Aróstegui looked down upon the town from a distance of two miles. The large expanse of land at the top was the domain of Martín de Aróstegui, the director of the Havana monopoly company founded in 1740, and his brother Martín Estéban, a captain of the mounted dragoons who had been lieutenant governor of Puerto Príncipe.[14] A twinge of shame mixed with anger struck Morales as he recalled that the hill was the site where British forces were able to land one contingent in 1762. Between the Loma de Aróstegui and the town, two watchtowers, La Chorrera and San Lázaro, had proven ineffective in sounding an alarm to prevent the enemy landing.[15]

As yet the suburbs did not intrude upon the unmistakable predominance of the city over its hinterland.[16] As if to reinforce the dichotomy between rural and urban life, a cleared parade and military practice ground, the Campo de Marte formed an effective line of demarcation, and beyond the Campo de Marte thick underbrush impeded travel except on a few roads leading to the west.[17] Rural folk from small hamlets followed the roads into town to sell the products of their farms, to marry, to have their children baptized, or simply to catch up on the latest news brought by the many vessels in port. To the east of Havana, across the bay, the sanctuary of Nuestra Señora de Regla, clearly visible to the south, housed approximately 117 friars and 20 families.[18] The *villa* (town) of Guanabacoa, home to nearly 6,000 persons, peeked out from behind the Loma del Indio, so named because the town was a haven for indigenous visitors and immigrants since its designation as a site to consolidate and congregate the declining indigenous population in the sixteenth century.[19] Even farther still, the watchtower at the mouth of the Cojímar River stood guard over the coastline that stretched toward Matanzas, the closest port to the east.[20] Like their rural counterparts from the west, farm families from the eastern villages rowed across the bay, disembarking at the Muelle de la Luz, or walked the long way around, drawn by the very cosmopolitanism of the city.[21]

Like most Spanish American cities, Havana was laid out in a grid pattern. It occupied an area extending approximately one mile north-to-south and a half-mile east-to-west. To the east, north, and south lay water—the famed harbor, which dominated most aspects of the city's defense and commercial activity.[22] To facilitate political administration the city was divided into two sections, or *cuarteles,* Campeche at the southern end of the city, named for *indios* (Indians) and mestizos from New Spain, who in the sixteenth century had made that area their home. The northern portion of the city was officially named the Cuartel de la Punta but was known locally and colloquially as Cangrejos for the thousands of land crabs that shared the swampy area with the human residents.[23] Ecclesiastical boundaries differed from the political boundaries but slightly. The northwestern quarter of the city was occupied by Parroquia (Parish) Santo Angel del Custodio, established in 1693, and made famous in the nineteenth century by Cirilo Villaverde in his novel *Cecilia Valdés, o la loma del Angel.*[24] Santo Angel's population contained many military members housed in the Cuartel de Artillería or its successor, constructed in 1789, the Cuartel de las Milicias.[25]

Directly adjacent and south of Parroquia Angel was Parroquia Santo Cristo del Buen Viaje. Its parish church marked the westernmost terminus of Calle de la Amargura, the street that divided the city into northern and southern sections. However, the ecclesiastical boundaries of Parroquia Santo Cristo itself overlapped the official boundaries into the southern portion of the city. Dating from 1694, Santo Cristo was closest to the primary city gate, the Puerta de la Tierra, and was one of the busiest parishes in terms of pedestrian and vehicular traffic moving in and out of the city. Because of its proximity to the ever-expanding hinterlands, by the first decade of the nineteenth century a market was officially established in its plaza. On market days rural inhabitants walked through the twin arches of the primary gate bringing their produce into town to sell.[26] To the east of Parroquias Angel and Santo Cristo lay the Parroquia Mayor, the oldest and most affluent of the city's parishes. The Parroquia Mayor, established in the sixteenth century and upgraded to cathedral status in 1788, catered to most of the city's wealthy families, whose houses, like the church, were located close to the Plaza Mayor (major plaza) near the governor's residence, the Castillo de la Fuerza, Havana's first fortification, and the customhouse.[27] At the far southern end of the city, the priests of Parroquia Espíritu Santo, the poorest of the city's parishes (dating from the 1630s), were charged with ministering to the 11,000 impoverished souls who were packed tightly within the confines of the Barrio de Campeche. Most of the parish was home to marginal members of Havana's society, but a few square blocks of Espíritu Santo immediately south of the Parroquia Mayor extending inland from the bay was considered part of the *zona noble* (noble zone) and housed affluent families. For the most part, however, the southern portion of the city was known for its taverns, gaming houses, and houses of ill repute, a distinction the area could claim well into the twentieth century.[28]

In order to enter Havana harbor, the ship, still under sail, had to traverse a narrow entrance canal, which when threatened by enemy forces, was closed by the raising of a chain boom stretched across its mouth.[29] The still formidable—if no longer impregnable—Castillo del Morro looked down upon all arrivals, and just outside the city walls to the north, the Castillo de la Punta guarded the northern gates of the city. The wall itself loomed over the city's north, west, and south sides, and from its heights unwelcome visitors arriving by sea would be greeted by cannons emplaced within four batteries facing the canal and the bay.[30] Safely inside the harbor, one could see that the continuity of the walls was broken by one small aperture at the end of Calle de Empedrado, where fishermen peddled their wares, and by three wharves: the Muelle de la Luz, used by the rural folk from across the bay; the Muelle de la Factoría, for the use of the royal tobacco monopoly; and the Muelle de la Real Contaduría, the official entry and exit place for passengers and products arriving on the island.[31] Between the wharves, small boats were beached in the sand in places that took their names from prominent families whose houses and commercial establishments flanked the waterfront.[32]

From his position at the rail, the lieutenant could discern the outlines of important buildings, for although not able to rival the architectural splendor of the viceregal capitals of New Spain or Peru, Havana of 1762 held its share of impressive structures. The harbor area was guarded by the ancient Castillo de la Fuerza, the city's first fortification, built in the early sixteenth century and reminiscent of its namesake, a medieval castle with its moat and drawbridge. La Fuerza was a multipurpose building, serving as a barracks, a jail, and the royal governor's residence.[33] Across the Plaza Mayor from the Castillo de la Fuerza was the Aduana (customhouse) and immigration offices, whose representatives descended upon the Muelle de la Contaduría to greet all arriving ships, avid to extract the requisite royal revenues on imports.[34] Rising above the roofs of Havana's private residences, the spires of the four rather modest parish churches rose in sharp contrast with the lavish domes of the eleven well-endowed monasteries

and convents belonging to the regular orders.[35] However, the available urban space was occupied primarily by private residences. The most substantial of these were built of stone quarried on the opposite side of the bay just
below the Cabañas hill and were roofed with tiles, which were made into
their characteristic U shape by molding the wet clay over a man's leg and
laying the tiles in the sun to dry before firing in a kiln.[36] Several of the
residences were two-storied and at least three had three stories, the ground
floor of which often doubled as space for commercial establishments.[37]
Much to the dismay of the authorities, however, some 470 houses (about
14 percent of the city's total) were made of an adobe-like material and
roofed with palm thatch that together was known locally as "guano." Contemporary writers complained that the houses of irresponsible owners de-
tracted from the appearance of the city, yet such structures survived in
spite of repeated prohibitions against the use of guano as a building material within the city limits.[38]

Ringed with hamlets that provided for its needs, Havana was the area's
primary city and dominated the agricultural and maritime hinterland that
stretched throughout the island and across the water to Florida (now ceded
to the British). The island officially came under the jurisdiction of the
Viceroyalty of New Spain, and the senior royal official on the island was
the governor, who also held the title of captain general, indicative of his
dual administrative and military function. The closest rival in terms of
population, Santiago de Cuba, located at the other end of the island, had
been important in the early years of contact, but its influence had diminished as that of Havana had increased. In 1607, the island had been divided
administratively into two jurisdictions, with the governor of Santiago de
Cuba becoming subordinate to the captain general in Havana.[39] The Bish-
opric of Cuba had been established in Santiago de Cuba in 1522 but the
bishop himself lived in Havana most of the time, rarely undertaking the
arduous journey to his official seat. The primary court of appeal was the
Audiencia de Santo Domingo, located on the neighboring island, Hispaniola, to the east.[40]

In light of Havana's being the military, administrative, and religious
center of the Spanish Caribbean, it is not surprising that it was also the
island's population center. Using several sources, a modern-day analysis
estimates that on the eve of the British occupation, approximately 35,000
people lived in Havana and its hinterland—affectionately named "Havana
Campo."[41] Another estimate attributes 60,000 persons to the area. The
first official island-wide census was conducted in 1774 and revealed that

approximately 171,620 people occupied Cuba's 44,028 square miles.[42] A more thorough count conducted in 1778 broke the census down into its component parts—white, free colored, and black slave, and men, women, and children—and produced a more refined total of 40,561 persons in Havana and 41,338 more people in Havana Campo.[43] Regardless of the absolute numbers, two characteristics made Cuba's, and specifically Havana's, population unique: the predominance of persons of European extraction, termed *españoles* or *blancos,* even living in the countryside, and the unbalanced sex ratio in both the white and black populations, with men outnumbering women.

Unlike other areas of Spain's Empire in America or other islands of the Caribbean, Cuba's population of European descent was numerically dominant. While Mexico's and Peru's population distribution was characterized by cities inhabited by españoles and a rural population of mestizos and indios, and on other Caribbean islands the black slave population was numerically dominant, Cuba's urban and rural populations were (or described themselves as and were considered to be) predominantly white. After their precipitous decline in numbers in the sixteenth century, few indigenes survived on the island. Most lived in the eastern part of the island, close to Santiago de Cuba; elsewhere persons of indigenous blood were subsumed into the free population of color, although a small group of persons of indigenous blood lived across the bay in Guanabacoa.[44] Elsewhere in the empire, by the eighteenth century, an elaborate system of social categorization based upon race had developed, while in Cuba, social classification was tripartite, based on status and further limited by race into white, free colored (both mulatto and negro), and slave (also mulatto or negro).[45] The second important characteristic of Havana's population was its unbalanced sex ratio. The census of 1778, which excluded military personnel (whose inclusion would have skewed the distribution even further), demonstrated that white males outnumbered white females in all age cohorts. Free women of color outnumbered their male counterparts within the city limits, but if the population of the surrounding countryside is included in the analysis, the numerical predominance of males over females remains.[46]

For Lieutenant Morales the unbalanced sex ratio would have important personal consequences. Respectable females occupied a privileged position in the marital market, and parents of marriageable daughters enjoyed more flexibility when arranging a suitable marriage. For widows the potential for remarriage was probably greater than elsewhere. Although he arrived with a built-in degree of cachet by being peninsular and military, he still would have much competition when the time came to choose a wife and establish a family. The ability to marry would be further complicated by restrictions on the choice of a marriage partner formulated as a consequence of the reforms of the 1760s. Morales, like thousands of other immigrant men, would marry late in life, after his professional and economic standing had been assured. When he did decide to marry, he contracted marriage with the daughter of a family from Santiago de Cuba, María de Medina.[47] He, in turn, would enjoy the favorable position as the father of a marriageable daughter of impeccable lineage when he arranged the marriage of his daughter, María Josefa Morales y Medina to Francisco de Varela, a young captain who served with him in the Fixed Regiment of Havana.[48]

Morales's position in the royal armies and his peninsular birth guaranteed his status in Cuba's hierarchical, status-conscious society. He would enjoy an advantage in choosing a mate and would marry successfully. Many of his colleagues, however, would not marry at all (a not uncommon occurrence). In such a case, their desire for female companionship would be satisfied by the numerous free women of color who often formed long-term liaisons with white males. In the absence of a free mulatta mistress, white men routinely satisfied their sexual desires with slave women. Either option served to increase the population of color.[49]

Yet, at that instant, the prospect of establishing a family was far from the lieutenant's mind, for the ship was through the entrance canal and inside Havana bay. Now the captain could safely lower the sails as one of the many *guadaños* (rowed pilot boats) hastened to guide the larger vessel through the busy harbor into port.[50] From his position at the rail he could see the Muelle de la Contaduría, crowded with ships unloading cargo and restocking with products to take back to Spain or to other ports in the Indies, such as Vera Cruz or Campeche.[51] Off to one side, a group of soldiers destined to reinforce Havana's garrison lounged in the shade of a building awaiting transfer to one of the several barracks in town. To another side, a ship's captain muttered in English complaining about Havana's market being glutted with British goods. Although the occupation forces had left the city in July 1763, British ships still arrived in Havana harbor—under the pretext of being in distress—to unload their cargoes of contraband.[52] Like most of his peers in the officer corps, Morales was not only literate but, like many of his time, understood several languages; perhaps the Englishman did not realize he could be heard and understood over the noise of the docks.[53] Indeed, the noise level reflected the activity going on all around the waterfront area. Black and mulatto stevedores unloaded products destined for Havana's commercial market, such as wines and brandies from Spain, textiles from the *obrajes* (workhouses) of New Spain (that had to compete with the contraband British textiles on board the English captain's vessel), or cinnamon from Holland arriving via Cádiz, through which all European commerce to and from the Indies was controlled. Others worked to load departing ships with the products of the island: tobacco, whole-leaved or ground into snuff; casks filled with fine white sugar or the less-refined muscovado; dried and salted beef and pork; and hides. The island's newest commercial products for export were beeswax and honey, produced across the bay in Guanabacoa in hives brought to the island by refugees from Florida.[54]

The agricultural products being loaded into ships had been the foundation of Cuba's economy since the sixteenth century. Tobacco was the mainstay of Cuba's economy and was stringently regulated under Spain's mercantilistic system. A Crown monopoly was implemented in 1717 that purchased limited amounts of the crop at controlled prices at terms favorable only to the company.[55] Cattle raising and its subsidiary industries were also important sources of income. Cattle provided fresh meat for the cities, and what could not be consumed immediately was salted or dried for future use. Hides from slaughtered cattle were an additional commercial product, destined for Spain to be crafted into shoes, saddles, and tack.[56] In addition, Havana was the only official port of disembarkation for slaves supplied by the British South Seas Company, whose monopoly, the *asiento*, was gained in 1713 under the terms of the Treaty of Utrecht that ended the War of the Spanish Succession (1702–14).[57] When the contract with the South Seas Company expired in 1739, the asiento was replaced by the Real Compañía de Comercio de la Havana, a Havana-based monopoly financed by a group of investors including Aróstegui, several members of the Havana elite, and the Spanish royal family. The company enjoyed an exclusive privilege to import slaves into the island, to promote the immigration of Canary Island colonists, and to provide food for the presidio in Florida.[58]

Another major source of income was the Real Arsenal, or Royal Shipyard, located outside the city wall. While Havana had long been important for careening and provisioning ships in the flota, and for constructing smaller ships for local commerce, large-scale ship construction had begun only in the first decades of the century after the destruction of the Spanish fleet at Cape Passaro. The city's importance and that of its shipyard, the "pride of Havana," had accelerated in the 1740s, when the Real Compañía accepted the financial responsibility to build ships for the Royal Navy. Moreover, the island had an abundant supply of suitable hardwoods that could be cut only with royal permission. Careening of ships provided employment for significant numbers of men, skilled craftsmen and day laborers alike. Revictualing of the fleet provided income for the hinterlands, and while in port, thousands of sailors needed lodging, food, and entertainment that the citizens of Havana provided.[59]

Although not yet queen of Cuba's economy, sugar ultimately would in the next century become the reigning commercial product of the island. Several current works maintain that military spending in Havana provided an economic boost for the expansion of sugar cultivation and slavery. These works quite correctly argue that the beneficiaries of the militarization of the island were the hyper-elites, that is, Cuba's titled nobility, including planter families who would become the island's sugar magnates and royal governors, and Cuban, British, and North American merchants and slave traders, who profited from the sugar boom after 1792. Some historians argue that the monopolistic regulation on the importation of slaves contributed to a labor shortage and retarded Cuba's ability to grow sugar, a situation that changed during the British occupation, during which time perhaps 10,000 slaves were introduced to the island.[60] Other interpretations (this work included), however, argue that by mid-century Cuba's elites had diversified their economic holdings to include sugar, tobacco, and cattle production to spread the risk amongst many sources of income.[61]

The chronology, enterprise, politics, and social consequences of sugar cultivation have occupied the scholarly efforts of several generations of historians. Historians can neither ignore nor discount the consequences of the sugar boom, given impetus by the Haitian rebellion of 1791, and though they might quibble over the chronology, few scholars doubt that the economic transition to sugar represented a watershed in Cuban history. The issue, however, is tangential to this research. Acknowledging that the spread of sugar would effect important changes in the future, this research seeks an alternative yet complementary interpretation to understand changes in eighteenth-century Cuba to place alongside the important body of scholarship dedicated to perpetuating the myth of the importance of sugar cultivation.

Just on the economic horizon, significant changes were in store for the people of Havana. The Royal Havana Company's monopoly and that of the

Consulado (merchant guild) of Cádiz were soon to be broken by the declaration of a limited degree of free trade. In return for higher but simplified taxation, a proposal under consideration would eliminate the monopolies by opening eight Spanish ports to direct commerce to and from Cuba. The Real Decreto de Comercio Libre, promulgated in October 1765, was the first of a series of fiscal reforms implemented by Charles III and his ministers, including the creation of an intendant system in the Indies to supervise tax collection. The appointment of an intendant for the island was an undisguised attempt to make revenue collection more efficient and profitable, and did away with the previous system of tax farming and its opportunities for graft and corruption. The man destined to be the first intendant of the island, Miguel de Altarriba, would arrive within weeks, in February 1765.[62]

But in late 1764 Havana's citizens were unaware of the future reforms that would grant them a large degree of commercial autonomy, and the lieutenant entered a city bristling with resentment. The Havana Creole oligarchy, representing old, entrenched interests, seethed because they had agreed to—even had suggested and promoted—increased taxation in return for commercial concessions, which, as yet, had not been granted.[63] At the same time, a schism developed among the elite based upon their behavior during the siege and occupation, as it became obvious that Sebastián de Peñalver would become the scapegoat for the imperial wrath while others, particularly Pedro Calvo de la Puerta, would manipulate the confused postwar situation to their advantage.[64] The military establishment was being streamlined under the direction of Field Marshal Alejandro O'Reilly, who had been sent to Cuba specifically to reform and to reorganize the obviously ineffective military structure. Old, infirm, and incompetent soldiers who were still on the payroll were furloughed or forced into retirement, and regular military units had been forced to accept a cut in pay, prompting widespread protests bordering on mutiny.[65] Merchants, always chafing under the restrictive mercantilistic policies of an era long past, were unable to sell their goods in a market still depressed by the oversupply conditions that lingered from the time of the British occupation.[66] The Factoría de Tabacos and the Real Compañía still clung to their monopolies, although prior to the war former governor Juan de Prado had limited the privileges of the Real Compañía by limiting its exclusive right to ship and market tobacco. Slaves were always in demand, and Cuban planters had enjoyed unlimited imports during British occupation. Now they faced a reduction in supply as yet another monopoly contract had been granted to a Basque company. Foodstuffs, too, had risen in cost as the large numbers of troops that had arrived with O'Reilly from 1763 onward forced demand and price up.[67]

As the passengers awaited the launch that would ferry them to the wharf of the Contaduría, the lieutenant had an opportunity to survey his new surroundings. Looking to his left he could see the Muelle de la Factoría, constructed for the use of the two monopoly companies.[68] Barrels loaded with tobacco were being loaded onto ships by a giant wooden crane, La Machina, from which the wharf and the surrounding area took its popular name. The wheel of La Machina was of recent construction, since the old one had been wrecked by the British before leaving, but the wood was already weathering in the sultry tropical climate. Water to run the wheel and for a fountain was supplied by tubes made of mahogany and joined together by copper rings that gleamed green in the sunlight.[69] The lieutenant would learn that the water, a precious commodity, was supplied to the city by a ditch, the Zanja Real (euphemistically termed an aqueduct), from a distance of three miles.[70] During the recent siege, the British army had diverted the city's water supply from the Zanja Real into the bay, which was one important factor contributing to their victory.[71] Indicative of how vital the Zanja Real was to the city, strict regulations prohibited bathing in or the watering of livestock in the ditch itself or in the city fountains.[72] Because the slaughterhouse needed copious amounts of water to process the meat, the *ayuntamiento* (town council) of Havana extracted a tax of three *reales* per head of cattle and one per hog that entered the city for slaughter, which yielded around 70,000 *reales* annually for the aqueduct's upkeep.[73] The most enterprising of Havana's families, however, collected rainwater in cisterns for daily use.[74]

The military contingent disembarked as a group while to one side a dour-faced immigration official waited for the civilian passengers. Morales watched pityingly as a long line formed while the official inspected the civilians' paperwork with more than the customary slowness. The delay was puzzling, since the ship had sailed from Spain and all passengers were required to carry a special license necessary to emigrate to Spain's American colonies.[75] Only a very few foreigners were allowed into Spanish territory, and they needed particular naturalization papers to enter and to remain permanently in the Indies. The civilians became even more restless when the reasons for the delay became apparent: one of the new arrivals had failed to offer the official an amount of money, a *propina*, or tip, designed to facilitate the speedy approval of his visa. Apparently the prohibition on officials' accepting bribes to process paperwork enacted during the British occupation had been quickly discarded once Spanish rule returned to the island.[76] Old habits die hard, thought the lieutenant, and when the required propina appeared, the remaining passengers were approved instantaneously for entry into the city.

Once on land, several fresh-faced youths from Havana's Noble Corps of Cadets waited to escort the arriving officers and soldiers to their barracks in town. Unlike the majority, who would be lodged in the barracks until other arrangements could be made, Morales had come prepared with the name of authorized lodgings on Calle Empedrado that were close to La Fuerza and the public baths on Calle Tejadillo. The boardinghouse had been recommended prior to his departure and was run by the widow of a man who originated from his home province in Spain. Although a new postal system between the Spanish port of La Coruña and Havana had been implemented only a few months previously,[77] Morales carried several letters to deliver to persons in Cuba, including a letter of introduction to the proprietress from her sister in Cádiz. At his request, one of the cadets hailed a waiting carriage, a curious contraption with overly large wheels, known locally as a *volante* and drawn by a single horse or mule, for the short ride through the dusty narrow streets. Luckily it was not the rainy season or the transit from the docks through the city would have been more difficult, the rain turning the city streets into quagmires. Indeed, the day was bright and sunny, and as the lieutenant looked down the side streets he could see shop owners pulling out awnings to shade the storefronts from the tropical sun that even in December could be intense.[78]

Upon leaving the wharf, the mulatto driver turned north and crossed the primary square, the Plaza Mayor, which was bustling with the activity of midmorning. On such a beautiful day, the plaza was full of people. Mulatto and black produce vendors sold local fruits such as pineapple, avocados, plantains, and sapotes. The scribes had been in their booths since seven that morning, offering their services to the illiterate majority of the population. Priests in their robes of black and grey engaged in lively conversation, discussing politics or the current economic plight of the island. Soldiers stood in groups of three or four, some guarding the entrance to La Fuerza and keeping out a wary eye for thieves and pickpockets, while others made little pretense of doing anything more than lounging or watching processions of Havana's maidens, out for a morning ride in their carriages accompanied by their ever-present *dueñas* (chaperones).[79]

Arriving at his place of lodging, Morales presented his letter of introduction to the proprietress, who welcomed him warmly. Nevertheless, she was forced to verify his identification papers to comply with laws prohibiting lodging common soldiers, vagrants, and persons of ill repute. She offered to have one of her slaves accompany him to the Cuartel de Artillería later that afternoon, where he would present himself to his commanding officer and be formally inducted into the city's forces. Although he was authorized to partake his *ración de la mesa* (day's ration) at the barracks, she suggested that he would probably prefer to dine with her, given the notoriously poor quality of barracks food. The midday meal, at the boardinghouse and elsewhere, was customarily served at twelve, and almost immediately thereafter, the afternoon siesta would bring all activity within the city to a halt. Most people would be asleep by half past the hour.[80] Morales was assigned to the best room in the establishment, on the upper floor of the building, as was customary for one of his status, to be able to enjoy the breezes that made living inside the city walls bearable. (If a house was two-storied, only slaves and people of color would occupy rooms on the primary floor.)[81] From his window he could see the entrance canal the ship had traversed earlier and behind it the escarpment leading up to El Morro. A refreshing breeze blew into the room when the shutters were open. The temperate December weather was deceptive, though, for at times dangerous winter storms blew in from the north bringing cold rain, deadly wind, and destructively high tides.[82] The furniture was massive, fashioned on the style of the south of Spain but constructed of the abundant native wood, such as cedar or mahogany, which was found in the interior of the island and which, as noted earlier, could be harvested only with special permission.[83] Exhausted from the events of the morning, the lieutenant fell asleep under the mosquito netting that only slightly impeded the feasting of the hundreds of flies, mosquitoes, and sand gnats that plagued humans and animals alike.[84]

Late-afternoon noise from the street outside his window signaled that the neighborhood had awakened from siesta. Morales descended the staircase that led to an interior patio flanked with plants growing in large earthenware pots, where the woman's slave awaited to guide him to the Cuartel de Artillería. As they were leaving the house, the widow suggested that if he were able to conclude his transfer paperwork, he might like to accompany her in her volante for a *vueltecita,* or nightly turn through the city. The guided tour would provide an opportunity for the new arrival to see the sights and sounds of Havana close up and have the added benefit of being escorted by a resident. If he chose to join her, the carriage and driver would be ready at the customary hour of six-thirty.[85]

As it turned out, the lieutenant was unable to present his papers to his commanding officer, for the man was not in Havana, having been called out to the surrounding province on an inspection tour.[86] So, at the appointed time the two departed in the woman's volante, which was considerably more ornate than the one that had brought the lieutenant to the house.[87] The top was left open to the evening air. The hostess explained that unless it was raining, the authorities prohibited owners from putting the top up, as thieves could use a closed carriage as a getaway vehicle. For the unwary, Havana could be a dangerous city. Thieves, vagabonds, and prostitutes lurked on every corner waiting to prey on newcomers, and in their many proclamations of *"buen gobierno,"* royal officials were merely doing their duty to protect the law-abiding majority from those who would disrupt the tranquility of society.[88]

As the carriage departed, the woman explained that the usual route was to proceed west on Calle Empedrado; turn south on Calle de la Havana to the massive Convent of Santa Clara; then east on Calle del Sol to Calle de los Oficios, then north on Oficios through the Plaza Mayor to Empedrado, on which they would return to her house. The paseo (promenade through the city) would take the two passengers through much of the fashionable parts of Havana while avoiding the unsavory areas in the southern portion of town. As dusk approached, the streets were crowded with open carriages of the well-to-do. It seemed as if everyone of consequence in the city owned a carriage and was out in the street on their nightly paseo.[89]

As the volante set out toward the west, the first building encountered was the Hospital of San Juan de Dios, on the corner of Calles Aguiar and Empedrado. The woman explained that the hospital had been founded by Royal Governor Pedro Menéndez de Avilés in the sixteenth century as a military hospital. Also serving the male population was the Convalescent Hospital of Nuestra Señora de Belén. The Hospital of Belén was perhaps the best-endowed hospital in the city, thanks to the generosity of a merchant who left his entire fortune for its maintenance in 1718.[90] Female patients in the city were cared for in Hospital de Paula, located along the waterfront. The building of that hospital was relatively new, having been rebuilt after a hurricane had destroyed the original structure in 1748. The new building, designed by famed architect Antonio de Arredondo, had separate floors for white patients and patients of color, and had separate facilities for surgery and pharmacy.[91] Once past the Hospital of San Juan de Dios, the carriage turned south on Calle Havana. The woman explained that Calle Havana was the longest street in the city, traversing its entire distance north to south, beginning at the land gate to the north, Puerta de la Punta, passing the Loma del Angel, with its relatively recent church, and continuing south to the wall at Calle de los Desamparados.[92] With the arrival of the Conde de Ricla as the new governor, a system of numbering the houses and buildings had been implemented. Nevertheless, the popular custom of sending a message to an address located between two cross streets—for example, at the house on Calle Oficios between Obispo and Obrapía—prevailed over the administration's innovation, designed to improve and modernize the city.[93]

Continuing southward of Calle Havana, the carriage approached the intersection with the Calle de la Amargura, which divided the city into its northern and southern sections. The widow said that during Lent, Franciscan friars would lead processions of worshipers carrying a large wooden cross symbolizing the same walk taken by Jesus on his way to the crucifixion, thus giving the street its name. The processions would leave the Franciscan monastery, located on the Plaza of San Francisco to the east on the waterfront, and proceed westward along Amargura, ending in the Plaza del Santo Cristo.[94] Looking westward, the lieutenant could make out the twin towers just inside the city walls that characterized the Iglesia Santo Cristo. As the volante continued its paseo, the odor of meat—some drying, some rotting—permeated the air. The woman explained that the carriage was approaching the town's slaughterhouse and one of the royal meat markets located one block to the east on the adjacent street, Aguiar. Two markets providing fresh meat operated in the city, one that had cheaper prices for military members and for those in royal service, located close to the Plaza Mayor and La Fuerza, and another for the general public. Price did not always equate with quality, as their noses told them. The contamination of the air by putrefying meat was blamed for much of the sickness in the city, the sea breeze rarely penetrating inland to the narrow streets to blow away the objectionable odor. In later years the authorities would address the problem by moving the slaughterhouse outside the city walls.[95]

Ahead, the massive Convento de Santa Clara marked the place where the carriage would turn eastward toward the bay. The woman explained that the convento was the place where many of Havana's wealthy families placed their daughters who either willingly desired to retire from the world or had incurred their parents' wrath through some infraction of behavioral norms. After a year of apprenticeship was completed, women were secluded for the remainder of their lives behind its imposing walls. Beyond Santa Clara began the most impoverished and most dangerous section of town, the Barrio de Campeche. Four blocks further south, Calle de Merced marked the line beyond which few respectable people would go. From the open carriage the man could look down Calle Havana to where he could see that the houses became poorer and the streets narrower as one penetrated further and further into Campeche. Music with a distinct African flavor could be heard over the rattle of the carriage wheels. His hostess related that the rhythmic sound was being made by processions of members of one of the twenty-nine *cabildos de negros* (brotherhoods of mulattos and blacks). During the Fiesta de los Tres Reyes, the cabildos, dressed in colorful costumes, would parade through the streets ending at the governor's residence. As he strained to hear the music emanating from Campeche, the lieutenant saw black and mulatto women wearing neither blouses nor chemises. He would learn that such public display was commonplace amongst the population of color and was a sufficient source of concern to warrant a decree banning such nakedness on the city streets.[96]

As the two passed through Havana's streets engaging in conversation, they had the opportunity to get acquainted. He was surprised to learn that she too was a peninsular: she had come to Cuba as a young bride more than fifteen years before in compliance with royal regulations that mandated that men in royal service must bring their families with them. Like Morales, her husband had served for a time in the European and African campaigns, but eventually he had transferred to Havana as one of the refuerzo regiments. He had taken part in the sea battle between Spanish admiral Reggio and British admiral Knowles in 1747, and afterward he had been reassigned to the garrison at Havana in 1759. Both had the good fortune to survive the seasoning process and the subsequent myriad of diseases that plagued the tropics, and she had survived the rigors of childbirth. Two of her four children had lived to adulthood, and both boys were serving in the Fixed Regiment of Havana.[97] Her husband had died in 1759, and she had considered returning to Spain, but the war had intervened and she had changed her mind. Her husband had been a good man, temperate and not given to gaming or dueling. His worst habit had been his love of the quality Cuban tobacco from Vuelta Abajo, the province to the west of Havana that produced the bulk of the premium tobacco sold to the factory. She too confessed to a love of the small cigars that the women of Havana smoked regularly in the privacy of their salons.[98] She lived on a small pension in her house that the couple had purchased with the dowry monies she had brought into the marriage.[99] The lieutenant surmised her age to be about fifty years. She had to be at least forty years old, otherwise she would have been prohibited from living alone, and she could not have gone into the streets with no other person accompanying her but her mulatto slave who drove the carriage.[100]

As the carriage approached the Plaza de Santa Clara, the driver stopped the vehicle to allow a procession going northward on Calle de Cuba to continue. The woman explained that it was a religious brotherhood organized within the Church of Espíritu Santo. Every night the members of that confraternity paraded through the streets of Havana in tribute to their patron saint, Nuestra Señora del Rosario.[101] Their church was two blocks to the south, and if the lieutenant looked down Calle de Cuba, he would be able to see the spire of Espíritu Santo, with its distinctive clock in the bell tower. As the carriage continued, the widow pointed out the house of the Zayas Bazán family on the corner of Calles Cuba and Sol, one of the many richly appointed houses that graced the area of the city close to the waterfront. A similar house greeted the two at the corner of Calles Sol and Inquisidor that belonged to a representative of the Holy Inquisition from whom the street took its name.[102] There the carriage took a detour from its customary route, turning to the left and entering the Plaza Nueva, one of the most fashionable plazas in the city. With the approach of darkness, the plaza was emptying of people, as vendors closed their stands for the day and common laborers hurried home after their day's work. The official working day ended at eight; soon the city gates would be closed, shutting out the rest of the world until dawn.[103] Several carriages were parked along Inquisidor and Teniente Rey, the streets that came together at the northeast corner. The woman explained that on that corner was a popular tavern where people out for their nightly paseo often stopped for a refreshment and lively conversation, while their drivers lounged by the volantes or surreptitiously played games of chance.[104] The houses of Havana's elite families ringed the Plaza Nueva, including those of the Cárdenas sisters and Field Marshall O'Reilly.[105] Now close to the waterfront, the unmistakable tang of salt air reached their noses. The freshness of the atmosphere close to the bay contrasted sharply with the stultifying closeness they had experienced in the interior portions of the city. Small wonder the wealthy chose to locate their urban residences in the most pleasant portions of the city.

With a quick turn right, then left, the carriage was in the Plaza de San Francisco. On the south end, the Franciscan convent, from which the Plaza took its name, fronted the bay, separated from the water only by the wide Calle San Pedro that ran parallel to the bayfront.[106] The lieutenant recognized the wharf located farther south on San Pedro as the one with the giant crane that he had seen upon his arrival. He felt a sense of familiarity as he began to recognize landmarks that he had passed upon his entry. Proceeding northward on Calle Oficios, they passed many elegant buildings as they approached the Plaza Mayor. It was almost nine o'clock, and there they would pause and descend from the carriage to enjoy a musical presentation held in front of La Fuerza.[107] Perhaps the governor himself would come out on his balcony on the top floor and listen! The woman confessed that she was delighted that Morales had been able to accompany her, otherwise custom and community censure would dictate that she must remain in her carriage. On the eastern edge of the Plaza Mayor, the ancient ceiba tree, where the first Mass had been celebrated upon the foundation of the city, had stood until 1753.[108] The widow could remember that the tree was the first thing she had noticed upon her arrival so many years ago. On the plaza itself, some structures looked dilapidated. In particular, the building housing the Parroquia Mayor was in a terrible state of disrepair. The lady told him that the building had suffered significant damage in 1741, when one of the most important ships to be produced by the Real Arsenal, the *Invincible*, had been struck by a bolt of lightning while anchored in the nearby harbor. The ensuing fire had burned the ship to the waterline, had killed several people, and had damaged several buildings located close by on the docks.[109] The coup de grâce for the old building would be a hurricane in 1768, which caused the steeple, containing the clock and heavy brass bells, to come crashing down to the street, leaving the interior of the church open to the elements and effectively destroying what remained of the structure.[110] In 1767, the Jesuits would be expelled from the Spanish dominions, and their building on Plaza de la Ciénaga (now that the land crabs had also been expelled) would be confiscated by the administration. With their building totally unfit for service, the Jesuits' buildings would be awarded to the secular priests of the Parroquia Mayor and consecrated as the Cathedral of Havana. For the time being, however, Havana's wealthiest families had to be content with the old structure that served as their church.[111]

When the music finished, the two returned to where the woman's slave was tending the carriage and boarded it for the ride home. Although only a few blocks from her house, they would have been unwise and in violation of the law to walk about at night. The safety and welfare of the community precluded persons from being on the city streets at night except in emergencies, and those who were forced out had to carry a torch or candle to light their way.[112] Soon, soldiers organized as urban patrol units would ensure that the public order was maintained throughout the night.[113] Others leaving the square and boarding their carriages were headed for the innumerable *tertulias* (social gatherings) held in wealthy homes almost nightly, and the more adventurous headed for the taverns to drink and engage in games of chance that no amount of legislation could eradicate.[114]

In the coming years Morales would become comfortable in the city he would adopt as his home. He would adjust to the particular structures of everyday life that characterized living in the third largest city in Spanish America.[115] Being of Andalusian origin, many things in Havana would be familiar, yet enough was different to make his life a challenge. He would learn of the local prohibition against racing horses in town, as so many of the leisure class were fond of doing.[116] His slaves would purchase bread at prices fixed according to the cost of flour imported into the island.[117] When he frequented the numerous *pulperías* (small stores) he would partake of classic items that distinguished the upper ranks from the lower —*vino tinto* (red wine), olives, white bread, and the distinctive serrano ham—just as he would have had he still been in the south of Spain.[118] He would get official news from proclamations posted in several public places around town and from newspapers, the *Gaceta de la Havana*, begun in 1764, and its successor, the *Papel Periódico de la Havana*, begun in 1790.[119] In 1775 he would become embroiled in the controversy over whether the community needed a *casa de recogidas* (house to incarcerate wayward women) or a theater. He would agree with the sensible solution envisioned by the Marqués de la Torre to use the profits from the admission fees at the theater to fund the women's jail.[120] When he was an old man, he would delight in the new foodstuff brought to the city, called snow. The Protomédico de Havana bitterly opposed the product, claiming that it could do grave damage to one's system in the tropical climate. On the other hand, no less learned a person than Francisco de Arango y Parreño supported the sale of the crystalline water flavored with fruit syrup, and it certainly tasted good, especially in the summer, when the heat seemed to envelope one's body.[121] International events beginning with Spain's entry into the American Revolutionary War would affect how comfortable or uncomfortable his life would be, as consumer products such as the instantly popular snow or flour from North America alternately became scarce or abundant. In 1781, he would celebrate with the rest of the inhabitants of the island when the news of Bernardo de Gálvez's victory in Pensacola became known and would mourn the death of Charles III in 1788.

More important, and more that any of the thousands of men who came and remained in Cuba after 1763, Morales would contribute to the dynamic processes of social change that swept Cuba in the aftermath of the

Seven Years' War. The military and fiscal reorganization of 1763–64 would create a climate of opportunity for Havana and all of the cities and towns that depended upon her well-being. The lieutenant would capitalize upon the prosperity engendered by the millions of pesos spent for defense, and the prestige that came with being associated with the transformative body, the Spanish army. Upon his arrival on the island, he was assigned to the Voluntarios de Cuba, a regiment that was garrisoned in Santiago de Cuba, where he would serve until November 1773.[122] There he would meet and marry Santiagüera María de Medina, and the daughter of that union, María de Morales, would follow in her mother's footsteps and marry another peninsular military man, Francisco de Varela. They, in turn, would become the parents of "the man who taught [Cubans] to think," Félix Varela.[123] In 1774, Morales would come to the attention of the Marqués de la Torre, who would select him to transfer to the reorganized Fixo of Havana, even though he had been designated to serve in the newly formed Second Battalion of Cuba in Santiago de Cuba.[124] Morales ultimately would become the commander of the Third Battalion of Cuba in St. Augustine in 1791, and his grandson would accompany him to that post, an event that would have lasting repercussions for the history of Cuba.[125]

But such events were in the unforeseen future. In the morning when the lieutenant awakened, the sound of a man's voice from the patio announced that Morales's commanding officer had returned and awaited his arrival at the barracks. As Morales descended the stairs, a fellow officer whom he recognized as a colleague from the Portugal campaign greeted him warmly with the characteristic hug close friends and family share with loved ones. Properly welcomed into kin and community networks, the foundation of Hispanic society, Lieutenant Morales was no longer a stranger. He had become Havana's newest invisible immigrant.

Good for Farmers but Not for Soldiers

Bartolomé de Morales's arrival in Havana was a direct consequence of the greatest disaster to befall the Spanish American empire in its 250-year existence, the fall of Havana to the British siege in August 1762. During the winter of 1762–63, the Spanish court of Charles III could not have been a pleasant place to be. The humiliation sent shock waves through his royal administration; all involved knew that the coming years would be but an interlude and prepared for another war with Great Britain.[1] In preparation for the anticipated conflict, the Crown consciously and deliberately expanded the military presence throughout the island. Such militarization had important economic effects and triggered widespread spatial reordering, but it also included social consequences. The human dimension of military expansion hinged upon the restructuring of the armed forces in all of Cuba's cities, but the effects were particularly visible in the Havana jurisdiction, that is, the western half of the island. As the scope of the military presence expanded to interior cities through reorganized militia companies, large segments of the general population became liable for military service, and in some areas, between one-third and two-thirds of the eligible males were militia members. Military service extended privileges to such men and their families but also involved the acceptance of many responsibilities. Such privileges and immunities set men in military service and their households apart from ordinary citizens but also brought them under the constant scrutiny of officers whose authority overlapped from professional to daily life. Disciplinary measures implemented in the years after 1764 to punish persons responsible for the defeat set important precedents for future behavior. Because such a large proportion of the population were directly involved in military service or gained their livelihood from the military presence, the Spanish regime enjoyed widespread acceptance. The army in Cuba, thus, differed from the military presence in other areas of Spanish America, for in Cuba the military establishment was not an army of occupation but rather an army of co-optation.

While the extensive literature dealing with military and reforms in Cuba has been introduced in chapter 1, certain pertinent concepts bear repeating. The fall of Havana served as the catalyst for military reform throughout the empire, but such reforms were generally unsuccessful except in Cuba. Some historians have argued that such was the case because Spanish America lacked a military tradition. Other historical studies maintain that training Creole units in the art of military engagement contributed to their ability to fight against royalist troops in subsequent conflicts. Studies by Lyle N. McAlister and Christon A. Archer for New Spain, Allan J. Kuethe for New Granada, and Leon G. Campbell for Peru detail how most military reforms fell far short of metropolitan goals.[2] Jorge I. Domínguez's work details the important differences between Mexico, Chile, Venezuela, and Cuba, and proposes a political and economic solution to the conundrum of why Cuba remained loyal to Spain while other areas did not.[3] In most areas of the Spanish American mainland, the majority of the population did not benefit from an increased military presence, and the Spanish army was viewed as an army of occupation sent to enforce unwelcome and unfair taxation. In areas other than Cuba, Bourbon reform measures were actively resisted by Creoles at all social levels; it was only in Cuba that this was not the case.[4]

While Cuba's post-1763 situation was unique as compared to other areas of Spanish America, the fall of Havana had not occurred because the area lacked a military presence or a military tradition. Indeed, nothing could be further from the truth. Havana and her sister cities in the circum-Caribbean area had survived and prospered *because* of their strategic importance to the empire's defense.[5] Still, the showplace of Spain's Caribbean defenses had broken down, reform was in order, and obviously the monarch had nothing to lose, since the existing system had proven to be a failure. The problem for the men sent by Charles III to Cuba, Ambrosio Funes de Villapando, the Conde de Ricla, and Field Marshall Alejandro O'Reilly, was to identify the reasons behind the inability of the defenders of the "Key to the New World" to withstand the British assault in 1762.[6]

A series of complex and interrelated causes had contributed to the fall of Havana, and Ricla and O'Reilly recognized that the solution must be as multifaceted as were the reasons for the defeat. Before ever setting foot on Cuban soil, these two architects of reform, along with head engineer Agustín Crame (or Cramer) and the director of engineers, Silvestre de Abarca, had occupied the hours spent aboard their ship mulling over plans to refortify the city.[7] Although immediate priority was given to the repair of military facilities, what emerged from their discussions was a comprehensive plan to revamp the defensive position of the city and its surrounding area. The first order of business was the rebuilding and expansion of El Morro, the primary fortress that guarded the city, and the Castillo de la Punta, its counterpart on the other side of the entrance to Havana harbor, both severely damaged during the British shelling.[8] In addition, teams of craftsmen, criminals, and slaves were assigned the task of augmenting and reinforcing the original fortification in the city, La Fuerza, repairing the wall, and refortifying the watchtowers of La Chorrera, San Lázaro, and Cojímar.[9] The second order of business was to address the reasons for the defeat. Two centuries previous, Spanish engineers had warned that whoever controlled the heights of the Cabañas hill to the east would be master of the city, an observation that the British victory had proven all too true.[10] Enemy forces had been able to encircle the city by blockading the harbor with their ships positioned to the north and by landing contingents of soldiers to the east and west. With the city surrounded, the British forces shelled El Morro into submission, and after El Morro's surrender the remaining defenses fell quickly.[11]

Acknowledging the vulnerability of the city that lay below the unguarded hill, on November 4, 1763, Ricla ordered work to begin on San Carlos de la Cabaña, located directly south of El Morro. To guard the southern flank and the important ship construction in the Real Arsenal (royal shipyard), the Castillo de Atarés, designed by Agustín Crame, was erected atop the Loma de Soto. The last potentially vulnerable position, the western approach to the city, and in particular the Loma de Aróstegui where a regiment of British troops had landed in 1762, was provisionally fortified in 1771. In 1774 ground was broken for yet a third massive fortification, the Castillo del Príncipe atop that hill to the west of the city.[12]

Ringing the city with fortifications only partially addressed the problems of defense. Military engineers recognized that an attacking army had been able to approach the city with impunity and divert the vital water supply from the Zanja, the aqueduct that supplied the city with water, by taking shelter behind buildings constructed in clear violation of the Laws of the Indies. To prevent a similar occurrence, Silvestre de Abarca proposed extending—and this time, enforcing—prohibitions against such construction near forts, watchtowers, the north coast, the wall, or other structures or features such as a swampy area that fed the Zanja, all of which were necessary for the defense and provisioning of the town.[13]

Thenceforth, all construction would be prohibited within a distance of

1,500 *varas* (about three-quarters of a mile) of designated structures. Houses, barns, and tobacco mills not in compliance with the new regulations would be demolished. No exceptions would be permitted. Since the city wall was included in the definition of a defensive structure, the building prohibition served to enlarge the Campo de Marte, which would be stripped of all existing buildings and most large vegetation, to extend to the requisite distance beyond the city gates. In times of war, the cleared ground would help defenders by depriving an approaching enemy of shelter. Withering fire could be directed toward any approaching force from a new battery in the wall, El Polvorín, erected to defend the western flank.[14] In times of an ever-vigilant peace, the cleared area would be utilized for a variety of military exercises, which could only serve to maintain the troops on a ready and alert status.[15]

Although the comprehensive plan was created to revamp the defense of the city, ancillary structures also became beneficiaries of the renovation. The royal administration envisioned the creation of multifaceted complexes that combined military, administrative, and fiscal functions in one area. One such complex was planned for the now-secure southern end of the Campo de Marte, which, in 1762, had been occupied by the Real Arsenal and a dilapidated building that served as a warehouse for the Factoría de Tabacos. By 1767, the Real Arsenal, under watchful eyes in the Castillo de Atarés, had been rebuilt and had launched the first of several ships, including two with eighty guns each in the first year of operations, amidst celebrations and much fanfare.[16]

New construction worked to benefit the general public in that enormous sums of money were pumped into Havana's economy. Much to the chagrin of Mexican taxpayers who "complained that their silver disappeared into Havana's financial maze," Habaneros enjoyed financial prosperity.[17] During the period in question, the Mexican *situado* (subsidy) rose from 437,000 pesos in the 1750s to an annual average around 1,485,000 pesos from 1763–1769. During the last years of the American Revolutionary War, the situado reached an all time high of 10,610,785 pesos in 1783, this in addition to revenues generated by taxation and the commerce of the island itself.[18] By the late eighteenth century, Havana was "the most fortified city on earth."[19]

The extensive building and rebuilding programs addressed only part of the problem, and in addition to administrative and fiscal measures, Bourbon reformers sought to address the human dimension behind the failure to hold the city. Two kinds of troops serving in Charles III's armies in Cuba had faced the British invaders. The first type was the regular troops, who were professional, career soldiers; the second type was the militia, consisting of ordinary citizens who could be mobilized in time of need. Regular professional troops were, as the name implies, responsible for the business of defense. The regular army was made up of men from Europe and Spanish America, but peninsular troops were considered to be the more elite units.[20] Military forces recruited in and sent to the Indies from Spain were divided into two armies, the army of *dotación* and the army of *refuerzo*. The army of dotación was the more permanent unit and was assigned to a particular post for a long period of time, while the army of refuerzo—such as the regiment in which Bartolomé de Morales arrived—was specifically recruited as a relief unit and was sent from Spain in times of crisis. Although intended to be temporary, individual members of the refuerzo could remain in their destination city by transferring to another military unit or by retiring after the crisis had passed. Moreover, although the purpose of the two units was different, their internal command structure was virtually identical.[21]

One difference between the two units was the social origin of their members. The army of dotación drew its officers from the most elevated social levels in Spain and from the recognized peninsulars living in Spanish America. Officers of the army of refuerzo were primarily peninsular but could contain a small contingent of foreign-born men. In general, refuerzo officers were of the second-line nobility and below. Both armies' regiments were raised in specific geographic areas and retained their geographical identification in their name, for example, the Regiment of Navarre (Morales's unit), or the Regiments of Asturias or Lombardy. In addition, regulars joined the military for a specific period of time. Commissioned and noncommissioned officers usually were appointed for life, but ordinary rank-and-file soldiers enlisted for a specific period of years that varied depending upon the location where they had been recruited.[22]

Joining the peninsular units who were intended to be rotated back to Spain were Creole, professional troops, who were recruited and stationed locally, forming fixed battalions, or *fixos*. Fixos were originally intended to be manned by locally recruited soldiers, but by the late eighteenth century, fixo units increasingly came to be staffed by peninsular troops who had arrived as part of a refuerzo unit, had remained, and had transferred to the local unit.[23] Both types of professional troops were supplemented by militia companies. Militia units were made up of ordinary men who held regular employment (artisans, shopkeepers, or bakers, for example), who trained on a regular basis (usually on Sunday morning after church), were provided with arms and ammunition, and were called up only in times of emergency. Militia units were also of two types, the provincial, or "disciplined," militia that had its origins in the militias of Castile, and urban militias that were sponsored and recruited by guilds or other corporate groups and saw little if any military action.[24]

Several recent studies have enriched our historical understanding of the growth and importance of militia service to the Crown and to the civilian population; however, the militia and the regular troops should not be confused.[25] Regular troops were professional soldiers whose sole function was to train in the art of military engagement, to practice military maneuvers, and to be ever alert. By contrast, militia members were the community's grandfathers, fathers, brothers, and sons who engaged in everyday occupations and only served when the security of the island was threatened. In addition, significant qualitative differences in status and function existed between regular troops and militia companies, eloquently expressed by Juan Marchena Fernández: "A militia officer cannot take a commission in the regular command structure of a plaza, he receives no salary, and he has no authority whatsoever, not even over a regular troop. The (militia) officer has not studied military doctrine . . . he has no garrisoning responsibility nor the obligation to be lodged in barracks, and he might use his uniform a dozen days a year."[26] The militia companies formed a vital component of the overall program of defense, "but at no time should [the militia member] be considered to be a professional soldier."[27]

Strict rules of conduct governed military life, and a professional, career soldier could be sentenced to death or to many years of hard labor for the slightest infraction.[28] Rigorous entrance requirements governed the entry of both officers and rank-and-file soldiers into the regular army. For officers, quality of station and purity of blood were implicit in being accepted into the officer corps and became even more important as the professionalization and ennobilization of the corps proceeded throughout the century.[29] Between the rank-and-file and the officer corps existed an "abyss" of prestige and rank.[30] Ideally, in recruiting rank-and-file soldiers in Spanish America the Crown hoped to attract españoles or their descendants. Since few peninsulars were found to fill the quotas, early in the eighteenth century a percentage of recruits from Spanish America—in Havana, up to twenty Creoles per company—were permitted. Limitations on Creoles remained in effect until the 1770s, when they became less rigorously enforced and more Creoles made their way into the recruit ranks.[31] Additional criteria for enlistment included being no less than fifteen years of age or no more than forty upon first entry, being of a certain minimum height (five feet and one inch in Havana), and signing on for a fixed period of years.[32] To be part of the regular forces was tacit acknowledgment of one's purity of blood, and outwardly, at least, the military maintained the fiction that the "legal race" of regular troops be undeniably white.[33]

The fall of Havana had tested the mettle of both the regulars and the militia and both had been found to be lacking. Leaders had failed to lead, regular troops had failed to perform, civilians had acted in their own self-interest, and someone had absconded with over 4,000 pesos of money for troop salaries, although all involved swore that the monies had been seized by the British.[34] Both Ricla and O'Reilly recognized that the problems extended far beyond military issues. Civilian militia members had performed poorly in the face of the enemy attack and after the capitulation had continued their shameful behavior by profiteering and collaborating with the enemy.[35] O'Reilly formulated several proposals to address the issue of economic profiteering and to overhaul the commercial structure of the colony (see chapter 2). He suggested—and the monarchy listened—that commercial regulations should be relaxed because restricted commerce only played into the hands of civilians who willingly purchased from British smugglers because of existing shortages of necessary goods. While promoting greater freedom of trade within the Spanish imperial system, another facet of his proposal included strict enforcement against contraband activities and vigorous punishment of violators of the new decrees.[36]

Addressing the problem within the regular army proved a formidable challenge, and the Bourbon reformers sought to punish the men responsible for the humiliation. Starting at the top, the blame fell to governor Juan de Prado, the men who constituted the Junta de Guerra who had advised him, and troops of the regular regiments assigned to the city during the siege, the Havana Fixed Regiment and the Edinburgh Dragoons.[37] Juan de Prado and naval commander Guitierre de Hevía y Valdés, the Marqués de Real Transporte, were sent to Spain to face the wrath of Charles III and a military tribunal. There they were tried for treason before a military court and received a death sentence.[38] Ultimately their sentences were commuted and both men were punished by the loss of their military commissions, the payment of restitution, and banishment from court.[39] Carlos Caro, who was a colonel in the Edinburgh Dragoons, Juan Antonio de Colina, and engineer Baltasar Ricard all were removed from military service in disgrace, and subordinate officers and soldiers not only were dishonorably discharged but also received sentences of hard labor.[40]

To his horror, O'Reilly discovered that indiscipline and insubordination permeated the ranks. Many soldiers from the Havana Fixo and the Regiment of Edinburgh had married without permission, and the responsibilities of family life interfered with their attention to military duty. In some instances, men officially assigned to a regiment housed in the city lived outside the city walls, where they could augment their salaries with other activities to provide for their families. In addition, many aged and infirm soldiers also lived in the countryside and only came to town once a month for review and to collect their five-and-one-half-peso pay. Some soldiers were derelict simply due to lax discipline on the part of their superiors.[41] Many fell prey to the opportunities for graft, theft, and the ability to engage in contraband because of a lack of supervision.[42]

Like the fate that had befallen their superiors, punishment was meted out to many soldiers for their unacceptable behavior. Utilizing existing prohibitions, O'Reilly weeded out the men he deemed unfit for service. His plan included culling the useless, aged, and infirm, and the enforcement of strict military discipline to instill a sense of pride and an esprit de corps.[43] As had been done with their superiors, the field marshal sought to make examples of some to serve as a warning for all. While many men were prosecuted under existing military regulations, especially the prohibition against unauthorized or clandestine marriages, most violators were pardoned in a blanket pardon issued upon the marriage of the Prince of Asturias in 1766, which generosity was extended to the command staff, including Hevía and Caro.[44] The worst incorrigibles, however, were sent back to Spain or to the various presidios in Africa in disgrace.[45] Invalid or infirm soldiers were ordered into the Castillo de la Punta, where they could be cared for at minimal cost to the Crown.[46] By the end of 1763, the purged soldiers from the Fixo and the Regiment of Edinburgh were replaced by battalions from Navarre and Cantabria, and those regiments were supplemented with the majority of the men from the evacuated presidios in Florida.[47] More important, however, the precedent had been established that cowardice, insubordination, or a failure to perform one's duty would not be tolerated in the reformed military units.

O'Reilly's response to the challenges of reforming Cuba's military reflected a tension between the reforming tendencies of Charles III's ministers and centuries of traditional military policy. Although the conquest of the New World in the sixteenth century was accomplished through the use of quasimilitary operations, in its aftermath, a centralizing monarchy sought to prevent the development of a powerful faction of Creole landowners. Hence, the Crown prohibited the development of a standing army from which a powerful Creole resistance might develop.[48] As late as 1763, military units were primarily of European origin and were intended to return to the Continent. Upon his arrival in Cuba, O'Reilly echoed this traditional attitude, and after his inspection of the Havana forces, he vigorously advocated the abolition of all fixed regiments, believing it would be more beneficial to replace local fixo units with peninsular troops who themselves would be replaced every two or three years. Not only would it solve the problem of men forming close ties with local interests, but also it would "relieve the repugnance with which soldiers from Spain viewed duty in the Indies," since they would be guaranteed that their stay would be temporary.[49] Battalions recruited in Spain or elsewhere in Europe would consist of *gente útil* (useful men), and they would be fit and ready for duty if they sailed in winter. They would arrive when Havana's climate was healthiest and losses from the seasoning process would be reduced. Moreover, O'Reilly believed that should a man desire to leave the royal service for any reason, he should be returned to Spain immediately.[50]

O'Reilly's draconian plan to abolish fixo units and replace them with continuously rotated, fresh, loyal, competent peninsular troops proved impossible to implement. For all of his idealized rhetoric, he was forced to alter his position when faced with the realities of the situation in Havana after 1763. Quite apart from the difficulties and cost of transportation, there simply were not enough veteran peninsular troops available for duty or to rotate so quickly.[51] Much to his dismay, when the first replacement unit, the Regiment of Lisbon, arrived on the island, he found the majority of its members to be (in his words) "*gente ratera*," or low-lifes, certainly not what he had envisioned when requesting replacement peninsular troops.[52]

But the final event that caused the field marshal to alter his thinking and led to the formulation of a new, comprehensive plan occurred during the winter of 1763–64, when Havana faced a "refugee crisis." Over that winter the inhabitants of Spanish Florida from St. Augustine, Pensacola, and the Castillo de San Marcos on the Apalachee River arrived in the city. Under the terms of the Treaty of Paris, to recover Cuba, Spain ceded Florida to Great Britain. Virtually without exception, all of Spanish Florida's inhabitants, over 3,000 persons, evacuated the province. Within six months, the Florida evacuation increased Havana's population by approximately 10 percent and severely strained the resources of the area. Most of the evacuee community were affiliated with the garrison and were absorbed into Havana's various regiments. But nearly one-fifth of the émigré population, about 600 persons, were civilian farmers. This group consisted of Canary Islanders, German Catholics, members of the free black community of Mosé, a small number of acculturated Florida Indians, and a few low-ranking peninsular soldiers who had illegally married local women. Although the male heads-of-household were obligated for occasional militia service, O'Reilly described these men as being "good for farmers but not for soldiers."[53] They were clearly unfit to be part of his new, professionalized corps. His ideal solution was to relocate such families on lands similar to those that they had been forced to abandon. However, most arable land around Havana had been granted into private hands since the earliest settlement of the island.[54] In addition, land reforms in 1754 and the ongoing fortification projects had further diminished what little land had been available near the city.[55] Clearly, other arrangements needed to be made.

The urgency of the situation called for decisive action even if it meant abrogating previous policies. The solution O'Reilly came up with not only reversed his own policies but challenged those of three centuries of Iberoamerican military tradition. To obtain royal approval, O'Reilly needed to justify his proposal to the monarch and his ministers, and to do so, he struck at the heart of the issues that most concerned the Spanish court. For his plan to be acceptable, it had to be effective in defending the island and it had to do so at little or no cost to the Crown.

Thus, in late 1764, O'Reilly formulated a radical but yet sensible new policy that would alter the human landscape of the island. His multifaceted plan dealt with the immediate crisis, incorporated cost-effective measures, addressed the critical issue of defense, and promoted population increase. One portion of his proposal capitalized upon the expertise of men already in service to the Crown. Rather than sending unseasoned troops of dubious quality, men of proven ability and loyalty like Bartolomé de Morales who were already serving in Spanish America would be encouraged to transfer to the Cuban regiments such as the Regimento de Voluntarios de Cuba or the Havana Fixo. Another portion of his proposal sought to spare the Crown excess transportation costs by suggesting not to rotate regiments as often and then only in royal ships.[56] However, the idea that would affect Cuban society and transform the island was O'Reilly's idea to save return costs by allowing officers and soldiers to retire or separate in place. When a man's enlistment expired, when he retired (voluntarily or otherwise), or when the time came for a regiment to be rotated, those who wished to stay in Cuba could do so. To this end, a decree issued on October

4, 1766, permitted men to leave royal service in any city of their choice. As a further enticement, after 1773, soldiers serving in America enjoyed the same salary and retirement pay as those serving in Spain.[57] For career officers, their monthly pension was calculated at half of one's normal salary. Progressively similar incentives were extended to certain noncommissioned officers with long years of service.[58] And if a man should die before his retirement, another concession included the establishment of pensions for their surviving widows and orphans.[59]

Even after their retirement or separation, though, the veterans had not outlived their usefulness to the Spanish Crown. Once retired, veterans and their families could be used as settlers in underpopulated areas where enemy activity was the greatest. O'Reilly proposed that new villages could be established on the south coast and to the east of Havana on the north coast, the areas most plagued by rampant smuggling and British encroachments to cut timber and introduce slaves into the island.[60] The field marshal astutely recognized that contraband was a time-honored local activity that was often aided and abetted by local citizens.[61] Encouraging both retiring and separating soldiers to remain in Cuba would provide a way to create new population centers with men of established loyalty who already possessed military training. Soldiers who were simply separating without retirement privileges would be given land grants in these areas, and for the first year they would continue to receive their military salary. If they received additional amounts of money, cattle, or implements, they would be allowed up to six years to repay their debts. The royal coffers would be spared the cost of transporting such men back to Spain, and the retirees would form an effective corps of veteran militia, who, in addition, would instill a martial spirit in their children.[62] As former military members, the veterans would be imbued with a sense of loyalty that would be reinforced, since they owed their land grants, cattle, slaves, and seed money to royal generosity. Veterans of higher ranks could be used as *capitanes del partido* responsible for policing the area.[63] Lastly, the veterans would be organized into reserve units of militia companies close to the major cities who could be called up at a minute's notice if another invasion threatened. The settlements of veterans could be augmented by allowing enterprising foreigners, particularly Germans, to emigrate, though they must be Catholic. Under such measures, O'Reilly believed Cuba's population would increase by 600 families per year.[64]

The only thing that would stand in the way of O'Reilly's plan involved the acquisition of land for the communities. For this, the Crown needed sponsors who could promote the creation of towns and the division of lands for agricultural activity. Town founding by private citizens had an established precedent on the island. In the 1730s the Conde de Casa Bayona created his own private fiefdom in Santa María del Rosario, and in the 1750s Bartolomé Antonio de Silva founded Holguín in the eastern portion of the island.[65] This carryover from a feudal era fed upon Cuba's landowning families' pretensions to grandeur, and since the island was plagued with a chronic shortage of labor, relinquishing part of their land for a town at least guaranteed their supply. In addition, the usual reward for such service to the Crown was a title of nobility.

Several wealthy landowners responded to O'Reilly's plan and offered their land for the settlement schemes. The first was Gerónimo de Contreras, who donated a large tract of land outside the city of Matanzas, located some one hundred miles to the east of Havana. Designated as the resettlement location for the agricultural component of the Florida refugees, appropriately the new settlement was named San Agustín de Nueva Florida.[66] The civilian farmers, free black population, and men who were cashiered out of service were offered the opportunity to "retire" and relocate to Nueva Florida to form the backbone of the agricultural community O'Reilly envisioned.[67]

Over the winter of 1763–64, seventy-three refugee families accepted land grants, implements, cattle, seed, and at least one slave. Within two years, most families had abandoned their grants and had returned to Havana. As tales of misery filtered back to the remaining families awaiting transportation, the majority simply refused to leave the extraurban barrios where they had been lodged upon their arrival.[68] When it became apparent that the Nueva Florida settlement was destined to be a disaster, other settlements were authorized closer to Havana to accommodate the refugees, once again rationalizing that such concessions would not only benefit the inhabitants but also promote commerce and benefit the royal purse as well. Gabriel Beltrán de Santa Cruz offered his land at the foot of the Escalera de Jaruco specifically to accommodate the families from St. Augustine, Pensacola, and Apalachee.[69] José de la Guardia, the proprietor of a large cattle-ranching enterprise on the bay of Jagua on the southern coast of the island, received royal permission to found a similar settlement to resettle at least thirty of the displaced families.[70]

The implementation of O'Reilly's settlement plan displays an ad hoc quality that was a response to a crisis rather than a carefully crafted, well-thought-out program. Clearly, though, by April 1764, his position had

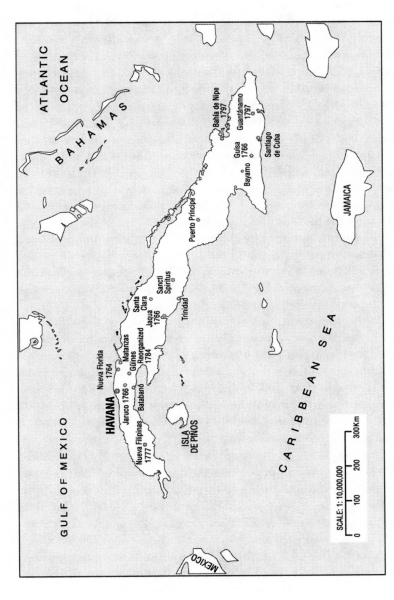

Fig. 3.1. Eighteenth-century map showing the location of newly created settlements established between 1764 and 1800.

undergone a total reversal of his original policies. The field marshal's plan to allow veterans to remain on the island had not been formulated prior to his arrival; he conceived the proposal when he was confronted with the resettlement of over 3,000 refugees, most of whom offered no positive contribution to the city's defense. Drawing upon the twin precedents of military resettlement policies of the Roman army and the medieval practices of town sponsorship, his solution captured the imagination and won the approval of Charles III.[71] The change in royal policy is illustrated in the case of militia colonel José Antonio de Silva, the son of the man who had founded Holguín. In 1754, the younger de Silva had requested permission to found a town on Nipe Bay on the north coast of the island. With virtually no debate, the Council of the Indies denied his petition. Undaunted, de Silva submitted a new request in 1762 asking permission to organize his ranching operation into a town, Guisa, in a picturesque little valley on the north slope of the Sierra Nevada on the far eastern end of the island. The Council of the Indies, obviously occupied with more important matters, delayed action on his request until the end of the war. With wartime behind them and in the spirit of rebuilding, in 1764, the council suggested to Charles III that now it would be "in His Majesty's best interests" to permit de Silva to proceed with his project.[72]

Was the Council of the Indies correct in assuming that O'Reilly's plan was in Charles III's best interests? Throughout Spanish American history, what the Crown mandated was not always what was achieved. More often than not, the consequences of royal policy were unforeseen, unintended, unworkable, and unwelcome. Did the royal initiatives in 1764 foster population growth and create a community that retained its military affiliation and loyalty to the Crown? Certainly, on both points, a combination of many sources suggest that they did.

The first indicator is evidence of population increase. As a whole, the province of Havana, which, in the eighteenth century, comprised the entire western half of the island, increased its population by 45,000 persons, or over 80 percent, in the course of the twenty-three years from 1755 through 1778. The city of Havana alone increased its number of residents by 18,000 people, an increase of 78 percent, and the population of its immediate suburbs rose by 81 percent. The outlying areas in the province to the east, south, and west of the city experienced a similar degree of population growth, adding nearly 24,000 new persons and reflecting a growth rate of 88 percent.[73] The second generation, from 1778 through 1810, experienced equally spectacular population increase, but with significant differences in specific areas that were affected. While in terms of absolute numbers, the explosive growth continued, in the city of Havana the trend slowed in the second generation. Between 1778 and 1810, the total population of the city of Havana rose but slightly, by approximately 2,900 persons, an increase of only 7 percent. The minute increase in absolute numbers suggests that the city had reached a saturation point, and further population increases could not be absorbed by the available land within the city limits. With regard to the *barrios extramuros* (neighborhoods outside the walls), particularly in the Barrio de la Salud (Guadalupe) and Barrio Jesús, María, y José, the impressive figures for the first period pale in comparison to the increases recorded for the second generation, the period from 1788 through 1810. The population of the suburbs rose from 3,761 persons in 1755, to 6,823 persons in 1778, to 47,102 persons in 1810, reflecting a sixfold increase in the number of inhabitants in only two generations!

The outward growth from Havana was accompanied by changes in spatial organization. Until 1763 little competition existed to challenge the cattle and swine that grazed on the *hatos* and *corrales* that encircled the city.[74] In the following fifty years, the population density in the suburbs rose from only 941 inhabitants per square mile in 1755 to 13,854 inhabitants per square mile in 1810.[75] At times both the residents and the authorities were at a loss to deal with the changes thrust upon them. By the 1780s the increase in inhabitants led to a vacuum in enforcement in the interstices between areas assigned to particular capitanes del partido. When residents complained that neither the captaines of Marianao nor Arroyo Arenas could control the number of *vagos* who had "infested" the suburbs, Diego José de Navarro was forced to redraw suburban jurisdictional limits because "the population had grown so much."[76] By the 1790s, Havana's urban sprawl reached to the foot of the Castillo del Príncipe, nearly a mile away from the city walls.[77]

Population growth was also evident by an increase in the number of new towns and villages outside the city. Most were evolutionary settlements, that is, towns that were not deliberately planned but rather arose in response to demographic needs, for example at a junction between two important roads, at a ferry crossing, or surrounding the barracks of a detachment of soldiers. The census of 1778 lists ten such new towns that had been created spontaneously or by hiving off from existing settlements. The creation of new settlements is reflected in ecclesiastical documents that provide data to extend the chronological scope through the end of the century. When church and state recognized that a sufficient number of residents had settled in a particular area to warrant the keeping of a separate set of vital records, church officials created new parishes. From the time of Havana's founding in 1519 through 1763, fourteen churches served Havana and its hinterlands. However, in the thirty-five years between 1765 and 1800, the growing number of residents required the founding of seventeen new parishes, more than twice as many as had been necessary for the previous two and a half centuries.[78]

Alongside the evolutional communities, the original planned communities grew and new settlements were authorized. From a rocky beginning in the 1760s, Nueva Florida survived, if not exactly prospered. The settlement on Jagua Bay also survived as a support center for the *castillo* (fortification) of the same name, and the villages Jaruco and Guisa grew steadily. In addition, the number of planned communities also increased. At the far western end of the island, a civilian settlement at Nueva Filipinas was organized and promoted by Miguel Peñalver alongside a watchtower that housed a detachment of mounted cavalry to provide advance warning against the approach of an enemy fleet.[79] To the southeast of Havana in 1786, Gabriel Beltrán de Santa Cruz, the founder of Jaruco, reorganized the tobacco-producing hamlet Güines into a created community specifically to supply the royal monopoly.[80]

Moreover, the initiative for settlement expansion and town founding did not abate as the century drew to a close. Quite the contrary, the population expansion was given additional impetus in the crisis years after the Haitian Revolution in 1791. In 1793, a Royal Order once again clarified and promoted population initiatives, this time focusing on the eastern end of the island. The proposed inhabitants were similar to those of the 1760s: immigrants fleeing the violence in the former French colony St. Domingue and evacuees from the Spanish colony Santo Domingo, lost to Haitian military forces in 1794 and ceded to the French Republic in 1795. Among the many schemes to resettle and populate the eastern end of the island were several advanced by royal officials Juan Bautista Valliant in 1794, by Juan Nepomuceno de Quintana in 1797, and by Isidro de Limonta in 1800. With the transferal of the Audiencia de Santo Domingo to Puerto Príncipe in 1796, these efforts represented a desire on the part of the eastern end of the island to break away from the influence of Havana.[81] While the desire for provincial autonomy fell on deaf ears, the king and his council did wholeheartedly approve of colonization schemes, especially those initiated by private citizens at their own expense. By 1797, the son of Beltrán de Santa Cruz received permission to develop Nipe Bay, the area that the Council of the Indies had specifically refused to permit José de Silva to develop thirty-five years earlier.[82]

Macro data such as islandwide censuses establish that the population continued to grow, while micro data—sequential, annual reports from every village around Havana—allow a closer analysis of the type of inhabitants that spilled haphazardly out into the hinterland. As late as 1796, the population of European descent was numerically dominant, and at no time until the mid nineteenth century did the population of color, free and slave, exceed the white inhabitants.[83] The majority of the rural inhabitants who constituted *el pueblo cubano* were humble folk—never addressed as don or doña—who engaged in a variety of agricultural activities revolving around production for Havana's urban markets and tobacco farming.[84] Contrary to historiographical tradition, sugar *ingenios* (plantations) had little impact on the majority of Cuba's rural population, and reports from a variety of capitanes del partido from the 1790s demonstrate that even during the first "Dance of the Millions," the number of ingenios was far exceeded by those of other agricultural enterprises.[85] From the far western district in the heart of tobacco country in Pinar del Río, the pueblo Palacios reported it had 10 hatos, 8 corrales, and 32 *vegas* (tobacco farms) but no sugar was produced in the district.[86] From Wajay, also west of Havana, the captain reported that 25 *potreros* (pastures) and 63 *sitios de labor* (farms) were located in his jurisdiction, but just 2 ingenios.[87] To the east, where sugar expanded so rapidly in the nineteenth century, Gibacoa's agricultural production was concentrated on its 5 potreros and 66 *estancias* (cattle ranches) rather than on its 4 ingenios.[88] Even in the heart of the contemporary sugar-producing zone, Río Blanco del Norte, with 13 ingenios, had the largest concentration of sugar mills; nevertheless, the majority of Río Blanco's rural population toiled instead on 17 potreros, 1 corral, and 177 estancias.[89]

The hamlet Güines, which enjoyed the legal distinction of villa, provides an example of the character of rural production that challenges its historiographical reputation as the epicenter of eighteenth-century sugar expansion.[90] Güines grew not because of the advance of sugar mills but rather because of the expansion of tobacco vegas. In 1770 Güines had 168 vegas, which employed 429 workers and produced 184,310 *cujes* (bundles of tobacco).[91] A year later the number of vegas rose to 279 and employed 586 workers in the production of over 250,000 cujes for the monopoly.[92] By 1796 the number of vegas had risen to over 600, and, along with the 30 potreros and 11 cattle ranches, challenged the attempts of the 11 sugar plantations to encroach on their land.[93] The town itself also exhibited similar growth. In 1774, the "villa" was, in reality, a motley collection of huts with 300 people that grew to house nearly 3,000 persons by 1786.[94] By October 1792, Güines's 9,070 inhabitants living in the villa and its hinterland consisted of 6,359 white persons, 491 free people of color, and 2,220 slaves.[95] Residents who did not own or occupy land probably worked as *jornaleros* (day workers) on the vegas or in a variety of trades and crafts catering to the tobacco industry.[96]

Perhaps because the sugar planters bore the stigma of collaboration during the British occupation in 1762–63, the Crown was only marginally interested in advancing their interests. In fact, Charles III worked against sugar's expansion when in 1771 he prohibited cutting Cuba's cedar trees for sugar boxes, which began the long-running battle between sugar growers and the intendant of the navy. From 1771 onward, Cuba's plantation owners were forced to turn to Louisiana for lumber for their boxes.[97] The Crown did permit the plantation owners to lease excess space in royal ships of the mail system to ship sugar to Spain, but clearly the arrangement was conducted on a space-available basis. In 1777 an unusually small harvest reduced the revenue considerably, thus adding to the Crown's reluctance to promote the industry.[98] In 1779, with the exigencies of war looming over the island, the administrator of the mail system, Raymundo de Onís, refused to allow the merchants to ship their products, primarily sugar, in royal ships.[99] Yet while the Crown refused to allow the transatlantic shipment of sugar, it never failed to purchase tobacco during wartime, as it did from Trinidad and St. Spiritus in 1778 and 1779.[100] In 1781, during the height of wartime, tobacco production continued without interruption. Not surprisingly, Güines led the island in its production.[101] Although the families most thoroughly invested in sugar ingenios repeatedly maintained that sugar was the *ramo principal* (principal industry),[102] royal officials remained unconvinced, especially since population figures and economic data demonstrated otherwise.

Thus, until the 1790s, and probably long afterward, Cuba's rural economy was as diversified as its inhabitants. The dangers of dependence upon a single crop were evident to even to Cuba's eighteenth-century leaders, and in particular, Captain General de la Torre also worked toward diversifying Cuba's agricultural bases. When arrivals from Florida brought beehives, de la Torre promoted beekeeping and wax production and actively fought commercial restrictions that prevented Cuba from exporting its wax to Mexico.[103] The marqués even wrote to the Council of the

Indies suggesting that artillery colonel Antonio Raffelín, a classic example of elite diversification, deserved royal accreditation for his efforts in cultivating bees.[104] Coffee production was also promoted by royal officials, especially after 1792 and the arrival of many refugees from Santo Domingo and St. Domingue.[105] Countless examples demonstrate that the agricultural product that most occupied the attention of the captains general and the capitanes del partido after 1763 was tobacco, perhaps since the nature of its production by small farmers was conducive to the population dynamic on the island and the symbiosis between small producers and retirees.

If sugar cultivation did not stimulate the demographic explosion on the island, what did? Populations can only replace themselves when the birth rate exceeds the death rate or through immigration. Given the island's climate and the prevalence of disease, it is unlikely that the birth rate outstripped the death rate sufficiently to account for the large increase in population. The scanty demographic evidence currently available—summaries of births and deaths for the city for 1793 and 1794—suggests that, at best, the birth rate equaled the death rate.[106] But that would mean that the population would remain static. Thus, only immigration of freemen or slaves can sufficiently account for such a large population increase. Large-scale slave imports, both legal and illegal, may be ruled out, because until 1789, trade restrictions limited the number of slaves brought to Cuba. Even with the free-trade declaration in slaves, Cuba's slave population did not increase significantly until after 1809.[107]

For the free and primarily white component of Havana's population, the most likely explanation lies in an increase in the number of European immigrants arriving after 1763. The reorganization of Cuba's military structure looms large as *the* reason for a significant increase in the number of white persons in the city. Given the limited ability of Spanish citizens and foreigners alike to migrate prior to 1778, the likelihood that nonmilitary arrivals made up the bulk of immigrants is small.[108] On the other hand, when in July 1763 British governor William Keppel returned the city to the Conde de Ricla, 2,675 newly arrived Spanish troops looked on.[109] O'Reilly's reforms resulted in the evolution of a regular troop structure more suitable for the conditions necessary to defend Havana, but it also resulted in the need for substantial numbers of peninsular soldiers. By 1776, professional soldiers permanently assigned to the vicinity were concentrated in the Fixo, in one squadron of mounted dragoons, in one company of artillery, and in three companies of light infantry that could move through the dense underbrush outside the city with ease.[110] The army of refuerzo remained responsible for providing rotation troops, but the average rotation cycle grew to be around four years and during times of crisis could be extended to longer periods.[111] In the following seventeen years, eleven Spanish regiments averaging 600 men each arrived to reinforce soldiers already serving in the city, and the wooden *barracones* (barracks) built on the Campo de Marte to accommodate just the transient units held twelve battalions.[112] Using these figures, a conservative estimate of the number of peninsular soldiers who were garrisoned in Havana from 1763 through 1782 would exceed 17,000 men. More concrete figures establish that in preparation for the attack on British territory, more than 7,700 men made their way to Havana, and on the eve of the first expedition in 1779, 5,300 army personnel alone were lodged in Havana and in the barracks.[113] By April 1780, 11,752 infantry soldiers were stationed in Havana.[114] As a basis for comparison, Havana's white male population in 1778 totaled 11,919 men and boys, which meant that between one in two and one in three adult white males walking Havana's streets was a peninsular soldier. Countless more naval personnel also interacted with the city's population.[115] Eventually, as men transferred from refuerzo units, the ever-growing Fixo would be divided into two, and then three, battalions. The second battalion of Cuba would be sent to garrison Santiago de Cuba permanently, and after 1789 the third battalion would be assigned to duty in St. Augustine once the province of Florida was returned to Spanish control pursuant to the Treaty of Paris of 1783.[116]

Military reform, however, was not the sole means of arrival. Administrative reforms, including the reorganization of the Real Hacienda and the implementation of an intendant system, brought widespread changes and a large bureaucracy to the island.[117] In 1708, the Crown had awarded the practice of tax farming to José Carmona, whose number of subordinates is impossible to calculate, but a recent estimate maintains that the entire western district of the island contained 122 Royal Treasury posts, of which 37 were located in the immediate vicinity of Havana.[118] Levi Marrero has demonstrated that at least 20 offices were part of the Real Hacienda in Havana in 1759.[119] In the reforms of 1764, the office of intendant was extended to the island, and by the 1790s, seventy-nine men assisted Intendant Pedro José Valiente serving as upper-ranking administrators for the offices nominally under Valiente's stewardship. The number of employees grew exponentially as responsibility filtered downward through the ranks. Twenty-nine lesser officials were assigned to Havana and the suburbs in charge of collecting the royal revenues, and twenty-four more were sent to the towns and villages in the province of Havana. They, in turn, supervised fifty-five collectors who personally received the taxes and fees due to the monarch.[120] Eight *guardacostas* (coast guard cutters) assigned to the Real Hacienda to minimize smuggling called Havana their home port after 1763, employing 214 sailors and an additional 493 criminals and slaves.[121] The creation of a consolidated and comprehensive mail system between Spain and the Indies with Havana at its hub made the city the nexus for communications to and from the Continent. While in 1763 two men handled the volume of communications between Spain and Spanish America, the expanded *sistema de correos* (postal service) required nineteen administrative officials in Havana, three in Tallapiedra (near the Real Arsenal), eight ship captains, eleven lieutenants and pilots, and at least one representative in each of the villages and hamlets scattered across the island.[122] In addition, new departments were created, such as the *junta de maderas* (timber industry board) which employed eleven men in Havana, with additional representatives assigned to provincial substations in the cities of Matanzas, Caciguas, Remedios, and Alquízar.[123] After O'Reilly organized the city into barrios, Havana needed eight *comisarios de policia* (police stations) and outside the city walls fourteen *jueces pédaneos* patrolled the five *barrios extramuros* and the settlements of Calvario, Jesús del Monte, and Luyanó.[124] As the Bourbon bureaucracy expanded, the new positions were awarded to men of proven loyalty to the Crown—veterans who had served many years in the army or navy—or to their children.

Of course, not all soldiers, sailors, or functionaries remained in the city. Given Havana's well-deserved reputation as a pestilential hellhole, certainly a portion of new arrivals did not survive the seasoning process. No study currently exists of troop mortality for eighteenth-century Cuba; however, contemporary estimates for such areas as St. Domingue maintain that troop mortality ranged between 30 and 35 percent throughout the period.[125] In addition, some soldiers served their tour of duty and were repatriated to Spain. But if 1771 is any example, two regiments, the Seville and the Hibernia, returned to Spain, and then these two regiments were replaced with three additional regiments, adding an additional 600 men to the military contingent in the city.[126] Members of the regular military were specifically excluded from the various censuses taken beginning in 1774, but their wives, children, mistresses, bastards, and other sundry dependents were counted as part of the total population.[127] Individual civilian immigrants made up only a small portion of new arrivals. Until the 1790s merchants who were not affiliated with the Real Compañía de Comercio de la Havana or with the Gremio de Longistas de Madrid had a difficult time in gaining a foothold in the city. In spite of the increasing declarations of Comercio Libre, Cuba's trade remained in the hands of a few select families.[128] On other occasions individuals arrived as a servant or governess in the household of a legally licensed arrival.[129]

The utility of demographic data lies not in absolute numbers but in their indication of trends. The intersection between population growth and military reform is crucial to understanding the dimension of social change in Cuba. Even those persons who were not part of the regular forces or were not directly associated with regular military service (such as suppliers of goods or services, for example) came under military scrutiny by serving in the militia.

A concomitant part of O'Reilly's plan for reform was the reorganization of the island's militia. In and around Havana, ordinary citizens were organized into two infantry companies of whites, one mounted cavalry company of whites, one infantry company of *pardos* (mulattoes), and another infantry company of *morenos* (blacks). Wealthy civilians were awarded figurehead positions of command in the militia companies; however, veteran commanders with true authority were assigned to each white militia unit, and the entire command structure of the pardo and moreno militia units consisted of veteran officers. After organizing the Havana militias, O'Reilly embarked on a journey throughout the island during which he organized all able-bodied male citizens fifteen to forty-five years of age into local militia units. Units were organized in Santiago de Cuba that included men from the neighboring town of Bayamo, in Puerto Príncipe, and one composite unit was formed in Cuatro Villas, encompassing the towns Santa Clara, Remedios, Sancti Spíritus, and Trinidad. In addition, a regiment of foot dragoons was created for Matanzas out of the disbanded foot cavalry from St. Augustine.[130] Except for Santiago de Cuba, which received a full battalion of veteran officers and soldiers from Havana, small veteran detachments were stationed in outposts to provide advice and training for local units.[131] Militia service for civilian males was universal and mandatory with a fine of twenty ducats imposed on men who failed to report, but some men such as *escribanos* (court clerks or notaries), doctors, sacristans, and teachers were exempt.[132] Similar exemptions were extended to European merchants and their employees.[133]

The impact of militarization on virtually all ranks of Cuba's society, for Havana and for the remainder of the island, may be gauged if simple quantifications are introduced to demonstrate how large a portion of the community came under the influence of military life. Moreover, such quantifications are important to show that the military presence was not seen as an invasion of outsiders but rather embraced significant portions of free society.

To define more thoroughly the percentage of the population directly affiliated with military service, a "military participation ratio" may be calculated by borrowing a technique employed by historians to calculate the number of men affiliated with military service in relation to the overall population. Such a technique was employed in a recent study that compared the military participation in Cuba in the late eighteenth and early nineteenth centuries with the military participation ratios of Mexico, Venezuela, and Chile. The study identified pre-independence Chile as the most "militarized" society with a per thousand figure of thirty-six men. The island of Cuba as a whole ranked second, with thirty-two men per thousand inhabitants. Thus, because of their low military-participation ratios, Venezuela and Mexico were more prone to rebellion, since fewer inhabitants were imbued with a military ethos. Conversely, because of their high military-participation ratios, Chile and Cuba were more co-opted into the imperial system.[134]

The analysis for Cuba, however, suffers from an acknowledged lack of precision in data stemming from the sources then available, but based upon recently available documents, the problem may be revisited. The following reevaluation eventually will be extended to encompass the entire island; meanwhile, the analysis will be centered around Havana, which had emerged as the dominant urban center of the island. Concentrating the analysis upon the Havana area has certain justifications in addition to being able to utilize precise data. O'Reilly and his successors expected that any attack would be conducted against Havana. Officers and regular troops temporarily assigned as advisers and training officers to outposts such as Nueva Filipinas, Puerto Príncipe, or Matanzas could call out their militia companies and return to defend the city if necessary.[135] As was painfully obvious from the events of 1762, if Havana fell into enemy hands, so fell the entire island.

To determine how pervasive the military presence in Havana was, troop numbers and population figures may be estimated for the years immediately after the reforms in 1764, and may be buttressed by another series of calculations using more precise military inspection records of 1776 and the population figures contained in the census of 1778.[136] To find the total urban population for both years, the numbers of professional troops in the city, who were not included in censuses, were added to the reported urban population. Such computation yielded an estimated total urban population of 36,800 for 1764 and a calculated total urban population of 42,737 for 1778. Once the total urban population was identified, two separate comparisons for each year were calculated. The first identifies the military-participation ratio based upon only the regular professional troops who were serving within a civilian population; the second military-participation ratio adds the number of civilians serving in the militia to the number of professional troops to yield a military-participation ratio based upon the total number of men who had any military affiliation whatsoever. In the first instance, the military-participation rate in 1764 was 49 professional soldiers per thousand within the general population; in 1778 it was 47 soldiers per thousand persons. The results are even more dramatic if militia members are included. In 1764, Havana exhibited a per thousand military-participation ratio of 149 men, and for 1778 a slightly lower per thousand military-participation ratio of 140.[137] Such figures stand in sharp contrast to the figures for Chile, which recorded only 36 men per thousand, and for Venezuela, with a military-participation ratio of 16 men per thousand, and are very different from the figures for Mexico, where only 7 men per thousand had any affiliation with military service. Put another way, Havana's military-participation ratio of 140 men per thousand inhabitants in 1778 was twenty times that of Mexico.[138]

Yet even such dramatic numbers fail to impart a sense of the depth of military participation within the community. Indeed, if commonsense qualifications are placed upon the figures chosen for analysis, a better idea of the pervasive military presence may be conveyed. For example, females were excluded from all military activities, so, logically, they should be omitted from the sample population.[139] Slaves, who were forbidden to bear arms, were also excluded from military service but 95 male slaves formed a select unit within the artillery brigades to perform menial tasks.[140] Additionally, among the population of white and free colored males, boys below age fifteen and men over age fifty were exempt from regular military or militia service except in cases of war or dire emergency.[141] Thus, the pool of males eligible for military service would necessarily be drawn from the white and free colored population between the ages fifteen and fifty, precisely that segment of the population organized by O'Reilly into the island's militia companies.

Using census and military data, among eligible white adult males ages fifteen to fifty, whose numbers totaled 14,503 (2,019 soldiers and 12,484 civilians), the military participation rate for Havana may be calculated at 409 per thousand.[142] In other words, approximately 41 percent of Havana's white adult male population was given military training, was inculcated with a sense of belonging and an esprit de corps of military life, benefited from privileges associated with military and militia service, and came under the jurisdiction of military law. The figures for the adult male free colored population are even more dramatic. Of 2,668 free colored males between the ages fifteen and fifty, 1,672 served in the free pardo and free moreno militia units, yielding a per thousand participation rate of 627. Put more succinctly, two-thirds of all adult free colored males in the Havana area chose to serve in the militia, since it was the only official avenue open to them.[143] Assuming that many of the adult males were heads of households, the privileges and responsibilities associated with military service would be extended to their wives, children, and household dependents.[144] As noted above, the dimension of militarization in the artificial situation prior to the assaults on Pensacola would skew the figures even more in favor of militarization. A report in August 1779 listed 9,331 men under arms in the city, including 5,308 in the regular forces and 4,023 militiamen. Thus, within the white population the military-participation ratio on the eve of battle was 524 per thousand, or just over 50 percent.[145] Comparable studies of militarized societies argue that if 20 to 25 percent of the population is under arms, the society is fully mobilized.[146] Accordingly, given a population in which, even in normal circumstances, between 30 and 66 percent of the eligible men bore arms, on a personal level, the extent of militarization on Havana's society must have been truly staggering.

The analysis may be extended to include the population centers throughout the entire island where local militia companies were organized and supervised by small troop detachments. The results, obtained by adding the members of the troop companies to the numbers of eligible males from fifteen to fifty years of age, range from a low military-participation ratio of 160 in Cuatro Villas to a high military-participation ratio of 510 in Matanzas.[147] Put differently, in Cuatro Villas, with one white infantry militia battalion, 16 percent of all eligible males were in the militia, and in Puerto Príncipe 30 percent of eligible males were in that city's white militia battalion. In Santiago/Bayamo, with a company of whites and a company of pardos and morenos, of the eligible white male population 28 percent were in militia units, and among the free population of color, 40 percent of eligible males likewise served in defending the city. In Matanzas 51 percent of eligible white males were members of the Matanzas foot dragoons.[148] Except for Cuatro Villas, which military participation ratio resembled that of New Granada, even in the provinces the military-participation ratio remained significantly higher than in other areas of Spanish America. Moreover, the degree of militarization did not diminish with population growth, and as towns and villages evolved, new militia units were organized. The war with Great Britain provided the primary impetus when Captain General Navarro decreed in 1781 that new urban companies could be formed.[149] From the original 9 militia companies organized by O'Reilly in 1764, 57 new companies were created between 1765 and 1795, including 35 additional companies of disciplined militia and 22 urban militia units.[150]

Certain enticements did exist to compensate for the dangers and uncertainty of military life. The primary ideological impetus came from a long tradition of military glorification that dated back over a thousand years beginning with the reconquest of Spain. After a millennium, the aggrandizement of military service pervaded the Iberian mentality.[151] For members of the officer corps, military service truly was a way of life and came with an inherent acknowledgment of their prestige and status. In periodic troop inspections men under review informed His Majesty's inspectors that they "derived their merits and services from their fathers (or grandfathers) who had served . . . for forty years."[152] In spite of the abyss that separated the officers and the noncommissioned officers from the rank-and-file, even the lowliest common soldier (usually) could count on being paid regularly, and their military salaries went further in Spanish America than in Spain. The rank-and-file could enjoy a degree of security that the average jornalero did not possess.[153] Officers and their families enjoyed *raciónes de la mesa,* or meal allowances, and military members had their own commissary close to the Castillo de la Fuerza.[154] Military members and king's slaves received medical treatment courtesy of the Crown.[155] Uniforms were indispensable for promoting military discipline and set the military member apart from the ragtag ordinary urban dweller.[156] Military maneuvers—sometimes as many as four per day—conducted on the Campo de Marte provided an opportunity to display one's prowess and competence.[157] Pensions paid to a military man upon retirement continued to be paid to his widow upon his death, and on occasion, retired military families were provided with housing free of charge.[158]

Another less tangible—but no less important—enticement for serving in the military was the enjoyment of the *fuero militar*. In general, fueros were a wide array of privileges extended to certain corporate groups that provided special exemptions from civic obligations and benefits not available to the general population. For example, the *fuero criminal* gave military members and their families the privilege of being tried by special military tribunals under military law, or in case of arrest to be held in barracks rather than in ordinary prisons. In addition, officers and some enlisted men in the regular armies were granted special privileges, *preeminencias*, which were exemptions from certain civic obligations such as local levies or from the attachment of their personal property for debt. Military privileges also provided for the pensions for mothers, widows, and orphans of military members.[159] In areas of Spanish America other than Cuba, the extension of the fuero militar usually was limited to men and their families serving on active duty. Under these circumstances regular troops, who always were on duty, possessed the active fuero all of the time. Militia, however, possessed the fuero only when they were mobilized. When deactivated, only officers of the disciplined militia and their wives retained complete fueros; enlisted men were entitled only to the fuero criminal. In contrast, the royal approach to the extension of fueros in Cuba underscores the singular importance of military service. After several years of debating whether and to what degree privileges should be enjoyed by militia members, a royal order in 1771 extended active fuero privileges to all military members, regulars and militia, regardless of their rank. Thus, all men with any military affiliation and their wives and children enjoyed the privileges and responsibilities such association entailed.[160]

Militia service was a powerful force in the accommodation process for the members of the ordinary ranks.[161] In 1770, on the heels of O'Reilly's expedition to New Orleans, a report from the *alcaldes del barrio* (ward selectmen) revealed that 175 men residing in the city served in Havana's white militia companies.[162] Their occupational distribution demonstrates that, as a whole, they came from the lower laboring ranks. Surprisingly, however, within the larger group, the majority of militiamen were students (26), a practice that ended in 1774 when the rector of the Colegio de San Gerónimo reached an agreement with the Marqués de la Torre to end the practice.[163] The second largest group were bakers (25), including 19 men who worked in the royal bakery close to the government center in the northern end of the city. Twenty-one militiamen were *pulperos* (proprietors of stores or taverns), 11 were day laborers, 9 each were scribes and *boticarios* (pharmacists), and 7 were carpenters. In addition, the militia units contained 2 haberdashers, 1 mason, 1 sailmaker, 1 barrelmaker, and 1 lamplighter. Not surprisingly, the occupational distribution reflected the social ordering of the city. Fishermen lived near the wharves and the fishmarket close to the entrance to the bay to the north; silversmiths and merchants clustered in the affluent areas by the Plaza de Armas; and most common laborers lived in the marginal southern end of the city.[164]

Militia service was an even more powerful force in forging an accommodation and an esprit de corps between the European sector of Havana's community and the free population of color.[165] As demonstrated above, approximately two-thirds of Havana's free colored males served in two militia companies of free pardos and morenos. Within society as a whole, militia service acknowledged and reinforced their elevated status, both within civilian society and within the military ranks. For example, in 1783, when the need arose to replace Captain Pedro Menéndez, who had died, royal officials took the job as seriously as they would have within the white units. As was customary, three men were suggested for the position: Juan de Flores, Antonio Pérez, and Cristóval Carques. First in line was Juan de Flores, captain of the company of grenadiers from an established military family, who had served in the militia units over forty-three years. During the siege, he was a member of the forces who defended the Cojímar bridge, he accompanied O'Reilly's forces on the New Orleans expedition in 1769, and he had served on both of the Pensacola expeditions.[166] The second nominee, José Antonio Pérez had served thirty-eight years and also defended the city in 1762. Later he was assigned to the frigate *Galga*, where he joined the hunt for Spain's enemies on the high seas. The third nominee, Cristóval Carques, whose life history will be explored more fully, was also a veteran, with thirty-eight years of service. In making the final selection, Inspector of the Troops Bernardo Troncoso explained that all of the men were meritorious but his decision weighed in favor of Flores because of his longer time in service.[167]

Although he lost out to Juan de Flores in the selection round of 1783, Cristóval Carques, who was from a prosperous free colored family and whose illustrious career spanned more than fifty years, demonstrates the importance of militia service in increasing a man's prestige and personal wealth. Born in Havana, he was the legitimate and literate son of free colored militia captain Francisco Xavier Carques and Gabriela Pérez.[168] He entered the Havana pardo militia in 1744. As a young man, he served on the famous ship *Invincible* in her sortie against British admiral Vernon in 1748. Like many of his comrades, he participated in the defense of the Cojímar bridge in 1762 and in the two expeditions to Pensacola.[169]

Carques's exemplary militia service mirrors his personal life, in which he enjoyed enviable capital accumulation. At the time of his first marriage, to María Josepha de Flores, he already owned his family home on Calle Obrapía 151 and enjoyed personal wealth of 1,000 silver pesos. During his second marriage, to María Rosa Alvarez (who was also literate), he increased his personal wealth to 6,000 pesos, and acquired considerable clothing, gold jewelry, and a female slave (named Catalina). He and his third wife, María Isabel Alvarez, owned in addition to the house on Calle Obrapía, a two-story house on Calle Compostela, another on Calle Jesús María, a fourth house on Calle Paula plus their personal property and six slaves. At the time of his death in 1794, Carques was a captain in the Battalion of Pardos, a post he had earned with distinction. In death, he chose to take one of his two most important possessions with him, his military uniform. The other, his silver medal with the bust of Charles III, he left with his family as a symbol of his service to Spain.[170]

While military service clearly led to a group of free colored elites who owned substantial property, it also seems to have contributed to freedom for some of Havana's slaves. To begin with, Charles III kept the promise made in his name by Governor Juan de Prado to free the slaves who fought for Spain during the British invasion in 1762.[171] Although not enslaved himself, during his lifetime of militia service, free black Juan de Dios Arenciba and his wife of twenty-five years, Ana Josepha Marroto, acquired a farm of one and a half *caballerías* (approximately 49.5 acres) in Santiago de las Vegas and three slaves. On his deathbed, Arenciba requested that his wife free the youngest of their slaves, Josefa Rafaela.[172] Antonio José Díaz, a retired captain from the Battalion of Morenos, was the son of free black Juan Bautista Arenciba; however, his mother, Catalina Díaz, originally was from Guinea, so she probably arrived as a slave. By the time of his death in 1795, Díaz owned a house that he had purchased with his own money that he passed on to his four children, Tomás, José, José María and María Soledad.[173] The family also owned a wattle-and-daub house located on a lot owned by the Cabildo de Negros Carabali purchased by the youngest sibling, María Soledad, from free morena María Rosario Oquendo thirty years before.[174] Even more exceptional were Antonio Abad del Rey from Guinea and his Conga wife, Rosalia Sabiona, who, within their lifetimes, went from being property to being property owners. The details about how they earned their freedom are unclear, but by 1796, Abad del Rey was a veteran of the Battalion of Morenos who enjoyed full fuero privileges. During the course of their lives, the couple acquired a wattle-and-daub house on Calle San Juan de Dios across the street from the pardo militia barracks. They also owned one female slave and a mulatto youth, José Cecilio. In spite of his obvious success, though, the militiaman requested to be buried in a humble fashion in the habit of San Francisco.[175]

Both Crown and community recognized the importance of the free colored militia units. Three soldiers in the Battalion of Pardos and seven in the Battalion of Morenos perished in the Pensacola campaign, and their survivors were awarded half of their monthly salary for the remainder of their lives.[176] After years of meritorious service, members of the pardo and moreno militia units were granted retirement just as were members of the white militia units.[177] Another way the Crown recognized meritorious service was to bestow service medals such as the one that Cristóval Carques left to his heirs. Francisco Antonio Alvarez of the Infantry Battalion of Pardos received the privilege to use a silver medal with the image of Charles IV, as did brothers Captain José Sánchez and Sergeant Juan Sánchez of the pardo artillery company.[178] Grenadier Juan Daniel Rivera received a greater honor when he was awarded a similar medal fashioned of gold.[179] Service medals represented not only a financial windfall, since they were crafted of precious metals, but also honor and intangible status. The receipt of the medal came with an announcement in the *Papel Periódico de la Havana*, a public declaration that the militiaman was exempt from sumptuary laws that prohibited the free people of color from wearing certain articles of clothing and jewelry in public places.

In recent years, a rich historiography has emerged evaluating whether and to what extent the life of Cuba's black and mixed-blood population differed from the life experiences of slaves and lower ranks elsewhere. Such scholarship, however, is usually based upon the symbiotic relationship between plantation slavery and sugar cultivation, and plantation slavery was far removed from the real lives of most of Cuba's free population of color and only slightly less so from that of most of Havana's slaves. Cuba's free coloreds enjoyed privileges unique in relation to free people elsewhere, a situation whose significance was not lost on metropolitan policy makers. In 1792, the ministers in the Council of the Indies acknowledged that Cuba's free people of color were less numerous than elsewhere, and "they are treated better" in comparison to the free colored population in the neighboring French colony, St. Domingue.[180]

Thus, the importance of military service in Cuba must be evaluated within an imperial context. The privilege and prestige granted to Cuba's military members—both regulars and militia—stand in sharp contrast to the experience of military personnel in Mexico or New Granada, where 7 and 16 percent of the population, respectively, enjoyed military privileges, but only a portion of the time.[181] Cubans were well aware that they enjoyed special status within the imperial context. From disgrace in 1762, by the 1780s, and in the aftermath of the American Revolutionary War, the island had emerged as the darling of His Majesty's colonial family. Virtually total militarization had allowed the regular troops to sail with Bernardo de Gálvez on his successful expedition to capture Pensacola while leaving a skeleton force in charge of militia units to defend the island. The subsequent events in the Caribbean after 1764 have led Allan J. Kuethe to conclude that military reform in Cuba was a success.[182]

Indeed, most of O'Reilly's contemporaries would have agreed with such an evaluation. After reforming Cuba's military structure, O'Reilly went to Puerto Rico, where he attempted a similar reorganization for that island. He returned to Spain briefly only to be ordered back to Cuba in 1769 to lead an expedition to New Orleans to subdue recalcitrant French inhabitants. His overwhelming success in bringing the former Frenchmen into line, in spite of the harsh measures he employed, contributed to the meteoric rise of his career, and O'Reilly returned to Spain once again to the accolades of the population and the court alike. He was promoted to inspector general of the army and was charged with accomplishing a similar reorganization in the Spanish army.[183] A number of men who had distinguished themselves in the New Orleans campaign chose to return to the peninsula with him. Theirs was a fateful decision that for some came with fatal results.

Meanwhile, on the island of Cuba, as a consequence of military reform, the population structure was altered dramatically. By the 1780s the social structure of the island had taken on a new profile based upon the presence of thousands of troops who had arrived from 1763 onward. Population growth cannot be attributed to natural increase alone, and immigration from other colonial areas was negligible. Census documents from the mid 1780s for the towns and villages that surrounded Havana support the hypothesis of a dynamic population constantly on the move. The censuses confirm what other evidence suggests: that persons from Havana were moving outward to the evolutionary and the planned communities. The majority of the outlying-village residents came (in descending order) from Havana; from the Canary Islands; from the various provinces in Spain; and from other areas, such as other Cuban towns or places in Europe. These figures hold true for evolutionary communities such as Jesús del Monte,

Bauta, and Arroyo Arenas, as well as for the reorganized community Güines.[184] When these findings are combined with population figures for the city and the immediate suburbs, they confirm that Havana was gaining population, and when the city had reached a saturation point, the inhabitants were migrating outward and were being replaced by new residents in the city.

O'Reilly's plan to settle veterans in the countryside may not have proceeded as rapidly as he would have liked, but the legal mechanisms to allow retiring soldiers to settle in Cuba remained in place and the end result was the same. Many men took advantage of royal concessions and made Cuba their home. Others soldiers died, but their widows and families chose not to return to Spain. Yet regardless of the circumstances surrounding their decision, their presence changed Cuban society irrevocably. Even if the new arrivals had no contact with the local population, their presence alone affected the human landscape, but surely it is naive to suppose that the military community lived unto itself. From the evidence available, it appears that the military community had a spectacular effect upon the social structure of the island. A majority of veterans remained in the vicinity of Havana, contributed to the explosive growth of that city and its immediate hinterland, and became the prime motivators in a dynamic process of population movement. More important, their social interaction with Creole families became one of the most visible and significant features of military reform. These issues will be discussed in the following chapters.

4

Honor Is Life

On a warm December day in 1794, aging artillery commander Colonel Vicente de Garcini rode in his carriage through the primary city gates of Havana. As he passed through the Campo de Marte, the colonel viewed with distaste the shacks that clung to the perimeter of the parade ground, hovels that pressed ever closer to the city and impinged upon the effective training of his troops.[1] His carriage driver needed no directions, as he knew to take the new central road that branched from the Calle de la Zanza leading toward the Loma de Aróstegui and the almost completed Castillo del Príncipe. As the colonel sat back to enjoy the ride, he never failed to be amazed at the changes in the once-pristine countryside where he and his companions had come for recreation in the 1770s. Now a substantial road that had been a footpath twenty years before led to his destination, his newly acquired farm (estancia). The colonel was filled with pride as the carriage approached and he saw the estancia's name carved in the ornate gatepost, "El Retiro," a name so evocative of the circumstances that contributed to its establishment.[2]

Garcini, like many others, had come to Havana in the 1770s with a regiment of replacement troops when war with Great Britain was imminent.[3] During his years of service in Cuba, the colonel, with the inherent prestige of being peninsular and military, had contracted an advantageous marriage to the daughter of *regidor perpetuo* (hereditary magistrate) Sebastián de Peñalver and had arranged a similar marriage for his brother Jaime to his wife's sister.[4] The marriage brought the two brothers into an extended kinship network that ultimately extended to the family of the Conde de Casa Barreto, the Marqués de Ameno Prado, and the Conde de Jaruco y Mopox.[5] Looking forward to his retirement, with local kinship and *compadrazgo* links established, the colonel had purchased the estancia that previously had belonged to the Urrutía family, thus following the economic winds of change and establishing himself as a landowner with diverse agricultural interests. There, like so many other peninsulars who had retired from His Majesty's armies, he intended to pass the days of his retirement, surrounded by his children and grandchildren, enjoying his military pension and the profits of his growing enterprise. But even though he had branched out into a quasicommercial venture, the name of his estancia, El Retiro, echoed the years of military service that were the foundation upon which the man's enterprise was built.[6]

The experiences of Vicente de Garcini exemplify the fortunes of military personnel who were assigned to Cuba in the wake of reform measures implemented after the return of the island to Spanish sovereignty. In the years immediately following the restructuring, the Crown, of necessity, drew upon the experience of men who had been serving in the Caribbean ambit prior to the defeat. Such men, incorporated into the reformed Fixed Regiment of Havana, enjoyed unparalleled advancement as the Caribbean theater grew in importance. Moreover, officers' career patterns changed as service in the Caribbean eclipsed peninsular experience as a measure of a man's ability to command. As permanence replaced transience for the officer ranks, Creole sons of peninsular fathers were allowed to advance to important positions in the military structure, and with their sons established in positions of importance, peninsular officers accepted royal incentives and elected to retire on the island rather than return to Spain. The officer corps, however, was only part of the floodtide of immigration that contributed to social change in the city. A prosperous economy beckoned lower-echelon officers and the rank-and-file alike, and from 1764 onward, military spending and construction on fortification projects benefited all sectors of Havana's society.

Cuba's re-formed military required a command structure of experienced and capable men. First and foremost were defense considerations, but equally important was the tradition of placing the reins of government in the hands of military men. In the fortified cities throughout the Caribbean, the governor was always a career military officer, as was his lieutenant governor, his secretary, his legal adviser, and the engineers responsible for building and maintaining the fortifications.[7] In the major towns and cities, veteran troops were responsible for maintaining the peace and for policing the streets. In outlying districts, the small veteran detachment formed the local arm of central government, and the ranking officer of the local unit represented the governor in absentia.[8] Veteran troops patrolled the roads, acted as escort for payroll shipments and for visiting dignitaries, and always were charged with the responsibility to ferret out contraband activity.[9] Veteran officers served as advisers to local militia units and as drill instructors for practice sessions on Sunday morning.[10] In addition, the administration of justice also fell to military men. In 1764, Alejandro O'Reilly had proposed the establishment of a *tribunal de apelaciones* (appellate court) in Cuba as part of his overall reform plan, arguing that the distance from the Audiencia in Santo Domingo, exacerbated by having only one regularly scheduled ship traveling between Havana and there, served to impede the swift implementation of justice.[11] O'Reilly's plan was not carried out until the transferal of the Audiencia to Puerto Príncipe in 1796, and in the interim, locally stationed officers acted as courts of first instance. Judicial proceedings might begin locally but were carried up through the military chain of command to the captain general in Havana. The quasimilitary judicial system reinforced the Caribbean tradition of overlapping jurisdictions divided among military service, governance, and justice, while, at the same time, it gave locally stationed military officers extraordinary powers over ordinary citizens.[12]

The immediacy of the post-1763 situation demanded talented, judicious, and experienced men, and in reorganizing His Majesty's forces in Cuba, O'Reilly and his successors relied upon men with experience in the Caribbean. Some career officers had survived the postsiege scrutiny with their reputations and careers intact. Sergeant Major of the Plaza Antonio Remírez de Esteñóz, who at the time of the occupation had accumulated more than forty years' service, was entrusted with delivering the articles of capitulation to the British. After the return of the city to Spanish sovereignty, Remírez de Esteñóz retained his position as sergeant major and the family suffered no loss of prestige by his conduct during the siege.[13] Lieutenant Mariano Gelabert survived the fighting, the siege, and the subsequent purge and remained a member of the fixo through 1770.[14] Second Lieutenant Manuel de Aldana had taken part in the defense of the Chorrera watchtower and the Cabaña Heights. He had been among the command force who voluntarily left for Spain on British transports after the capitulation, but he had returned to Havana in 1763, and resumed his career in His Majesty's armies, being posted in several places throughout the Caribbean through 1797.[15] Another cohort of the upper-echelon troops had been assigned to circum-Caribbean posts such as Pensacola, St. Augustine, or Santiago de Cuba at the time of the siege, so they could not be held responsible for the fall of Havana. These experienced men formed the nucleus of the new command structure, and even though O'Reilly initially had sought to limit the influence of permanently fixed regiments, the fixo would evolve as the mainstay for leadership on the island.[16]

In 1765, the cohort of officers of the Fixo contained 65 commissioned officers, 47 noncommissioned officers, and 25 cadets. Two-thirds of the commissioned officer corps were peninsular-born men (45 out of 65), and the noncommissioned officers were overwhelmingly peninsular, with only 4 of 47 being born in Havana. The cadet corps exhibited exactly opposite characteristics, with 24 of 25 cadets being Creole.[17] Although they would have been unaware of their fate, the majority of the officers serving in the Fixo in 1765 were destined to remain in service in Cuba or her dependent cities. All 5 lieutenant colonels retained senior positions in the army and were assigned almost immediately to positions of command throughout the island.[18] Of 14 captains, 1 elected to retire on the island within three years, but 9 remained in service and 3 still served at the rank of lieutenant colonel in 1795.[19] Lieutenants, younger men whose careers would have spanned the thirty-five years from 1762 through the 1790s, were most affected by policy decisions stemming from international circumstances and the preparation for another war with Great Britain. Among this group, 15 of the original cohort of 18 remained in service in Cuba.[20] So did 17 of 25 second lieutenants, of whom at least 5 were lieutenant colonels by 1795.[21]

In the years following the reorganization of 1763, the typical man placed in a senior leadership position would be Spanish-born and would have served a number of years in European campaigns, often in Italy, Portugal, or North Africa, before transferal to the Indies. Some officers had participated in the defense of Santiago de Cuba during the siege in 1738 by British admiral Vernon, or had been part of the defense of Havana in 1748 against the naval forces of Admiral Knowles.[22] One such example, Miguel de Muesas would be moved from Bayamo to serve as interim governor of Santiago de Cuba upon the death of the Marqués de Casa Cagigal before being promoted to the position of captain general of Puerto Rico.[23]

Lieutenant Colonel Juan Dabán, as sergeant major of the Second Battalion of Havana, was also sent to Santiago de Cuba before being designated inspector general of the troops in 1773.[24] Career officer Vicente de Zéspedes had been serving in Pensacola during the time of the siege.[25] Recalled to Havana, he became the commander of the Third Battalion of the Fixo, a post he held until he was assigned to Santiago de Cuba as interim governor in the late 1770s.[26] When Dabán was promoted to the captaincy general of Puerto Rico (in what appears to have evolved as the normal career progression for upper-echelon officers), Zéspedes assumed the post of inspector general of troops of the island before receiving his own governorship in Florida in 1784.[27]

The cadre of fourteen captains and eighteen lieutenants could look forward to their careers following lines similar to those of Muesas, Dabán, or Zéspedes, with one important difference. In the past, European and African campaigns provided the training in military strategy, tactics, and leadership necessary for promotion. Now the Caribbean replaced and eventually eclipsed the required peninsular experience. With the establishment of military outposts in hamlets such as Bayamo, Jagua, and Nueva Filipinas and the assignment there of small detachments of regular troops supplemented by local militia, younger officers received the opportunity to learn the art of command and the organization of drills while maintaining an ever-vigilant eye on the coast.[28]

A review of the chain of command of outlying detachments reveals the dependence on officers of the fixo. Captain Ventura Díaz, who ultimately accumulated over forty years of service in the Caribbean, was placed in charge of the newly created garrison in Jagua, where he served from 1771 through 1778.[29] Díaz was replaced by Manuel de Aldana, who commanded the detachment from 1779 to 1785 before advancing to the position of sergeant major of the plaza under Zéspedes in Florida in 1785.[30] When an anchorage was authorized at Batabanó in the 1770s, fixo captain Antonio López de Toledo was chosen to lead the garrison and militia unit that guarded the new port.[31] Baracoa resembled a revolving door as fixo officers were assigned to replace and were relieved by their comrades-in-arms. Between 1773 and 1784, the lieutenant governorship of Baracoa was occupied sequentially by four fixo captains: Miguel de Olea, who was replaced by Francisco del Río, replaced, in turn, by Rafael de Limonta and he by José de Saavedra.[32] By 1784, the responsibility for overseeing the defense of Baracoa was assigned to José de Horrutiner, who had entered as a cadet when the fixo was reorganized in 1763.[33]

Service in His Majesty's army could be extremely rewarding but was not without its perils. Career officers had to cope not only with the constant danger associated with warfare and the continuous vigilance required to prevent contraband activities, but also with the petty jealousies inherent in royal service and the overlapping jurisdictions created by the fiscal, judicial, and military reorganization. For example, the career of Captain Miguel Ibáñez Cuevas seemed promising when he was first assigned to command the outpost in Bayamo in 1766, and in little more than a year he was promoted to the position of lieutenant governor of Puerto Príncipe.[34] However, his career was seriously jeopardized when he became embroiled in a controversy with the intendant, Miguel de Altarriba, and other ministers of the treasury, who accused him and three other conspirators of embezzling funds in his care.[35] In spite of his military rank and its attendant privilege, Ibáñez Cuevas was arrested by another fixo member, Ramón Vuelta Flores, and was returned to Havana in chains wearing only the clothes on his back, where he was imprisoned with common criminals, a treatment clearly unbefitting his station as a military member and in violation of his rights under the fuero militar.[36] After the proceedings relating to his case wound through the existing judicial maze, Ibáñez Cuevas was exonerated, and because of his "unjust persecution" was reinstated and promoted to lieutenant colonel.[37] Not content with simple reinstatement and largely through his own perseverance after he was absolved of all wrongdoing, he brought his case to the attention of the Council of the Indies in Madrid, and in 1782, Charles III granted him a special royal grace for restitution and a promotion to full colonel.[38] Another case, though not as extreme as that of Ibáñez Cuevas, was the reprimand of Juan Antonio Ayans de Ureta, the governor of Santiago de Cuba, who was punished for apparently overstepping his authority, thus running afoul of the previous captain general, in pursuing a case involving contraband in 1779.[39] Similarly Vicente de Zéspedes and the third intendant of the island, Juan Ignacio de Urriza, constantly bickered about money matters back and forth between Havana and St. Augustine when Zéspedes served as the governor of Florida in the 1780s.[40]

In spite of the possible pitfalls of entering the royal armies, for young Creoles the luster of a military career remained undiminished. In 1764, O'Reilly established the Noble Corps of Cadets, thereby creating a means through which Creole youths could enter military life.[41] Although supposedly open to any qualified youth, the cohort of cadets in 1765 was composed of sons or grandsons of officers or of those who, like Estéban de Menocal and Antonio Fernández de Velasco, were appointed because of their noble birth.[42] A bit of imagination brings to life the ceremony such as the one that occurred on August 11, 1764, inducting two of the four López de Toledo brothers, sons of the fixo captain who would become the commander of the outpost at Batabanó. The brothers, following their father and grandfather into Charles III's army, were joined by Juan and Joaquín de Landa, also sons of a captain, and by José de Repilado, the son of a lieutenant who died in royal service.[43] Few who were present could fail to be impressed by the gathering of notables. O'Reilly himself would have presided over the ceremonies. After all, as head of the corps of cadets, conducting induction ceremonies was part of his designated responsibilities. The Conde de Ricla, as the governor and a military man, would have attended this important function. The entire First Battalion would be present dressed in their white uniforms with the royal coat of arms emblazoned on their shoulders. In their blue cadet uniforms trimmed in gold, the boys would have presented a sharp contrast to the gathering of veterans. Flags of the various infantry, artillery, and cavalry companies would have fluttered in the breeze, and the boys could make out the motto of the militia company of Matanzas: "Honor Is Life" proclaimed the banner. The motto must have struck home to the youths, who, surrounded by friends and family, could not help but feel proud as the pomp and ceremony reinforced the mystique and exclusivity of being accepted as members of the Royal Army of Spain.[44]

The case of Ibáñez Cuevas being exceptional, young men entering His Majesty's armies could expect their careers to encompass a much more mundane existence. After several years of study and training, graduation would come with a promotion to second lieutenant that normally occurred at the end of eight years.[45] A young man would expect to remain a second lieutenant an average of twelve more years, until he reached his mid-thirties, and the promotion to captain would normally come only after the age of forty.[46] Certain exceptions allowed more rapid promotion, although none as unusual as the case of Ibáñez Cuevas, who was promoted to rectify an injustice.[47] More representative of accelerated advancement was Pedro Remírez de Esteñóz, who, as the grandson of the former sergeant major of Havana and by volunteering for the Gulf Coast expeditions with Bernardo de Gálvez from 1778 through 1782, advanced through influence and merit.[48] Juan José Escañes had been singled out for preference in promotion because of the exceptional bravery and leadership he had shown when his party was ambushed by hostile Indians while on patrol in Florida.[49] On occasion, the successful capture of a shipment of contraband could earn an aspiring officer a promotion and even a portion of the spoils as a reward for his exemplary service to the Crown.[50]

The career of Juan Gemir y Lleonart, of impeccable lineage, represents the quintessential track serving in the Caribbean theater would take. The youth drew upon generations of tradition as the son of a military officer from Cataluña, Lieutenant Colonel Juan Lleonart, who ultimately served as the captain general of Guatemala, and Mariana Crespite y Mora, who arrived with her first husband, the lieutenant governor of the island.[51] Lleonart began his career as a cadet and was assigned to Santiago de Cuba in 1754, where he distinguished himself by making fifty-eight arrests for contraband and apprehending sixteen deserters while assigned to the detachment at Puerto Príncipe.[52] From Santiago, he was sent to Havana in 1762, where in 1764 he welcomed his father, who had been part of the evacuation force from Florida that relinquished the province to the British.[53] In 1766 he was assigned the lieutenant governorship of Bayamo, remaining there until 1772, when he returned to Puerto Príncipe as the lieutenant governor of the more important garrison.[54] After having gained the requisite experience in the provinces, Gemir y Lleonart returned to the *plana mayor* (high command) of the Second Battalion of Havana stationed in Santiago de Cuba, from which eventually he ascended through the senior ranks to attain the position of its commander in 1785.[55] By 1792, he was at the peak of his career with the rank of lieutenant colonel after having served in His Catholic Majesty's army for forty-six of his sixty-one years.[56]

The attainment of high rank and the promise of retirement awaited at the end of one's military career. After serving a lifetime in Cuba, separating soldiers took advantage of a decree issued in 1766 that permitted them to leave royal service in any city of their choice. For career soldiers the retirement option included a monthly pension of half of one's normal salary.[57] Captain Gabriel de Zubieta from Bilbao, who had commanded the watchtower at Chorrera during the siege, retired leaving his son, Bernabé, to carry on the family military tradition.[58] Sixty-year-old Captain Juan de Landa could retire from his command of the garrison in Bayamo after seeing his sons, Juan and Joaquín, safely ensconced in the corps of cadets.[59] Manuel de Aldana, another veteran of the siege, served until 1797, when he was granted his retirement in Santiago de Cuba.[60] Often, the veteran's retirement was proudly proclaimed in the local newspaper in announcements such as the one that appeared on August 25, 1791, informing Havana that "His Majesty has granted retirement to Miguel Alvarez, Pablo Alfonso, and Manuel Meriño Serraquín at home with full privileges [fuero] and the use of their uniforms."[61] Many officers separated from active service but retained their affiliation (*agregación*) with their former units, or secured a new position in the militia, which provided them with uninterrupted military privileges and an increased pension based upon their higher rank.[62] As older officers retired, they made room for the younger men whom they had trained and who were ready to succeed to their command.

For many officers, however, retirement appears to have been forced upon them because of illness or an inability to serve effectively.[63] Many supernumeraries showed no inclination to retire and served to an advanced age. Brothers Isidro and Rafael de Limonta, born in Santiago de Cuba of noble parents, spent more than fifty-five years apiece in military service, culminating their careers by both attaining the rank of full colonel in 1795.[64] During a periodic review in 1792, mounted cavalry colonel Antonio Fernández responded proudly that his health was "robust" at seventy-one years of age![65] Although he could have requested his retirement in 1792, Juan Gemir y Lleonart remained on active duty in 1793, and he was chosen with Colonel Matias de Armona to lead the ill-fated expedition to Santo Domingo.[66] Even though they may have retired, their obligation to defend the island could never be abrogated. When the security of Cuba was threatened, the old warriors dusted off and donned their uniforms in response to the call to arms. Lieutenant Colonel Francisco de Paula Oñoro officially retired in 1788 because of the wounds he suffered when a bomb exploded close to him during one of his many campaigns.[67] Nevertheless, during the crisis in 1793 and the declaration of war against France, Oñoro returned to active duty and earned a promotion to full colonel in 1795.[68]

Although the fixo was most representative of military service in the Caribbean, the permanence of its officers was by no means unique. The career patterns of men who served in the artillery and in the mounted cavalry units paralleled those of men in the fixo.[69] Similarly, men in the Engineer Corps once assigned to duty in Cuba and the Caribbean would spend the better portion of their professional lives overseeing the repair of fortifications in Havana or Santiago de Cuba, or supervising the construction of new structures in Batabanó, Nueva Filipinas, or St. Augustine.[70] Fixo officers from the cohort of 1765 were joined by peninsular officers who arrived with refuerzo units during the 1770s when another war was imminent. Men such as Vicente de Garcini, Vicente Risel (Garcini's successor as commander of Cuba's artillery units), and Bartolomé de Morales arrived in Cuba in the 1760s and '70s and never returned to Spain or sought to transfer to another area.[71] Indeed, the opposite was more often the case, as officers and soldiers assigned to mainland regiments avidly sought transfers to Cuban units.[72]

The assignment of career officers of peninsular origin in the 1760s and '70s may have been a response to the exigencies of the moment; however, the advancement of fixo cadets through the ranks demonstrates that Crown officials sought, promoted, and retained Creoles in positions of responsibility. The only difference that distinguished the career of cadets in 1765 was their Caribbean birth, a distinction that would become less meaningful as Charles III's reign drew to a close. The induction and promotion of Creole sons were engineered by their peninsular fathers, and, significantly, the fathers saw their sons' best avenue to success as being or remaining in service in the Caribbean. Perhaps the urgency of the moment allowed peninsular strategists to overlook a man's Creole birth, or perhaps being Creole was no longer seen as a detriment to one's career. Within Charles III's highest ministries, a new importance was attached to experience in the Americas after 1773, when the positions of the Council of the Indies were made equal to those on the Council of Castille.[73] Nevertheless, the "Creolization" of the Cuban military should not be overstated. While the cadets were overwhelmingly of Creole birth, they were, without exception, either the Creole sons of a peninsular family with a long-established military tradition or of noble birth. And in spite of the tendency to allow American-born youths into the Noble Corps of Cadets, Creole officers and their families still had to pass the strict scrutiny of royal officials at every turn. However, particularly after 1782 what it meant to be "Creole" had different resonance in Cuba than it did elsewhere in Spain's American dominions, and with the new urgency of defending the Caribbean against the enemy, Cuban Creoles clearly were able to overcome the ostensible stigma of being born in the colonies.

Thus, in the wake of military reforms after 1763, a "new group of elites" arose to prominence.[74] Although military officers were but a small and privileged sector of Havana's society, they represented the highest echelons of the largest and most important group on the island. More important, their experiences differ but little from that of the noncommissioned officers and the rank-and-file, the men who would become O'Reilly's invisible immigrants and whose presence would contribute so much to changing the social and spatial landscape of Cuba.

Junior and noncommissioned officers left a less prominent profile on the documentary record. Because they earned less to begin with, their pensions were not as large as those awarded to senior officers. Many such men petitioned the royal administration for favors and concessions in the hope of augmenting their pensions with additional income.[75] Frequently such men were forced to seek employment after retirement, and the rapidly expanding Bourbon bureaucracy, and in particular, the Royal Treasury, provided just such an opportunity. For example, Felipe Magriña, a senior noncommissioned officer, secured a position in 1794 upon his retirement from the Light Infantry Company of Cataluña.[76] Captain Raymundo de Arrivas, after forty-two years of service, including being taken prisoner of war, was forced to leave active duty as a result of his injuries. With two sons, a stepson, and two sons-in-law already in military service, he obtained a position for himself and for his youngest son, Tadeo, in the expanding treasury.[77] Francisco de Quijano accepted a position fraught with almost as much peril as military service—collecting rents from properties that the treasury owned outside of town.[78]

Lieutenants and sergeants constituted one of the key elements in O'Reilly's plan to install retirees in the local settlements to repel enemy incursions and to prevent smuggling. At his suggestion, the Conde de Ricla created the post of *capitán del partido* (district captain or constable), combining police functions and patrol functions for prevention of enemy incursions at the local level. Intendant Juan Ignacio de Urriza took O'Reilly's idea one step further and suggested to the royal governor under whom he served, the Marqués de la Torre, to expand the police powers of the capitanes del partido. Urriza argued that the capitanes could be even more effective in maintaining internal order by acting as the king's eyes and ears. The governor included Urriza's suggestion in his proclamation, the Bando del Buen Gobierno, three weeks later.[79] If ordinary incentives were not sufficient inducement, a bounty system was established that offered cash payments for the apprehension of "desertores . . . y otros mal hechores, vagos, y viciosos," who would be summarily dispatched to the fortification projects.[80] In his farewell address to the city, the marqués boasted that he was responsible for expanding the scope of responsibility of the capitanes del partido (although it was indisputably Urizza's idea), and de la Torre proudly reported that he had sent more than fifty "delinquents" to presidios in Africa, San Juan de Ulloa, Puerto Rico, and Omoa.[81]

The job of rounding up such delinquents fell to men such as Antonio Ruíz, who in 1774 received permission to remain in the Santiago district with a sergeant's rank.[82] José Rafael Lasquetti, formerly a second lieutenant of the Regiment of Flandes, retired in 1791 and was granted the lieutenant's position assisting the capitán del partido of the district of Guatao.[83] Closer to Havana, the extraurban barrios were policed by retired lieutenants Juan José Escuder, who became the capitán del partido of the Barrio del Salud, and Vicente de Castilla, who upon his retirement assumed a similar position in the neighboring barrio, El Cerro.[84] To aid these men in their task, rules were established for the apprehension of criminals and for the conduct such capitanes must obey, aided by local press that printed and sold the decree for one real.[85] By 1795, ninety-seven jueces pédaneos patrolled the hamlets surrounding Havana.[86]

The bulk of the retirees, however, came from the rank and file. The implementation of the program, like its conception, displays an ad hoc quality that eventually evolved into an elaborate institutionalized and bureaucratic process. In the beginning, when the plan was still in its tentative stages, military officials kept few records of retirees—after all, once retired, the man was no longer a concern of the treasury. Accordingly, rank-and-file soldiers rarely appear in the early records, not only because of their low status but also because of the nature of the documentation. When a man separated or retired, he was presented with his discharge papers, which remained with him or his family.[87] Retirement documents, such as those granted to invalid Francisco Muñoz in September 1776, were treasured as a precious testimony of the veteran's status that set him apart from the ordinary man.[88] More important, such papers also were evidence that he could not be subject to forced reinduction or, worse still, be arrested as a deserter.[89] For example, Antonio López Díaz had obtained his discharge license and had returned to Trinidad, where he was mistaken for a deserter. Apprehended by overzealous local authorities, he was transported to Havana, and ultimately was exonerated and released only after a lengthy judicial process.[90]

Extraordinary circumstances such as the unfortunate arrest of López Díaz allowed copies of an ordinary soldier's discharge to survive in a context other than the man's separation from service. Even more exceptional, the original documents were surrendered by the soldier's family to add support to their particular claim. Such was the case in the pension request of Margarita Escovedo, who needed her husband's retirement certificate to verify her own eligibility for support. Contained within the verification papers that granted her a pension of two reals per day were the original discharge papers of her husband, artillery soldier Francisco de Otero, who left active service in 1764. While it is unclear whether his retirement was voluntary or was forced upon him, his papers were approved and signed by O'Reilly himself.[91] The daughters of Juan Manuel Ximénes provided a copy of their father's discharge papers to royal officials when they too came before the treasury requesting financial assistance.[92] More commonly, however, retirement patterns for rank-and-file soldiers can only be established by inference. Prior to his arrest, Miguel Ibáñez Cuevas relayed that he had permitted seven unnamed men to remain in his jurisdiction in Santiago rather than have them return with the regular rotation of the Dragones de América.[93] Almost as an afterthought, de la Torre informed the lieutenant governor of Santiago de Cuba that he had granted permission to remain on the island to artillery soldiers Andrés Padilla and Pedro del Castillo.[94]

In the early years, one area in which Bourbon officials did keep meticu-
lous records was in documenting the returnees, that is, persons for whom
the treasury paid the return passage to Spain. For example, in 1772, at least
119 veterans and their families returned to Spain courtesy of the Crown.[95]
Similarly, in May 1776, Captain Estéban Fontanet, commander of the
Compañía de Fucileros de las Montañas (Company of Mountain Riflemen)
led five of his men back to Barcelona after serving fourteen years in Florida
and Cuba.[96] Yet these members of the Compañía de Fucileros left fourteen
of their comrades-in-arms in the garrison in Puerto Príncipe where they
had been assigned in 1771.[97] Put simply, soldiers who can be documented
as returning to Spain in 1772 could not begin to offset the 1,800 troops that
had arrived the year previous. By the mid-1770s, the number of requests
to return to Spain began to decline. One obvious reason was the imminent
entry into the war with Great Britain that propelled the Caribbean theater
to imperial prominence. The demand for increased forces was coupled with
progressively liberal royal decrees to encourage men to remain in
America, and in 1775 the monarchy officially extended royal privileges to
retire in place with a portion of their salary to lower ranks that officers and
noncommissioned officers had enjoyed for nearly a decade.[98]

Inevitably, as the military presence spread throughout the island, the
nameless and faceless veterans could no longer remain anonymous. As
time went on and the requests for *retiros* and *premios* (retirements and
remunerations) increased, royal officials were forced to account for the
hundreds of men who left military service, not only because they were
eligible for retirement pensions but also because they would retain their
fuero militar. For example, at the end of 1784, Brigadier General Bernardo
Troncoso conducted an inspection of the troops in the various regiments
that served in Havana. Thirty-seven men in the Regimento de Voluntarios
Blancos de Havana, 5 men in the Voluntarios de Cavallería, 11 men in the
Battalion de Morenos Libres, and 5 men in the Battalion de Pardos Libres
were unfit for service, and Troncoso suggested that they should be granted
their separation because of twenty or more years of service.[99] Regardless
of whether these men served in the regular forces or the militia, or
whether they were white, brown, or black, military officers agreed that
they shared the experiences of having served Charles III well and with
dignity for half a lifetime, they were all similarly "tired," and they all deserved retirement with pensions and the military privileges.[100]

But acknowledgment by local officials was only the beginning of some
soldiers' long battle to receive their retirement pay; now the request
needed to be verified and approved at higher levels. In 1782, grenadier José

Nicolás Hernández, of the Infantry of Havana but originally from the Canary Islands, petitioned military officials for his retirement based upon his
more than twenty years of service rather than the less-generous pension
for invalids. While on sentry duty in the defense of El Morro in 1762, he
had received a bullet wound that had cost him two fingers on his left hand
and one on his right, but he had never left his post, continuing to fire at the
enemy in the futile defense of the fort. During O'Reilly's purges, he had
been spared from reassignment to the Castillo de la Punta like the majority
of the invalids, and instead had been allowed to reside with his family and
continue in military service. Twenty years later, when the old, tired soldier
sought to separate, he needed the confirmation of his commanding officers
to verify his status as a retiree, not as an invalid. One by one his superior
officers, Captains José de Rivas and Manuel Gallegos de Viamonte, con-
firmed that in spite of his infirmity, Hernández had never failed to perform
his duty, but it was the testimony of Colonel Vicente de Zéspedes that won
the day. Zéspedes related that the soldier had participated in the siege and
capture of Pensacola and had, after the capitulation, remained there and
gone on several sorties into the hostile countryside to eliminate the resistance by the Indian allies of the British. Bolstered by certifications from
the parish priest of the Parroquia Mayor that Hernández was a responsible
citizen, married to a local woman, and the father of several legitimate children, royal officials approved his request to retire in Havana with pension
privileges in April 1785.[101]

For ordinary soldiers, the decision to leave royal service—with or without benefits—may have been a logical choice. From the onset of O'Reilly's
reforms, the ordinary classes had enjoyed prosperity because Havana was
plagued by a severe shortage of labor. In April 1777, the royal engineer in
charge of Havana's fortification projects, Luis Huet, wrote to Captain General de la Torre, complaining of the difficulties he was experiencing in advancing his projects. The official complained that "the scarcity of labor and
the multitude of other enterprises" made it difficult to get and retain sufficient workers.[102] He had particular trouble in obtaining manual laborers
for construction on the Castillo del Príncipe and for digging a moat around
the watchtower at the mouth of the Chorrera River. A call went out for 300
day workers, and when the requisite number failed to appear, the captain
general approved Huet's request to offer the additional employment to
off-duty soldiers, ironically encouraging the same moonlighting activity
that had infuriated O'Reilly a decade before.[103] Huet's complaints, combined with demographic evidence, point to an increasing sector of free

workers, both Europeans and free coloreds, who enjoyed a prosperity associated with militarization and who were ubiquitous in trades and mechanical crafts inside and outside of the city.[104] Moonlighting probably made the transition from soldier to settler relatively easy, as many men secured employment prior to separation.

In addition to veterans, particularly after 1782, skilled workers began to immigrate to the city. Some arrived on their own, such as master carpenter Joaquín Zavala, who came to Havana from Navarra in 1791.[105] Miguel Antonio de Arrayal's talents as a master craftsman were so prized by his employer that the man wrote to his wife in Spain requesting that she do whatever necessary to send Arrayal to Cuba.[106] The expansion of skilled crafts, especially in service to the garrison, encouraged families of minimal means to apprentice their sons to master craftsmen. At the request of the young man's father, master silversmith José Estanislao Melexo agreed to accept Bernardo Rondón from Bayamo as his apprentice.[107] Craftsmen who catered to the garrison were particularly in demand. Juan Montero, the master armorer of the fixo, had two boys, Fernando Palacios and Manuel Guinol, apprenticed to him on the same day.[108] So great was the demand for labor that the city of Puerto Príncipe repeatedly attempted to recruit skilled workers in Havana to migrate to that city in the eastern district of the island.[109]

The solution to everyone's problem of labor was unfree workers, both slaves and criminals. Crimes such as treason or murder demanded execution; desertion and smuggling usually were punished by exile to such places as the presidios in Africa or New Spain.[110] Nonviolent crimes such as drunkenness, possession of contraband, antisocial behavior, or vagrancy, however, earned the "delinquent" a sentence on Havana's various construction projects. For example, the captain of Managua, Felipe Cantón, sent José Antonio Carabali to the city for repeatedly abusing his wife, and Juan Farina was transported from Marianao for impregnating widow Ana Lorenzo Pacheco. Farina was sentenced to work on the coliseum until he agreed to marry the woman.[111] Free black Mariano de Roxas was sent to Havana by the capitán del partido of San Pedro. In spite of convincingly demonstrating his free status, he, too, was sentenced to labor on the new coliseum to correct his incorrigible behavior and his fondness for drink.[112]

As Roxas's sentence demonstrates, free status did not guarantee freedom for Cuba's lower orders, and as if to reflect the wider society, the lines of demarcation between free and unfree labor were extremely muddled. Public works and private enterprise were often interconnected. Agustín

Piña, a private contractor charged with paving the main streets of the city, requested and was rewarded with 100 forced laborers, who, in spite of being employed in a private enterprise, remained on the royal ration lists.[113] Slaves and criminals alike were organized into brigades identified by letters and labored side by side on Havana's public works projects.[114]

Incongruous though it may seem, even the worst of circumstances could be mitigated within a climate of scarcity, and in rare cases, a measure of esteem was extended to unfree workers, both slaves and forced laborers. A most unusual example is José Gregorio de la Guerra, a Christian slave from Guinea, who was not only literate but also multilingual in Latin, Spanish, Italian, French, and Arabic. Royal officials were so impressed by de la Guerra's abilities that he was entrusted with the position of supervisor and interpreter for the royal slaves of Brigade F in the quarry of San Lázaro.[115] In another instance, the "wives" of royal slaves assigned to the fortifications sewed uniforms for the garrison, for which they earned more than 3,300 pesos from the Royal Treasury.[116] Havana clearly represented a better opportunity than New Spain to furloughed criminal José Ramírez, for when he completed his sentence of four years on Havana's fortifications, he refused repatriation to his home at royal expense. Instead he asked for and received a license to remain in Havana from Captain General Luis de Unzaga y Amézaga, who also wrote the equivalent of a letter of recommendation for the man.[117] A group of twenty-three furloughed criminals took matters into their own hands when they failed to board the ship that would have returned them to Campeche.[118] Tanner Francisco de Oliva arrived as a prisoner of war from Jamaica in 1780, obtained his freedom, and subsequently enlisted in the urban militias in the barrio extramuro Jesús María.[119]

Convicts jumping ship and the occasional individual immigrant could never supply sufficient labor to meet demand. Within a growing economy plagued with a chronic shortage of labor, soldiers who had been artisans and tradesmen prior to their enlistment would have had many opportunities to prosper. José Prieto was forthcoming about his motives, stating to royal officials that he "had come to improve his luck" ("*mejorar su suerte*"). Indeed, he was successful, because by 1790 he had acquired two houses and a pulpería in Guatao.[120] Enrique José Ystace came as a soldier in the Hibernia Regiment, but he clearly saw better opportunity in separating and returning to his trade as musician. He retained his affiliation with military service by enlisting in the militia.[121] The details surrounding the personal decision of shoemaker Antonio Montes de Oca are less clear. In

1764, he was a twenty-five-year-old member of the disbanded foot cavalry, a regiment that had fallen victim to O'Reilly's reforms. As a single man he may have joined his (similarly "retired") comrade-in-arms and brother-in-law Juan Chrisóstomo González, whose family had attempted to settle in Nueva Florida but had returned to Havana. When and where Montes de Oca learned his trade is impossible to determine, but both he and González relinquished their military affiliation and contributed to the increase in population in the barrios surrounding the city.[122] Sergeant Vicente Chicharo, upon his retirement in 1792, set up a small shop outside the city walls where he sold a variety of comestibles, as well as wine for four reals a bottle.[123] Similar ancillary industries, such as Vicente Quintana's small shop to bake bread and biscuit for the chain gangs, blossomed outside the city walls in response to the demands of the garrison.[124]

As time passed and increasing numbers of troops arrived in Havana, population pressures became more acute. Reconstructing the residential patterns of the rank and file provides evidence that ordinary soldiers and their families were part of a dynamic movement of population to and through the city beginning in the mid-1760s. During a soldier's tour of duty, he and his family were required to live in town, but on his retirement or separation, the prospect of resettlement in remote agricultural communities was singularly unappealing. Instead of accepting the Crown's offer of agricultural land, the veteran and his family simply migrated outward to the extraurban barrios beyond the Campo de Marte, thus increasing the population of Guadalupe, Jesús María, or other such places. At the same time, he was replaced by men in incoming regiments whose residential patterns ultimately would follow similar lines. This forced transience is reflected in the residential progression of much-traveled infantry soldier Antonio de Almeyra, who initially lodged in Guanabacoa in 1764 after his arrival on the island.[125] From 1775 through 1784, the family lived in the parish Espíritu Santo, but by 1793, Almeyra's widow, Juana Rodríguez de Arfián, had moved to Guadalupe.[126] Pinpointing when infantry soldiers and brothers Romualdo and Juan Serrados left active duty and resettled outside the city walls is more difficult. They served on active duty during the 1760s, but by the 1790s the two men and their families had moved to the extraurban barrio Jesús María.[127] Similarly, determining when brothers Juan Martín and Francisco Carmona retired and settled their extended family in barrio Guadalupe may only be approximated as having occurred during their period of active duty from the 1760s to the 1790s.[128]

Often entire family clusters would migrate outward to the countryside.

Such moves may have occurred en masse or more likely were accomplished through chain or relay migrations, whereby one family member migrated outward, surveyed the prospective new territory, reported favorably, and other family members would follow. This practice is evidenced by the family cluster that revolved around infantry compadres Antonio Monzón and Cristóval del Castillo. Initially the men lived in the northern part of Havana, probably in the barracks, where they became brothers-in-law in 1767.[129] In the 1790s, Monzón and his family retired outside the city, where he became the head of a large extended family that included himself, his wife, his two spinster sisters, his aunt by marriage, and her daughter. The family retained linkages with del Castillo and his wife, who remained in town, and with his widowed sister-in-law, who lived in a nearby extraurban neighborhood.[130] The family cluster organized around foot cavalry soldier Juan Manuel Alvarez ultimately moved even farther afield. During his years on active duty the family lived in town, but upon retirement they settled in the hamlet El Cerro (also called Prensa), one of the evolutionary communities that grew up around several mills that utilized water from the aqueduct that supplied the city. Perhaps, as was customary, when the time came for him to retire, the patriarch, Alvarez, accepted housing for his family in usufruct granted by royal favor. By 1795, three of his four children and their families had joined the old man and lived in the growing village.[131]

Official policy greatly influenced such migratory residential and retirement patterns. The primacy of the military mission and the expendable nature of veterans were evident in Captain General Diego de Navarro's 1778 declaration that any soldier who had been issued his separation papers must retire from the city unless he was a resident of long standing or was married to a resident.[132] Such a decree would compel many officers to seek comfortable country estates to establish new homes, and the impetus to acquire rural property extended to the highest echelons of power on the island. In 1792, José María de Cárdenas, Captain General Luis de Las Casas's aide-de-camp, retained his military rank but also received the governor's permission to cultivate lands outside the city on the road to Güines.[133] Even Captain General Luis de Las Casas acquired an ingenio close to Güines that had recently been granted the status of villa and incorporated as a tobacco-producing center.[134] Navarro's decree was likely what motivated Garcini, introduced at the beginning of this chapter, to sell his urban residence and to establish a new homestead at El Retiro, and was what probably influenced Captain Francisco Valiente and Second Lieutenant José Figuredo to purchase tracts of land when such were made available through the sale of *realengos* (untitled, unoccupied land belonging to the Crown) in 1784.[135]

Rural property was a sound investment in many respects, and diversification was the rule rather than the exception. To begin, rural property values increased as Havana's population grew and continuously moved outward from the city.[136] Acquiring an estancia (garden plot) close to town allowed the military member to provision his urban household. The village of Cano was the site of artillery commander Vicente Risel's potrero (horse farm) that covered seventeen caballerías of land. The family headed by brothers Captain Felipe and Lieutenant Manuel de Lima owned more modest farms, including three estancias and one potrero, each encompassing one caballería.[137] Like the de Lima family, Colonel Antonio Raffelín diversified his agricultural enterprises into beekeeping, and he also purchased one of the confiscated properties that had belonged to the Jesuit order.[138] Rural property also represented a source of additional income. Juan Batista Arango, a captain in the Infantry Regiment of Guadalajara, rented his estancia for five years to José María de la Cruz.[139] Engineer Bruno Caballero also rented his estancia San Antonio for three years prior to selling it to his tenant, Diego Peñalver.[140] Military members continued to receive their salaries even while they pursued their agricultural interests, and thus, to a certain degree, military expenditures contributed to the development of the countryside.[141]

For ordinary soldiers whose lives were marginal to begin with, the possibility of a comfortable retirement home was clearly beyond their financial resources. These men, with their families, concubines, and bastards simply became part of the more than 40,000 new inhabitants of the suburbs. Indeed, by the 1790s, so many former military members had migrated outward that the extraurban barrios had become synonymous with "marineros y tropa," who in June 1795 were sternly warned by the voice of the government, the *Papel Periódico de la Havana*, to be on their best behavior at an upcoming public performance.[142] No doubt, countless other soldiers passed from the historical record without a trace, leaving the only record of their residence on the island to be reflected in the ever-escalating population data for Havana and her province.

The "invisible immigration" of retiring and separating military personnel is just one part of Cuba's population explosion and just one aspect of the social impact of militarization; even harder to document are the women who formed liaisons with soldiers and the children born of those liaisons.

While the extensive integration of peninsular men into Cuban society through marriage will be treated in detail in the next chapter, a few examples bear examination at this time, since the arrival of but one soldier often contributed exponentially to the increase in Havana's population through the birth of legitimate and illegitimate offspring. Such a process is exemplified in the life history of Doña Jacinta Escañes. Daughter of a peninsular officer, sister of another, wife of a third, and daughter-in-law of a fourth military man from Bilbao, she was the mother of five children in 1781, when her husband, Captain Bernabé de Zubieta, failed to return from the Pensacola campaign.[143] The same campaign brought even greater tragedy to the Bermúdez family when both Captain Pedro de la Rosa and his brother-in-law, Sergeant Second Class Diego Bermúdez, did not survive the expedition. De la Rosa left his wife, Ana Bermúdez, with six minor children; her sister-in-law, Diego's widow Petrona Labate, was left with four children. Each woman had to raise her family thereafter on half her husband's military pay.[144] These extraordinary cases allow a fleeting glimpse of the personal lives of Havana's women via the service records of their husbands, but they also underscore the issue that in many cases, the arrival of but one soldier increased the population of the city by an average of five persons. Even more elusive than a soldier's legitimate children—and impossible to quantify with any degree of certainty—were the children born out of wedlock under the many varieties of illegitimacy of the eighteenth century.

Several reasons suggest why officers and soldiers sought to transfer to or remain in service in the Caribbean. From a materialistic perspective, especially for the rank-and-file soldier, Havana was a place of opportunity. Military service afforded a means to arrive; military policy provided an opportunity to remain; a burgeoning economy offered a chance to prosper. If he chose, a discharged soldier could take up farming, and the government would do everything in its power to accommodate him. On the other hand, most veterans simply separated and squatted immediately outside the boundaries of the Campo de Marte, where their talents were in demand by the growing population.[145] Equally important was the ideology of military service. During the purge of 1763, being returned involuntarily to Spain was viewed as punishment.[146] Moreover, to military men, their honor truly was their life, and honor and duty demanded that an officer and his men wanted to remain where the danger to the empire was the greatest.[147] Between 1763 and 1779, international circumstances propelled the Caribbean theater to a position of importance, and increasing numbers of military personnel were needed to participate in campaigns in New Orleans in 1769, in Pensacola in 1781, and in New Providence in 1782.[148]

As important as factors on the island in changing the imperial dynamic, however, were events in Spain. After 1775 the prestige of the peninsular army sunk to an unprecedented low owing to Spain's military failures, particularly the invasion attempt of Muslim North Africa at Algeria. The expedition, led by Alejandro O'Reilly, was a defeat of monumental proportions that led to over 5,000 casualties, including the deaths of over 1,500 soldiers. While the political machinations surrounding the Spanish involvement in North Africa were beyond O'Reilly's control, the expedition's failure was unquestionably his fault. The political repercussions in Spain and Spanish America, however, were enormous, and the debacle effectively closed the career alternative of returning to Spain.

At the time of the expedition, Charles III's court was characterized by political cronyism and factionalism and the bitter enmity surrounding the minister of state, Jerónimo Grimaldi, Marqués de Grimaldi. Grimaldi, who accompanied the royal court from the Italian peninsula, was the leader of the court faction Golillas. His political and personal adversary was the Conde de Aranda, president of the Council of Castille, and the leader of the opposing Aragonés faction. On the eve of the invasion attempt, Grimaldi and his Golillas enjoyed the monarch's favor. The Aragoneses enlisted the support of the Prince of Asturias, the future Charles IV, and his wife, Princess María Luisa de Parma. Grimaldi scored a political victory in 1773 when he convinced Charles III to appoint Aranda to the post of ambassador to France, effectively removing his rival from the locus of power and the intrigues of court in Madrid. Meanwhile, the Prince of Asturias and the Aragonés faction continued to scheme while their leader presented a rustic, unkempt appearance to the sophisticated French court in Paris.[149]

In 1775, the international crisis with North Africa demanded immediate attention when the Muslim Sultan of Algeria attacked Spanish shipping in the Mediterranean. Both Golillas and Aragoneses clamored to teach the Algerians a lesson. While the political fortune of Grimaldi suffered most from the disaster, in reality, all of Charles's other ministers had supported the invasion, and both factions had been encouraged by Pope Clemente XIV, who likened the campaign to a crusade.[150] Charles III, however, was reluctant to invade North Africa, and he sought the counsel of his most distinguished military advisers.[151] Ultimately, he chose the hero of Cuba and New Orleans, O'Reilly, to accomplish the task for him.[152]

The attempted invasion of Algeria was destined for disaster even before it was launched. Spies in Valencia kept the North Africans apprised of the progress of outfitting the expedition, and since they were aware of the coming invasion they were prepared to meet the invaders. The military planners relied upon an outdated map drawn fifteen years previous that did not take into account recent improvements in the Algerians' fortifications. When confronted by a well-armed, well-fortified objective, O'Reilly was gripped with indecision. He vacillated for several days while navy troop ships under the command of Pedro de González de Castejón, a political enemy of the general, rode at anchor just off the North African coast in sight of the Muslim fortifications. When O'Reilly finally decided to go ahead with the invasion, a tactical mistake landed Spanish soldiers on a sandy beach where the artillery bogged down in the sand. Caught in a crossfire, the flower of the Spanish army—over 1,500 young men—died, including the majority of the cadets at the school of infantry at Avila that O'Reilly himself had founded.[153]

The disaster at Algeria came with wide-reaching political consequences for Spain. When the news reached the capital, the Madrid press excoriated the general. Capitalizing upon antiforeign sentiment, the press questioned whether O'Reilly was loyal to the Spanish cause because he was Irish-born. In the following days, accounts, hypothetical conversations, *décimas* (Spanish stanzas of ten octosyllabic lines), and *quartillas* (Spanish stanzas of four lines) in the Madrid press taunted the general using descriptive epithets such as "traitor," and "crippled, deaf, and blind" ("*cojo, sordo y ciego*"). One particularly vicious attack inflamed popular passions in demanding that O'Reilly should be hanged for his incompetence.[154] Another account dubbed him "Alejandro Argelino" ("Alejandro the Algerian") and "General Disaster," epithets he carried with him for the remainder of his life.[155] In turn, O'Reilly sought to shift the blame away from himself, and he accused some of his military comrades of cowardice.[156] This, in turn, prompted an angry response from many military leaders, and the general alienated many more when he failed to recommend them for promotion even though they had performed with courage and heroism during the battle and bloody retreat.[157] An incensed Madrid press published a fictional last will and testament in which O'Reilly confessed that "to cover his sins he had imputed disobedience to those who died . . . that they never committed."[158] Public opinion was so negative that Charles III sent the disgraced leader on an inspection tour to the Chafarinas Islands off the coast of Africa. Upon his return, he was named captain general of Andalusia and he took up residence in Cádiz.[159]

Soon thereafter, over the winter of 1776–77, Minister of State Grimaldi, who was of Italian birth, also fell victim to the antiforeign sentiment engendered by the disaster at Algeria. When he resigned in November 1776, the Aragoneses hoped that their time had come. Grimaldi's resignation was followed by the death of Fray Julián de Arriaga, who had held two positions in Charles III's cabinet, minister of the Indies and minister of the navy. While the Count of Aranda waited to be appointed to the ministry of state that Grimaldi had been forced to resign, Charles III stunned everyone by rejecting the politics-as-usual approach in favor of a complete reorganization of his group of advisers. Instead of Aranda, he appointed José de Moñino, the Count of Floridablanca and a protegé of Grimaldi, to the position. Pedro de González de Castejón, who participated in the Algeria expedition as head of the naval forces, was rewarded with the Ministry of the Navy. The appointment that would have the greatest consequences for Cuba, however, was that of José de Gálvez to the position of minister of the Indies. These appointments represented a great disappointment to the Aragoneses, and especially Aranda's most vocal supporter, the Prince of Asturias, for Charles's decision meant that they would remain isolated from the center of power at court.[160]

The political reorganization as a consequence of Algeria meant that O'Reilly's followers would be forced to make a choice: align with the Aragoneses and wait for another day or align with one of the new ministers and hope for success. To remain with the disgraced general meant that they too would suffer a similar decline in fortune. The consequences of Algeria and the political decline of both Grimaldi and O'Reilly were obvious: "No one wished to be associated with policy failures stretching from the Falklands to North Africa."[161]

The choice for O'Reilly's brother-in-law, Luis de Las Casas, was clear. The ties of kinship were unequivocal, and Las Casas was promoted to the rank of brigadier as a consequence of Algeria. He participated in the failed siege of Gibraltar in 1779 and in the successful recapture of Minorca in 1781. After Minorca, he slipped into obscurity for more than a decade as the inspector of troops on Spain's Mediterranean coast, where he watched from a distance as the Gálvez family and their followers increased their prestige and expanded their circle of supporters.[162] As a follower of Aranda and the Aragoneses, only after the deaths of Charles III and the members of the Gálvez clan would Las Casas return to the locus of power in 1790.

Just as Las Casas remained isolated from power, Francisco de Saavedra, O'Reilly's secretary and one of his strongest supporters prior to the invasion of Algeria, took the opposite decision and aligned with the Gálvez faction. The young man remained loyal to his mentor throughout the bloody fighting and the ignominious retreat; only when O'Reilly sought to blame others for his mistake did Saavedra request his release from the general's entourage. In retaliation, the general failed to send Saavedra's name up for promotion for his heroism, even though the young man saved many of his comrades who had been wounded. Finding himself without employment, Saavedra intended to join the entourage of the Conde de Fernán Núñez, who also participated in the disaster. From his past acquaintance with Bernardo de Gálvez, however, Saavedra came to the attention of the new minister of the Indies, José de Gálvez, and because of his exceptional talent, he was recruited to join Gálvez's functionaries in the Ministry of the Indies. Thus, Saavedra went over to the Gálvez faction, and as the family became more and more influential, so, too, would his political fortune rise.[163]

Neither choice was an option for young Lieutenant Tomás de Aróstegui, a scion of the Havana patriciate, the son of a colonel in the Dragoons of America, Martín Estéban de Aróstegui; the nephew of Martín de Aróstegui, the founder of the Havana company; and the nephew of Brigadier Vicente de Zéspedes, commander of the Third Battalion of the Fixo. Young Aróstegui died on the sandy beach of North Africa.[164] His father, Martín Estéban, gained O'Reilly's favor in 1763 for his actions during the siege, for which he had been awarded a colonelcy in the cavalry regiment.[165] No doubt, the older man believed that his son's future was assured when the youth returned to Spain in O'Reilly's entourage. From the perspective of 1764, a Creole cadet would have a better chance for distinction serving in the peninsula than would his Creole cousins who remained in the Fixo.[166] No one could have foreseen the fatal consequences of Algeria.

Three young sons of the Havana patriciate survived the carnage at Algeria. Ignacio Peñalver began his military career in the navy, but in 1766 he transferred to the infantry, and by the time of the invasion, he was a captain in the Regiment of Príncipe. After Algeria, he left the army and accepted a reduction in rank to secure a commission aboard ship once again. He served with distinction in the Spanish navy operating in European waters, but after the ineffective blockade of Gibraltar in 1779, his ship joined the convoy led by Admiral José Solano that provided naval assistance in the assault on Pensacola.[167] By casting his fortune with the Gálvez faction, Peñalver eventually was inducted as a Knight in the Order of Santiago.[168] Like Peñalver, Manuel Eligio de la Puente remained in Spain without promotion until O'Reilly finally agreed to allow him to transfer back to the Americas in 1779.[169]

The consequences of Algeria weighed heavily on Francisco de Montalvo, who was but twenty years old when he landed on the beach of North Africa. He, too, was passed over for promotion, but his transfer to the American theater and service in the Gulf Coast earned him a lieutenant colonelcy in 1784.[170] After the war with Britain was concluded, Montalvo volunteered to return to Andalusia, not to serve in the peninsular army but rather in service to the Regiment of America. Armed with an extraordinary commission issued by José de Gálvez, Montalvo became the commander of a recruitment party designed to entice soldiers to enlist for service in Cuba in the heart of the territory assigned to O'Reilly and Las Casas. Although the blanket commission permitted the Regiment of America to search for and enlist recruits anywhere, it broke with a tradition that normally recruited youths in the Canary Islands. More important, it represented an incredible insult to O'Reilly and his followers. Accompanying Montalvo on the recruiting party was a peninsular lieutenant who also had transferred to the land forces under the Gálvez family, Francisco de Varela.[171]

Small wonder, then, that officers under O'Reilly's command did everything in their power to obstruct Montalvo and Varela in their mission, even more so when the two enlisted ninety-six men in just six weeks. On one occasion, the head of the Cádiz commissary refused to provide food for the Cuban recruits, and on another occasion the head officer of the port refused to allow the enlistees to board a ship destined to take them to Havana.[172] The minister of the Indies maintained a formal but frigid correspondence with the captain general of Andalusia, reminding him that the men were just doing their duty. For his part, Montalvo was scrupulous in maintaining a distance from O'Reilly's forces, and he appointed two sergeants to interview each of his recruits carefully to ensure that they were not deserters from O'Reilly's army.[173] Peninsular recruitment duty was not to Varela's liking, and by 1786 he had transferred into the Havana Fixo, where he served under his future father-in-law, Bartolomé de Morales. Montalvo, however, remained in Cádiz until 1789, when he, too, returned to Cuba.[174]

The decline in prestige of the peninsular army coincided with a rise in importance of Spanish America that was directly linked to the ascendancy of the Gálvez family. José de Gálvez's previous experience as visitor-general to New Spain in 1769 made him a strong advocate of the importance of Spanish America. After 1776, with war with Great Britain looming on the horizon and the loss of Florida and the Malvinas (Falkland Islands) in the collective military consciousness, Gálvez recognized that operations in the Indies would be of enormous significance. The successful campaigns would require talented and loyal men. Whatever had been the norm prior to the capitulation of Havana, new circumstances dictated that an officer in Caribbean service could choose to spend the majority, if not the remainder, of his life there. Many men took full advantage of the status of being peninsular in a Creole world and faced a not-so-difficult choice between "adjusting to life in Castille or being a true señor in the Indies."[175]

And the move to the Indies became still more attractive, for after 1782, Havana clearly became the imperial darling. Yet the favor of the monarch would not be earned without cost. It would take discipline, sacrifice, and heroism, and Cuba and her people would be sorely tested when Spain faced off against Great Britain in 1779. This time, unlike 1762, Cuba would not be found wanting.

Díme con Quien Andas

(Tell Me with Whom You Walk)

On June 17, 1782, the Marqués de Casa Tremañes, Don Pedro Regalado de Tineo, a lieutenant general in the Royal Army and a member of the royal court of Madrid, married Doña Bárbara María Montero de Espinosa y García Menocal, the Habanera daughter of the commandant of the Castillo del Morro, Don José Montero de Espinosa.[1] The choice represented more than just the union of two families. Although it was but one of over 4,400 marriages celebrated in Havana from 1753 to 1800, it was typical of a social trend that diverged from matrimonial patterns elsewhere in Spanish America. Between one-third and one-half of the marriages in Havana occurred between immigrant men and women born in Cuba (Creoles). Beginning at the highest level with the marriage of Bernardo de Gálvez of Cuba to Felicité de St. Maxent of Louisiana in 1777, the phenomenon of peninsular-Creole intermarriage extended through all ranks of society.[2] The conscious and deliberate program to integrate peninsular men into Creole society "brought the colony . . . closer to acceptance of Spanish rule than it had been barely a decade before under the successful, but strong-armed Governor O'Reilly."[3]

After 1776, with José de Gálvez as minister of the Indies, the Americas commanded singular importance in imperial policy for the next twelve years.[4] Havana, as the staging ground for the military and naval operations throughout the Caribbean and the Gulf Coast, benefited from changes in the political and military realm. The military initiatives came with important social consequences in the form of increased numbers of soldiers, sailors, marines, and their commanding officers. Soldiers arrived as bachelors and married Creole women in such considerable numbers that the process takes on historical importance as an indicator of a trend distinct from other areas of Spanish America. Even after the reforms of the 1760s and the clear intent of Charles III to implement stricter regulation of the population as a whole in 1776, the trend continued. Because so many Spanish men were permitted to marry Creole women, it is clear that the metropolis viewed Cuban society differently from the way it viewed the societies of Mexico and Peru. Peninsular-Creole intermarriage practiced and promoted under the stewardship of the Gálvez family was the final step in sealing the metropolitan-Creole compact between the island and the monarchy of Charles III.

While their approach to the Americas was unique, the Gálvez clan was typical of the politics of their day. Cronyism, nepotism, and favoritism were the rule rather than the exception. Within the intrigue-filled atmosphere of European court politics, men in power installed their friends and relatives of unquestionable loyalty in key positions.[5] For the Gálvez clan, rewards began at home. José's brother, Matias, began his bureaucratic career as governor of the Canary Islands. During the war he was transferred to Honduras, where he led the expeditions that drove the British from logcutting camps on the Central American coast. At war's end he was rewarded with the viceroyalty of New Spain.[6] Another brother, Miguel, was Charles III's counselor of war.[7] A third brother, Antonio, was wartime commander of Puerto Real, the strategic naval center across the bay from Cádiz, on the south coast of Spain.[8] In 1778, Antonio also served as emissary to the Muslim states in North Africa to negotiate a settlement to the hostility that the invasion of Algeria had caused.[9] In 1776, fast on the heels of José de Gálvez's appointment to the Ministry of the Indies, the scion of the Gálvez family, Bernardo de Gálvez, Matias's son and José's nephew, was appointed to one of the most difficult assignments in the empire, the governorship of Spanish Louisiana.[10]

Bernardo de Gálvez's tenure in Louisiana and his subsequent Gulf Coast exploits represent some of the most celebrated episodes in the history of the Americas. His military expeditions that expelled the British from the lower Mississippi Valley, Mobile, and Pensacola resonate through many national historical narratives.[11] With the arrival of the official notification of the young man's victories, the exultation in Spain was tangible. The correspondence between uncle and nephew reflects their jubilation: "His Majesty has received the news with the greatest satisfaction," wrote José de Gálvez after the Mobile campaign.[12] Rewards for Bernardo's bravery and audacity followed on the heels of each victory. After the Mississippi Valley victories, his post as governor and captain general of Louisiana was separated from the authority of the viceroyalty of Mexico and granted complete autonomy.[13] After Mobile and Pensacola he was awarded the title of Conde de Gálvez and made captain general of Cuba.[14] His brief tenure in Cuba preceded more honors, when, upon the death of his father, Matias, in Mexico City, Bernardo was chosen to succeed the older man as viceroy of New Spain in 1785.[15]

Following custom and precedent, Bernardo de Gálvez surrounded himself with loyal followers, and by 1782, the governance of the northern half of Spain's American empire was in the hands of a personalized clique of his partisans. The list of men who participated in the military expeditions and were rewarded with government posts reads like a who's who of Spain's postwar colonial government. Some were veterans of the disaster in North Africa. Francisco de Saavedra's illustrious career after he fell from O'Reilly's favor after Algeria hinged as much on his association with the Gálvez family as on his prodigious talent. During the war of 1779, Saavedra was the monarch's personal messenger to the governors and military commanders throughout the Caribbean, and he was reunited with his old friends in the expedition to Pensacola in 1781.[16] After Pensacola, he was promoted to the intendancy of Caracas and later served in many capacities in Charles IV's monarchy as minister of war, minister of the treasury, and as interim minister of state until his death in 1819.[17] Diego José de Navarro, governor of Cuba during the War of 1779, was another veteran of Algeria.[18] José de Ezpeleta, a member of the Mississippi River expeditions, was named governor of Mobile after that city fell in 1780, and he served as interim governor of Cuba twice.[19] Estéban Miró succeeded Gálvez as governor of Louisiana in 1782.[20] Arturo O'Neill became the first governor of Pensacola after its restoration to Spanish sovereignty.[21]

The veterans of the Africa campaign were complemented by veterans of the Caribbean theater whose loyalty to Gálvez was unimpeachable. Matias de Armona, the brother of the administrator of the mail system in Havana, accompanied José de Gálvez on the grueling inspection tour of the northern Mexican frontier in 1767.[22] Armona subsequently served in the difficult position as governor of the frontier province, and in late 1782 he participated in the expedition to New Providence Island in the Bahamas.[23] Domingo Cabello, interim governor of Cuba on two occasions in the 1780s, guarded Spain's internal frontier as governor of San Antonio de Bexar from 1778 to 1786, and protected the cattle supply for Gálvez's expeditions, while his son, Manuel, served with Bernardo on the Gulf Coast.[24] Families with experience dealing with international matters were particularly important to the war effort. Juan José Eligio de la Puente was the head of an extensive espionage network that utilized former Florida residents who spied on British positions throughout the Caribbean.[25] Floridanos were crucial not only for their knowledge of the coastal waters surrounding the peninsula but also because of their linguistic talents, especially as interpreters of Indian languages.[26] From the 1770s onward, Florida Indians acted as valuable sources of information for the captain general in Havana, and they were indispensable allies during the Gulf Coast campaigns.[27] Merchant-observer Juan de Miralles, who had extensive linkages throughout the Caribbean, represented the Spanish government in Philadelphia to solidify relations with the leaders of the new United States.[28] No less important was the home front, which also needed talented and loyal men to protect against a repetition of the invasion of 1762. Juan Bautista Valliant, future governor of Santiago de Cuba, supervised one of the key components of the strategic defense system, the mounted cavalry detachments stationed in the countryside surrounding the city.[29] Bartolomé de Morales and his future son-in-law, Francisco de Varela, served in the Fixo and held down the fort in Havana while younger men sailed on the expedition to Pensacola.[30]

Such favoritism was taken one step further by the Gálvez family, who changed the social dynamic between metropolis and colony by deliberately forging kin linkages with Creole families. Bernardo, always in the vanguard, married Felicité de St. Maxent, from one of the most distinguished families of New Orleans.[31] Three men—all in-laws of Bernardo—further exemplified the close connection between military service and kinship strategies. Juan Antonio de Riaño, a young naval captain, followed his future brother-in-law over the dangerous shallow entrance into Pensacola Bay and into marriage with another daughter of the St. Maxent family, Victoria. After his service in the Gulf Coast, Riaño was named intendant of Michoacán and later was assigned to Guanajuato.[32] Another brother-in-law, Luis de Unzaga y Amézaga, a veteran of O'Reilly's expedition to New Orleans in 1769, remained in the Caribbean and became Captain General of Cuba in 1785.[33] Gilbert de St. Maxent, Gálvez's father-in-law, appointed lieutenant governor of West Florida on his son-in-law's recommendation, represented the family in their proposal to regulate Indian affairs after the territory was returned from Britain.[34] The importance of these extended personal and professional networks cannot be overstated. More than simply representing time-honored kinship strategies, the social transformation represented a deliberate and calculated strategy designed to tie the residents closer to the Spanish Crown.[35] The new direction in kinship policies was even more important because it represented a source of power and prestige of which the O'Reilly faction was not a part.[36]

The significance of the process can best be understood when it is placed in its imperial context, for it represents a significant contrast to marriage patterns in other areas. In Cuba, unlike other areas of Spain's American empire, persons who called themselves "españoles" and were acknowledged as such by their peers and royal officials formed the majority of the island's population and constituted the largest and most affluent sectors. Free coloreds amounted to less than 15 percent of the total free population.[37] Slaves, whose numbers, though considerable, were not predominant, were rarely permitted to marry other slaves or free partners of color and even less frequently married Europeans. Moreover, except for creating tangible linkages between the families of their masters, slave marriages did not shape policy decisions.[38] Thus, to understand the degree of integration of the peninsular and Creole populations, this chapter will focus upon marital relationships between members of white society, that is, between persons judicially defined as being racial equals. The very nature of being peninsular implied that the immigrant could demonstrate his or her purity of blood *(limpieza de sangre)*, that is, that she or he was completely European. If a soldier were of Creole birth, regardless of the phenotypical reality, military service came with the implicit assumption that the soldier's "legal race" was español, and as such, he and his family enjoyed elevated status in comparison to other members of the lower ranks. Consensual unions were commonplace, but such unions, whether interracial or intraracial, by definition, implied no legal commitment, although on occasion a parent could legitimize his illegitimate offspring.[39] A Spanish jurist in the nineteenth century summarized the legal dimension of the issue: "Without equality there can be no marriage." This became a maxim well known to all who entered into the marriage contract, a serious matter that involved neither frivolity nor free will.

A body of civil and canon law placed limitations on marriage and the choice of marriage partners.[40] The Leyes de Indias, laws particular to Spain's overseas possessions, prohibited Spanish officials from marrying locally, and if married, the official was required to bring his family with him. Such regulation was intended to discourage royal officials from forming kinship obligations to local families which could interfere with an official's ability to enforce the royal will.[41] Military marriages were governed by special regulations. Prior to the 1760s, men stationed in Spanish America were prohibited from marrying locally without first obtaining permission from their superiors. Priests and chaplains attached to military detachments were prohibited from performing marriage ceremonies if the parties could not produce the proper licenses.[42] Yet these prohibitions were rarely enforced vigorously in either the military or bureaucratic corps.[43]

With the empire-wide military reorganization beginning in 1763, Alejandro O'Reilly was charged with correcting the problems that plagued Cuba's military structure. As introduced in chapter 3, in many cases O'Reilly enforced existing regulations regarding military marriages to weed out undesirable elements from military units.[44] New regulations were codified in 1769 in which important distinctions were drawn between officers and enlisted men.[45] Officers' brides now were required to post a dowry bond, provide evidence of their father's military service to the Crown, and demonstrate an impeccable lineage.[46] To be eligible to marry and receive a pension, men had to have attained the rank of captain or above, a measure which precluded marriage until men reached a mature age.[47] Treasury, intendancy, and royal tobacco factory employees were warned that they, too, would be relieved of their posts if they married without permission.[48] Lastly, in 1776, Charles III promulgated the Real Pragmática sobre Matrimonios in response to his horror at the marriage of his younger brother, who married far beneath the royal family. The Pragmática extended royal scrutiny to the civilian population, which until then had escaped scrutiny except under canon law.[49] Thus, after 1778, challenges to one's choice of a marriage partner could come from the Church, the government, one's superiors, or from other family members, male or female. If a couple dared contract a marriage that offended community norms, some sort of challenge to one's choice of a marriage partner could be virtually guaranteed.

If reform measures truly represented more stringent metropolitan involvement in local affairs, then the year 1764 should represent a watershed in the enforcement of laws, evidenced by the number of judicial proceedings. Throughout the island, the effects of the military reform of 1764 on matrimonial alliances were immediate and highly visible. Prior to 1764, only four atypical cases have been discovered that allude to the regulation or that establish that permission had been granted in some form. For example, as early as 1752, Habanero Juan José de Justíz, who would become the Marqués de Justíz y Santa Ana in 1758, wrote to inform the governor of Cuba that he had granted permission for the marriage of his niece and ward, Doña Gerónima, to Antonio Guaso, who would become governor of Puerto Rico.[50] Two years later, Justíz's son, Gerónimo, wrote to inform the governor of his own marriage.[51] In 1756, Francisca Antonia del Rosario y Silva wrote that she had contracted to marry Francisco de la Torre, sergeant major of the garrison of Bayamo. She enclosed permission granted by her father, who was in bed with a fever and unable to inform the governor of his own accord.[52] Yet pre-1764 enforcement of bans on nonsanctioned marriages appears sporadic at best and seems to have been limited to families that had pretensions to titles of nobility.[53] Other prominent couples married without royal permission, including María de Concepción Aróstegui, the daughter of the head of the Real Compañía de Comercio de la Havana, and Vicente de Zéspedes, who at the time was a junior officer but who would advance to the position of inspector general of the troops and to the governorship of Florida.[54]

In the post-reform years between 1764 and 1770, fourteen different judicial proceedings involving military marriages came to the attention of the captains general of Cuba, as compared to four in the previous twelve years. Each major garrison city had at least one representative case which was pursued by local authorities at the direction of the captain general in Havana. The reasons for prosecution varied. In some cases, local authorities were instructed to return errant wives to their husbands and to punish the men with whom the women had consorted. Other sins included soldiers' marrying without permission or marrying women who were not their social equals. Transgressors could expect punishment ranging from a dishonorable discharge from service to a sentence of hard labor, depending on the severity of their disobedience.

Far away from home and the scrutiny of superiors and family, soldiers fell victim to the charms and ambitions of provincial women. The love triangle involving Manuel Varela of Havana, Felipa Santiago of Bayamo, and Manuel de los Reyes, also of Havana, serves to illustrate the nature of such proceedings. In spite of warnings to the contrary, Varela, a forty-year-old sergeant second class with the Second Regiment of Havana assigned to Bayamo, eloped with Santiago, who previously had pledged to marry Reyes.[55] Varela's crimes could not go unpunished, since he had ignored several warnings by his superior officer not to marry and had compounded the problem by stealing the betrothed of another military member. Citing Varela's lack of foresight in marrying, not only because he could not provide for his wife on his paltry salary but also because he would be away during times of war, Acting Governor Luis de Unzaga y Amézaga sentenced Varela to six months in prison, his case "serving as an example" for the rest of the garrison.[56]

Matrimonial regulations provided a convenient rationale to cleanse the incorrigibles from the ranks, but more often than not, royal officials sought to implement a policy of determined but benevolent enforcement. For his "falta de amor de su soberano," demonstrated by his marrying Ursula Melo who was "notoriamente desigual," Joaquín Caballero was to be punished by being discharged from service, thereby losing his fuero militar and its concomitant honor and prestige. However, O'Reilly's intervention in consultation with the Conde de Ricla led to Caballero's reinstatement because of his previous good conduct. At the same time, the official communication warned superiors that because of the honor, perquisites, and privileges associated with military service, they must be on guard that similar incidents did not occur.[57] In 1770, a young and foolish cadet, twenty-six-year-old Francisco del Río, Jr., of the Regiment of Havana, was whisked back to that city after precipitously contracting to marry Angela Ferrer in Santiago de Cuba. The intervention of his father, Francisco del Río, Sr., a captain of noble lineage with over thirty years of service to His Majesty, prompted the cadet's ignominious departure, which served to prevent a marriage that likely would have ended the youth's career and brought disgrace to his family.[58] Tomás Gil was dishonorably discharged in 1770 for entering into a secret marriage, but by 1777, on the eve of the conflict with Great Britain, he was reinstated into his former position of adjutant major of Matanzas.[59] Indeed, on the occasion of the marriage of the Prince of Asturias, Charles III granted reprieves to all soldiers in Cuba who had married without proper permission.[60] Nevertheless, the wholesale purges in 1764 of men who had married without permission, the increase in the number of soldiers brought up for prosecution after 1764, and the obvious resolve to prosecute flagrant violators, indicates a tightening of enforcement policy on the part of royal officials.

Additionally, military authorities began to enforce the financial requirements for military marriages. Military brides' families were required to post a dowry bond *(fianza)* of no less than 2,500 pesos, which was increased to 3,000 pesos in 1789.[61] The content of the dowries varied. Some were outright gifts of cash, such as the 3,000 pesos that merchant Pedro José Rodríguez del Junco deposited with the Marqués del Real Socorro so his daughter, María del Mercedes, could marry Second Lieutenant Vicente Folch of the Infantry Regiment of Catalonia.[62] Others dowries involved tying real property into a mortgage or an outright gift. When María Rosa del Castillo married Bernardo Carillo de Albornóz, who attained the rank of lieutenant colonel of the Fixed Regiment of Havana, she brought a dowry worth over 20,000 pesos consisting of various urban and rural properties. He, like innumerable military men, "brought nothing" but his position as lieutenant in the Fixo.[63] For families with fewer resources, provisions were enacted to allow them to apply to the Royal Treasury for a loan against the value of the property.[64] The obligations could be lifted if and when the requisite 3,000 pesos was accumulated or if something interfered with the consummation of the marriage.[65] One poignant entry relates the deathbed testament of Rosalia Morejón, who had agreed to marry Lieutenant Dionisio Valdéz. On the night of her death, as one of her last conscious acts, she enumerated the 1,100 pesos from her aunt and the four slaves from her father that had been given to her to fulfill the requirements for her dowry.[66] So important was the establishment of dowries that not just immediate relatives but also grandparents, aunts, cousins, in-laws, and stepfathers contributed to accumulate the requisite 3,000 pesos.[67] In a few instances, the intended groom used his own resources to provide the necessary money for his bride's dowry bond.[68]

The trend toward more stringent regulation in the 1770s stands in sharp contrast to regulations of alliances formed prior to O'Reilly's reforms. Before 1765, royal officials did not enforce the requirements for military marriages, and posting the required dowry bond was of even less concern even when marriages involved officials at the highest levels. For example, a member of one of the most prestigious military families in the city, Hilario Remírez de Esteñóz, entered the Royal Army in 1755 and eventually rose to the position of commandant of the Castillo de Atarés.[69] Yet when he married Nicolasa Mancebo Betancourt in the 1760s, she brought only a negro slave valued at 85 pesos and a *china* (servant girl) valued at 150 pesos.[70] María Carillo, married for over forty years to captain of dragoons Joaquín de Arteaga, brought only a few gold and pearl necklaces and the clothing she wore to her marriage in the 1740s.[71] Likewise, in Captain Gabriel de Zubieta's two marriages, neither wife contributed any property to the union.[72]

The next major shift in enforcement policies is evident in the wake of the Real Pragmática in 1776, when royal scrutiny was extended to civilians. As a consequence, civilian parents and guardians were required to grant permission to their children or wards. The most immediate visible effect of the Real Pragmática in Cuba was to require civilian parents of military brides to begin approving their daughters' marriages, over and above the requisite permission from military officials. The early "licenses" were short and to the point, such as the three-sentence approval that merchant–royal emissary to the United States Juan de Miralles granted to his daughter Antonia in July 1777.[73] A month later, widow María Teresa Chicano granted permission to her daughter María Rafaela Brito.[74] María de los Nieves Sotolongo as the oldest sibling granted permission to her youngest sister Josefa Dolores to marry Martín Ferran, and to another sister, Ursula, who sought to marry Manuel Fernández de la Puente.[75] Quickly, though, the process of obtaining governmental permission became an elaborate ritual. Military requests became so numerous that clerks collected and stored the documents in separate *legajos*. As if to influence the decision of their superior officers, the dossiers became increasingly more ornate, and one beautiful volume presented in 1801 was bound in leather, embossed with the intended couple's names in gold lettering, and tied up with a green silk ribbon.[76]

Yet the glitz of the presentation could not take away from the seriousness of the proceedings. In the cases involving civilian families, the bride and groom simply needed to demonstrate parental permission and their equality of station. In the case of military or bureaucrats' marriages, two issues occupied the attention of royal officials: that the bride's family demonstrate their impeccable lineage beyond any doubt and that they demonstrate their financial stability through the establishment of the bride's dowry. In the first instance, royal instructions were explicit. Writing in 1789, Brigadier General and Acting Governor Domingo Cabello admonished that bureaucrats and military officers must choose women "of the same quality, customs, and circumstance" for the marriage to be acceptable.[77] The woman's family had to establish that they were of the highest caliber *("de la primera calidad")* and of renowned repute. In her petition to marry Baron Federico Witenfeld, Clara Perdomo y Pacheco included an elaborate family tree delineating her family's genealogy for three previous generations, carefully demonstrating the members of her family who had served in the Royal Army and in what capacities.[78] The daughter of a ship's captain who had received royal recognition for his espionage activities against the British during the American Revolutionary War brought a parade of witnesses to verify that she and her family were *"notoriamente blanca"* in her marriage petition to marry the *guarda mayor* of the Third Battalion of Cuba in 1786.[79] Before the marriage of Juan de Montes and María Antonio de Herrera could be approved in May 1799, the intended bride had to produce a certificate verifying her family's noble status, in addition to the other documents required by military officials.[80]

Civilian marriages technically were outside the purview of the captain general, so judicial proceedings fell under the jurisdiction of the Audiencia de Santo Domingo. Ultimately, from 1776 through 1801, that agency came to be the adjudicating body for challenges to military and civilian marriages alike.[81] Like the early cases involving military marriages exclusively, the evidence in the Audiencia de Santo Domingo is scanty but suggestive. Fourteen relevant petitions involving matrimonial issues survive in Cuban archives. In addition, sixteen suits are available in the Archivo General de Indias, suggesting that these petitions may have been heard initially in neighboring Santo Domingo but ultimately were carried to the highest levels of royal judicial authority, the Council of the Indies in Madrid. The petitions filed between 1776 and 1799 deal with a variety of matrimonial issues and provide a general idea as to the nature of the proceedings.[82]

Challenges, or *disensos,* could come from parents or guardians of one or more partners or from the partners themselves. One such petition filed by Doña Francisca Morera in 1776 sought to compel her reluctant suitor, Don Manuel Pérez, to comply with the *palabra de casamiento* he had given. After hearing the testimony, the tribunal ruled that the young man must take Doña Francisca as his legitimate wife, over the strong objections of his father.[83] Similarly, in 1797, Don Diego de Sotolongo successfully averted his father's challenge to his marriage to Doña Dorotea de Flores Quijano.[84] In another incident, Juan de Flores and his wife, Gregoria Gonzáles, seeking to prevent their daughter Manuela from marrying Miguel Casiñas, confined the girl in the Convent of San Juan de Nepomuceno. Undaunted, Casiñas enlisted the help of his friends and the naval squadron commander to rescue the girl he called "his wife." After being reunited, the couple defended their actions to royal officals, and throughout the proceedings Manuela referred to Casiñas as her "husband."[85]

On the other hand, some parents and guardians were successful in preventing their child's marriage. Don Martín de Aróstegui, son of the founder of the Compañía de la Havana and one of the city's wealthiest and most powerful men, successfully opposed his son Martín in the young man's desire to marry his cousin Doña Tomasa Ugarte.[86] Wealthy merchant Raymundo Gabriel de Azcárate successfully prevented his thirteen-year-old daughter from marrying Lieutenant Máximo du Bouchet, who, as Azcárate argued, only sought his daughter's hand because of her enormous dowry (*"gruesa dote"*).[87] The brother-in-law of María Concepción de Lisundia convinced the Council of the Indies that his sister-in-law was not only embarrassing the family, but also flouting the law of titles of

Castille by her scandalous affair with a suitor so beneath her and her family that he never dignified the lover by identifying him by name.[88]

Not surprisingly, disenso proceedings often became bitter and acrimonious. On becoming involved in a disenso, a family had to be prepared to defend its status, honor, and limpieza de sangre. The strategy involved presenting a parade of witnesses, some to bolster the family's prestige, others to engage in character assassination of their adversaries. In 1785, Don José Morejón sought to block his daughter María de Regla's marriage to soldier Guillermo Molina. Determined to proceed with her marriage, she hired a lawyer to have her father's challenge declared irrational. In presenting his case, Morejón argued that Molina's family, composed of drunkards, thieves, butchers, and shoemakers, was mixed with Indian blood. One of them, Andrés, was in jail in Guanabacoa. "Please," the old man successfully pleaded with the judge, "my daughter could not have chosen a more vile person."[89] When María Josefa Pita and Juan José Pérez sought to marry in 1786, his mother challenged her lineage, claiming that her family "were not descended from españoles but vile pardos of ill repute," to which María Josefa retorted that her betrothed's father "had been a carpenter and a carter."[90]

Although challenges were infrequent, their importance should not be casually dismissed. Losing a case meant that the reputation and honor of one's family was irreparably tarnished. The only avenue available was an appeal to higher offices, either the Audiencia in Santo Domingo or to the Council of the Indies and the monarch himself. Either action was a costly proposition, but was the only recourse available to Angel Tejera, who sought to compel his daughter's suitor, Antonio de los Reyes Gavilán, to marry the girl. Tejera lost the case, and in an interesting reversal of roles, the young man entered a monastery. Tejera's only recourse would have been to appeal to the Council of the Indies, which would present its recommendations to the king.[91]

Successful challenges represented a victory for the guardians of a family's honor in defending that honor against intrusion by unworthy suitors, but instituting such suits were not for the fainthearted. The lengthy proceedings taxed a family's financial resources and often exposed the participants to a scandal that would delight the modern-day tabloid press. One such scandal exploded in 1787 involving the Conde de Lagunillas, Felipe de Zequiera and his wife, Mariana Duarte, who sought to prevent her brother, Bonifacio, from marrying María Aniceta de Valdespino. The scorned woman enlisted the sympathy and support of attorney Pedro de Ayala, and their scandalous account of the Zequieras' and Duartes' sexual escapades made the rounds of Havana's taverns and bawdyhouses until Zequiera's suit for libel brought the story to a halt. While Aniceta suffered only insofar as she was prevented from marrying young Duarte, the lawyer, Ayala, was imprisoned and subjected to a lengthy and costly legal battle in which he lost his privileges to practice law.[92]

Findings for other areas of Spain's American empire demonstrate that most parental challenges were unsuccessful.[93] The condition and quantity of documents does not allow a conclusion regarding the rate of success or failure of marriage challenges in Havana. It is possible, however, to evaluate the impact of increased enforcement and parental challenges on the overall marriage patterns in the city. Prior to 1764, challenges were rare and, when initiated, often involved the Church. After 1764 challenges to marriages increased, though the small number of challenges (26), whether military or civilian, represents a minuscule portion of the more than 4,000 total marriages that took place during the period in the city.[94] Thus, on one hand, the evidence suggests that the impact of reform and the concomitant potential for challenge was negligible. On the other hand, the lack of evidence may also imply that parental challenges were unnecessary. In all likelihood, the promulgation and implementation of more stringent laws represented a mechanism by which the royal administration or parents could exercise greater control over social ordering, if only as a deterrent against frivolous or rebellious behavior.[95] With the clear-cut wishes of the monarchy and the precedent set by O'Reilly, military members and bureaucrats alike who were interested in advancing their career were cautious men when it came time to choose a life's partner and a suitable mother for one's children. If one married according to family and community standards, one could easily comply with the ordinary procedures implemented by the Spanish government. The majority of Havana's couples conformed to the explicit standards set by the royal administration and the implicit standards set by the administration, their parents, and the community. Simply and obviously, therefore, if no challenge occurred and a marriage took place, the match could be considered suitable to family members and the royal administration alike.

Accordingly, between 1753 and 1800, more than 4,400 suitable marriages occurred in the four parish churches that existed within the city in the late eighteenth century, the Cathedral of Havana, the Iglesia Santo Angel Custodio, the Iglesia Santo Cristo del Buen Viaje, and the Iglesia del Espíritu Santo.[96] An analysis of the marriage records of these four churches can provide twenty-first-century observers a glimpse of what contemporary society considered to be the proper social order. Evidence to evaluate marriage patterns was collected from parish books of Matri-monios de Blancos or Matrimonios de Españoles, including data identify-ing the origin and status (Don or Doña) of the partners.[97] Distinct indica-tions of social ordering may be established by identifying whether and to what extent social or ethnic groups intermarried. How pervasive were dif-ferent categories of marriage, for example, peninsular-Creole versus Cre-ole-Creole marriages, in relation to the rest of the population? What years represented peaks in peninsular-Creole marriages, thus signifying social processes operating in concert or conflict with political and economic trends? Was intermarriage confined to particular areas of the city, suggest-ing a geographic distribution by rank and/or occupation? Was intermar-riage and social co-optation confined to the elite (military, bureaucratic, landowning) stratum or was the process shared by many social ranks? Who amongst Havana's social groups provided wives for government bu-reaucrats and military personnel, men who occupied the highest social po-sition in the community? What were the differing prospects for men and women, and did whether a person was a widow or a widower affect mar-riageability? What effect did "foreigners" have upon the marriage market and the social structure of the city? The overall trend in the data demon-strates that the phenomenon of peninsular-Creole marriage pervaded the period but that after the war of 1779 and the victories in Pensacola and New Providence it reached epic proportions.

Prior to 1778, peninsular-Creole–Creole-Creole marriage ratios stayed fairly constant at 2:3, that is, two peninsular-Creole marriages for every three Creole-Creole marriages, a 40 percent to 60 percent distribution. Af-ter 1778, however, the rates become equal—in other words, for every Cre-ole-Creole marriage a peninsular-Creole marriage also occurred, probably since the militarization in preparation for the war brought many more soldiers and sailors to Havana. Absolute numbers are more precise and more understandable than ratios, and in such terms, from 1778 to 1785 throughout the city, peninsular-Creole unions actually were more numer-ous than Creole-Creole marriages![98]

A closer look at the data provides insight into the geographic and demo-graphic distribution of marriages. The phenomenon of marriage over-whelmingly involved peninsular grooms and Creole brides. Peninsular-Creole marriages were most prevalent in terms of numbers and frequency in the most "militarized" or elite parishes, La Catedral and Santo Angel, logically because of the high degree of royal activity and because many Creole families were affluent, so their daughters would have been suitable as wives. The poorest parish, Espíritu Santo, had the least degree of inter-marriage, which is logical, too, since that parish contained most of the city's least desirable families, who likely would not pass scrutiny. None-theless, Espíritu Santo's percentage of peninsular-Creole unions (35 per-cent of all marriages represents the lowest figure, which occurred in 1775) was still substantial until the boom years after 1778. Then, too, that par-ish's absolute numbers become roughly equal, and in the most active years, 1782–1785, Espíritu Santo's marrying population mirrors the that of the rest of the city, in that peninsular-Creole unions outnumber Creole-Creole unions.[99]

With the return of the troops from the successful campaigns of Pensa-cola in 1781 and New Providence in 1782, Havana and its inhabitants were caught up in the jubilation brought by military victory and revenge over Spain's old enemy, Great Britain. Gálvez's victories at Pensacola and other outposts on the Gulf Coast demonstrated beyond any doubt that Cuba's reinvigorated regular army and militia had comported themselves well, redeeming their honor that had suffered so much after the British occupa-tion of 1762–63.[100] When word of the negotiations leading to the Treaty of Paris, officially signed in 1783, became common knowledge, Havana's couples celebrated with a matrimonial frenzy that was without equal. As soldiers returned to the city, men and women rushed to tie the knot. The total number of marriages in the city rose by 25 percent, and in the par-ishes of La Catedral and Santo Angel, the ratio of peninsular-Creole mar-riages to Creole-Creole marriages skyrocketed to an all-time high of be-tween four and a half and five to one.[101]

Who, then, were the families that provided spouses for peninsular im-migrants, whether military personnel, royal employees, merchants, or other civilians? In simple terms, almost everyone with sufficient status to be entered into the parish books of matrimonios de españoles, which in light of the demographic evidence presented in previous chapters, repre-sents the majority of Cuba's free population. The most visible were Ha-vana's elite families, who married their daughters to peninsular grooms, and on occasion, some elite Creole sons married daughters of peninsular high officials. Most such families were landowners, but civilian fathers of such families regularly held positions in the militia.[102] As Allan J. Kuethe has demonstrated, militia positions took on increasing importance and prestige after the reforms of the 1760s and the victory years after 1782.

However, the phenomenon was by no means restricted to civilian hyper-elites with titles of nobility.[103] Even more prevalent were daughters of members of the professional military ranks, and among this group the majority of Creole sons were wed to peninsular daughters.[104]

The members of the Fixed Regiment of Havana provide individual insights as to the phenomenon of peninsular-Creole intermarriage. The ninety members of the officer ranks in 1765 may be separated into two groups for the purpose of analysis, upper-echelon officers (captain and above) and lower-ranking officers and cadets. Such a distinction is logical because single men in the upper echelons would be eligible to marry immediately if permission could be secured. The behavior of the younger cohort, all of whom would not be eligible to marry for several years, would demonstrate change or continuity over time. Of course, some members of the Fixo must be excluded from such an examination. For example, some officers were already married, others died within a few years of the reorganization, and still others were assigned to other locations on the island so their marital preferences cannot be established at this time. Colonel Melchor Feliú, for example, died a bachelor.[105]

As demonstrated, O'Reilly used the existing legislation to remove some undesirables by rationalizing that their marriages were unsuitable according to existing regulations. Thus, if a soldier was unfit and he was married to a Creole women, the legal precedent for cashiering him was clearly established and could be utilized if the commanders saw fit. Yet in spite of the established regulations and their legal rationale, the punishment for marrying Creole women was seldom carried out. Indeed, the majority of the officer corps already married suffered no censure. Quite the contrary: many married officers enjoyed significant career advancement. Lieutenant Colonel Vicente de Zéspedes, married to María Concepción de Aróstegui since 1754, exemplified the unification of peninsular and Creole families, and Zéspedes enjoyed steady career advancement.[106] Of course, the Zéspedes-Aróstegui marriage may be exceptional given the unquestionable status of the participants. However, other men married to Creole women suffered little, if any, career discrimination. While other men had been discharged because of their unfortunate marriages, Captain Ventura Díaz had been promoted to lieutenant colonel, in spite of his marriage to a Creole widow.[107] Clearly his marriage to a Creole woman had no effect on his potential for career advancement, as he continued the normal career pattern, serving in the many garrisoned cities on the island. Similarly, Lieutenant Antonio López de Toledo, who would become the commander of the garrison at Batabanó, found that his marriage to a Floridana woman was no impediment in his progression up the career ladder.[108]

Since the militarization of the island required experienced men, royal officials might have chosen to overlook such existing marriages, especially if the men in question had otherwise performed satisfactorily. However, if the Crown truly sought to prohibit peninsular-Creole unions, then the new regulations should signal a change in policy after which peninsular-Creole marriages would have ceased or have been greatly reduced. Even though a greater degree of enforcement is clearly evident, exactly the opposite occurred, as the intermarriage of peninsular officers and Creole women continued apace. For example, fixo lieutenant Mariano Gelabert married a daughter of militia captain José Arango in 1767.[109] Captain Benito Ramírez, who would be promoted to lieutenant colonel by 1795, followed suit in 1773, as did Second Lieutenant Rafael Contador from Cádiz, who married a Creole bride in Cathedral parish in 1776.[110] Even more significant was that peninsular-Creole intermarriage involved men in the highest echelons of military service. Lieutenant Colonel Juan Dabán, who would become inspector general of the island, married the Habanera daughter of an *oidor* (judge) of the Real Audiencia in 1766.[111] In May 1773, Captain José García de Valverde of the Regiment of Dragoons from Valladolid married the daughter of navy commander José de Acosta.[112] His marriage obviously had the approval of his commanding officer, Paris-born Lieutenant Colonel Antonio Raffelín, who chose a Habanera bride a short four months later, in October 1773.[113]

The printer's ink was barely dry on the published copy of the 1764 version of the Reglamento para las Milicias de Cuba, which detailed the strict new regulations that, thenceforth, would be enforced, when Lieutenant José Montero de Espinosa from Navarra married into one of the most prestigious families on the island, that of Pedro García Menocal, whose family had grown rich by provisioning the garrison since the seventeenth century.[114] A daughter of that union, Doña Bárbara, introduced at the beginning of the chapter, followed in her mother's footsteps by marrying a member of the royal court in 1782, as did her sister, Ana María, who had married Jaime de Carvajal of the Regiment of Aragón four months previously.[115] Both unions clearly were complementary in status, as, in the intervening years, their father had risen through the ranks to become the commander of the Castillo del Morro in spite of—or perhaps, because of—his marriage to a Creole woman.[116] Moreover, their unions linked the Havana family to the highest echelons of imperial society. Doña Bárbara married a member of court and Doña Ana María married the son of one of the commanders of the fleet at Algeria, Luís de Carvajal. Their sponsor was the governor and captain general of the island, Juan Manuel de Cagigal.[117] Montero de Espinosa was not unusual in arranging his own marriage to a Creole and that of each of his daughters to a newly arrived peninsular man of noble birth. Countless other men in military service united their families with families of similar status through the marriage of their sons and daughters. Sevillano widower Diego Fons y Monsalve stood in as proxy groom in the 1773 marriage of his daughter, Mariana, to Captain Antonio Chinchilla from Málaga, and arranged an even more prestigious union for his second daughter, Brigida, to Francisco de Albuquerque, the commander of the Castillo de Atarés, from Ceuta.[118] Sons of military personnel, the youths of the cohort of cadets, were more discriminating in their choice of a mate than was impetuous cadet Francisco del Río. At the same time that del Río was scandalizing the garrison at Bayamo, his comrade, cadet Ignacio María de Acosta, whose sister married José García Valverde, married the daughter of royal engineer Bruno Cavallero in Havana in Parroquia Santo Angel.[119] Likewise, the sons of retired Captain Juan de Landa, cadets José and Joaquín, were married to Creole brides in Havana in 1767 and 1781, respectively.[120]

While the previous examples may give the impression that peninsular-Creole intermarriage was an elite phenomenon, such was far from being the case. Upper-echelon military members and the Creole familes into whom they deliberately integrated themselves simply were more visible and more traceable in their careers than ordinary soldiers and civilian families; however, the practice of marrying Creole women was not confined to the upper ranks. Ordinary soldiers such as Manuel Gutiérrez, a corporal in the Regimento del Príncipe from Toledo, Sergeant Fernando de la Puente from Ciudad Algeciras, and Pedro del Olmo, a sergeant from Burgos, were representative of many lower-echelon peninsular men who married locally born women.[121] Parish priests were less rigorous in entering the personal details in marriage entries of less affluent couples than they were for couples of elevated status. That the poorer men and their brides could barely afford the requisite ecclesiastical fees and rarely added an additional offering accounts for the perfunctory manner in which parish priests recorded their ceremonies.[122]

With regard to individual characteristics of the participants in marriages, one visible trait that can be demonstrated at this time from the matrimonial data is that in most Creole groom–peninsular bride unions, the bride was a widow, suggesting that she had arrived with her previous husband. Foreigners had little effect on Havana's marriage market. Grooms from other areas of Charles III's dominions (Genoa, Naples, Caracas, Cumaná, etc.) did marry, but their numbers were not high either relative to the rest of the population or in absolute numbers. The majority were members of the Spanish army.[123] Grooms from New Spain usually were men attached to the regiments of Mexico or Guadalajara. For example, peninsular Jaime Garcini was a member of the Regiment of Guadalajara who transferred to the Regiment of Havana. Garcini obviously found marriage to a Cuban bride more promising than contracting a marriage in New Spain.[124] Several men from provinces in France—from Paris, Normandy, and Languedoc, for example—married locally; again, many were military personnel. Some Frenchmen arrived via Martinique, bringing their intended brides with them. Persons of Irish Catholic descent were few (less than twenty), and mostly were men assigned to the Hibernia Regiment.[125] Although some historical interpretations argue that the penetration of British or North American mercantile interests had wide-reaching economic effects, the presence of Anglo ship captains and sailors had a negligible effect on Havana's marriage market. The appearance of British subjects in Havana's parish records are extremely rare, obviously since few were Catholic. One poignant entry in 1780 relates how an English child, María Francisca Varela, was orphaned when both of her parents died in 1762 during the occupation of the city in the aftermath of the siege. Raised in the Casa Cuna (the orphanage), the brief story of how she came to reside in Havana was related in the entry detailing her marriage to a man recently arrived from the Canary Islands.[126]

The act of contracting a marriage represented significant legal, religious, and social commitments, a step not to be taken lightly. "Till death do us part" was literally the case. For their part, Havana's Creole population could secure a privileged social position through alliances with bureaucrats, military personnel, and other peninsular immigrants. Creole social aspirations at many levels could be fulfilled through such kin networks, and many otherwise unprepossessing Cuban families could gain a measure of status previously reserved for only the most wealthy Creoles. Their sentiments were expressed succinctly in the phrase: "Better a pygmy from Spain than a giant from the Indies."[127]

In addition to the intangible reward of increased status, military pensions represented obligations on the part of a grateful monarch to reward men who had served him well and to care for their surviving widows and children. In Cuba, three separate welfare measures for military and bureaucrats' families were in operation: the general *montepío*, or pension system, to provide for families of bureaucrats and treasury officials; the *montepío militar* for military families; and the specialized *limosna de Florida*, created in 1731 specifically for surviving mothers, widows, and children of military personnel stationed at the presidio in Florida.[128] While pensions were granted to dependents throughout Spain and Spanish America, the Cuban montepío militar in particular would come to represent a significant concession to the widows and orphans of the island.[129]

As true watchdogs of the monarch's money, however, Bourbon treasury officials were not willing to part with a single peso without a fight. Thus when the more than 350 women from Florida displaced by the cession of the province to Great Britain came to get what was due them, they formed a virtual vanguard in an assault on treasury officials' tightfistedness. The subsequent expansion of the limosna de Florida is a story of repeated efforts between bureaucrats intent on preserving the king's money and perseverant military women equally relentless in their pursuit of the privileges they had been granted under the 1731 decree. Their petitions for relief began in 1764, but officials effectively delayed implementation until the early 1770s, pleading confusion in how to implement the royal concession. A July 1773 royal order in favor of the *limosneras* broke the logjam, and military women who had fought the decade-long struggle finally saw their efforts come to fruition. The victory of the Florida women ultimately benefited all military widows, children, and mothers.[130] In the beginning the drain on the treasury was minimal. María Carillo, who began her marriage to Joaquín de Arteaga with just the clothes on her back, was awarded a pension of ninety pesos a year.[131] As the century wore on, however, pension requests became more numerous and awards became larger. Nicolasa Mancebo Betancourt and her two maiden daughters each received 280 pesos annually upon the death of her husband, Hilario Remírez de Esteñóz, in 1789.[132] María Candelaria Perdomo, widow of Ventura Díaz, was awarded 292 pesos annually in 1789.[133] Colonel Miguel Ibañez Cuevas's career was a checkered one that included his withstanding false charges of smuggling in addition to the late-1760s charges of embezzlement mentioned; upon his death a royal order established a pension of 500 pesos per year for his widow, Francisca Clara Fernández de Beranes.[134] Brigadier General Matias de Armona, who had served on the northern Mexican frontier with José de Gálvez, had an equally checkered career, yet his widow, María Dolores de Lizundia, and six minor children also received a pension of 500 pesos annually after he died on July 29, 1796.[135]

Almost as quickly as royal policies underwent a volte-face in the 1770s, the situation began to get out of hand. At times the women's requests appear preposterous and the subsequent approval extraordinary by twentieth-century standards, but in the euphoria in the aftermath of the Pensacola Campaign, Charles III was determined to reward the men and their families who had served him well. Estefanía del Valle y Rosas, widow of Miguel de Olasagasti, received seventy pesos annually even though he died over twenty-seven years before she submitted her request and thirteen years before the establishment of the pension system.[136] Yet upon her request and substantiating letter from Vicente de Zéspedes, she became a beneficiary of the grateful monarch's generosity.[137] Margarita O'Neilly, an English widow living in Florida, requested a pension based upon the services of her husband, Enrique O'Neilly, who was murdered by "banditti" while defending His Catholic Majesty's interests on the frontier. The family were refugee British Loyalists who had fled to Florida when their plantation in Virginia was confiscated by patriot forces. In 1784, when the province was returned to Spanish rule, O'Neilly chose to remain in Florida under the Spanish regime. In spite of having fought for Spain's enemy, Zéspedes's recommendation also earned his widow a pension in 1791.[138] Not only widows and orphans were eligible for pensions: in the case of Marcos Martínez of the Battalion de Morenos Libres of Havana, his father, Juan Antonio Martínez, was awarded half of his deceased son's salary for the remainder of his life.[139] The most unusual case that came to the governor's attention occurred in 1774, when Felipe de Acosta presented the petition of Doña Ana María Larios, over one hundred years of age, who wrote from Santo Domingo asking for a pension and 6 percent interest from the year the pension system was implemented. Not only did she request the pension for herself, but she also asked for the back pay that was due her deceased husband, Francisco Ruís, who had been a sergeant in Santiago de Cuba. According to the documents she entrusted to her spokesman, the Crown owed her 797 pesos 5 *reales*. De la Torre responded that he would try to honor her request, especially with regard to her advanced age, but because it was such a large sum, the outcome would be favorable only if it did not harm the overall interests of the Crown.[140] He sent the request to the intendant, Nicolás José de Rapún, who expedited the petition and secured royal approval based upon Doña Ana María's dire circumstances.[141]

If kinship alliances with royal officials brought increased prestige and lifetime pensions, they also brought significant responsibilities. Military men literally pledged their lives to royal service. Time and again military men—perhaps agonizingly—wrote into legal documents, *"debo seguir mis banderas"* ("I must follow my flag"), but both they and their women recognized that their families took a subordinate position to their obligations to the state.[142] Women and their families who chose to ally themselves with officers or soldiers accepted the responsibilities such alliances entailed. These included not only the normal obligations of being a wife and mother but also the additional burdens of military life. In normal circumstances, wives were expected to help and support their husbands, manage the home, bear and raise children, and remain loyal, honorable, and pure in spirit. A woman's greatest contribution was the proper upbringing of children, and "enlightened motherhood" was the goal for women defined by proscriptive literature of the time.[143] However, in cases of emergency, women were empowered—even expected—to act as "deputy husbands" and take an active role in conducting the family's affairs.[144] Widows were venerated as models of exemplary feminine behavior, and were entrusted with the instruction and care of younger women.[145] But unlike families who lived in more secure areas of the empire, the women of Havana were charged with obligations over and above normal female responsibilities. The military community was always in a state of readiness; thus, women needed to be prepared to manage their households and to care for their family by themselves at a moment's notice. And while it matters little whether such responsibility was for a short period or for the remainder of their lives, male family members recognized that their wives were equal to the task.

The likelihood of frequent and unavoidable absences demanded that men leave proper documentation so their women could "act in all matters" in their stead.[146] On one hand, with the expectation that he would survive the campaign and return, men drafted powers-of-attorney in favor of their wives.[147] These documents allowed wives to carry on the daily business of managing the family and providing for their needs. It also allowed women to cope with minor emergencies and to buy and sell family property, particularly slaves. More serious was the very real possibility that the husband may not return, and in this contingency, men regularly named their wives as executors of their wills. Jacinta Escañes (introduced in chapter 4), widowed as a result of her husband's death during the siege of Pensacola, was one such example, and she, in turn, named her daughter, María Josefa de Zubieta, to act in her stead should anything happen to her.[148] Havana's women lived with the continual possibility of widowhood being suddenly thrust upon them, so in a way their behavior was a rehearsal for the inevitable.

In either case, women were forced to take over many of the administrative tasks that were not normally theirs. While there was a tangible difference, both legally and emotionally, between being a wife and a widow, in actual practice, there was little difference. Havana's women proved themselves capable of shouldering the responsibilities that inevitably would be theirs. One area where women were particularly visible was in making the financial arrangements for brides' dowries. Victorina Guillén, wife of Colonel Antonio Fernández of the Mounted Dragoons, made arrangements for her daughter's dowry in her husband's absence. The property she pledged as collateral came from properties she inherited from her mother's family.[149] In 1784, widow Melchora Ponce de León granted permission for her daughter's marriage. She turned to her mother, Catalina Cabrera, also widowed, to provide the necessary collateral, one and a half caballerías of land.[150] María Dolores Guerra's arrangements for Rita Gonzáles de Guerra's marriage to a lieutenant of the Regiment of Aragon included a provision garden (*sitio de labor*) in Arroyo Naranjo.[151] Women also arranged their sons' military education. Manuela Maroto set up a fund for the maintenance of her son, Manuel Ponce de Leon, until his brother returned from Spain.[152] María Concepción Morejón petitioned the Council of the Indies for her sons to be admitted as cadets in the Fixed Regiment of Havana when they came of age.[153] Tomasa María Noroña arranged a position in the Infantry of Nueva España for her son, Diego González de Barrera, and provided fifteen pesos a month for his maintenance.[154] Rather than asking for a position in military service, Josepha Gabriela de Ambulodi sought a title of nobility, that of the Conde de Valle Llano, for her son José Antonio de Arredondo.[155] Notarial records are full of examples in which Havana's women acted independently, particularly in financial matters. At the very least, such action demonstrated a financial acumen unique for their time. But in other instances, women stepped beyond the mundane and actively confronted royal officials and the system. For mothers and wives, it was perfectly acceptable and expected for them to confront the system in defense of their family.

"Díme con quien andas y te diré quien eres" ("Tell me with whom you walk and I will tell you who you are") quotes an old Spanish proverb. Clearly Spanish and Creole families considered their status to be complementary, as they walked hand-in-hand down the aisles of Havana's churches. The prevalence of peninsular-Creole intermarriage reveals the dynamic social changes that occurred in Cuba after 1763, even after the implementation of strict new regulations. Simply put, Cuban Creole women were acceptable brides for peninsular royal officials, military men, and merchants. Such acceptance represented an important change in metropolitan policy towards Cuban-born Spaniards, a change which must have been obvious to all. Certainly, regulations regarding choices of a marriage partner were articulated clearly in the new legislation. The degree to which the regulations were enforced buttressed by the evidence of behavior demonstrates that Cuban Creole women had the opportunity to marry Spanish men of similar status and to have their match approved by the appropriate royal officials. Thus, unlike mainland families, who were viewed with suspicion, Cubans enjoyed a privileged position in the imperial system.[156]

But if further proof was needed, in early 1782, after the victories along the Gulf Coast but before the matrimonial frenzy, a letter from Madrid addressed to the governor of Cuba arrived in Havana. It conveyed the gratitude of Charles III for the "fidelity, love, and diligence with which the city, the local officials and public alike, distingushed itself . . . showing, at the same time, new proof of the constant interest that [Havana's] citizens take toward the glory of arms."[157] This tangible acknowledgment of their status in the eyes of their sovereign, combined with the intangible verification of their equality with peninsulars, sealed the social contract between the island's inhabitants and the Crown. From that moment onward, Habaneros and all the rest of the Spanish imperial world recognized that Cuba had been restored to the royal grace.

6

There Is No Subordination in These People

Al pueblo como a los niños,
Preciso es tratar,
Mostrárlelas cariño,
Y también severidad.

When dealing with the people,
Like with children,
It's necessary to give them love,
But also strictness.

Perhaps no other Spanish American city mourned the death of Charles III in December 1788 so genuinely as did Havana.[1] The father-monarch had chastised, corrected, and tested the city, and finally had brought it back into royal favor. Its citizens had reciprocated his "paternal benevolence" with "love and filial recognition."[2] In the aftermath of his death, Cubans praised their beloved monarch as "a beneficent sun that in his rotation transmitted his ardent kindness to his vassals. . . . Virtuous even into his old age that same virtue made him worthy of the eminent place he had obtained on earth."[3]

The island had good reason to mourn. The decade after the close of the war with Great Britain had been very good to Cuba in spite of a mild economic downturn that affected primarily the sugar interests.[4] At the same time, however, a lively trade had developed with the United States to both parties' benefit. Cuba needed food; the United States needed markets, since its traditional trade networks had been severed with independence.[5] In and around the city the population continued its spectacular growth, spilling out from the city to the hinterlands. In contrast to other areas of the empire during the turbulent decade of the 1780s—while mixed-bloods and Indians in Peru rebelled against taxation; while comuneros in New Granada ran wild in the streets, and while urban mobs in Mexico City rioted over severe food shortages—Havana remained tranquil, basking in royal favor and economic prosperity.[6] From disgrace after the shameful capitulation to the British in 1762, the city had redeemed itself in the wake of Cuba's stellar performance in the American Revolutionary War. The victory was even sweeter when compared to the peninsular army's dismal performance in Europe. Cuba's "faithful vassals . . . could do no less than feel deeply the loss of such a great monarch."[7]

Barely five years later the island teetered on the brink on anarchy. The countryside was a simmering cauldron ready to boil over in revolt. City inhabitants hid behind closed doors fearful of an uprising of French Republicans, free coloreds, and/or slaves. The military was in a mutinous mood in response to the cavalier and disrespectful treatment it had received. Slaves in El Cobre and Puerto Príncipe took advantage of disarray in the free population to make their bid for freedom. The borders were under assault by partisans of Republican France, and merchants fought with royal governors and among themselves. In less that a decade love and filial affection had evaporated, and in its place suspicion and resentment ruled the population's emotions. What on earth could have happened?

Incredible though it may have seemed to contemporaries, barely a decade after the euphoria that gripped the island after the Spanish victory against Great Britain in 1782, the carefully crafted social contract between Crown and colony began to fall apart. The decline of Spanish America in general and of Cuba in particular began with the deaths of key members of the Gálvez clan: Matias, viceroy of New Spain, in 1785; his son Bernardo, who had succeeded him as viceroy in 1786; and its most powerful member, José, minister of the Indies, in 1787. The final straw was Charles III's death in 1788, and thereafter, Spain embarked on a path toward self-destruction. While the European nation would survive, its sovereignty in the New World would end, and although Cuba would not follow its mainland Creole brethren to independence, its filial affection for Spain would be seriously compromised.

The causes for the loss of Spain's empire in America are well-studied, and most interpretations place the blame upon the legendary ineptitude of Charles IV. The bumbling monarch inherited a peaceful, prosperous empire poised to enter the mainstream of European enlightenment. During the first years of his reign, Charles IV seemed dedicated to retaining the ministers who had served his father well, particularly the minister of state, the Conde de Floridablanca. For their part, royal ministers seemed dedicated to continuing the reforms Charles III had implemented. Quickly, however, the morass of court politics complicated by the revolution in

France engulfed the untrained and incompetent monarch.[8] Many of the accomplishments of Charles III's reign were dismantled, a setback summarized succinctly by Jacques Barbier: "Gálvez's successors brought in the final fruits of reform only to have their work eventually destroyed by circumstances beyond their control."[9] From the perspective of Spanish America, the most important institutional casualty was the Council of the Indies, which was abolished in 1790, its functions being taken over by the Council of State.[10] On a personal level, Floridablanca's ministry was undermined by his uncompromising opposition to France, which Charles IV believed placed the French royal family in jeopardy, and ultimately, "Charles IV sacrificed his minister for his relatives."[11] Floridablanca's old rival, the Conde de Aranda, returned to Madrid, and at last he succeeded in gaining the long-coveted appointment as minister of state in February 1792, only to be dismissed six months later in favor of Manuel de Godoy, and finally, exiled in 1794.[12]

Few historical figures have generated the controversy that Godoy has.[13] Reputed to be the lover of Queen María Luisa, he occupied an elevated position in the royal household. Within the realm of court politics, Charles IV relied heavily on the royal favorite, and in four years Godoy rose from anonymity in the junior officer corps to the position of minister of state.[14] As the titular head of Spain's defense—but without the experience or the respect of his troops and detested by the Spanish public—he led Spain into disastrous European conflicts, first against Republican France, later against Great Britain.[15] In the Caribbean, Godoy's corrosive influence embroiled Spain into an invasion of the French colony St. Domingue, which shared the island Hispaniola with the Spanish colony, Santo Domingo.[16] Charles IV's reliance upon Godoy struck at the very fabric of the Spanish national character, the reconquest ideology, and the glorification of military exploits and gradually eroded the support of the Spanish and Spanish American subjects alike.[17] By the end of the century, so too, the fabric of military life in Cuba was slowly unraveling.

Unlike in 1762, however, the sorry state of the Spanish military could not be blamed on the Creole military units that had protected the front lines of the Caribbean and had taken the offensive and recaptured Mobile, Pensacola, and New Providence. Their exploits stood in sharp contrast to those of the men who had chosen to return to the peninsula. Some of the best and brightest veterans of the Caribbean theater had accompanied Field Marshal Alejandro O'Reilly back to Spain, and their European careers were as undistinguished as his. In addition to the humiliation that accompanied the defeat at Algeria, when Spain joined France in support of the rebellious British colonies in 1779, her immediate European goal was to wrest Gibraltar from British control.[18] After two years of laying siege to the fortress, Silvestre de Abarca, the engineer who supervised the refortification of Havana in 1764, was unable to dislodge the British forces.[19] Luis de Las Casas, O'Reilly's brother-in-law, had followed his kinsman to the Caribbean, to Spain, to Africa, and into obscurity during the decade that the Gálvez family dominated Spain's political culture. With Charles III's death, the Aragonés faction returned to royal favor, and Las Casas, Aranda's protégé, reemerged from his position as inspector of the troops along the Mediterranean coast and secured the lucrative post of Cuba's governor and captain general.[20]

A veteran of the reforms of the 1760s and the New Orleans pacification, Las Casas took up his position in Cuba in July of 1790.[21] The timing appeared auspicious. One of Las Casas's first positive accomplishments was to begin publication of a twice-weekly newspaper, the *Papel Periódico de la Havana*, a successor to the *Gaceta de la Havana*, which had provided news to Havana's literate sector during the 1770s and 1780s.[22] Before his death, Charles III had approved a Sociedad Económica de Amigos del País for Santiago de Cuba in 1787; Las Casas proposed a similar society for Havana, and that of the latter city quickly eclipsed that of the former.[23] Other enlightened ideas followed. A Sociedad Patriótica was born in 1793 in the throes of the campaign to end the rebellion in St. Domingue, and a Real Consulado was established in Havana on April 4, 1794.[24]

Because of these seemingly progressive accomplishments, Las Casas's reputation has weathered the historiographical storm well. Based upon nineteenth-century antiquarian accounts, many traditional historians maintain that his administration was wise, prudent, or fair.[25] Historians of the dependency school, however, see the Basque as a tool of the plantation interests and his administration as contributing to the spread of Atlantic world capitalism.[26] A recent study rescues his negative image and describes the man as "a son of the enlightenment," who championed forward-looking ideas while promoting internal social order.[27] On one hand, Las Casas was responsible for fostering commerce in general and favored the sugar industry in particular, a development that would resonate through Cuba's future. On the other hand, in collaboration with his group of henchmen— Francisco de Arango y Parreño, Pablo Estévez, José de Ilincheta, and Pedro Pablo O'Reilly—he would be responsible for destroying the metropolitan-colonial social compact that Charles III had created. Far from being an "Amigo del País," he was, in the long run, no friend of Cuba.

The new governor arrived with a philosophy that was diametrically opposed to that which had dominated the relations between Cuba and Spain for the previous two decades. To begin with, he was a member of the rival faction who was forced to watch Gálvez's partisans' successes while he was associated with the failure at Algeria. He also represented a monarchy ill equipped to deal with matters of government and whose policy vacillated from one extreme to another. On one issue, however, royal policy was constant: dealing with an impending financial crisis. Even from its early years, Charles IV's monarchy was not known for its fiscal responsibility, and the task of its representatives was to make their jurisdictions profitable.[28] Cuba, with its costly defense-based economy was a continual drain on the metropolitan treasury. Certainly, no one needed to convince Mexico, the imperial cash cow, that excessive amounts of money were spent on Cuba. Ways to reduce the costs of maintaining the island were obvious: lower its costs and increase its profitability. Moreover, Aranda and the Aragoneses had never favored the interests of the Indies over those of the peninsula, and they were convinced that cost-cutting measures were in order. They turned to men with experience with the island, and Cuba's most famous Creole intellectual, Francisco de Arango y Parreño, was eager to offer his suggestions as he lobbied for the plantation interests in Madrid.[29]

Arango presented his now-famous *Discurso Sobre la Agricultura* to the Council of the Indies in 1789.[30] By his own acknowledgment, his proposal was limited to the potential contribution that the sugar industry could make to the empire; therefore, by design, his suggestions were limited to the area surrounding Havana. In the first draft, Arango in fact admitted that he did not speak for the rest of the island. The *Discurso* explained the condition of Cuba's agriculture and contained several suggestions as to how the island's problems could be resolved, presented as requests for permission to do so. These requests including asking for permission to form a junta to promote sugar cultivation, permission to visit Jamaica and learn from the British how best to develop the industry, and for a subsidy to be provided from the Royal Treasury in Mexico to further the trade. A continuous thread of Arango's missive to the Crown was that Cuba suffered from a chronic shortage of labor that contributed to the island's backwardness. The situation could be remedied only by increased slave imports.[31] In his closing argument, Arango sought to convince royal ministers that profits were slipping through their fingers through commerce with foreigners. The need to increase Cuba's sugar industry was manifest when Arango appended a table that demonstrated that the majority of aguardiente and rum introduced into Cádiz from 1786 to 1791 came from England.[32]

With the benefit of historical hindsight, the victory for Cuba's sugar planters has been seen as natural and inevitable. It is a mistake to believe, however, that the triumph of the sugar interests was either quick or easy. Rather, the gradual approval of portions of Arango's proposal took more than four years to obtain, and the most controversial, the subsidy from Mexico, was never approved. Part of the reason for the delay was that Arango originally presented his *Discurso* to the Council of the Indies, and that the ministry that was subsequently dismantled and its functions taken over by the Council of State. In addition to delays in transferring responsibilities, there were delays as leadership of the Ministry of State passed through three men during the course of deliberations, Floridablanca, Aranda, and Godoy, all of whom held widely divergent political positions. Overall, however, royal ministers on both councils were unsympathetic to Arango's proposal, and on some issues they were clearly obstructionist.

One of the first of Charles IV's advisers to advance his opinion, Diego de Gardoqui, minister of Hacienda, reported favorably on the proposal. The Council of the Indies, however, moved with its customary glacial slowness, and it took them more than two years to approve the first particularly innocuous portion, the request for permission to form the junta to promote agriculture.[33] Three more months elapsed before the notification of their approval was finally sent back to Gardoqui for his signature.[34] Meanwhile, the spokesman for the plantation interests was growing impatient with the failure of royal ministers to act on his requests, and the rebellion in neighboring St. Domingue gave new urgency to his campaign as its effects were felt immediately throughout the Atlantic world.[35] Although Arango exulted that the destruction of that colony removed competitors of Cuban producers, nevertheless, he had only minimal success to show for nearly three years' work. Throughout 1792, he pressed for the approval of other, more serious concessions, such as permission to travel to Jamaica to consult with British producers on how best to grow and process sugarcane. Gardoqui and the now-defunct Council of the Indies, men with experience in Spanish America, saw little harm in learning from foreigners. The Council of State was not convinced, and yet another year passed before it took up the issue in October 1792. They relied heavily on the previous decision in Arango's favor when in November 1792 they granted permission for a group to travel to Jamaica.[36] Once again, the council took no action on the portions of the request to increase slave imports or to provide a subsidy of Mexican silver for the sugar producers.

Indeed, in spite of Arango's blasé assurance that the disturbances in Guarico worked to Cuba's advantage because they eliminated the French competition, the issue that caused the most unease among the ministers was the request to permit more slaves to enter the island. Their concern was shared by the Marqués de Casa Peñalver, who wrote that the island already had more than 90,000 enslaved blacks. According to Peñalver, a better solution would be to encourage Canary Islanders to immigrate to Cuba, and even transporting Mexican Indians would be preferable to encouraging slave imports.[37] Arango's recommendations were also not enhanced when the captain of San Lázaro, a barrio immediately outside the city walls, wrote that nearly 1,500 newly imported slaves were "infesting" his neighborhood because they did not have a place to be lodged.[38] Periodic missives from various capitanes del partido throughout the island reinforced the image that fugitive slaves were uncontrollable. Particularly troublesome were reports such as that from the captain of Guayabal, Pedro Monza, who wrote that a fugitive slave had broken into the house of Bartolomé Pachecho and stolen several objects. To survive during the course of his flight he also killed a horse for food.[39] South of Havana near Güines, thick forest was ideal territory for communities of runaway slaves. In 1792 eight slaves belonging to Domingo de Ugarte escaped and fled to a *palenque* (runaway slave community) on the hacienda Carairas.[40]

Such disturbing missives contributed to the Council of State's reluctance to approve Arango's requests, even though they believed him that Cuba's blacks were few *("son pocos")* and they were better treated than those of St. Domingue. They were also concerned with Cuba's free black militia units, a "dangerous policy that did not exist in any other colony." The council took under consideration his recommendation that black militia units were no longer necessary because "there were enough whites" to defend the island. Even though Cuba's free black men were "accustomed to work, frugality, and subordination and made very good soldiers . . . in the end, they were still blacks, and in any conflict . . . would be fierce opponents."[41]

Four years later, after the original proposal was introduced, no action had yet been taken on the remaining two portions of the *Discurso*. In May 1793, Arango wrote a furious letter to the ministers. "Hurry up," he told them, "or I'll renounce my position as your adviser."[42] Clearly the issue was at an impasse, and with Spain now involved in a war against France, the proposal was passed on to yet another group of ministers in the hope that they could resolve the issue "with the least embarrassment to the Council of State."[43] After four years, Arango had accomplished little, and while four years in historic time are but a moment, four years in human time could mean the difference between solvency and ruin.

Given the downward spiral of Spain's economy, the appeal of Arango's proposal to make Cuba profitable must have been very tempting. Realistically, however, sugar production was the only agricultural product that could be manipulated, since the other agricultural products were limited by structural restraints. Tobacco and mining were regulated by royal monopolies. Similarly, the shipbuilding-and-timber industry was governed by the Royal Navy and the Timber Board. Concomitantly, while searching for quick solutions to long-term problems, the Crown proposed to exacerbate the situation by cutting back on the island's most important source of income, defense spending, a decision that would affect thousands of active-duty soldiers, retirees, and petty producers who provided goods and services for the garrisoned cities. As royal ministers frantically searched for ways to balance the Bourbon budgets, the seduction of Arango's eloquence and logic was compelling. Yet even though the monarchy needed money and Mexico was tired of paying for Cuba, the Crown's acceptance of Arango's opinion was far from a foregone conclusion.

Arango's position vis-à-vis slave imports was especially difficult to reconcile in light of the evidence that the island's population continued its explosive growth even after 1792 and the onset of the sugar boom. Indeed, both the Council of the Indies and the Council of State concluded that "because of the number of Spaniards who had immigrated to Cuba," there were enough white inhabitants to meet defense requirements.[44] On the other hand, Arango's complaints about a shortage of labor and demographic data are, in fact, complementary and mutually supportive. The problem for the plantation interests was that while there was an ever-increasing number of workers, they were the very people who could not be compelled to work in sugar cultivation: free workers of European descent and free people of color.

Indeed, the problem of obtaining laborers in Cuba was more complex than in other areas of the Americas because Cuba's marginal ranks were not Indians or mestizos but rather European men, their legitimate family, their illegitimate offspring, veterans, militia members, or some combination thereof. Accordingly, Cuba's underclasses enjoyed privileges that the marginal people of other areas in Spanish America did not. Furthermore, because so many ordinary citizens were the beneficiaries of militarization, either as pensioners, active militia, or suppliers of goods and services, Havana's common people were not economically dependent on the whims of the local colonial elites. Worse still, because of militarization they enjoyed the complete fuero militar, so they were not subject to the arbitrary measures of social control. Las Casas's historical reputation as a champion of increased social control demonstrates that their autonomy infuriated him and his compatriots among the plantation interests. This observation was not lost on Alexander Von Humboldt, who wrote that Las Casas's efforts were nothing short of a "guerra contra los habitantes de los arrabales" ("war against the inhabitants of the suburbs").[45] Militarization had created a monster, and the root of the lower orders' unruliness stemmed from their inherent status as españoles, their economic prosperity, and their access to privileges unique to the island. Arango's impatience at the imperial level was reflected in the efforts of his counterpart on the island, who was unable to coerce the island's inhabitants to "promote agriculture" by working for the sugar planters.

At first, the relationship began on a positive note, and the new governor received the customary letters of welcome and thanksgiving for his safe arrival from the capitanes del partido throughout the island.[46] Las Casas reciprocated the feeling of goodwill in the inaugural issue of the *Papel Periódico de la Havana*, which appeared on October 24, 1790. The undisguised voice of his government praised the Habaneros for their "excess of patriotism," engendered because of their love of their island.[47] Cordiality disappeared rapidly as the Basque made his forceful presence known. By December 1790, an editorial lauded the arrival of many Basques, "whose numbers have grown not only in commerce but also in the bureaucracy and in the military corps."[48] The editor went on to praise the newcomers for their healthy lifestyle that would be received favorably even by classical societies such as the Romans.[49]

The implication, of course, was that while the Romans would have provided a welcome for Las Casas's compatriots, el pueblo cubano did not, and while the depth of the inhabitants' hostility is difficult to gauge, the cause is clear. Las Casas had been in his post but a few months when the sugar harvest of 1790–91 approached. Although the lower ranks could refuse to work in agriculture, there were other ways to ensure their contribution. One way to increase production was to make sure that sugar got to the wharves quickly to be shipped to Spain. Because the finished product was so heavy and bulky, its efficient marketing required building and maintaining roads and bridges. In late 1790, Las Casas decreed that all able-bodied citizens were to present themselves to the capitanes del partido immediately in order to volunteer their personal labor to maintaining the bridges and the roads.[50]

Popular resistance to his decree was immediate. The first suggestion that trouble lay ahead appeared during the Christmas season, when the captain of San José de las Lajas, Pablo José Interian, reported that a disturbance occurred on Christmas Day in the *plazuela* of the village. The disturbance was apparently organized as a protest against the order to present themselves for work detail, and when Interian attempted to enlist the residents to dispel the unruly crowd, nobody came to his aid. The captain reported: "There is no subordination in these people," and requested a party of mounted dragoons to restore the peace. Las Casas's fury and outraged response were characteristic of a pattern that began early and that was maintained throughout his tenure in which he routinely placed himself in implacable opposition to the inhabitants of the island. A lieutenant and four soldiers were dispatched to aid Interian in his police-keeping duties. The ringleader, Carlos Ruíz, and the individuals who refused to help were sent to Havana to answer to him personally. Las Casas concluded his letter with the admonishment that the citizens of San José de las Lajas must be chastised because they were obligated to respect the position of the captain, who derived his authority from the government.[51] Thus began the battle with the inhabitants of the countryside that would last until Las Casas was relieved of his position in November 1796.

Quickly it became clear that the disorder in San José de las Lajas was symptomatic of more widespread resistance that continued into the new year. By the end of January 1791, Las Casas was exhorting the captains of Jesús, María, y José and Prensa to be zealous in their duty to force the residents to work on the roads and bridges.[52] In Río Blanco del Norte, in the heart of sugar-growing country on the north coast to the east of Havana, the captain ordered Miguel Barsaga three times to help clean the roads. After his third refusal, he, too, was summoned to Havana to explain his disobedience.[53] By April, along with praises to the Lord, the parish priest of Santa Cruz de los Piños advised his parishioners that neither they nor their slaves were obligated to report for road duty.[54] The alcaldes of Guanabacoa, Miguel Núñez and José Pérez de Medina, were less confrontational. In early May they wrote that because of the lack of rain the harvest was poor, and the scarcity of food had contributed to widespread sickness that prevented their residents from complying with Las Casas's order.[55]

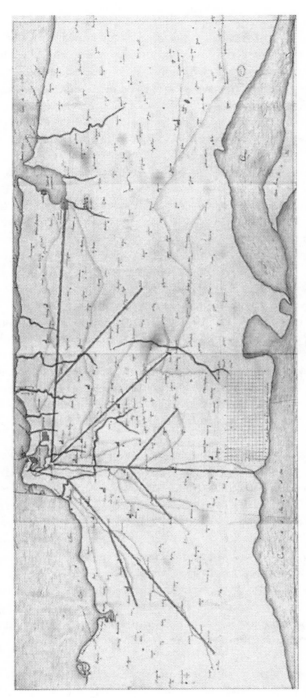

Fig. 6.1. Luis de Las Casas's plans for road construction, c. 1790–96. MP Santo Domingo 583 "Plan de Caminos," reproduced by permission of the Ministry of Education, Culture, and Sport, Archivo General de Indias.

Amid the growing rift between governor and governed, Mother Nature intervened in the form of a furious storm in June 1791. The resulting flash flood swept away everything in its path including humans, homes, cattle, crops, roads, and bridges. As reports from the capitanes del partido arrived in the captain general's residence, it became clear that the storm caused human suffering of epic proportions. The disaster would also severely affect the harvest of the following winter. Existing bridges across rivers on the main arteries into the city on both sides of the bay at Luyanó, Puentes Grandes, Puente Nuevo, and Cojímar, had been washed into the sea.[56]

Las Casas's response displayed none of the concern for human suffering that had characterized the captain generalcy during Charles III's reign.[57] Instead, he ordered the captains in the areas where the bridges were destroyed to get out and mobilize the citizens to repair the bridges immediately. Cristóval Pacheco, the captain of Quemados, where many casualties had occurred, questioned whether a temporary bridge to get food to the people should be built at the expense of the inhabitants who had already suffered so much.[58] His reward for his concern for the survivors in his village was a letter that criticized his responses to the disaster, from the recovery of the bodies to the burial the victims.[59] The captain of Luyanó received a similar reprimand when Las Casas ordered him to get up out of his sickbed, enlist twenty men, and fix the bridge over the river.[60] Places that were not directly affected by the floods were ordered to take a census of rural inhabitants so that every able-bodied male would be counted and expected to report for road maintenance.[61] No resistance would be tolerated.

Because of the extent of the devastation, work proceeded slowly, and with the harvest approaching, sugar producers recognized the potential for economic disaster if they could not get their sugar to market. Led by Las Casas's friend and fellow Basque, Raymundo de Azcárate, in August several residents approached the cabildo of Havana with a solution to one of the problems. At present, a toll was collected for every carriage that used the most heavily traversed bridge, the Puente Nuevo, the "esophagus" of the city.[62] Citing the recent rains as a cause for their petition, Azcárate and his colleagues proposed that instead of the usual ways of building the bridge over the river, all who used it should contribute to its reconstruction. Petty producers to the west of town who drove their cattle to market should be charged a fee for every head of cattle or hog that passed over the bridge.[63]

Las Casas's reply was enthusiastic. After reviewing their suggestion, he ruled that their petition was not in violation of any of the Laws of the

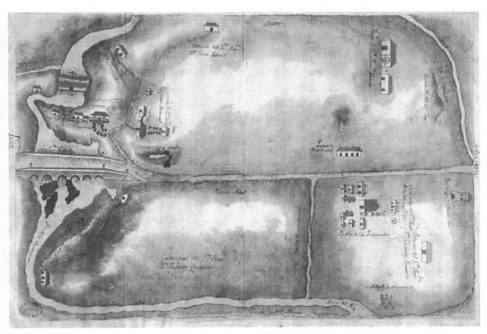

Fig. 6.2. The Puente Nuevo prior to the storm of 1791. MP Santo Domingo 526 "Puentes Grandes" reproduced by permission of the Ministry of Education, Culture, and Sport, Archivo General de Indias.

Indies. The captain general thanked the citizens for their initiative in offering a solution that "extended the spirit of sharing the burden [*repartimiento*]."[64] The announcement of the new regulation in the *Papel Periódico* prompted the captain of Horcón to write an agonized letter to Las Casas pleading with him to reconsider the new regulation because the bridge was the only way that the farmers in his district could get their produce to market.[65] Characteristically indifferent to the consequences to ordinary citizens, Las Casas allowed the regulation to take effect in September 1791, and the only exemptions were military detachments sent on patrol or citizens or soldiers on official government business.[66]

As the harvest of 1791–92 approached, resistance spread to the higher ranks, particularly to the leaders of the villa Guanabacoa. The major artery along the coast to the east of town was also closed because the June storm had washed away the bridge at Ricabal over the river at Cojímar.[67] On Las Casas's orders, a royal engineer had drawn up plans for its reconstruction, and Las Casas sent those plans to Guanabacoa's cabildo with the demand that they mobilize their citizens and begin work on rebuilding the bridge.[68]

From their conciliatory—albeit evasive—stance the previous year, now their response was an absolute refusal to contribute workers for the bridge's reconstruction. Since the bridge was farther to the east than the limits of their jurisdiction, they suggested that Las Casas should call upon the towns that would derive the most benefit, the sugar producers from Río Blanco del Norte, Río Blanco del Sur, and Jaruco.[69] Guanabacoa's disobedience posed a problem for Las Casas: as an autonomous villa, it enjoyed exemptions from certain duties and obligations, and the town's leaders were using their status as the basis for their refusal. The subsequent suit, if it were taken to the Council of the Indies, could take years to resolve, and the sugar harvest was fast approaching. Worse still, news of Guanabacoa's rejection spread to other areas, and so, too, San José de las Lajas sent a list of ingenios that would benefit from the new road and the numbers of workers each could contribute to work on the road.[70]

Clearly Las Casas's arbitrary and autocratic mandates had not worked, and faced with resistance now spreading out from the city and to the leaders of the small towns around Havana, he tried a new tactic: feigned cooperation. A conciliatory missive was sent to the leaders of Guanabacoa. Citing the example of the residents of Güines, also an independent villa, who the previous year had declared themselves "ready to assist in the construction of a new road to that village,"[71] Las Casas "invited" Guanabacoa to join the bandwagon and "contribute to the progress" of road building with as many workers as they could spare.[72] The captain general also took seriously the suggestion that towns at the eastern terminus of the road contribute to its construction. He wrote to the captain of Gibacoa, thirty miles to the east of Guanabacoa, mandating that they too would be responsible for the bridge's reconstruction. He ordered that the captain convene the leading citizens of his area to decide how to proceed. Las Casas suggested that the best place to announce his order was at the exit from Mass on Sunday morning.[73] The same order to convene a meeting of town leaders at the end of May 1792 was sent to captains on the west side of the bay in Govea, San Antonio, and San Luis de la Seiba del Agua. To ensure their cooperation, he appointed the Conde de Buena Vista, his nephew Pedro Pablo O'Reilly's father-in-law, to be in charge of the proceedings.[74]

The end of May came and went, and cryptic reports from the captains of San Antonio and Govea arrived in Havana. On the assigned day, they and their deputies were conspicuous as the only representatives who showed up for the meeting. They were particularly angry because Antonio José Morejón y Sotolongo, the captain of Seiba del Agua, had ignored the order.[75] His absence prompted a very strongly worded rebuke from Las

Casas, warning Morejón that he dared not disobey an order from the captain general again.[76] A few weeks later, Morejón sent a long, exculpatory missive that attributed his absence and his inability to attend the meeting of local leaders to the poor condition of the local road. His letter ended with a plea to Las Casas: "Please forgive me as I've really done everything in the past to try to comply with your wishes."[77] Apologies also arrived from the captain of Arroyo Arenas, who wrote that the rain prevented the residents of his jurisdiction from fixing the road.[78]

Las Casas experienced equal difficulty in getting the captains to count the number of able-bodied citizens in their areas. Felipe Núñez Villavicencio, the captain of San Pedro, blamed the rains and swollen rivers as the reason why he did not send the *padrón*.[79] An angry Las Casas felt the evasion was deliberate, and Núñez Villavicencio responded to Las Casas's charges: "I really have not failed to comply with your order. Any officer who served in three wars on this island cannot fail to take the census much less [fail to obey] your Excellency's orders."[80] Even normally complaisant Güines tried a bit of sleight of hand and sent the previous year's tally. Las Casas returned it with a strict admonishment.[81] Some captains, such as the men in charge of Melena, Marianao, and the Isle of Pines, avoided the issue entirely and sent neither the population figures nor excuses.[82]

The growing disobedience in nearly every village surrounding the city prompted a furious tirade in the *Papel Periódico de la Havana*. In May 1792, its editor asked the rhetorical question: "What has the city done for itself lately?" Among the many causes for the problems that each day seemed more numerous, the editorial criticized the people, particularly retirees, for their laziness because so many of the island's residents lived on pensions and had no incentive to work.[83] Worse lay ahead. Barely a month later, in June 1792, Las Casas promulgated a Bando de Buen Gobierno for his regime. Virtually a direct copy of the decrees of his predecessors, the Bando targeted the lower classes in particular in that it sought to eradicate idleness and vice by sentencing the "vagos y mal entretenidos" to the public works projects.[84] In addition, the enforcement capabilities of the capitanes del partido were expanded by creating a level of subordinates (lieutenant captains) to each local captain. While the establishment of the lieutenant position increased the captains' ability to carry out Las Casas's decrees, its more sinister purpose was to provide Las Casas with a means to investigate the insubordinate captains themselves.[85] Hailed as one of the legislative hallmarks of Las Casas's administration, in reality the Bando reflects a hardening of attitudes on both sides of the conflict.

The harvest season of 1792–93 approached with the new decree in place that gave the captains the authority to arrest and transport recalcitrants who refused to report for road duty. Throughout the winter, virtually every local official blamed the unusually rainy season for their failure to comply with Las Casas's orders. Excuses arrived almost daily. The captain of Santiago de las Vegas, Manuel Machín, wrote that one of the reasons he was dilatory was the poor weather and the impassible roads.[86] The complaints of Santiago de las Vegas were echoed by the captain of Río Blanco del Norte, who reported that the road to his jurisdiction was similarly impassible.[87] In Luyanó, the Pastrana bridge was also intransitable.[88] The most hard-pressed were the residents of Quemados, who had been forced to build a temporary bridge after the storm of 1791. The following year Cristóval Pacheco informed Las Casas that the makeshift bridge was washing away, and in order for horses to pass they had to be unloaded and led carefully through the mud.[89] A far more disturbing report arrived from Antonio de la Torre, the captain of Gibacoa. De la Torre wrote that he was having trouble containing the "serious disorders" on the smallholdings of his jurisdiction. Instead of working to promote agriculture by growing foodstuffs, some of the petty farmers had introduced cattle and pigs into the fields normally used for vegetables. De la Torre ended his report saying that the lower classes of his area "do not want to work . . . even after I have required them to do so. They even fail to respond to the exhortations of the parish priest."[90]

As the dynamic of popular resistance passed into a more rebellious stage, towns and villages began to foist the blame for noncompliance onto their neighbors. Las Casas's reprimand to Santiago de las Vegas's Captain Machín prompted a reply that his jurisdiction had too few people and he needed the cooperation of other villages to build a substantial bridge.[91] A three-way dispute began among Jaruco, Río Blanco del Sur, and Río Blanco del Norte about working on the hill that separated Jaruco from the two towns to the east. Both Río Blanco del Sur and Río Blanco del Norte maintained that they had too few *vecinos* (residents) to complete the task themselves.[92] For his part, Las Casas was growing more infuriated with the island's recalcitrant populace. In March 1793 he gave the *ayuntamiento* (town council) of Havana the charge of naming a commissioner to oversee the composition of the Pastrana bridge in Luyanó.[93] Throughout the winter, the cabildo of Guanabacoa fought tooth and nail against building the bridge at Cojímar themselves. By April 1793 Las Casas told them to stop delaying or he would call new municipal elections guaranteed to return people who would be more punctual in fulfilling their obligations as citizens.[94] Predictably, Guanabacoa responded with a petition to the Council of the Indies requesting that the council uphold their authority to elect their own municipal officials.[95] In addition, one of Guanabacoa's beleaguered leaders, Manuel Josef Domínguez, sent his own appeal, charging that "every oppressed vassal has an unquestionable right to solicit the protection of his monarch."[96]

The arrival of the new year of 1794 portended a bleak future for Las Casas and the plantation interests in the ayuntamiento of Havana. In February, the governor was forced to admit that he had been unsuccessful in coercing the island's residents to build and maintain the roads, and Mother Nature had been as uncooperative as the Cubans. Las Casas's report lamented that the beautiful new road to Vibora was now impassible during the rainy season. The Puente Nuevo, where the toll schedule was inaugurated in 1791, was also impassible, and farther out along the same road, the "stones were so dislodged from the roadbed that it was of no benefit even for foot traffic. On some days traveling on the road was so difficult and uncomfortable both for carriages and for riders on horseback that it would be better if the road did not exist."[97] Las Casas's remedy was twofold. The toll schedule to raise funds for the road and bridge maintenance would remain in place, but voluntary compliance with the labor requirements would be replaced with an involuntary, forced-labor draft of all men who could not demonstrate that they were gainfully employed. To make sure that no "vago" escaped the snare, the captains were ordered to round up all the vagrants and also to send reports of all the foreigners and nonresidents living in their jurisdictions.[98] The last, and most offensive provision, was the appointment of a public magistrate, Pablo de Estévez, who was given the status of lieutenant governor and to whom was delegated the authority to arrest and bring in vagrants and unemployed. The provision was particularly objectionable because Estévez was paid a bounty for each worker he delivered.[99]

The appointment of Estévez put the captain general in direct opposition to the Cuban people, and the position of capitán del partido, which once represented a coveted source of prestige, became a thankless chore. From April 1794 onward, the captains were caught in the middle between their constituents and a tyrant. Their carefully crafted letters attempted to deflect blame from themselves individually and from the inhabitants of their regions collectively. In the ongoing battle among Río Blanco del Sur, Río Blanco del Norte, and Jaruco, the captain of Río Blanco del Sur, José Belén Gonzáles, responded that none of his residents lived close enough to work on the road, and in any case they did not use that road, but rather the one that ran through Río Blanco del Norte, where the church was located.[100] Guanajay's problems were multitudinous. Not only did the river flood and ruin the bridge and the drinking water, but a fire a week later burned down nine houses.[101] Resistance spread to the east as far as Matanzas, where tenants at the Hato de Canímar, militia lieutenant Bernardo del Junco, his brother Feliciano, and militia cadet Felipe Ximénes, refused to report for road duty.[102] From Jesús del Monte, Félix González wrote a conciliatory letter explaining that he was unsuccessful in gaining the support of his residents. Las Casas responded with a disparaging letter chastising González for his inability to lead.[103] Faced with the captain general's uncompromising stance, González discarded his moderate tone and bluntly informed the captain general of the widespread and open hostility to repairing the roads and bridges.[104] The responsibilities of his jurisdiction weighed heavily on the captain of Laguna, Diego Ruís, who had to deal with a number of escaped criminals and delinquents in the neighboring area, Alvarez. The lawbreakers were committing so many robberies in his territory that in complying with the requirement to patrol the roads to maintain order in his area, he was unable to find time to implement the road-building draft.[105] Las Casas responded in a circular letter to Ruís and to the captains of Guamutas, Laguna Grande, and Alvarez, ordering them to get out and arrest the disorderly, confiscate the property of the recalcitrants, deputize honorable men as necessary, and above all, fix the roads.[106]

Throughout the six-year battle between the Cuban people and the governor, few men acted with the creativity and courage of Antonio José Morejón, the captain of Seiba del Agua. The captain of Seiba was a constant thorn in the side of neighboring capitanes del partido and the captain general alike. From the outset of Las Casas's demands, Morejón contrived innovative ways to evade compliance. In the beginning, like most of his fellow captains, he blamed the rains and the impassible roads for his village's resistance.[107] In 1792, when Las Casas ordered rural leaders to share the burden for road building, Morejón ignored the decrees. His ability to shield the inhabitants of Seiba del Agua came at the expense of other villages, and with every new mandate by the government, complaints from the neighboring captains of Wajay, Aguacate, Govea, and San Antonio arrived in Las Casas's residence.[108] Morejón's defiance was common knowledge among the residents in his jurisdiction on the west side of the bay, where he took on the dimension of a local hero.[109]

The decrees of August 1794 were intended to close the loophole and shut down the potential for evading road-maintenance obligations. Morejón's response was to make his entire village "disappear" by deliberately undercounting the number of Seiba's inhabitants. While he did submit the obligatory census figures, the number of residents he reported for 1795 and 1796 differs so dramatically from previous years that his count could only be a fabrication. According to Morejón's tally, Seiba's population, which held steady from 1790 through 1794, declined by 75 percent, from 3,000 inhabitants to approximately 670.[110] Seiba's drastic decline in residents stands in diametric opposition to population trends for the rest of the island. Furthermore, it cannot be explained by redistricting to other jurisdictions, because no neighboring area increased its population figures by 2,300 persons. Morejón's idea quickly caught on with other disobedient captains. After the acrimonious exchange in 1794 in which Las Casas accused Félix González of dereliction of duty, González's jurisdiction, Jesús del Monte, also "lost" nearly half of its 6,600 inhabitants between 1795 and 1796.[111]

While Morejón and González made their people disappear figuratively, others began to disappear literally. The captain of Guanajay, Francisco José de Roxas y Sotolongo, tried many ways to convince his people to obey Las Casas's orders. At first he appealed to their pride and sense of civic duty by flattering them as "patricians of the island." When flattery failed to persuade, Roxas resorted to coercion and began to enforce the laws regulating movement without a specific license from local captains. Roxas's coercive measures proved ineffective, and the people of Guanajay "began to run away when threatened with the possibility of imprisonment."[112] By late 1793, the pattern of flight spread and took form in an epidemic of resignations within the ranks of the captains who recognized that their position was intolerable. Manuel Benítez of Naranjal was among the first asking to submit his resignation, citing as his reason his uncertainty about how long he would remain in the area.[113] From Hanávana, Miguel de Sotolongo requested to be relieved of his post because of his infirmities.[114] When the captain general failed to respond, Sotolongo sent a long letter describing how his feet and hands were so crippled that he was unable to enforce Las Casas's orders.[115] In October 1794, Juan Joseph Díaz de la Cruz Peñalver of San Gerónimo requested his release, and Las Casas appointed Juan Joseph Díaz Amador, who previously had served as captain of the same area.[116]

More often than not, however, Las Casas refused to relieve men of their obligations, so captains who sought release began to suggest eligible residents to whom their responsibility could be transferred. Thomas Borrego tendered his resignation from the captaincy of Wajay and recommended that Las Casas appoint Francisco Franco to the post. According to Borrego,

Franco had retired in 1789 because of his illnesses, but by 1793 there was no reason why he should not be appointed, since he was completely recovered.[117] As a former military member, Franco was unable to refuse. He served in the difficult post for three years until he obtained his retirement based upon permission granted in 1789 by interim governor Domingo Cabello. Persistence, at last, paid off, and after his second appeal, Las Casas granted Franco's request in July 1796.[118]

Filling the position in Managua was similarly challenging. Francisco Péres de Oliva initially tried to resign his position in July 1796 based upon his illnesses. When he received no answer, he repeated his request in September, reporting that he was so sick that he required help just to accomplish the normal tasks of daily life.[119] Once again, Las Casas ignored the man's request, so in October, Péres de Oliva sent a request guaranteed to get the captain general's attention. In it he admitted that because he had been so sick he had "inadvertently omitted" some details from his reports.[120] The unusual candor finally gained the captain general's attention, and Las Casas relieved Péres de Oliva in favor of his lieutenant, Juan del Castillo.[121] The position was equally unattractive to Castillo, for immediately upon receipt of the notification, he acknowledged his appointment accompanied by a letter of resignation. In turn, he nominated Juan Crespo, a retired sergeant, who lived within Managua's jurisdiction.[122]

The winter of 1794–95 represented a critical juncture in the deteriorating relationship between Las Casas and the Cuban people. As other areas of the Caribbean entered a dangerous "Turbulent Time," resistance to the captain general's demands escalated into undisguised defiance bordering on rebellion.[123] Under the circumstances, it was inevitable that news of the discontent on the island would make its way to Spain and to royal advisers on the Council of State. By late October, rumors of a popular uprising spread throughout the city of Havana and, ultimately, reached metropolitan ears. In its various versions, the source of the rebellion centered around a slave rebellion, a popular commotion, a mutiny among French prisoners of war, and an uprising incited by French infiltrators. With the Council of State aware that all was not well in Cuba, ironically, the tables were turned on the captain general. Now, he, too, was forced to justify his actions to his superiors in Spain just like the captains on the island were forced to justify their actions to him.

Las Casas's letter sought to reassure the Council of State that he had the situation under control. He explained the events that might have given rise to the rumors. The most frightening was an attack on a girls' school by a male slave wielding a machete. The slave was subdued by a retired military captain and a free mulatto, but only after he had mortally wounded three girls and an elderly man who lived in the household where the school was located. The slave subsequently died in the hospital of the blows to his head he received in the incident. After the attack, there were four isolated reports of insolence by individual slaves, but nothing that would indicate an impending slave conspiracy. Moreover, there was little to note in the free population. Francisco de Basave reported that he had overheard two Canary Island immigrants using republican language and criticizing the government. There were rumors about a rebellion among French prisoners of war, and someone had reported to the town council that French spies had infiltrated the island to incite the population. These rumors were fostered by reports that some key posts were unguarded and the rebels (whoever they were) would have access to cannons and powder. Lastly, a *pasquín* (lampoon) was posted in public view on the night of November 8, that exhorted the public: "Let's put a guillotine in the plaza—long live the French nation."[124]

Las Casas assured the Council of State that all of the rumors were untrue. Basave, a man "of a good family but of poor personal habits," had capitalized upon the existing tension to accuse the Canary Islanders because of an ongoing dispute. The prisoners of war were being well treated and, furthermore, the inspector of prisoners had stationed spies within their ranks and in the prison where they were being held. There was no plot by French infiltrators, and nobody had access to cannons or powder without proper authorization. The author of the pasquín was of so little consequence in the public esteem that the offending poem was removed and delivered to the captain general the same night that it appeared in public.[125] Several days later, the captain general was able to report even more felicitous news. The author of the pasquín had been arrested, and he had confessed that he was the author of the offensive lampoon. He admitted that he had no plan, and that the heat of the moment and rumors of a rebellion in the Viceroyalty of Santa Fe (present-day Venezuela and Colombia) had prompted his behavior. Upon hearing the rumors, a group of leading citizens reconnoitered the countryside, and they reported that everything was quiet. There were no foreigners except those who had permission to reside on the island from the government. In response to the ostensible threat, Las Casas's solution was a decree prohibiting commerce and contact with foreigners, especially Frenchmen, because of the upheavals in France and in St. Domingue.[126]

Blame for starting the "unfounded rumors" was placed upon gossip mongers, and the rumors were deliberately abetted by people who were interested in "intimidating" the government. Once started, it was easy to convince women and weaklings of the imminent uprising, since they were already terrorized by the horrors in France and Santo Domingo. Rumors of rebellions in the Viceroyalty of Santa Fe and New Spain only added fuel to the fire. Such behavior played into the hands of those who wanted to "inconvenience" the government. The populous city was plagued with a number of vagrants and idlers who were acting out of revenge against his campaign to conscript the *"gente perniciosa"* (pernicious people) of Havana. Las Casas closed his first letter with the assurance that he would do everything to maintain the "greatest [degree of] tranquillity" on the island.[127] Eleven days later, he confidently assured the Council of State that "the rumors have totally dissipated."[128]

Las Casas's letters sought to reassure the Council of State that he was in control of Havana, but he pointedly omitted any mention of the recurring disturbances in the villages surrounding the city. Indeed, the reports from the countryside contradict his claim that tranquillity was the rule. Instead, the gente perniciosa were growing more restive, and if anything, discord in the countryside during the winter of 1794–95 was worse than ever. The correspondence between the captain of San Gerónimo, Joseph Díaz, and Las Casas dealt with little else but the jurisdiction's disobedience against the captain general's orders for road duty.[129] From Río Blanco del Norte, Antonio Visiedo reported on the undisguised complaints by the citizens of his town.[130] The obvious resistance on the part of the countryside prompted yet another circular letter in April 1795 with the familiar demand that the island's residents contribute to promoting agriculture.[131] Instead of motivating the people to get out and work, the letter brought more protests: Yaguaramas's inhabitants met to complain to captain Benito Hernández about the "unjust extractions" that were made upon them.[132] The annual harangue spurred a conflict between the villages of Bauta and Cano, and when Cano wrote to complain about its neighbor, the captain of Bauta replied that he was powerless to deal with the resistance to paying the taxes for the roads.[133]

The escalation from such open defiance resulted in harsher measures on the part of the government. The forced-labor draft targeted the lower classes, while more affluent citizens who resisted became liable for arrest and the confiscation of their property. Some were subjected to punishment usually reserved for common criminals, such as public humiliation. When one of the leaders of the resistance in San Gerónimo, Josef Bello, refused to respond to an order, Las Casas ordered that he be placed in the town stocks for twenty-four hours. Two men who had aided Bello were similarly punished. The insolent villagers were to be informed of the sentences at the customary entrance to Mass with the warning that they would receive the same treatment if they were not punctual in their compliance with his orders.[134] Las Casas ordered the arrest and confiscation of the cattle of the men who had complained about the unjust taxes in Yaguaramas, Manuel López, Andrés Hernández and Juan Gregorio Arranzola, accusing them of being responsible for a "commotion" in their village (which he failed to mention to the Council of State).[135] Ironically, in Río Blanco del Norte, fines paid by the residents were used to finance the construction of stocks for the public punishment of their fellow villagers.[136]

Such direct intervention occurred because Las Casas had lost the support of the local captains who, regardless of the consequences, refused to obey his orders. The captain of San Pedro conspicuously absented himself when rumor of the forced-labor draft reached his village. To complicate matters further, he took the censuses with him, so neither his lieutenant nor officials sent from Havana could determine how many men were liable for road duty. An enraged Las Casas wrote to San Pedro's lieutenant: "I've heard that the captain has absented himself from the pueblo taking with him the book of Instructions and Orders. Tell me when he left and where he went. I want to know how many able-bodied men there are, and don't forget to tell me about the slackers, whom we'll pick up in the levee."[137] Las Casas was also furious at Manuel Benítez of Narajal, who was ordered to send a list of eligible men in his town. At the same time, he was ordered to provide four men whom he surely would be able to apprehend if he diligently implemented the levee.[138] Francisco Franco, who unwillingly accepted the captaincy of Wajay, was also chastised when he reported that there were no men eligible for forced conscription in his jurisdiction. Las Casas's response: "Don't tell me that, and in the future, you'd better be more punctual in your compliance."[139] When the captain general criticized the captain of Prensa for his tardiness in conscripting men in his district, the man replied: "My slow response meant no disrespect, but I was employed in carrying out your other orders."[140]

If the captain general was unable or unwilling to discern the depth of popular discontent, it was well understood by the Cuban people. By early 1795, leaders such as Antonio José Morejón, the captain of Seiba, were looked upon as folk heroes. Their exploits were celebrated in popular culture in events such as one that occurred in Batabanó, a village south of Havana. In the years since the hamlet was organized into a support center for the garrison in the early 1770s, it had grown into an important gateway between the southern coastal cities and the capital. Consequently, the road that connected the village to Havana was constantly in need of repair. In August 1794, a group of landowners led by Luis Serrano addressed a petition to Las Casas requesting relief from their burdensome obligations.[141] Predictably, their request was ignored, and over the winter, popular sentiment in Batabanó mirrored the discontent throughout the island. Early in February 1795, three young men arrived from Havana with a wagonload of meat and other comestibles for the garrison. One of them brought a guitar, and upon arrival, they entertained the rustic townspeople with "obscene" songs that were circulating throughout the province. The local capitán del partido, George Josef de Roxas, caught the perpetrators in the act, and when he ordered them to cease, the impromptu concert moved to the house of Ramón Vilá, a sergeant from the Cataluña mountain riflemen who had secured a treasury post upon retirement. Outraged at Vilá's complicity, the captain attempted to enter and put an end to the singing, but the former sergeant confronted the constable and ordered him out of his house. Meanwhile, news of the entertainment spread, and merrymakers "of both sexes" from Batabanó and surrounding villages gathered at Vilá's house, where they sang, danced, and gambled at cards. Roxas tried once again to end the party, but Vilá now was reinforced by a number of provincial notables, including Serrano and his family, one of the garrison officers, and several of the guards. When Roxas persisted, the captain of the guards warned him that he would be escorted home at swordpoint if he persisted in trying to interrupt their party.[142]

Roxas prudently retreated to his house and stationed himself in his doorway, but the women who had joined the festivities followed him home and taunted him by passing back and forth in front of his house stamping their feet, shouting, and singing. Throughout the day the revelers moved through the streets between Vilá's house and the local taverns, where at sundown even the tavernkeepers disobeyed local regulations to close. The party lasted far into the night and into the early-morning hours. By then the group added blasphemy to their transgressions by singing a mocking parody of the Ave María *(en son de chuleo)*. At two o'clock in the morning, they assembled in front of Roxas's house and sang the same obscene song over and over again for half an hour. Finally, at dawn the exhausted revelers repaired to their houses.[143]

Batabanó's disobedience was symptomatic of a generalized malaise that pervaded the countryside. Traditional authority had broken down, and Roxas, as Las Casas's representative in Batabanó, became the target of the provincials' scorn. More important, the entire province was complicit, from the pillars of the community to the ordinary people. The leader of the local landowners, Serrano, already at odds with the captain general, was unlikely to come to Roxas's aid. Moreover, the constable had no support from the garrison or its officers or from the retired sergeant who had settled in the town. Even the commander of the outpost looked the other way and refused to interfere in the commotion. Batabanó's captain was at a loss at how to deal with the situation, as the impromptu concert and subsequent party clearly had the approval of the village residents. Like the incident in San José de las Lajas five years previous, the townspeople willingly and deliberately joined in the seditious chorus. Roxas dutifully reported the incident even while he was powerless to stop it.[144]

The behavior of the Cuban people demonstrates patterns of resistance in classic form. Beginning with feigned compliance and excuse abuse and escalating into more severe forms such as satire, whispering and rumor, group resistance, and ultimately flight, the people exhibit what has come to be termed "everyday forms of resistance," or "weapons of the weak."[145] These are all steps along a continuum that, if left to run its course, lead to full-scale rebellion. Throughout 1795, the island approached a breakdown of civil society as the incidents in the countryside escalated in their number and their severity. The increasingly harsh responses on Las Casas's part, culminating in Estévez's appointment and commission as his lieutenant, were last-ditch attempts on the part of a collapsing government to shore up its authority. A shadowy figure whose role is imperfectly understood, by the end of 1795 Estévez became synonymous with a hated regime. As Cuba entered 1796, criticism on Havana's streets was vocal and vicious, and confidence in the government was nonexistent.[146]

By 1795, Las Casas had lost the power to compel allegiance and to enforce his wishes. Unlike the punitive measures employed in San José de las Lajas in 1790 and in spite of clearly escalating resistance, the captain general did not send regular troops to quiet popular discontent. Why would Las Casas retreat from his antagonistic, bellicose stance, especially as the military leader of a virtually totally militarized society? Instead, his threats ran hollow, because not only did he lose the allegiance of the people—captains and commoners who were veterans—but he also had alienated the regular military forces to an unprecedented degree. The loss of loyalty and its internal and imperial consequences will be the focus of the following chapter.

A Tyrant without Equal

The deep discontent that pervaded Cuban civil society might have been remediable or even irrelevant had it not been mirrored in greater measure in the corporate ranks of the military. The seriousness of the situation was evident by late September 1792, when a disillusioned young lieutenant, Juan Estéban Eligio de la Puente of the Infantry Regiment of Cuba, shocked the military community to the core by requesting his release from the army. The news must have been greeted with disbelief, for the Eligio de la Puente family was synonymous with royal service. Indeed, their bureaucratic pedigree was already generations old when Juan Estéban's great-uncle Francisco had commissioned his *méritos* (merits) in 1733.[1] The young man's father, Juan José Eligio de la Puente, had held a position in the Royal Treasury, and in that capacity, he had supervised the transfer of the civilians and the garrisons from Florida in 1763.[2] During the British occupation of the Florida peninsula, the senior de la Puente was responsible for coordinating espionage activities against their old enemy throughout the Caribbean, and his brother, the lieutenant's uncle, José María, carried out secret missions to St. Augustine throughout the war years.[3] Another uncle, Juan de Miralles, had been specifically chosen by José de Gálvez as Spain's unofficial emissary to the thirteen rebellious North American British colonies because of his experience and his proven loyalty to the king.[4] Miralles had given his life for his sovereign, dying in George Washington's camp at Morristown in the severe winter in 1780.[5] Like his comrade Tomás de Aróstegui, who also gave his life for his sovereign (in Algeria), Eligio de la Puente returned to the Iberian peninsula and served in the campaign against Gibraltar. When that campaign proved fruitless, he came home to Cuba and contributed to the success of the Gulf Coast victories.[6] Ties of affection and compadrazgo bound the family to Field Marshal Bernardo de Gálvez, the hero of the Pensacola Campaign, who acknowledged the family's status by becoming a witness and sponsor at Josefa Eligio de la Puente's wedding.[7] Only six months prior to the lieutenant's request, Las Casas acknowledged the family's sacrifices, in particular those of his mother, Michaela Sánchez Casahonda, and his aunt, Antonia Eligio de la Puente.[8] The idea that an Eligio de la Puente would request to be relieved of his duty to his monarch "to attend to his family's interests" was unthinkable.[9]

Yet what was unthinkable in 1782 became the norm a decade later. For Cuba's military society, the world turned upside down on many levels. Political alignments in place for nearly a century were rearranged in a moment. France, suddenly, became Spain's enemy, and Great Britain its ally. The monarchy and royal ministries were in the hands of discredited and/or incompetent men, many of whom returned to Madrid bent on vengeance against those who had kept them from power for so long. The metropolitan malaise transferred to Cuba, and the decade of the 1790s has been described as one of "crisis" characterized by a "precipitous" decline in the numbers of the veteran garrison.[10] The precipitous decline was accompanied by a failure to enlist significant numbers of young Creoles into the regular ranks and a concomitant increase in the number of wealthy civilians, primarily members of the plantation interests, who were able to purchase commissions.[11] This congruence of events occurred because of Luis de Las Casas's conscious and deliberate campaign to curtail military privileges. Working in conjunction with his associates Francisco de Arango y Parreño, Pablo Estévez, and José de Ilincheta, and with Basque merchants and sugar interests, the captain general accomplished the almost-total alienation of the Creole military community.

The list of names of military families that incurred the wrath of the captain general reads like a who's who of Cuba's military establishment. That the alienation was politically motivated goes without saying, for the list of men who became Las Casas's targets is very similarly to a list of those who had earned rewards for their service in the Caribbean during the Gálvez years. In virtually every instance, the recipient, male or female, represented the third and fourth generation in service to the Crown in the Caribbean. Thus, whether applied to the ordinary ranks in the form of increased regulation of their activities and competition from slave labor, to widows and orphans in reducing or denying their pensions, to families in general in the violation of their privileges under the fuero militar, or to the officer corps in destroying their careers, the reforms of 1792 take on the appearance of a purge of an even greater magnitude than that of thirty years before.

The assault on the military society began with a campaign to undermine one of the fundamental perquisites enjoyed by Cuba's population, privileges granted under the fuero militar. Since such a large percentage of Cuba's population was militarized, any challenge to the fuero's protection represented a grave danger to society as a whole. The community had won a major victory in 1771 when the active fuero was extended to all who were in the regular army and all who served in the militia. In addition, protection under the fuero was granted to all soldiers who retired after twenty years with the stipulation that they still would be under the jurisdiction of the lieutenant governor of the district and the capitanes del partido.[12]

Protection under the fuero bordered on the sacred, and the procedures that were to be followed in a fuero case were explicit.[13] Even in heinous crimes (such as the murder of María Catalina de la Cruz by her brother, Fernando, a member of the Bayamo Light Cavarly, when he discovered that she was pregnant), protection and procedure were strictly observed by Captain General Diego de Navarro.[14] Protection for the families—especially the wives, mothers, and daughters—of men who enjoyed the fuero was also sacrosanct. For example, in 1772, the alcalde of Guanabacoa arrested the wife of a retired lieutenant. His actions prompted a quick response from the Marqués de la Torre, who chastised the man not only for violating the family's rights under the fuero, but also for acting in a disingenuous manner by denying his mistake. The same day the captain general wrote to the second-in-command of the town, Rafael Rivero, ordering the man to rectify his superior's mistake and release the woman. Indeed, in both cases, the issue was not whether the person was innocent or guilty, but rather that their rights under the fuero be observed.[15]

The fuero militar posed one of the greatest obstacles to Arango and Las Casas's plan to transform the island. Appalled that potential workers could refuse to work, and downright horrified that they could do so with impunity, the deputy governor, José de Ilincheta, led the assault against their privileges. Ilincheta determined to remove such protection and make large numbers of the population liable for discipline under his jurisdiction. One of his first acts was to challenge the widespread application of the active fuero that extended to militia members and retirees, who were technically civilians but came under military justice. Ilincheta argued that the application was unreasonably broad, but the Ministry of War disagreed and sided with those who came under the umbrella of privilege in February 1793. The announcement was greeted with jubilation, as Havana's residents took their celebration into the streets with shouts of "Long live the King!"[16] Undaunted, Ilincheta refused to honor the order and requested a clarification about the ministry's intent. In addition, falling back upon legal machinations, he refused to acknowledge the authority of the military order on the pretext that he was a civilian official in charge of the civilian population that fell under the jurisdiction of ordinary justice.[17]

Keenly aware of the deputy governor's malevolent intent, the military community did not take the threat lightly. Leading the charge was aging Lieutenant Governor Domingo Cabello, second-in-command in the military structure who, like many, had served on the island since the 1760s. Cabello challenged Ilincheta on the fuero issue and on the deputy governor's attempt to usurp his authority on the island should Las Casas leave or become incapacitated.[18] The battle ranged from the highest echelons of the imperial bureaucracy to the island's most modest households. In February 1794, retired soldier Cristóval Aguila, who enjoyed the fuero, became embroiled in an argument with the captain of Guanabacoa, Agustín Fleitas. Aguila's criticism was overheard by two sisters, Candelaria and Micaela Alvarez, who also enjoyed the fuero as daughters of a military man. When Fleitas summoned the women to appear before him to testify what they had heard, they refused, replying that "they were not the ones who were obligated to inconvenience themselves" to appear before the constable. Fleitas complained to the captain general, and Las Casas ordered that the women "had no justification to believe that they possessed greater status than the captain." He ruled that they must obey the summons, but like so many of their counterparts, no evidence suggests that they were ever forced to do so.[19]

The fuero controversy led to frequent jursidictional disputes between and among civilian and military authorities. In November 1791, Blas Sigler, the captain of San Miguel del Padrón, arrested a sergeant on active duty, an action that earned him a reprimand from the captain general. Las Casas chastised Sigler for "insulting the sergeant . . . while he was under my command. You need to understand more clearly the limits of your authority. The sergeant does not come within your jurisdiction. You should have called upon an active-duty lieutenant or another military commander."[20] Sometimes the implementation of Las Casas's "buen gobierno" took on the dimensions of a tragicomic opera. Nicolás Domínguez, a soldier in the Third Battalion, was caught in a compromised position while spending the night with a widow. He was apprehended by civilian Juan José de Basave on his regular patrol, jailed, and sentenced to prison.[21]

Although at times the disputes bordered on the ridiculous, Ilincheta's action posed a serious threat to almost every household on the island, and so it was a stunning victory for el pueblo when the Crown rejected both his attempts to usurp the people's rights. In the first instance, Ilincheta was severely reprimanded for his refusal to honor the application of the active fuero.[22] In the second, Cabello prevailed in his fight to maintain the established chain of command in case of an emergency.[23] Once again, Las Casas and his henchmen were thwarted, but the victory for el pueblo did not last for long.

The next—and certainly the most vulnerable—sectors of Cuba's society to fall victim to Las Casas's arbitrary rule were the widows and orphans of military personnel. As the 1780s wore on, treasury officials wrote with growing alarm about the considerable drain military expenditures placed on the royal finances. Las Casas was keenly aware of metropolitan desires to reduce costs, and the cost-cutting measures provided a perfect rationale to vent his own anger at the island. Unlike his "poor sister," Alejandro O'Reilly's widow, who was living in a "disgraceful" state unbefitting her status, Las Casas believed that Cuba's women received rewards out of proportion to their sacrifices.[24] Thus, one of his first acts upon arrival was to issue a decree reviewing the eligibility of many Cuban women who were receiving pensions, and he began to deny new petitions altogether.[25] In particular, he singled out the limosneras of the Florida community for scrutiny, since their numbers were considerable and since the reasons for their hardship no longer existed, the province having been returned to Spain in 1783.

In an effort to entice floridanos, particularly widows, to leave Havana and return to their homes, in 1791 Las Casas resurrected and expanded the resettlement plan originally conceived for Nueva Florida. For those who would return, their ancestral properties would be restored if they could prove prior ownership. In addition, with a few stipulations and based upon their status, they would receive additional farmland to cultivate and be provided with a slave and implements to help with cultivation.[26] Another significant concession granted floridanos preference in the awarding of government posts, which was unthinkable for the mainland colonies, where a preference for peninsular officials was the rule. Moreover, Floridians who could not afford the cost of the ocean voyage would be transported at royal expense.[27]

The response on the part of the Florida community as a whole was rejection, and the unwillingness to leave Havana was strongest among the limosneras. To make his proposal more palatable, if such women returned to Spanish Florida, Las Casas offered to double their pensions. This concession—that directly contradicted the cost-cutting goals and suggests that the captain general was motivated by reasons other than economics—met with widespread resistance on the part of most of the 318 surviving widows and children of the evacuation of 1763.[28] In exasperation, in 1793 Las Casas mandated that only women who were physically unable to make the trip back to Florida would continue to receive their pensions in Havana.

Immediately, royal officials were bombarded with a barrage of documentation from parish priests and doctors verifying the women's illnesses or their inability to travel.[29] From the sanctuary of Regla, the parish priest wrote that Francisca García was ill and she needed her limosnera daughter, María, to attend her, since her husband, Francisco Zapata, was away.[30] Several more women in that village across the bay and in neighboring Guanabacoa were too sick to make the journey across the harbor into Havana, never mind endure the long sea voyage to St. Augustine.[31] In town, the protomédico of Havana certified that Antonia Castillo's condition resulting from a high fever was "very grave," and the surgeon of the Royal Navy added the weight of his official position to affirm that Josefa Urrutía Cabeza de Vaca was "sick with various contusions."[32] Perhaps hoping to avert any suspicion of dishonesty, the hospital in Guanabacoa wrote that sisters María Concepción and Petrona Rita de Salas were "verdaderamente enferma" ("actually sick").[33] When royal officials tacitly acknowledged the futility of their task, most such women recovered from their ailments and were still alive and collecting their pensions in Havana in 1805.

The strategy, then, became to strike at the root of the problem and refuse permission for marriages that would make the bride eligible for a pension. In 1788, the Crown reiterated the "fatal consequences" that would befall officers who married secretly or without proper permission. Much as with the warnings and prosecutions of the 1760s, the men were cautioned once again that they would be deprived of their positions if they were caught in a clandestine marriage.[34] Second Lieutenant Francisco de Oñoro was granted permission to marry María Blasa de Oñoro y Amat but without the privileges under the montepío, unless he died as a consequence of combat.[35] Josepha de Corgaya, the intended bride of José Mariano de Quijano, second lieutenant of the Infantry of Castile, failed to meet the dowry requirements, so she could never claim the benefits under the montepío militar.[36] One of the most representative cases involved Juana Barriera, widow of Isidro Más, and her three orphaned children. Her husband's forty-five years' service—including being taken prisoner of war twice—counted for nothing, as Las Casas denied her pension request in 1790 because they had married while he was still a junior officer.[37]

But it was toward the men of Cuba's regular military forces that Las

Casas's animosity was most especially directed. The governor's attitude encompassed both professional and personal dimensions. One personal issue (touched on briefly in chapter 5) involved a battle between his friend, civilian Basque merchant Raymundo de Azcárate, and the son of an old military family, Máximo du Bouchet, of noble status from a long line of men who had served in Spain's armies, both in the Caribbean and in Spain. In 1788, prior to Las Casas's arrival, Azcárate's daughter, Josepha, was courted by the youth, an officer in the light infantry corps.[38] Du Bouchet had proposed marriage to the thirteen-year-old girl behind her father's back, and when Azcárate found out, he took the girl to his country house out of the lieutenant's reach. Undaunted, the lieutenant enlisted the help of Cabello, who was serving as interim governor and captain general, and he championed the boy's interests. Together the two secured an ecclesiastical order to marry, and the governor ordered Azcárate to bring the girl back into town and to comply with the order of *esponsales* (betrothal).[39] The merchant's frantic petition, presented to the Council of the Indies upon the death of Charles III, reflects equally the arrogance of wealth and the helplessness of a father trying to prevent his child from making an irreparable mistake. He claimed that du Bouchet intended to seduce María Josepha for her large dowry *("gruesa dote")*. Angrily, Azcárate charged that the governor was also complicit in that "he had infringed upon the tranquillity of the family." When the young girl came to her senses, she had repented her mistake of having encouraged the lieutenant, but in spite of her rejection and the "remote possibility that he could consider himself worthy of her affections," du Bouchet continued to fortune-hunt through every legal avenue available.[40]

The outcome of this case exemplified how metropolitan thinking had shifted away from the status quo, which had been in favor of military families. Now an officer of acknowledged nobility with at least three generations of men in service to the Crown was not good enough for a merchant's daughter! Las Casas's arrival prevented the marriage, but it fueled the enmity between Azcárate and the du Bouchet clan in particular and between the Las Casas–Arango faction and the military community in general. The new captain general blatantly promoted the mercantile interests and was determined to rein in the autonomy of his rivals in the military community. The du Bouchet family provided him with the perfect targets.

Las Casas's next victim was Máximo's younger brother, Juan Manuel du Bouchet, whom the captain general dismissed from the corps of cadets for disturbing the peace. In his youthful excess, exacerbated by repeated bouts of intoxication, the youth hurled insults accompanied by vulgar gestures at his neighbors, and on occasions, he assaulted passersby with sticks, stones, and buckets of water. For Las Casas, the final straw was when he accosted a "decent" woman neighbor and snatched a tortilla from a free black woman street vendor. When the street vendor attempted to recover the tortilla, he struck and wounded her. Juan Manuel was discharged from service for his bad behavior, and the intervention of the cadet's father, Lieutenant Colonel Blas du Bouchet, fell on deaf ears when he petitioned for his son's restitution in February 1792.[41]

The family's troubles continued when Máximo was singled out for rebuke for parking his carriage in front of a popular tavern on the Plaza Nueva. Although the local prohibition was routinely flouted by carriage drivers of all ranks, an official of the cabildo came upon du Bouchet's illegally parked carriage and released the carriage brake, causing the mules to bolt. After retrieving his carriage, du Bouchet confronted the official with his sword drawn, and predictably, a fight ensued. As a consequence, the family was further disgraced as du Bouchet received a fine for fighting with a town official, while the official received only a reprimand.[42]

While the behavior of the "Bad Boys du Bouchet" may stand as the worst excesses of the arrogance of military privilege, Las Casas's actions stand in sharp contrast to official responses to previous misdeeds by young military officers. Not long before, in 1785, Lieutenant Domingo de Oñoro had scandalized the troops by embezzling the salaries of the garrison in Matanzas.[43] The junior officer had been lucky, as Captain General Bernardo de Gálvez had listened to the pleas of his mother and had reassigned the youth to the Second Battalion in Santiago.[44] Even more incredible was that the young man had previously ran afoul of the law in 1772, and the intervention of his brother Francisco persuaded the Marqués de la Torre to set the boy free with only an admonishment that he reform his wayward ways.[45] Once upon a time, Cuba's captains general, all military men, would have shrugged off the du Bouchets' indiscretions or chosen to look the other way. By any standard, though, few could justify Las Casas's actions, since embezzlement of troop salaries that went virtually unpunished was infinitely more serious than disturbing the peace or parking illegally. More worrisome, the community that had been lauded by the monarch and enjoyed extraordinary esteem only six years previously now saw its privileges and position being eroded by, worse still, one of their own, a military man.

Junior officers were at the mercy of the governor, and even the intervention of their powerful families could not save them from punishment. No less so were the military governors of the various cities under Havana's jurisdiction, men who were partisans of the Gálvez faction. Las Casas wasted no time in replacing Estéban Miró, Bernardo de Gálvez's friend and the governor of New Orleans, with his brother-in-law, the Baron de Carondelet.[46] Brigadier General Juan Bautista Valliant, the governor of Santiago de Cuba, however, would prove to be a far more difficult adversary.

At the time of Las Casas's arrival, Valliant, of the mounted cavalry from Cataluña, had served in His Majesty's armies nearly forty years.[47] During the war of 1779, he supervised one of the strategic links in the defense of Havana, the string of cavalry detachments protecting the city.[48] Valliant was rewarded with the governorship of Santiago in 1788.[49] Las Casas stopped in Santiago on his way to Havana in 1790; perhaps the animosity began during the initial encounter between the two men.[50] Subsequent events would do little to improve the relationship.[51] One such event was a controversy initiated by the merchants of Santiago over the responsibility for paying for militia uniforms. In 1785, taxes were imposed upon selected imports and exports to fund the costs. In Havana, the majority of the expense was borne by sugar producers, who paid a tax on every box of sugar that cleared the port.[52] Although Las Casas collected the tax, he lent the money back to the ayuntamiento of Havana with generous repayment terms to provide liquid capital for their obligation to maintain public buildings such as the theater and jail.[53] On the other hand, since Santiago was not a major producer of sugar, most revenue came from a tax collected on the necessities of life, such as bread, meat, and salt, which placed a burden on all of Santiago's residents, including the poorest families. In 1791 the *síndico* (receiver) of Santiago petitioned the captain general for the tax to be removed from comestibles and be placed upon luxuries such as liquor, wine, and aguardiente.[54] The request went to Ilincheta, who in his position as *asesor general* (head legal adviser) of Havana refused to change the existing system.[55] With Valliant's blessing, the representatives of the cabildo of Santiago went over the captain general's head and petitioned the Council of State directly, and the change was authorized in May 1793.[56] Unaccustomed to having their authority challenged, Las Casas and Ilincheta were enraged.

By 1792, with the schism growing between Las Casas and the people of the island, Cuba could not have been less prepared to cope with the external pressures being brought to bear upon the Spanish Empire from several fronts. The revolution in France caused grave concern in Spain and in her colonies, particularly in Santo Domingo, French St. Domingue's neighbor. In 1789, the French National Assembly mandated the equality of all men, leading to intrigues on the part of St. Domingue's population of color. The highly permeable border between the two colonies offered a refuge from the republican violence that spread to St. Domingue in 1790. Alarmed, the Spanish governor of Santo Domingo, Joaquín García, put his forces on the highest state of alert, and the Regiment of Cantabria arrived from Puerto Rico to reinforce the border between the two colonies. As the violence in France spiraled downward, other European nations allied against the French National Assembly and the Republic in 1792. With the execution of Louis XVI, Spain declared war on May 30, 1793.[57] Suddenly the danger to Cuba was very real, and the families who recently had been targets of the captain general's malice now became those upon whom he would be forced to rely.

However torn the military community might have been at obeying a man they clearly despised, they nevertheless could not help but uphold their honor, follow tradition, and respond to the call to arms. An expeditionary force was organized in Havana to transfer to Santo Domingo, from which it would march overland and invade St. Domingue from the east. At the same time, British forces would assault the coastal cities on the west coast of the island.[58] To lead the expedition Las Casas chose Brigadier General Matias de Armona, a veteran peninsular officer, who had served in Spanish America since he accompanied José de Gálvez on the inspection of the northern Mexico frontier in 1767.[59] Armona was also the brother of the first administrator of the mail system, José Antonio de Armona, and he was married to the daughter of Domingo de Lisundia, from whom Armona had inherited his title, the Marqués del Real Agrado.[60] A veteran of forty years of Caribbean campaigns, Colonel Juan Gemir y Lleonart, was called upon to assist Armona as second-in-command.[61] Colonel Antonio María de la Torre and Captain Miguel Ortiz de Zárate were selected to serve under the two leaders.[62] The announcement in Havana was accompanied by frenzied preparation. Some veteran soldiers prepared by granting powers of attorney to their wives and other family members; others revised their last will and testament in case the worst occurred and they did not survive the campaign.[63] Some old warriors, like Francisco de Paula Oñoro and Alonzo García Caxares, came out of retirement and offered their services to the expeditionary force, offers that now were gratefully received.[64] Another contingent of soldiers, including the du Bouchet family, was dispatched to the other frontier in Florida to respond to the agitation of Citizen Genet and the possible invasion from North America by republican sympathizers.[65]

At first the Spanish expedition scored impressive victories over the republican forces in western Santo Domingo, and then in the fall of 1793 they crossed the border into St. Domingue. There they formed an alliance with black leader Toussaint Louverture, and together the Spanish, British, and black forces harassed the republican and royalist forces alike. By January 1794, the Spanish army led by Armona was in control of the major city, Bayajá, and it seemed as though the combined forces would prevail. Fatefully, though, in August 1793, the French National Assembly declared the end of black slavery in the empire. As the Spanish forces headed toward Yaguesi, Toussaint Louverture betrayed the Spanish cause. Once the French royalists were defeated, he joined the republicans and turned on the Cuban expeditionary force. The Spanish were forced to retreat in the campaign for Yaguesi all the way back to Bayajá. There they were attacked by over 4,000 former slaves and free coloreds. Badly outnumbered, the Cuban expeditionary army was forced to retreat even farther.[66] The insurgents gave the inhabitants of Bayajá three hours to evacuate the city with the Cuban army. Those who could not—642 civilians—were slaughtered, primarily by having their throats cut with the machetes that the insurgents had formerly used to cut cane.[67] One by one, the towns under Spanish control fell to the black nationalist armies.[68] While the expeditionary forces did not suffer a tremendous loss of life, they did suffer a tremendous loss of prestige and morale.[69] Joaquín García returned to the capital in a wheelchair, a broken man.[70] An even worse fate was in store for the members of the Cuban expedition upon their return to Havana.

Unbeknownst to the men of the Cuban expeditionary force, the war had grown increasingly unpopular at home. The disillusionment of Eligio de la Puente, whom Las Casas described as having "such little honor," was but the tip of the iceberg.[71] For the previous three years Havana's population had been characterized as "vagrants, idlers, and tricksters"; not surprisingly, they refused to step forward when Las Casas called upon them to enlist. At the same time, they watched while the incentives to serve in the armed forces were undermined both on the island and as a consequence of metropolitan policy. Within the regular ranks, recruiting goals fell far short of the required numbers.[72] In desperation, Las Casas turned to his merchant friends with a request for money to further recruiting, and the *Papel Periódico* announced an additional call for volunteers.[73] Along with the failure to enlist new recruits, Cuba's armed forces were plagued with desertions, and even a general pardon failed to encourage deserters to return to their units.[74] Among the officer corps, an increasing number of men refused transfer, which prompted an order that those who refused to move would not be considered for promotion.[75] Las Casas's troubles multiplied when a rebellion of French supporters, white, free colored, and slave, occurred in Louisiana. Almost simultaneously, Florida was threatened by an invasion from Georgia. The captain general opted to send the few available reinforcements to Louisiana to aid his brother-in-law, Carondelet, while the Havana free colored battalion was sent to St. Augustine.[76]

Meanwhile, the besieged commanders of the troops in Santo Domingo begged for reinforcements; none were forthcoming.[77] When it became clear that the expedition was in danger of annihilation, Las Casas ordered Valliant to transfer 2,400 replacement troops to Santo Domingo from Santiago de Cuba.[78] Rumors swirled around the Caribbean port cities, and with one corsair that arrived in port came news that an expeditionary force was being prepared to invade eastern Cuba.[79] Wary of an invasion attempt on his own territory, aware of the consequences of the fall of Havana in 1762, and even more aware of Las Casas's character and the precedent of Algeria, Valliant decided to retain enough troops to protect his area of responsibility. Nevertheless, he sent 1,224 men to aid his comrades under fire, slightly more than half the original number.[80]

If the expedition to Santo Domingo was a disaster for the men who had escaped with their lives, it was nothing compared to what awaited at home. Cognizant of the army's ineptitude in Africa and the public outcry that the defeat in Algeria had engendered, Las Casas and Joaquín García sought to shift the blame away from themselves.[81] The four primary leaders of the Cuban expedition, Armona, Lleonart, de la Torre, and Ortiz de Zárate, were brought up on charges in court-martial.[82] The Marqués de Casa Calvo and Colonel Francisco de Montalvo were left in Santo Domingo to pick up the pieces of an army that was seriously demoralized, not just by its military defeats but by the stunning news that Spain would cede Santo Domingo to France.[83] It was no longer 1763 or 1782, and the contrast, beginning with the leadership at the highest levels, could not have been more obvious. No longer did a fair and loyal monarch content with symbolic prosecution sit on the throne. Now the Spanish Crown was represented by intrigue, capriciousness, arbitrariness, and vindictiveness.

Suddenly, men and their families who had dedicated their lives to military service saw their fortunes and futures in jeopardy. The first to be prosecuted, Juan Gemir y Lleonart, wrote an anguished letter to Godoy, throw-

ing himself at the mercy of the minister of state. He was "an officer without a command, disgraced in his old age, his honor, which he had so diligently guarded throughout his long career, challenged." He explained how
during his forty-eight years of service he had served in many capacities in
several cities in Cuba. Upon arrival in Santo Domingo he was assigned to
defend the southern and western frontier. The poor locations made the
outposts indefensible and the shortage of troops, munitions, and provisions guaranteed defeat. The captain general ignored his repeated requests
for reinforcements, and in desperation he commissioned Mauricio de
Zúñiga to go in person to request help directly. Lleonart told Godoy that he
was not a wealthy man and he did not have the funds to defend himself. He
was placed under arrest in Santo Domingo, where he had no relatives or
kin networks. Upon his arrest he was treated like a common criminal and
confined in prison in Santo Domingo. He told Godoy: "Stripped of my
honor, the only hope I have are the principles . . . of justice and your media-
tion."[84]

While the trial of Lleonart and the other three leaders progressed, Las
Casas proceeded to dismantle the remainder of the old veteran garrison,
targeting its oldest and most prestigious members. Pedro Remírez de
Esteñóz, the grandson of the sergeant major of the fixo in 1762, was deliberately passed over for promotion in 1795. Las Casas's excuse was that the
man's health was delicate, in spite of his evaluation of being "robust" two
years before.[85] Las Casas also vetoed the request for promotion of Lieutenant Colonel Manuel Cabello, the son of interim governor Domingo
Cabello, Azcárate's and Ilincheta's adversary. Derisively, Las Casas reported that the younger Cabello had spent the majority of his career in
Havana, *"sin enemigos"* ("without enemies"), with the exception of the
Mobile expedition, for which he was awarded his lieutenant colonelcy.[86]
Not surprisingly, Blas du Bouchet, the head of the family targeted for discipline, was similarly denied promotion at the whim of the captain general,
and Manuel de Aldana, who had served in Cuba since 1748, was denied
promotion, transfer, and his privilege of retirement in Havana.[87] Francisco
de Varela, who had tweaked the tiger's tail in 1784 in the recruiting expedition to Andalusia, received but one curt word on his request for promotion
to lieutenant colonel: *"Negado"* ("Denied").[88] Even the dead could not rest
in peace. Julián Parreño perished in the fighting in Santo Domingo, but
when his widow, María Rodríguez del Toro, sought to probate his estate, it
was discovered that he had originally written his will in 1788. Citing the
birth of three legitimate children since the will was originally drafted, Las

Casas declared it null and void, thus forcing the family into probate court, where they were at the mercy of the civilian justices.[89]

Las Casas also seized the opportunity to strike at Brigadier General Juan Bautista Valliant. At first he attempted to discredit the general through the rumor that Valliant was secretly a French partisan, and that he had two sons serving in the insurgent republican armies in Guarico. Both the lieutenant governor of Santiago, Isidro de Limonta, and the síndico of Santiago, José Nicolás Pérez Garvey, replied that Las Casas's charges were nonsense.[90] For his part, Valliant inaugurated a mechanism initially implemented during the administration of Bernardo de Gálvez, direct communication with Madrid and the Council of State. Except for local matters, Valliant bypassed Havana entirely, thus removing himself from Las Casas's chain of command.[91] Las Casas then sought to have him removed from his post as governor of Santiago de Cuba for his ostensible ineffectiveness in containing a rebellion of former royal slaves in Santiago de Cobre.[92] Valliant refused to relinquish his post on Las Casas's orders, and once again, bypassed the captain general and fought against his removal by appealing directly to Madrid.[93] The ayuntamiento of Santiago also wrote to the Council of State, lauding the governor's good government and justice and lamenting how bad his transfer would be for the city.[94] The Council of State responded by extending Valliant's term until a new governor could be designated.[95]

The situation was equally precarious on the Florida frontier, where the Third Battalion of Cuba protected the border against the intrigues of Citizen Genet and the ambitions of adventurers from Georgia and the Carolinas. St. Augustine's governor, Juan Nepomuceno de Quesada, also boasted long experience in the Caribbean. Prior to his assignment in Florida, Quesada had succeeded Matias de Gálvez as the governor of Honduras from 1784 through 1791. The danger to Florida from Georgia made the position particularly difficult, and failure could bring a dishonorable end to his long career. A familiar case of administrative flight at the highest level, Quesada repeatedly sought to transfer elsewhere, the need for which, by March 1795, he attributed to his failing health. Predictably, his requests were denied.[96] Three doctors in St. Augustine were called upon to certify the governor's illness; meantime, Quesada and Las Casas bickered back and forth between Havana and St. Augustine, both over military policy detailing the line of succession to military command and over sick leave policy that allowed a commander to relinquish his command only in a grave emergency. On every occasion, Las Casas adamantly refused to allow Quesada to leave, and he rejected completely the governor's suggestion that he turn over the reins of government to the senior ranking military officer, Bartolomé de Morales.[97] Morales had been promoted to lieutenant colonel in 1786 and to full colonel in 1791 and, at the same time, was rewarded with the command of the Third Battalion of Cuba garrisoned in St. Augustine.[98] For Morales, it was the culmination of his fifty years of service. A capable leader who enjoyed the respect of the men under his command, Morales knew the successful defense of Florida lay with his leadership qualities and with the loyalty of the men who served with him.[99] Accompanying him was his young grandson, Félix Varela.[100]

By April 1795, two additional doctors certified that Quesada's health had declined to the point that he could not do the job effectively. With no other alternative and in consultation with his junta de guerra, he relinquished control of the province to Morales, an action perfectly consistent with royal orders and within established precedent throughout the empire.[101] Las Casas was incensed. His long letter to his superior, the Marqués de Campo Alange, reflects his malevolence toward the Creole military units in general and toward Morales in particular. Morales, who had been personally chosen by the Marqués de la Torre to serve in Havana in 1774 because of his ability and judgment, suddenly became an officer "who does not have the capacity to govern [the province]."[102] Las Casas described the colonel as being unschooled in military matters, inept, and guilty of a lack of restraint in his actions and words. Even more astonishing was Las Casas's solution to the crisis in command. He proposed to allow an officer junior to Morales and with ten years less time in service, Irish-born Carlos Howard of the Hibernia Regiment, which was stationed at a garrison north of St. Augustine, to take command of the province.[103] Worse still, a recent assessment of Howard's performance criticized him as being excessively fond of drink even on the frontier, and the men who served under him disliked his harshness and arbitrary behavior.[104] Las Casas swept the criticism aside, attributing the poor evaluation to jealousy on the part of the inspector of the troops, Ilincheta's adversary, Cabello. The captain general acknowledged that Howard had neither the rank nor the experience, but he rationalized his decision because the Irishman had extensive experience in Florida. He added his own personal commentary that it would be a shame if such a capable officer were overlooked simply because of one bad evaluation. His letter concluded that if Campo Alange did not feel that his solution was acceptable, then the governance of Florida should be shared by Howard and the *auditor de guerra*, peninsular-born José de Ortega.[105]

Las Casas's decision to undermine the authority of the governors in the provinces who opposed him was a particularly irresponsible course to take, given the potential danger in the Caribbean in the 1790s. Not surprisingly, by 1794, royal authority throughout the Spanish Caribbean began to spiral out of control. In Havana, the community was frightened and horrified at the palpable danger that threatened from all sides. As they watched the situation deteriorate, they laid the blame squarely at Las Casas's doorstep. Conversations on street corners spoke of the calumnies of the governor and his favorites, whom the captain general was accused of "protecting and rewarding in the face of the torrent of public opinion [against them]." The governor and his lieutenants were guilty of thousand instances of corruption, but "the Havaneros, . . . especially the families who served His Majesty stood face to face against his tyranny."[106]

The Havana community was particularly outraged at the governor's failure as a military leader. The conspiracy of the previous year and the rumored rebellion of slaves, free coloreds, and prisoners were fresh in their minds for the terror it brought to the city. Instead of protecting them, Las Casas sent Havana's troops to New Orleans to help his brother-in-law, leaving the citizens on the island vulnerable. Las Casas was accused of secretly being a French partisan and of intending to surrender the city to the Sanscullottes from St. Domingue. Because he had dismantled Havana to supply New Orleans, he was indirectly responsible for the disturbances in St. Domingue and the "throat-cutting" ("degollación") at Bayajá. The bright spot in his sordid administration was the gallant garrison in Florida, which had defended against the invasion on the St. Johns River and against an English corsair. No wonder "everyone including the military officials, the town council, the military corps, and absolutely all of Havana's inhabitants," spoke openly of the governor's indolence. It was rumored that during the threatened uprising, Las Casas locked himself inside his house on the Alameda de Paula on the harbor front so he could escape from the city should the rebellion prove true. There he cowered, hoarding powder and munitions to protect his person. This "gentleman" governor did nothing to protect the city, neither adding to the watch, nor taking any of the prudent measures in previous cases. There was not one person who was not terrified, and his recklessness and abandon caused the disturbance, like what had happened in Guarico.[107]

Similar acts of open defiance spread to the population in the cities in Havana's jurisdiction. In St. Augustine the crisis in government prompted old rivalries based upon the award of government contracts to surface. In

January 1795, pasquines appeared on the church door criticizing governor Quesada. One chided the governor for his preferential treatment of the commercial interests: "Who will save you? Bad man, bad judge, tyrant, fear God." When Quesada relinquished his command to Morales, another lampoon called to Floridanos, "Give thanks to God immortal who has liberated us from such a fatal evil."[108] The battle between Las Casas and Valliant over the position in Santiago de Cuba prompted similar verses to appear in that city. In March a "faithful vassal of His Majesty" wrote to the Duque de Alcudia (Godoy) warning him that four to six members of the city council were tricksters, and one of the alcaldes, Ysidro Palacios, was "a drunk, and somewhat demented." Pasquines appeared on street corners that called Valliant a liar, a hypocrite, and a thief.[109] Others characterized the city leaders as inept fools, suitable for a comic masquerade but not for city government.[110] The faithful vassal went on to describe the prejudicial effect that the battle between Las Casas and Valliant had generated: "The city is truly in [a state of] anarchy."[111] From New Orleans came the disturbing news that thirty-seven men were involved in a conspiracy to foment a rebellion. The group, consisting of free colored and white males, were caught and transported to Havana in July 1795, where they were condemned to hard labor until their cases could be adjudicated.[112] Twenty men were finally executed in Havana.[113] The Council of State did not take such unrest lightly, for, as the example of St. Domingue had proven, a restive and defiant population would not hesitate to attack their oppressors.[114]

The epidemic of resignations in the ranks of the capitanes del partido, in the officer corps, and even at the highest levels of society—as indicated by Juan Estéban Eligio de la Puente and Juan Nepomuceno de Quesada—is consistent with the charges of bad government, indiscretion, and incompetence leveled against Las Casas. In the new order, loyalty and service counted for nothing; favoritism, arbitrariness, and partiality were the new rules. As royal governors, veteran officers, and ordinary soldiers retired or resigned in disgust, serious manpower shortages developed. The European campaigns demanded that fewer troops could be sent to replace those who separated or retired during the 1790s. With the implementation of the British blockade in 1796, Charles IV, desperate for currency, began to sell militia offices and later commissions in the regular forces to Cuba's planter elites, men with no experience but with unlimited financial resources.[115] These men, like those who sold them their positions, embodied bad government and did not command the loyalty, obedience, or respect of the people.

Resignation fever reached its zenith in mid-1795, when the ayun-tamiento of Santiago de Cuba, weary of the *"desgobierno"* ("bad govern-ment") of Las Casas, requested "separation and independence from Ha-vana with the [ability] to create a captain generalcy" in that city.[116] The Council of State, faced with innumerable resignations, culminating with the entire eastern half of the island, opted instead to accept only one: that of Luis de Las Casas himself, written in the wake of the frightening days following the rumored uprising of 1794.[117] The notification of his trans-feral was made public knowledge by October 1796, and the Sociedad Patriótica of Havana, representing the plantation interests and disheart-ened at the loss of their champion, eulogized Las Casas as a "father of the country, whose absence will threaten our interests."[118] The majority of el pueblo, however, likely breathed a sigh of relief. Unlike the plantation in-terests, el pueblo would remember Las Casas as "a tyrant, the likes of which the island had never seen before."[119]

An Ungrateful People

How close Cuba came to the brink of rebellion may never be established, but by the harvest season of 1795–96, the Crown was forced to back away from its captain general's intractable stance. The situation was far more precarious than Luis de Las Casas admitted to the Council of State in 1794. Resistance had escalated into open defiance and had spread throughout the civilian and the military population. Although there was minimal restlessness in the slave population, the "horrors" of St. Domingue were never far from the minds of the metropolis or the colony.[1] The retreat represented a victory for the people of the island and possibly saved Cuba from going the way of St. Domingue. The final victory, obviously, was Las Casas's recall. Until now, his departure has been interpreted as part of a normal rotation that was a tragedy for the island. Clearly, though, the evidence of near anarchy in the countryside, disillusionment in the military, insubordination among other royal officials, rejection of Havana's authority on the part of the cities under her control, and Las Casas's own request to leave demands that such a conclusion be reevaluated.

Before el pueblo savored its final victory, however, a remarkable incident exemplified the tenor of the times. In early 1796, a curious pamphlet hoped to strike a conciliatory note in the form of an oblique apology to the people. Like all publications of the era, it required governmental approval, and it appeared "with a license [to present] truth, reason, and justice."[2] The didactic tone sought to influence public opinion—or, at least, deflect the wrath of Cuba's inhabitants away from the governor—in favor of Las Casas's lieutenant, Pablo Estévez, the man appointed to conscript men for road duty. Its ostensible author was Miseno de Laura, but the introduction by Estévez removed all doubt that Laura was a pseudonym for Las Casas's lieutenant himself. Its form was a (probably nonfictional) heated argument on one of Havana's street corners between a Cuban clerk and an elderly (*quebrado*) Basque merchant. They were arguing about Las Casas and Estévez and the "thousand evils they had wrought on the island."[3] Curiously, the mediator between the two men was an Anglo American merchant of long residency (an eerie presentiment of the future), who took a neutral stance between the two extremes. Within the course of the debate, the list of the inhabitants' complaints were spelled out in detail, and the extraordinary publication allows a revisionist evaluation of how desperate the situation had become.[4]

The pamphlet's goal was to convince the people that Las Casas and his henchman Estévez were justified in their actions and were beneficial to the island. The apology appeared as a preface to the dialogue, and in it, Estévez took responsibility for his "conduct and person regarding his part in carrying out Your Excellency's orders."[5] Since the publication was the product of the captain general's press, it is not surprising that the debate should finally turn in favor of the pair. At the end, the Cuban clerk repented and recognized that he had been unjust in his denunciation. The ghost writer harangued el pueblo for being "an ungrateful people." Instead of complaining, they should have been thankful that Las Casas was so reasonable, for he could just as easily have called upon the military forces to put an end to el pueblo's stubbornness.[6]

The publication, with its unprecedented apology, combined with the evidence of resistance in civil society and disillusionment in the corporate ranks of the military, leave little doubt that by 1796, Cuban society was in a deep crisis, a crisis that replicated itself over and over in the coming century. The very foundations of Hispanic society—loyalty to tradition and the glorification of military service and the privileges that it entailed—were under assault. Virtually overnight, the criteria for earning royal favor had changed, and the new metropolitan policies did not translate well to the island. All sectors of society came under attack, but the change in royal attitude was particularly significant in the case of the "families who served His Majesty."[7]

Las Casas's behavior reflected more than a lack of confidence in the ability of Creole units to perform their duty. His blatant favoritism toward O'Reilly's partisans and to his Basque compatriots represented his attempt to rein in the extensive privileges granted to the island. Long before his arrival, he was determined to destroy the accommodation between Cuba and Madrid, and his undisguised resentment of the Cuban military forces likely stemmed from a deeper motivation, jealousy over the consequences of Algeria and the fifteen-year alienation from power that he and his brother-in-law, Alejandro O'Reilly, endured. O'Reilly's star and those of the men who surrounded him faded with the defeat in Africa and the ineffective campaign against the British in the siege of Gibraltar while the men who allied with the Gálvez family increased their prestige and power. Without question the Caribbean forces shone while the European and African campaigns were embarrassments at best and disasters at worst. Las Casas's jealousy of the Creole military community was evident in his attempt to curtail military privileges at all levels, from the lowliest artisans, to the limosneras, to the leaders of the Cuban battalions and their families. Conversely, to Cuba's military society, Las Casas represented all of the worst characteristics of Charles IV's regime. He, not the Cuban people, was the very embodiment of ingratitude, who pandered to the basest elements for monetary gain. What made Las Casas's "desgobierno" unique, however, was that its consequences resonated into the nineteenth century.

Las Casas's departure in November 1796 represented a victory for Cuba, and the island breathed a collective sign of relief when he was replaced by Juan Procopio de Bassecourt, the Conde de Santa Clara, and he by Salvador Muro y Salazar, the Marqués de Someruelos.[8] The members of the O'Reilly faction were subdued, but they were not vanquished, and the fight was carried on by Francisco de Arango, José de Ilincheta, and Alejandro's son, Pedro Pablo, who inherited his father's title and married into the family of the Conde de Buena Vista. Meanwhile, the Crown extended an olive branch to the military community with the designation of Joaquín Beltrán de Santa Cruz, the Conde de Jaruco, as sub–inspector general of the army of Cuba.[9] His appointment has mystified historians, who view it as the worst example of partisanship and favoritism. To be sure, Beltrán de Santa Cruz was a man of immense wealth and power, so he is universally regarded as a classic example of the Cuban elite. He also is universally maligned for his association with Manuel de Godoy, an association that led to his appointment as sub–inspector general in 1795, to his receipt of the title Conde de Mopox in 1796, to his commission to survey and develop the Guantánamo Bay in the same year, and to his exclusive privilege to import flour from the United States in 1797.[10] Yet in spite of his negative historical portrait, the young man played an important role in mediating among the competing factions in Cuba.

Certainly, even before his success at court, Beltrán de Santa Cruz was one of Cuba's richest men. His wealth and power made him a good representative of the island's economic interests, which, by 1789, were seriously jeopardized by the impending financial crisis. To this end, Beltrán de Santa

Cruz acted in concert with Francisco de Arango, and one point on which both men agreed was the need to liberalize the slave trade. During their early years in Madrid, the two maintained a friendly correspondence in spite of their divergent opinions about the path for Cuba's economic development. While Arango argued vigorously in favor of promoting sugar production, Beltrán de Santa Cruz felt that diversification, the policy that had been successful since 1764, was a better course to maintain.[11] The amicable relationship between the two men began to erode when Beltrán de Santa Cruz's influence eclipsed that of Arango, and it became even more strained after Las Casas's recall. By 1796, Beltrán de Santa Cruz had received the additional title of Conde de Mopox and had obtained the exclusive privilege to import flour to Cuba from the United States in return for Cuban rum, aguardiente, and molasses. It was not long thereafter that Antonio del Valle Hernández, one of Arango's closest associates, complained about the "scandalous concessions that the King has conceded to the Conde de Mopox for the importation of flour and other provisions from North America."[12]

Yet Joaquín Beltrán de Santa Cruz was a far more complex figure, one who remains an enigma. As the war effort with Republican France deteriorated, he agonized over the defeats Spain suffered in Europe and in Santo Domingo. He caught the attention of Godoy, and, in turn, that of Charles IV, when he offered to maintain a company of eighty men at all times, and if the need arose, to raise and pay for an entire battalion of men to fight against France. In spite of his reputation as a sycophant, by mid-1794, weary of the artificial life at court—and against Arango's advice—he sought permission to return to Havana. In 1795, the king agreed to his request, promoted him to brigadier, and appointed him sub–inspector general of the troops of Cuba, making him the second most powerful man on the island.[13]

Whether or not he was qualified in a strict sense to become sub–inspector general of the troops, given his kinship and friendship networks, Beltrán de Santa Cruz's appointment could only have been a strategic move designed to placate several factions on the island. In spite of being distantly related to Pedro Pablo O'Reilly's wife through his maternal line, Beltrán de Santa Cruz was even closer to their adversaries. One of the most persistent opponents of the O'Reilly faction was Jacinto Barreto, the first Conde de Casa Barreto, who was Beltrán de Santa Cruz's stepfather.[14] In 1789, in the scramble for privilege in the new court, Barreto relied upon his stepson to advance his interests and press his claim for recognition. The affection and esteem between the two men comes through in their correspondence, as Barreto signed his letters "your very affectionate father" ("tu más afecto padre").[15]

Beltrán de Santa Cruz's appointment, therefore, sought to bridge the chasm among the interests in Cuba. The young man had a foot in both elite camps, and as sub–inspector general of the troops, he was in a position to influence opinion in the military ranks, both in the officer corps and in the common ranks of soldiers, veterans, retirees, and militia members. In addition, what he lacked in military experience, he made up for in pragmatism, and he became the driving force in rectifying many of the injustices perpetrated during Las Casas's tenure. Whether or not he actively encouraged those who had been wronged by Las Casas's vindictiveness, Beltrán de Santa Cruz's opinion weighed heavily in the outcome of their requests, and neither he nor the new governor, the Conde de Santa Clara, obstructed their petitions for redress.

Under Beltrán de Santa Cruz's stewardship, for some families, at least, the end of the century also came with a measure of vindication and a happy ending. Juan Estéban Eligio de la Puente was granted his retirement with an affiliation with the Fixo in 1798.[16] That same year, Juan Manuel du Bouchet was allowed to return to service based upon the merits of his ancestors and for the "usefulness that he could provide to military service."[17] Young Agueda Más, the daughter of the woman to whom Las Casas denied a pension in 1790, traveled to Madrid as a governess to beseech the monarch in person to grant her brother, José, a second lieutenant's position in the Fixo.[18] Manuel Cabello obtained the sergeant major's post in the Fixo, and Juan Nepomuceno de Quesada was granted his transfer from Florida, and he ultimately returned to Spain.[19] Along with the resentment in the military ranks, the tension in the civilian community abated. In late November 1796, a letter from the ayuntamiento of Guanabacoa related: "Even though we have tried to implement the division of responsibility [for bridge construction] many times, the scarcity of provisions prevents us from complying with Your Excellency's wishes."[20] The excuses from outlying villages had, once again, adopted their traditional stance.

For others, however, the rectification was a long, agonizing battle. While the four leaders of the Santo Domingo expedition were exonerated without repercussions in 1804, Matias de Armona never realized his absolution, for he died in 1796, shortly after the expedition's forces returned to Cuba.[21] Until the end of the century, Juan Gemir y Lleonart remained the scapegoat for the losses in Santo Domingo, but he ultimately was reinstated to his command of the Second Battalion of Cuba.[22] Juan Bautista

Valliant defended Santiago de Cuba from various threats, but his greatest battle was his successful defense of his own conduct before the Council of State.[23] Bartolomé de Morales gained a measure of satisfaction in his struggle with Las Casas's partisans in St. Augustine. Morales remained in his post as commander of the Third Battalion and governed Florida in the interim until a new governor, Enrique White, was named in 1796.[24] In 1797, he won a victory over the administrative challenge of the auditor de guerra, José de Ortega, and never again was his authority questioned in the chain of command.[25] He served as commander of the Third Battalion in St. Augustine until he was relieved by Manuel Martínez and returned to Havana in 1801.[26] His son-in-law, Francisco de Varela, disappeared from the historical record after he was denied promotion in 1797.[27] In all likelihood he died in Santo Domingo, his last known post in His Majesty's service.

True vindication for Morales and Varela would come long after their deaths in the universal renown of Félix Varela, who, as a boy, stood by his grandfather's side in St. Augustine during the difficult time between 1795 and his victory in 1797. Félix Varela's influence in the creation of Cuban identity in the nineteenth century is manifest, but the extensive literature dealing with his life never addresses the fundamental question of how a young man so thoroughly steeped in tradition could abandon his heritage. His grandfather, father, and uncle all served in the Royal Army; his mother and grandmother were quintessential examples of the social process of peninsular integration into Creole society.[28] Yet it was their experiences as victims of the royal abrogation of the implicit social contract that suggest how the youth could become so disillusioned with the status quo. For the man who taught Cuba to think, the attack on his grandfather and the sacrifices of his father cannot help but have affected how the youth saw military service in particular and the Spanish monarchy in general. Varela experienced firsthand how duty and honor could be subsumed by the greed of certain "particular interests."[29] What transpired between his family and the captain general provides an understanding of one of the most often quoted incidents from Varela's childhood. When asked whether he would pursue a military career, the young man answered, "My destiny is not to kill men but to save souls."[30]

Like the sense of inclusion, though, the sense of disillusion did not happen overnight. The uneasy equilibrium between the old and the new lasted until crisis once again gripped Spain and her empire in 1808 with the fall of Godoy, the abdication of Charles IV, the removal of the Spanish royal family, and the usurpation of the Spanish throne by José Bonaparte. In Cuba, the O'Reilly faction, led by Arango, Ilincheta, and Pedro Pablo O'Reilly, saw its chance to capitalize on the moment and to press their advantage. Their political aspirations found fertile ground in the merchant community, who, in spite of their internal differences, united in the face of a depression that began in 1806.[31] The O'Reilly faction under Arango's leadership gathered seventy-three signatures on a petition that called for the creation of a junta superior de gobierno modeled on the one that had been created as an emergency measure in Spain. For his part, Captain General Someruelos vacillated, unsure of the best course to take, while an opposing coalition of interests stepped forward to crush the movement at its inception. Led by José Francisco Barreto, the second Conde de Casa Barreto (who was also the half-brother of Joaquín Beltrán de Santa Cruz), the junta's adversaries included the former intendant Rafael Gómez Robaud, who had assumed control of the Tobacco Factory; the commandant of the navy, Lieutenant General Juan Villavicencio; and the commander of the army, Brigadier Francisco de Montalvo.[32]

Historians have attributed great political and ideological importance to the failed attempt to create the junta in 1808. Cuba's nationalist historians were bewildered that anyone could oppose Arango, the "great patrician" and "spiritual teacher," and label him a tyrant and a traitor. They attribute the failure of the junta movement to the misguided personal animosity of the leader of the opposition, Casa Barreto.[33] More-modern analyses see the key in Arango's failure to secure the support of the military establishment.[34] The various interpretations are all correct in a broad sense, and they each contribute partially to understanding the dispute, but reevaluating the composition of the factions and understanding that the legacy of confrontation was but a reemergence of long-standing grievances allows the controversy to be revisited.

Key to understanding the problem lies in recognizing that the deep personal enmity that motivated the junta challengers was a product of the rivalries than began as early as 1762 and were exacerbated by the near rebellion of the 1790s. In addition, the antagonism was not directed exclusively at Arango; rather, each member of the coalition in favor of the junta was an enemy of one or several members of the opposition. Because Arango was the most erudite spokesman for the junta's supporters, subsequent studies have seen the dispute in polarized terms and argue that the antagonism was directed specifically against him. In reality, however, Pedro Pablo O'Reilly and José de Ilincheta were as thoroughly disliked as was their spokesman. Finally, just as the movement in favor of a junta was

a coalition, so too was its opposition; however, events in the months following the junta's defeat demonstrate that the leaders of the opposition,
especially Montalvo, commanded the loyalty of the Cuban people.

Time had not softened the hatred between the O'Reilly faction and
their opponents, and the moderating influence of Beltrán de Santa Cruz
had waned with his premature death in 1807.[35] The crisis of 1808 exacerbated a personal feud between Pedro Pablo O'Reilly and José Francisco
Barreto that dated from 1762 and the British occupation of Havana. The
rancor began between Barreto's father, Jacinto, and the grandfather of
O'Reilly's wife, Pedro Calvo de la Puerta, both members of the Havana
ayuntamiento. On September 8, 1762, the British governor, Lord Albemarle, appeared at the door of the ayuntamiento building with a party of
grenadiers and demanded that the members swear vassalage to the king of
England. Nonplussed, the men hesitated; then Jacinto Barreto stood and
refused to take the oath. His action was seconded by José Martín Félix de
Arrate, and the remainder of the council followed their initiative. Their
rejection surprised Albemarle, who diplomatically refused to press the issue. In the confusion and uncertainty of the situation, however, when the
official version was recorded by the government scribe, Ignacio Ayala, the
proceedings reported only that the members had unanimously voiced
their opposition to the British governor's demand.[36]

In the following years, Calvo de la Puerta aligned with the O'Reilly
faction, and in 1766 he was awarded the title Conde de Buena Vista for his
ostensible patriotic stance in spearheading the resistance during the occupation.[37] Because he enjoyed the favor of the field marshal, no one dared to
challenge him, and he made himself even more unpopular by opposing the
appointments of Domingo de Barrera and Gabriel Beltrán de Santa Cruz to
local office, appointments that were eventually upheld by the Marqués de
la Torre.[38] With O'Reilly's fall, however, a chorus of disapproval surfaced
in the city. The most vocal critic was Jacinto Barreto, who also earned a title
of nobility in 1787. Now armed with equal status as his adversary and with
the O'Reilly faction in disgrace, Barreto initiated a judicial challenge that
sought to correct the record. He called witnesses such as the ayuntamiento's scribe, Ayala, and others who could testify to Barreto's leadership
in the ayuntamiento during the incident in 1762 and that Arrate had
seconded his defiant stance. Both men offered eyewitness testimony as
to the veracity of Barreto's claim. Governor and Captain General José de
Ezpeleta ruled in favor of the challenge, and the outcome of the judicial
proceedings was carried to Spain by Joaquín Beltrán de Santa Cruz. He, in

turn, entrusted them to another confidant, Lieutenant Colonel Ramón de Sentmanat, who made sure that they were entered into Barreto's dossier in the College of Nobles in Madrid.[39]

The next skirmish came in 1791, when Casa Barreto died, and his heir, José Francisco, had not yet reached majority age. Using the boy's minority as his pretext, Las Casas attempted to strip the family of one of its hereditary positions, Alcalde de Santa Hermandad, which granted the recipient the privilege to capture escaped slaves on the island. The position had belonged to Barreto since it was granted to his grandfather early in the century, but Las Casas awarded it to Manuel de Zequiera.[40] Barreto responded with a direct appeal to the Council of the Indies that forestalled the challenge for the moment.[41] Las Casas and his partisans countered with their own appeal, an appeal that would work toward the same end as Zequiera's appointment. Basing their argument on reports that the number of fugitive slaves had grown considerably in the previous few years—even while simultaneously petitioning to increase the number of slaves brought to Cuba—they requested permission to increase the number of patrols in the countryside. The Council of State temporarily shelved the matter but finally approved the measure in 1803.[42] Thus, by 1808, Casa Barreto's stance against the junta was but a continuation of forty-five years of bitterness and legal maneuvering that further revealed the wider schism in Cuban society.[43]

On the other hand, former intendant Rafael Gómez Robaud harbored specific grudges against Arango. Gómez Robaud was relieved in 1808, but he remained in Havana as superintendent of the royal tobacco monopoly. The feud originated when Arango served as the monopoly's adviser, and Gómez Robaud was his superior.[44] Time and again, Arango had been thwarted in his efforts to mold the free workers of the island into a submissive and obedient labor force. Neither Las Casas's mandates to work nor Ilincheta's attempt to bring the recalcitrant country dwellers under ordinary justice by removing their protection under the fuero militar were successful. The vegueros, whose numbers exceeded 10,000 families, were his greatest obstacle because they enjoyed a protected market in the tobacco monopoly.[45] Worse still, instead of becoming more cooperative, the tobacco producers won several victories against the plantation owners who sought to encroach on their land. Beginning in 1798, the Crown recognized the "need to assist the vegueros," and issued a series of orders that prohibited the large landowners from interfering with them. Santa Clara was authorized to use every means in his power to enforce the decrees, including the use of regular troops, and he warned that "in the name of His Majesty he would take the most severe measures against any of them [the large landowners] who contravened his royal intent."[46] Adding insult to injury, in 1801 the king extended an existing exemption from paying *diezmos* (tithes) for an additional ten years as long as the rural residents dedicated their lands "to producing abundant harvests of tobacco," and he named the captain general as the official guardian of their interests in 1803.[47]

Contrary to royal wishes, Someruelos exhibited none of his predecessor's diligence in promoting abundant tobacco harvests or in guarding the interests of tobacco growers. Encouraged, the ever-persistent Arango sought to remove the vegueros' protected market by calling for the elimination of the tobacco monopoly in 1805. Gómez Robaud opposed the plan, and so he became the tobacco producers' champion and Arango's adversary.[48] In 1807, he initiated the inquiry that exposed the irregularities in Las Casas's clandestine acquisition of an ingenio on the road to Güines, and he challenged Arango by establishing his complicity in the affair. As a royal official himself, he was well aware of the obvious conflict of interest among the captain general, the sugar producers, and their spokesperson.[49] The animosity between the two men ran deep, and Arango bitterly called Gómez Robaud "the venerable founder of the small but pious brotherhood of my persecutors."[50]

The remaining opposition leaders represented the military forces. Navy Commandant Juan Villavicencio harbored a personal enmity against the captain general based upon jurisdictional disputes, but he also represented the Crown in its long-running battle with the sugar producers who sought to encroach on the navy's monopoly on cutting trees in Cuba's forests.[51] Brigadier Francisco de Montalvo, however, was the most powerful force in crushing the junta movement. Since the fateful day on the beach at Algeria, Montalvo harbored long-standing grievances against the O'Reilly faction. Throughout his long professional career, he had clashed with O'Reilly's partisans from the time he led the recruiting party to Andalusia in the 1780s to his part in saving the lives and dignity of Cuba's troops after the military disaster in Santo Domingo. Now in charge of Cuba's army and second in command only to Someruelos, Montalvo knew the potential danger in allowing his enemies to gain the upper hand.[52] On the night of July 27, when Arango presented the signed petition to a meeting of Havana's leaders assembled in the captain general's palace as a fait accompli, Montalvo interrupted the speech, slammed his fist on the conference table, and shouted that neither a supreme nor a provincial junta would be formed as long as he lived and carried a sword.[53] Montalvo's resistance prompted an equally passionate speech from José Francisco Barreto, who exhorted the majority of his colleagues in the assembly to join the two of them in rejecting Arango's plan. In the face of such strong resistance, the petition for the junta was withdrawn.[54]

Like Beltrán de Santa Cruz before him, Montalvo's influence extended far beyond his position as commander of Cuba's regular troops. To begin, as the son of the first Conde de Macuriges, Lorenzo de Montalvo, he was born into one the most prestigious families on the island.[55] His half-brother, José Rafael, inherited their father's title in 1779.[56] The family's status was such that when the children of Macuriges's second marriage, Francisco's siblings, challenged José Rafael's succession, Charles III diplomatically solved the problem by creating another title of nobility for the family, that of Conde de Casa Montalvo, awarded to Francisco's older brother, Ignacio, in 1784.[57] By 1808, the title was in the possession of Montalvo's nephew, José Lorenzo.[58] The family's titled kinship network included their first cousin, the Conde de Vallellano, José de Arredondo y Ambulodi, who was also linked directly to the military community through his father, royal engineer Antonio de Arredondo, and through marriage to the daughter of Sergeant Major Manuel Cabello.[59] Equally important as his network among Havana's titled and landowning elites was Montalvo's position as the head of Cuba's regular forces in Havana, which, although reduced in numbers, still were a powerful force in keeping order.[60] In addition, among Cuba's militia companies, the junta garnered little support, and the majority of militia officers, also titled nobility, did not sign Arango's petition.[61] Military members of all forces—whether regular military or militia—had good reason to be suspicious of the junta's motives, especially those of Ilincheta, who so recently had tried unsuccessfully to rein in their privileges under the fuero militar. Thus, the majority of military leaders refused to sign the petition and supported the commander of the troops in his opposition to Arango's plan.

The failure of the junta underscores rivalries within the elite ranks, but the as-yet-unexplained factor in Cuba's political landscape was the ability to contain the passions of the ordinary people (el pueblo). Chaos in Spain and conflict in Cuba's leadership, unsurprisingly, led to confusion in the common people, although Someruelos's proclamations were sufficient to calm their fears for the time being.[62] Over the winter of 1808–1809, the island remained quiet, but that peace was threatened in March, when two

French immigrants on horseback rode toward the main city gate. The sentry demanded to see their identification papers, and when the men could not produce them, he was required to turn the Frenchmen over to his superior officer. As the immigrants were being escorted under guard to military headquarters, the procession passed through the marginal sections of the city. The streets were full of people, mostly decent citizens, but among the throng were a number of delinquents and troublemakers. Upon seeing the Frenchmen being escorted through town, the crowd mistakenly believed the men were under arrest, and they began to shout insults against France and Napoleon. Insults escalated into obscenities, and then into violence when the crowd began to throw stones. Now transformed into a mob, the enraged townspeople raided a shop belonging to a French silversmith. The man fought valiantly to save his property, wounding one of the rioters in the process, until he was killed by the uncontrolled crowd. Within an hour, six more houses belonging to French immigrants were looted, although the residents escaped. Upon hearing of the uprising, Someruelos responded by ordering the rioters to cease; his orders were ignored. Instead, even larger groups gathered in public squares with sticks and stones for weapons. The captain general then called upon the city's most respected residents and clergy to try and calm the rioters, but they were equally unsuccessful in quelling the disturbance. Nightfall brought a brief respite, but the rioting continued at dawn. Finally, on the second day, when all attempts to restore order had failed, Montalvo took the situation in hand and called out the militia, and peace was restored at the point of their bayonets.[63] Parties of armed soldiers were dispatched to the extraurban barrios and to the towns and villages in the countryside where several French families had settled, but fortunately the commotion had been confined to the city.[64]

The events from July 1808 to March 1809 suggest that Francisco de Montalvo was one of the most powerful and respected men on the island. Montalvo's opposition to the junta movement demonstrated that his opinion was very influential in convincing fellow elites and military officers to defeat the measure. More important, however, his ability to quell the popular disturbance established his leadership and support among the populace. Havana, like most Spanish American cities, was on the verge of anarchy. Traditional symbols of royal control had been deposed, a usurper sat on the Spanish throne, and the spectre of independent Haiti loomed large in the island's consciousness. The authority of the captain general was seriously compromised, but Montalvo still commanded the obedience and respect of the regular troops. In addition, the majority of the island's militia members were willing to accept the leadership of their commanders. At the first sign of popular unrest, Montalvo and his captains moved quickly to avoid a repetition of the disaster that happened on the neighboring island. Although the conditions for rebellion were propitious, a strong military leader drew upon a strong military tradition and order was restored.

In the coming decades, similar struggles would be played out as Spain and Cuba lurched from one political crisis to another. After 1808, conspiracies were frequent but none was successful. A brief period of constitutional government in Spain (1812–14) instituted a brief period of freedom of the press in Cuba, which prompted a series of venomous exchanges among the elite factions on the island. During the course of the dispute, Arango was branded a tyrant, a traitor, and a supporter of independence by the coalition's many enemies, and he left the city in voluntary exile to his plantation near Güines, where he remained until 1815.[65] Napoleon's defeat in 1814 led to the withdrawal of the French troops that maintained his brother on the throne of Spain, and in 1814, Ferdinand VII, the "desired one," was restored to power. Cuba's loyal citizens never dreamed that their fidelity would be rewarded by the return of a truly ungrateful and unworthy monarch. Ferdinand's absolute absolutism was responsible for losing the greater part of the Spanish Empire in America. The sad denouement for Cuba came after 1825, when the island remained as one of the few colonies in the once-glorious empire, and Cubans were transformed into prisoners of their own honorable behavior.

The political realities of post-Napoleonic nineteenth-century Europe and the independence movement in the Americas changed the political dynamic on both sides of the Atlantic. Peninsular veterans of the South American campaigns, Ayacuchos, carried home a very real revulsion for Creoles, and they did not differentiate between the inhabitants of Peru and those of Cuba.[66] Cuba's economy became more and more dependent upon the United States instead of upon Spain, and upon sugar cultivation instead of upon military spending.[67] Finally, the success of the Haitian Revolution drove a wedge into Cuba's free society, as Cubans began to fear that a similar fate would befall them.[68] The generation that grew to maturity in the early nineteenth century lived in a different Cuba and within the context of a different Atlantic world than had their parents and grandparents. The sons and grandsons who carried on Cuba's military tradition were increasingly excluded from the mainstream of power on the island that their ancestors had helped to create and to preserve. But new political options were available to intellectuals in the nineteenth century that had been unthinkable for their grandfathers. While the military community of 1790 had little recourse but to endure the tyranny of bad government and wait for change, their heirs in the 1830s enjoyed many more possibilities.

The intellectual mentor of this new generation, Félix Varela, was born and raised into a noble military tradition, but, paradoxically, he was at the vanguard of the new currents in political thought. With each betrayal by an ungrateful monarchy, an increasing degree of disenchantment pervaded Varela's many writings, from the time he taught in the San Carlos Seminary in Havana, to his service to the island as deputy to the Spanish Cortes (Parliament) in 1823, to his exile and subsequent writings in Philadelphia, New York, and St. Augustine.[69] He worked tirelessly to change the condition of those on the island and left behind a generation of his disciples to carry on his tradition. Varela's disciples are nearly as legendary as their teacher, and they all share, with minor variations, the ideological legacy of his tutelage. Some, however, share more than a common political ideology. At least two, Francisco de Sentmanat and José Cipriano de la Luz y Caballero, share direct kinship ties to and the political sentiments of the opponents of the Las Casas–Arango–O'Reilly faction in the century before.

Aptly described as a "personalist warrior-adventurer," Francisco de Sentmanat was a mysterious figure whose life history was interwoven with conspiracies and rebellions from Cuba to New Orleans to Mexico.[70] Time and again, whenever a crisis occurred in Cuba, Sentmanat was involved directly or behind the scenes. His political radicalization apparently came when he was jailed after Ferdinand's abrogation of the Constitution in 1823, and until his death in Mexico in 1846, he worked to frustrate Spanish rule in Cuba. Like his mentor, he was exiled from the island for his political activities. With the backing of Antonio López de Santa Ana, he planned an assault on the Morro Castle in Havana harbor in 1825, and a few years later he was implicated in the conspiracy of the Grand Legion of the Black Eagle, for which he was condemned to death. Pardoned in a blanket pardon in the early 1830s, Sentmanat established himself alternately in Mexico and New Orleans, where he kept company with an assortment of adventurers and conspirators who moved among the revolutionary groups organized in Caribbean and Gulf Coast cities. He was reported to have been in Havana in November 1843, just fourteen days before a rumored uprising in Sabanilla, and again in 1844 at an urban riot known as the Battle of Ponche de Leche. Finally, he was implicated as one of the leaders in the nearly successful conspiracy in the free population of color, the La Escalera Conspiracy in 1844.[71]

Unlike Varela, Sentmanat chose a violent solution to Cuba's problems, but like his mentor, his family roots went deep into the military society forged in the previous century. Francisco's uncle, Ramón de Sentmanat, was a lieutenant colonel in the Immemorial Regiment who arrived in Cuba as part of Gálvez's army of operations in the 1780s. Following the familiar pattern, the older Sentmanat opted for marriage to a Creole bride, María Josefa de Zayas, in 1785, and in doing so he joined the ranks of military immigrants who established themselves on the island.[72] Along with his father-in-law, Manuel de Zayas, he joined the quintessential measure of status in Havana, the Sociedad Económica, when it was founded in 1792.[73] Although the relationship remains unclear, the family was almost certainly related to the Condesa de Santa Clara, Teresa de Sentmanat, who was renowned in Havana for her charitable works during her husband's term as captain general.[74] More important, Ramón de Sentmanat was clearly aligned with the adversaries of the O'Reilly faction, with Jacinto Barreto, and with Joaquín Beltrán de Santa Cruz. It was Sentmanat whom Barreto and Santa Cruz entrusted to press their judicial claim against Calvo and O'Reilly at court in 1789.[75] Another of Varela's disciples and one of the key figures in the evolution of Cuba's literary tradition, José de la Luz y Caballero, also was directly linked to the Barreto family. His sister, Mercedes Luz y Caballero, married José Francisco Hipólito Barreto, the third Conde, who was the great-grandson of the man who refused to swear allegiance to George III and the grandson of the man who so perseverantly opposed the O'Reilly faction in 1808.[76]

Varela, Sentmanat, and Luz y Caballero represented different manifestations of Cuban resistance to Spanish colonialism, but they shared a common heritage in that their roots originated in social processes of the eighteenth century. More important, they shared a heritage that was opposed to the principles promoted by Las Casas, Arango, Ilincheta, and O'Reilly. But they also represented a society in deep crisis. On one hand, Cuba's loyalty to its military heritage remained very strong; on the other, it rejected the policies and practices of Spain. Cuba's ideological indecision was captured in literary form by another of Varela's disciples, Cirilio Villaverde, in *Cecilia Valdés, o la loma del Angel*, considered by many to be the prototypical *costumbrista* (social custom) novel of nineteenth-century Cuba. The story centers around interracial social relations, and is most often seen as being representative of the privilege of Cuba's elites and the abuses of slavery and sugar cultivation. Originally written and serialized in the 1830s, it was finally published in its entirety in the 1880s. Intent on the larger message, most readers overlook an obscure passage that speaks volumes to how Cuban identity in the nineteenth century was divided. The passage relates a scene in which the protagonist, Leonardo Gamboa, chats with his mother in her salon. The young man says how much he hates the Spanish soldiers garrisoned in Havana because of their arrogant demeanor. The mother chastises her son and reminds him that her brother, his uncle, had been an officer who arrived in the eighteenth century and that he had contributed significantly to the development of the island.[77]

Like the semifictional family of Villaverde's novel, long into the nineteenth century, innumerable Cuban families could recall their peninsular ancestor who had arrived in His Majesty's service, married a Creole bride and became the progenitor of the family. Indeed, even into the 1830s, grandmother might still be alive to relate stories of her peninsular husband to her grandchildren and great-grandchildren. She would treasure the tattered remains of his uniform that once had been a visible symbol of his elevated status and prestige.[78]

The legacy of such pride is imperfectly understood because existing histories of Cuba's colonial past are few and were written by patrician historians who operated under strict censorship policy, and not surprisingly, supported Spanish rule.[79] One notable exception was Domingo del Monte, another of Varela's disciples and a compatriot of Sentmanat and Luz y Caballero in Varela's seminars.[80] Del Monte, whose fame derives from his antislavery stance and from his literary *tertulias* in the 1840s, was commissioned by the Sociedad Económica to write a history of Cuba.[81] He assembled the documents and completed a rough draft of his history of the island that remains an unpublished manuscript. The selection of documents and the predominant theme of the work speak volumes as to what del Monte and the leading intellectuals considered representative of Cuba's history. Overwhelmingly, the documents privileged for inclusion highlight military exploits, including the siege of Havana, the victories in the American Revolutionary War, and the challenge presented to the island by independent Haiti. According to the impressive documentary array, the rise of the plantation complex, the spread of sugar, its concomitant slave labor system, and the factions that promoted and perpetuated it, were, at the same time, insignificant and detrimental to the formation of the Cuban nation.[82]

Cuba's heritage of loyalty and military service would gradually change from an identification with a vindictive and ungrateful mother country into a sense of its own identity, *cubanidad* (Cubanness). While the anonymous Creole in Miseno de Laura's 1790s document asserted to the peninsular and the Anglo American merchant: "I am as noble as any español," in Felix Varela's writings, identification with Spain was replaced with pride in being Cuban.[83] The alternative to the evolution of a distinct Creole ideology was a metropolitan policy dedicated to perpetuating Cuba in colonial status, to developing sugar as the island's primary export, and to maintaining slavery as the predominant labor system. Meanwhile, the Cuban people watched helplessly as an insensitive government pursuing a misguided official policy in service to special interests turned a blind eye to unrestricted slave imports to the island. Varela and his disciples became the vanguard in speaking out against such a policy, but independence sentiment would have to wait until the majority of Creoles could overcome their loyalty to an institution that long ago had abandoned them.[84]

La Voz Sagrada del Pueblo

(The Sacred Voice of the People)

During the dangerous winter of 1794–95, most of Cuba's inhabitants watched in growing horror as Luis de Las Casas and his partisans battled with el pueblo while political stability throughout the Caribbean disintegrated. Others refused to stand silently by as danger threatened from all sides, and they exercised their "incontrovertible right to solicit the protection of the monarch" in the form of a barrage of complaints to the Council of State in Madrid.[1] Few conveyed the sentiment of the island as succinctly as the writer of an anonymous letter in 1795. The writer condemned the behavior of the elites, who, he felt, put the rest of the inhabitants in grave danger, but his most damning criticism was reserved for Las Casas and government officials, whom he accused of "trying to usurp the sacred voice of the people."[2] Royal officials in Madrid heeded the voice of the people and took immediate action to remedy the reasons for popular discontent. Scholars, on the other hand, have been slow to recognize the plurality of voices in Cuba beyond a small, unrepresentative group of elites. To date, most scholarship is satisfied with the explanation that frames Cuban history in the context of sugar cultivation and plantation slavery. For their part, historians are content to accept the political and economic consequences of the plantation complex and concentrate their efforts on evaluating the relationships inherent in such a system.

Such was not always the case. As early as 1967, Herbert S. Klein suggested the pernicious influence of a historiography centered around sugar cultivation. Klein wrote: "It should be kept in mind that sugar did not become the all-encompassing mono-production industry of Cuba until *after* the end of slavery, and that even at the height of slavery in the nineteenth century, it did not control a majority of the Negro slaves on the island" (italics in the original).[3] The results of this research support and expand upon Klein's conclusions. While there is no question that Cuba in 1800 was

a slaveholding society, a wide variety of evidence contradicts the conclusion that Cuba in 1800 was a plantation society. Instead, data from many
sources demonstrate that the majority of Cuba's population had nothing
to do with sugar production, and they adamantly voiced their opposition to
Luis de Las Casas's demands. When the chorus of their complaints fell on
deaf ears in Havana, the faithful vassal, articulating the louder voice of el
pueblo, did not hesitate to appeal to higher authorities in Madrid.

The sacred voice of the people was, in reality, many voices with a common cause and a shared heritage, and understanding those voices demands
a reevaluation of who constituted el pueblo Cubano. Instinctively, perhaps,
such an analysis should begin at the top, with Cuba's "elites." Until now,
the elite ranks universally have been characterized as sugar producers. But
in reality, Cuba's powerful families were far more heterogeneous in many
respects. The island's elites were of both peninsular and Creole origin, and
prior to 1763 they drew their maintenance from a variety of economic
pursuits, usually based upon landholding and associated agricultural enterprises. Some had earned titles of nobility, and all aspired to such an
honor. Native-born elites were powerful in their own milieu, and some
even became powerful in an international theater. After 1763, Cuba's native-born elite families were reinforced and rejuvenated by the continual
influx of Spanish military men. Initially, Charles III and his advisers approved of peninsular immigration to Cuba as an emergency measure, but
as the Caribbean became more important to a larger imperial defense
strategy, increasing numbers of high-ranking military officers sought to
transfer to the island. They married the Creole daughters of elite families,
purchased or inherited houses, farms, ranches, and plantations, and raised
their children as Cubans. Military spending in general, and their military
salaries in particular, fueled Cuba's economic prosperity, but that prosperity rested upon far more extensive bases than solely upon sugar cultivation.

Just as they sought diversification in economic enterprises, Cuba's powerful families were far from monolithic in their approach to social, political, and economic issues. Ideology and factional loyalty divided the upper
strata, and bitter rivalries that were direct consequences of imperial politics pervaded their ranks as early as 1762. Factionalism endemic in Bourbon court politics was translated into similar social and political cleavages
on the island. Alejandro O'Reilly's meteoric rise to power and his subsequent fall, the rise of the Gálvez clan, their predominance in circum-Caribbean life, their deaths and the death of Charles III, and the arrival of Las

Casas all impacted the social dynamic in eighteenth-century Cuba. Some families, like that of Pedro Calvo de la Puerta, were partisans of the O'Reilly faction, and as long as O'Reilly maintained his influence, they rode his coattails to privilege and prestige. After Algeria and O'Reilly's fall, the ascendance of the Gálvez family brought a new group to power, power predicated, of course, upon their military accomplishments. This group included many of the well-known names in Caribbean and Gulf Coast history, such as Francisco de Montalvo, Bartolomé de Morales, and men linked to the Barreto family. Based upon previous experience, these families had good reason to resent and to fear the return of the O'Reilly faction, and Luis de Las Casas did not disappoint them. As expected, he sought revenge against the men who had kept his group from power, and he promoted his own clique, which included Francisco de Arango, José de Ilincheta, and several Basque mercantile families. But international conditions were far different in 1795 than they had been at any time in the past. New political currents threatened Cuba from all sides. An astute Council of State heeded the warnings from the Caribbean, and amid the complaints that came from almost every city under his command, Las Casas's resignation was accepted in 1796. Neither Charles IV nor Manuel de Godoy are normally hailed for their astute handling of political matters, but they may be credited for defusing a particularly dangerous situation in 1796. Throughout the remainder of Charles IV's reign, the Crown maintained a delicate balancing act, as both factions engaged in a tug-of-war for political supremacy on the island. As had happened in the past, the legacy of these enmities was carried into Cuba's future. Unresolved issues fueled the conflict that would resurface periodically throughout the nineteenth century, as a far less astute monarch and his/her ministers never felt the need to reestablish the accommodation between Crown and colony that had prevailed the century before.

The opposition coalition forged out of the followers of the Gálvez clan and coalescing around elite military families such as Morales, Montalvo, and Varela and his disciples in the nineteenth century could not have pressed their advantage time and again without the support of the ordinary families of the island. Their constituency ranged from the illiterate common laborer to lower military echelons to teachers, notaries, and lawyers. Some of the common families were native born; those who were not arrived in Cuba primarily from Spain or the Canary Islands as sergeants or soldiers. They became Cuba's invisible immigrants, and more than any other group, they changed the social dynamic of the island. When they

retired or otherwise left the military, they joined the rest of the free population of artisans and tradespeople who, once upon a time, were immigrants like themselves. Sometimes they were fortunate enough to secure a
position in the bureaucracy upon retirement. More often than not, they
became the armorers, the silversmiths, the coopers, the bakers, the musi-
cians, the tavernkeepers, the captains of small boats in the coastal trade, the
petty producers, the day laborers, the guajiros and the vegueros. They organized into militia companies and were proud that the military leaders
could depend upon them to defend the island. They married the daughters
of ordinary Creole families and formed consensual unions with women of
the lower ranks. Cuba's ordinary women were housewives, street vendors,
laundresses, teachers, governesses, proprietresses of boardinghouses, concubines, and prostitutes, and they were even less visible than their men
because of their gender. Over and over during their lifetimes, they waited
for the men in their family to return from the many Caribbean military
campaigns. If their men failed to return, Cuba's women assumed the responsibility for the family and raised their children to honor the memory
of their father and grandfather and the military tradition they had sacrificed their lives to uphold.

Eighty-five percent of Cuba's free population was of European descent,
but 15 percent of free society was made up of families of color. Most of
Cuba's free coloreds were of African descent, but a small number of indigenes survived in the eastern end of the island, and their numbers were
augmented by an even smaller number of indigenous immigrants from
Florida and Mexico. As in any status-based society, race and ethnicity were
important, but they were important in a different way than twenty-first-
century people are easily able to comprehend. Time and again studies demonstrate that the free population of color distanced themselves from the
slaves and aspired to advance their families as strongly as they aspired to
advance their race.[4] Militarization added another dimension to a social
dynamic based upon status, and the criteria for acceptance encompassed
not just ethnicity and status, that is, whether one was free or enslaved, but
also whether one was affected by militarization or not.

A better conceptual framework to understand popular sentiment lies
less in phenotypical categorizations, and more in how an individual identified with one particular group or the other.[5] Because of militarization,
Cuba's free colored population enjoyed privileges and status that were not
available elsewhere, either in the other Spanish colonies or in the remainder of the Caribbean. Based upon their shared military heritage, there

probably was a greater affinity between Lieutenant Colonel Manuel de Aldana and free colored militiaman Captain Cristóval Carques than between Aldana and Las Casas. Aldana and Carques both entered military service in the 1740s, Aldana in regular service, Carques in the pardo militia. Both men served on the ill-fated *Invincible*, both participated in the naval battle between Spanish admiral Reggio and British admiral Knowles in 1748, both defended Havana during the siege in 1762, and both contributed to the Spanish victory in the Pensacola expeditions. Carques, the families of Juan de Flores and Antonio José Díaz, the pardo militiaman who gave his life at Pensacola, and the free mulatto man who helped subdue the slave in the attack on the girls school in 1794, exemplify the accommodation reached and reinforced among the many sectors of Cuba's society. White, brown, and black families shared their loyalty to Spain, a fierce pride, and an even more fierce sense of privilege that was reinforced by the fuero militar. They were keenly aware of injustice and did not hesitate to protect the privileges their sacrifices had won. More important, this official practice was upheld by the monarch and his ministers until 1808. After 1823, when their sacrifices were no longer recognized by the Crown, the descendants of Carques and Flores would find common cause with the descendants of Morales, Barreto, and Sentmanat. Their chosen course of action might have been different, but they all shared the heritage of honor and the bitterness of betrayal.

A variety of evidence, particularly census data, contributes to the portrait of a complex and multidimensional society. Censuses are valuable tools that if used with care and common sense contribute immensely to a better understanding of historical processes. If used carelessly and without reservation, however, unrefined census data can lead to limited or unsupportable conclusions. Many excellent modern studies have drawn upon the varied censuses of Cuba, beginning with the first in 1774, and on a macro level, they all demonstrate that the island's population increased dramatically from 1763 through 1810. Yet for all of their utility, all of Cuba's eighteenth-century censuses are inherently flawed in that they deliberately did not count the most numerous and most influential group, active-duty military personnel. Fully one-third to one-half of adult white males were never officially recorded during the period of greatest militarization even though their presence impacted Cuban society irrevocably. Furthermore, the circumstances under which census materials were collected must be taken into consideration. The most important question to be considered is the purpose of the count, that is, whether it was taken to reward or to punish. When military officials were counting men to extend fuero privileges, all eligible men and their families had a vested interest in being enumerated. Conversely, when Las Casas's purpose was to know how many males were liable for road duty, not surprisingly, most men did everything in their power to avoid the census takers. More often than not, local captains were complicit in deliberately undercounting the population of their villages, as the examples of Antonio Morejón of Seiba and Félix González of Jesús del Monte demonstrate. By the same token, men who were adamantly opposed to the importation of slaves, such as the Marqués de Casa Peñalver and the captain of San Lázaro, had every reason to exaggerate the number of slaves and free coloreds in their areas.

When macro data demonstrating overall trends are supplemented by micro data on a local level, a more refined portrait of Cuba's urban and rural society is possible. The results demonstrate that demographically the population was increasing and moving outward from Havana. A close analysis of parish records and lists of inhabitants submitted by rural officials reveals the large number of peninsular immigrants, soldiers and sailors, who escaped notice in the macro data but whose presence made the population predominantly European both in urban and rural areas. Along with absolute population increase came a corresponding exponential increase in militia companies organized after 1763. Micro data also allow a more refined portrait of the nature of rural economic production. Taxation lists reveal that until the end of the century, the countryside around Havana was characterized by smallholdings owned or rented by free families who held but a few slaves. These smallholdings were estancias, potreros, hatos, corrales, and vegas, and their owners had nothing to do with sugar cultivation. Micro data, thus, confirm the existence and affirm the importance of several fundamental figures in Cuban history: the guajiro, the veguero, and the estanciero. These rural heads of household were quick to raise their voices in disapproval of the pretensions of the O'Reilly faction, not just once in the near rebellion in 1795, but again at the turn of the century, when they fought and won skirmishes against the large landholders who sought to encroach on their land. Meanwhile, the heads of household maintained their military affiliation, and by the nineteenth century, Cuban rural society could justifiably trace its military tradition to their ancestors of the century past.

Such close scrutiny of the composition and behavior of el pueblo Cubano calls into question many of the myths of eighteenth-century Cuban history. To begin, the chronology of the spread of sugar cultivation may be qualified, as it is clear that as late as 1796 ingenios were not the dominant agricultural enterprise in the countryside. In addition, it is clear that the expansion of sugar plantations was resisted strenuously by the rural inhabitants, and during Charles IV's reign, their possession and use of rural lands were upheld by the Crown. These findings lead to a reevaluation of the importance of the celebrated protagonists of the era. Among the casualties of this reevaluation are the historical reputations of several of the principal actors. The first is Luis de Las Casas, whose manifest unpopularity with the island's residents was evident in the behavior of the inhabitants of the villages surrounding Havana, in their numerous complaints sent to the Council of State in Spain, and in the captain general's own admission published as the unprecedented apology in 1796. The second casualty is Alejandro O'Reilly, who was recognized as a hard and arbitrary taskmaster by his contemporaries and subordinates. Spanish and Cuban historians have conferred a positive legacy on him while failing to look beyond the social and political consequences of his ineptitude in Algeria and his subsequent fall from power. The third, and certainly the most controversial, is the perception of Francisco de Arango, the most vocal spokesperson for reform, who subsequently has been enshrined in the pantheon of Cuban heroes. Few would question that he was a champion of new economic currents, and that his economic aspirations were, by eighteenth-century standards, modernizing and enlightened. Because he was resident in Madrid for many years, undoubtedly he was aware of the impending financial crisis and the Crown's intention to cut back on defense spending on the island. He may have been motivated by a genuine desire to improve the economic standing of Cuba and to find an alternative economic basis and to avert financial disaster before the threatened fiscal reforms took effect. Perhaps better than anyone, Arango knew that the majority of the island's workers were exempt from the demands that could be placed upon them, so his logical solution was to increase the labor force with workers who could not refuse the demands of their superiors.

Nevertheless, it is clear that Arango represented a small group of men who were not Cuban, who did not have the island's best interests at heart, and who promoted ideas that were diametrically opposed to the wishes of the Cuban people. Nowhere is the political tug-of-war between outside interests and el pueblo more apparent than in the outcome of the failed junta of 1808. The coalition led by Arango, José de Ilincheta, and Pedro Pablo O'Reilly was a continuation of the unsuccessful O'Reilly–Las Casas movement of 1790–96, but they were hardly a group of "notables." One reason for the confusion was that several merchants supported the Arango-O'Reilly initiative, and in later years they and their families did emerge as Cuba's elites. In 1808, however, neither they nor Arango enjoyed sufficient confidence in their abilities or motives to convince other elites, military members, or el pueblo to place the reins of power in their hands. On the other hand, the opposition coalition made up of Francisco de Montalvo, José Francisco Barreto, Rafael Gómez Robaud, and Juan de Villavicencio was powerful enough to prevent the Arango-O'Reilly faction from seizing control of the island. Their ability to block the formation of the junta demonstrated that they, not Arango, were the leaders of the elites and the military, and that they were the true power on the island. Moreover, the urban riot of 1809 further demonstrates Montalvo's influence, as clearly the troops and el pueblo followed his leadership. Contrary to historical opinion, Arango did not speak for the majority of Cuba's elites, nor did he speak for el pueblo. Furthermore, he and the interests he represented were feared and detested by commoners, military, intellectuals, and titled nobility alike.

These conclusions directly challenge a century and a half of celebratory history that sees the O'Reilly–Las Casas–Arango faction as proponents of positive and enlightened ideas for the benefit of the island. One of the enigmas of Cuban history is the evolution of a popular discourse against the expansion of sugar cultivation and slavery. This popular discourse directly contradicted the historical reputation of the captain general who was so thoroughly identified with the plantation complex. The discovery that Las Casas's government was ineffective and unpopular goes a long way in explaining the popular resistance to the expansion of sugar production beyond the standard interpretation decrying the evils of the spread of world capitalism. The evidence that the leaders of this resistance were the heirs of the families that were directly harmed by the followers of the O'Reilly faction adds weight this conclusion.

Evaluating social processes and conflicts of the eighteenth century contributes to an explanation of why Varela, Sentmanat, Montalvo, Luz y Caballero, Villaverde, and del Monte, in particular, became the leading proponents of opposition to Spanish rule. The importance of Félix Varela and his followers as proponents of a distinct Cuban identity in the mid nineteenth century is well established. In no instance, however, have their motivations been explored beyond traditional explanations, particularly the manifest righteousness of Cuban independence. Their antagonism toward the sugar interests grew out of several generations of animosity that was fueled by political competition in the early nineteenth century, but only after the restoration of Ferdinand VII and the constitutional interlude of 1820–23 did their opposition to Spanish rule become crystallized. Unlike his father and grandfather, Ferdinand VII was a monarch who abrogated the rights and privileges of the people, gave precedence to sugar cultivation, and sent in an army of occupation to enforce his arbitrary rule. The heirs to the conflicts of 1795 and 1808 grew to political maturity in a different world, and they enjoyed a wider variety of options that were not available to their grandfathers. Once consigned to play a waiting game, by the 1820s the opponents of a tyrannical regime could look to the examples of the United States, Mexico, and Gran Colombia and realize that their political destiny did not necessarily lie with Spain.

Neither Arango, O'Reilly, Las Casas, nor the metropolis could have imagined that their attempt to curtail the privileges of el pueblo for their own economic gain would destroy the metropolitan-colonial accommodation in the years to come. Even less likely was the possibility that Varela, a descendant of the military community, could transfer his disillusionment to generations of his students. Childhood impressions resonated through the life of the most influential intellectual in Cuba in the nineteenth century and provided a powerful ideological legacy for two centuries. Varela, Montalvo, and Sentmanat, among many others, were the heirs to tradition who became the voices of opposition in working toward reform and independence for future generations on the island.

This research has attempted to understand the connections between politics and society by an analysis of Cuban society beyond the elite, plantation complex ranks. It has sought to determine who constituted el pueblo and what they were doing, thinking, and feeling. Through demographic evidence and their behavior, conclusions may be drawn of a society significantly influenced by peninsular immigration as a result of military expansion after 1763. Not only did immigrant soldiers, sailors, marines, and their commanders arrive in Cuba in considerable numbers, but they also remained on the island and interacted with the island's Creole population. In the nineteenth century, while the political destiny of the island was inextricably linked to sugar, it remains unclear whether a majority of Cuba's free population was linked to sugar cultivation, either directly or indirectly.

The "sacred voice" of the Cuban people has been stilled for more than a century and a half. It has been buried by unrepresentative elite writings dedicated to promoting a particular point of view. El pueblo's beliefs have

been misunderstood and have often been taken out of context. This research has sought to give voice to el pueblo and demonstrate that the ideology of Cubanidad (Cubanness) took its root in eighteenth-century demographic and social forces. What remains is for historians to corroborate
or contradict whether and to what extent the voices of resistance of 1795
and 1808 grew into an "ideología mambisa" of 1868 and beyond.[6]

Appendix A

Population Distribution in the City of Havana and Its Suburbs: Comparison by Race, Status, and Gender, 1778

Havana

Males		*Females*		
Ecclesiastics	398	Ecclesiastics	149	71.3/28.7*
Whites	11,919	Whites	8,579	58.1/41.9
Free coloreds	1,960	Free coloreds	2,600	43.0/57.0
Free blacks	1,439	Free blacks	2,128	40.3/59.7
Mulatto slaves	363	Mulatto slaves	280	56.5/43.5
Black slaves	6,047	Black slaves	4,728	56.1/43.9
Total	22,096		18,465	54.5/45.5

Havana jurisdictions

Males		*Females*		
Ecclesiastics	0	Ecclesiastics	0	100.0/00.0
Whites	13,578	Whites	10,215	57.1/42.9
Free coloreds	1,049	Free coloreds	817	56.2/43.8
Free blacks	706	Free blacks	515	57.8/42.2
Mulatto slaves	242	Mulatto slaves	135	64.2/35.8
Black slaves	11,105	Black slaves	2,976	78.9/21.1
TOTAL	26,680		14,658	64.5/35.5

Source: Archivo General de Indias, Indiferente General, Legajo 1527, printed in *Revista de la Biblioteca Nacional Jose Marti* 29 (September–December 1987): facing page 25.
*Ratios are given in percentages.

Appendix B

Comparison of the Number of Households in Towns and Districts in the Province of Havana, 1755 and 1778

	1755	1778	Net Gain/Loss	% Change
Havana	3,497	5,172	+1675	+ 48
Havana Suburban[a]	669	1,312	+643	+ 98

Havana Province

	1755	1778	Net Gain/Loss	% Change
Alvarez	75	122	+47	+63
Batabanó	43	150	+107	+249
Calvario	331	124	−207	−63
Cano	310	190	−120	−39
Guamacaro	7	23	+16	+229
Guamutas	47	77	+30	+64
Guanabacoa	637	1,253	+616	+97
Guanajay	33	182	+149	+451
Güines	197	770	+573	+291
Hanabana	95	112	+17	+18
Jesús del Monte	232	348	+116	+50
Macuriges	44	88	+44	+100
Managua	135	214	+79	+59
Quemados	183	152	−31	−17
Regla (includes Potosi)	86	399	+313	+364
Río Blanco	61	126	+65	+107
San Felipe y Santiago	190	322	+132	+69
San Miguel	199	160	−39	−20

S. Cruz de los Pinos	65	88	+23	+35
S. Maria del Rosario	53	439	+386	+728
Santiago de las Vegas	40	375	+39	+11

Sources: For 1755 data: Augustin Morell y Santa Cruz, "Padron ecclesiastico de 1754–55," in "La configuracion del espacio colonial en Cuba (Estudio del sistema urbano en los siglos XVII y XVIII)," by Carmen Gavira, *Revista de la Biblioteca Nacional Jose Marti* 24 (January–August 1982): 81–93; John Robert McNeill, *Atlantic Empires of France and Spain: Louisbourg and Havana, 1700–1763* (Chapel Hill: 1985), 126–29. For 1778 data: Archivo General de Indias, Indiferente General, Legajo 1527, 1778, in "Presentacion de un censo ignorado: El Padron General de 1778," by Juan Perez de las Riva, *Revista de la Biblioteca Nacional Jose Marti* 29 (September–December 1987): 17–25.

[a]In 1755 the area outside the wall was known simply as Barrio de Guadalupe. By 1778 five separate settlements had evolved: San Lazaro; El Horcon; Jesus, Maria, y Jose; Prensa; and Nuestra Senora de las Salud (Guadalupe).

Appendix C

Military Participation Ratios Comparison: Havana, 1764 and 1778; Mexico, 1810; Venezuela, 1800; and Chile, 1800

	Troop Numbers	Population	MPR
*1764**			
Regular Troops	1,800	36,800	48.9
Regulars + Militia	5,550	36,800	149.4
1778			
Regular Troops	2,000	42,737	46.7
Regulars + Militia	6,000	42,737	140.4
Mexico—Regulars + Militia			7
Venezuela—Regulars + Militia			16
Chile—Regulars + Militia			36

Sources: Bibiano Torres Ramirez, "Alejandro O'Reilly en Cuba," *Anuario de estudios americanos* 24 (1967): 1374; John Robert McNeill, *Atlantic Empires of France and Spain: Louisbourg and Havana, 1700–1763* (Chapel Hill: 1985), 126–29; Archivo Nacional de Cuba, Asuntos Politicos, Legajo 2: 11, May 9, 1776; Archivo General de Indias, Indiferente General, Legajo 1527, 1778; Jorge I. Dominguez, *Insurrection or Loyalty: The Breakdown of the Spanish American Empire* (Cambridge: 1980), 76.

*Estimated, based on Torres Ramirez and McNeill

Appendix D

Military Participation Ratios (MPR) of Eligible Males in Militia Companies, 1778

Town	Militia Members	Population	MPR
Cuatro Villas	623	4,015	155
Puerto Principe	585	1,925	304
Matanzas	247	483	511
Santiago Bayamo:			
White Company	594	2,075	286
Pardo Company	644	1,540	418

Sources: Allan J. Kuethe, *Cuba, 1753–1815: Crown, Military, and Society* (Knoxville: 1986), 83; Archivo Nacional de Cuba, Asuntos Politicos, Legajo 2: 11, May 9, 1776; Archivo General de Indias, Indiferente General, Legajo 1527, 1778.

Notes

Abbreviations Used in the Notes

AGI—Archivo General de Indias, Seville, Spain
AGS—Archivo General de Simancas, Simancas, Spain
ANC—Archivo Nacional de Cuba, Havana, Cuba
BAN—Boletín del Archivo Nacional de Cuba
EFP—East Florida Papers, Library of Congress, Washington, D.C.
GM—Secretaría de Guerra Moderna
IG—Indiferente General
PC—Papeles Procedentes de Cuba
SD—Audiencia de Santo Domingo
SMI—Archivo de S. M. I. Catedral de la Habana, Havana, Cuba

Chapter 1. Sin Azúcar, No Hay País

The title of this chapter comes from José Manuel Casanova, Sugar Mill Owners' Association, 1940s, quoted in Pérez-Stable, *The Cuban Revolution*, 14.

1. Greene, *Pursuits of Happiness*.

2. Ibid., 28.

3. Ibid., 166–68.

4. Ibid., 141.

5. Kuethe, *Cuba*; Kuethe, "Havana in the Eighteenth Century," 13–39; Kuethe and Inglis, "Absolutism and Enlightened Reform," 109.

6. Domínguez, *Insurrection or Loyalty*.

7. Cepero Bonilla, *Azúcar y abolición*; Moreno Fraginals, *El ingenio*; Riverend Brusone, *Historia económica*; Franklin W. Knight, "Origins of Wealth," 231–53; Domínguez, *Insurrection or Loyalty*; Kuethe, *Cuba*; McNeill, *Atlantic Empires of France and Spain*.

8. Wallerstein, *The Modern World-System II*; Stern, "Feudalism, Capitalism, and the World-System," 829–73; Wallerstein, "Comments on Stern's 'Critical Tests,'" 873–96; Stern, "Even More Solitary," 996–1007; Seed, *To Love, Honor, and Obey in Colonial Mexico*, 233–36.

9. Moreno Fraginals, *El ingenio*, 1:126–33.

10. Liss, *Atlantic Empires*; Salvucci, "Supply, Demand, and the Making of a Market," 40–57.

11. McAlister, "Social Structure," 349–70; Mörner, *Race Mixture*; Seed, "The Social Dimensions of Race," 602–604; McCaa, "*Calidad, Clase*, and Marriage in Colonial Mexico," 477–501.

12. Levine, "Constructing Culture and Power," 10.

13. Greene, *Pursuits of Happiness*, 141.

14. Levine, "Constructing Culture and Power," 10.

15. Sagra, *Historia económico-política* (Sagra copied the data from Raynal, *A Philosophical and Political History*); Humboldt, *Ensayo político*, 103–7; Guerra y Sánchez, *Manual de historia*, 195–96; Riverend Brusone, *Historia económica*, 27–28; Knight, *Slave Society in Cuba*, 22–23, and *Slavery and the Transformation*, 16–17, 22; Sánchez-Albornóz, *The Population of Latin America*, 107–111; Kiple, *Blacks in Colonial Cuba*, appendix A and passim; Inglis, "Historical Demography," passim; Inglis, "Constructing a Tower"; Marrero y Artiles, *Cuba*, 9:169–95; Kuethe, *Cuba*, 38–40. The term "sugar determinism" was coined by Lisandro Pérez in "Iron Mining and Socio-Demographic Change," 383.

16. All censuses were inherently flawed in that they counted only the civilian population and did not take into account that as many as one in two adult males was an uncounted peninsular soldier or sailor.

17. Sánchez-Albornóz, *The Population of Latin America*, 134–35.

18. Quoted in Lynch, *Bourbon Spain*, 337.

19. Geggus, "Slave Resistance in the Spanish Caribbean," 131–55.

20. Geggus, "The Enigma of Jamaica in the 1790s," 274–99.

21. García Rodríguez, "Presencia Jesuita."

22. Klein, *Slavery in the Americas*, 194–227; Klein, "The Colored Militia of Cuba," 17–27.

23. Martínez-Alier, *Marriage, Class, and Colour*; Kuethe, *Cuba*, 123–26; Villaverde, *Cecilia Valdés*; Paquette, *Sugar Is Made with Blood*, 251; Kutzinski, *Sugar's Secrets*.

24. Deschamps Chapeaux, *El negro en la economía habanera*.

25. Twinam, *Public Lives, Private Secrets*.

26. Landers, *African American Life in Spanish Florida*.

27. Ferrer, *Insurgent Cuba*.

28. Valdés, *Historia*; Torre, *Lo que fuimos*, 167–70; Hart, *The Siege of Havana*; ANC, *Papeles*; A. Rodríguez, *Cinco diarios*; Syrett, *The Siege*.

29. Parcero Torre, *La pérdida*; Aiton, "Spanish Colonial Reorganization," 269–80.

30. Lynch, *The Spanish American Revolutions*, 8; McAlister, "*Fuero Militar*"; Burkholder and Chandler, *From Impotence to Authority*; Lynch, *Spanish Colonial Administration*; Barbier, *Reform and Politics in Bourbon Chile*; Fisher, *Government and Society in Colonial Peru*; Fisher, "Imperial 'Free Trade' and the Hispanic Economy," 21–56; Farriss, *Crown and Clergy in Colonial Mexico*; Fisher, Kuethe, and McFarlane, *Reform and Insurrection*.

31. Corbitt, "The Administrative System in the Floridas: Part I," 41–47; Corbitt, "The Administrative System in the Floridas: Part II," 57–67; Kuethe, *Cuba;* Delgado, "El Conde de Ricla," 88; Torres Ramírez, "Alejandro O'Reilly en Cuba," 1357–88; Parcero Torre, *La pérdida;* Lockhart and Schwartz, *Early Latin America,* 368.

32. Kuethe, *Cuba.*

33. McAlister, *"Fuero Militar";* Archer, *The Army in Bourbon Mexico;* Kuethe, *Cuba;* Kuethe, *Military Reform;* Campbell, *The Military and Society;* Phelan, *The People and the King;* Fisher, Kuethe, and McFarlane, *Reform and Insurrection.*

34. McAlister, *"Fuero Militar."*

35. Kuethe, *Military Reform;* Campbell, *The Military and Society.*

36. Archer, *The Army in Bourbon Mexico.*

37. Domínguez, *Insurrection or Loyalty.*

38. Kuethe, *Cuba,* 174.

39. Ibid., passim.

40. Moreno Fraginals, *El ingenio,* 1:65; Riverend Brusone, *Historia económica,* 143–44; Knight, "Origins of Wealth," 231–53.

41. Altman and Horn, *To Make America;* Altman, *Emigrants and Society;* Corbitt, "Immigration in Cuba," 280–97; Tornero Tinajero, "Emigración, población, y esclavitud en Cuba," 229–80; Tornero Tinajero, "Comercio colonial y proyección de la población," 235–64; Bitlloch, "Trabajo, inmigración y colonización," 109–43; Castillo Meléndez, "Población y defensa," 1–87; López Valdés, "Hacia una periodización," 13–29; Kiple, *Blacks in Colonial Cuba.*

42. Corbett, "Migration to a Spanish Imperial Frontier," 415–16; Robinson, "Migration in Eighteenth Century Mexico," 55–68.

43. Borah, "Marriage and Legitimacy," 948–1008; Ripodas Ardanáz, *El matrimonio en Indias;* Lavrin, "In Search of the Colonial Woman," 29–36; Lavrin, "Women in Spanish American Colonial Society," 325–26.

44. Balmori, Voss, and Wortmann, *Notable Family Networks in Latin America;* Elizabeth A. Kuznesof, "The History of the Family in Latin America," *Latin American Research Review* 24 (spring 1989): 168–88.

45. Martínez-Alier, *Marriage, Class, and Colour,* passim; Szuchman, "A Challenge to the Patriarchs," 141–64; Socolow, "Acceptable Partners," 210–51; Twinam, "Honor, Sexuality, and Illegitimacy," 118–55.

46. González-Ripoll Navarro, "Voces de gobierno," 152.

47. Laura [Pablo Estévez], *Parte tercera de las revoluciones periódicas de la Havana,* 10.

Chapter 2. Wherever I May Serve His Majesty Best

The title of this chapter is from a letter by Juan Bautista Valliant, in AGI, Estado, Legajo 14, Numero 104: 1, 20 March 1797.

1. Torres Ramírez, "Alejandro O'Reilly en Cuba," 1370.

2. AGS, GM, Legajo 7259, Expediente (Cuaderno) 2, folio 9, 1788.

3. Altman and Horn, *To Make America;* Altman, *Emigrants and Society,* 170–90.

4. Arrate, *Llave del nuevo mundo*, 70; Wright, *Early History*, 20–55; Guerra y Sánchez, *Manual de historia*, 22–32; Piño-Santos, *Historia de Cuba*, 21–30.

5. Arrate, *Llave del nuevo mundo*, 70; Guerra y Sánchez, *Manual de historia*, 79; Torre, *Lo que fuimos*, 102–103; Marrero, *Cuba*, 7:97–102.

6. Cook, *Born to Die*, 15–59; Cook and Borah, *Essays in Population History;* Henige, "On the Contact Population of Hispaniola," 217–37.

7. Hoffman, *The Spanish Crown*, 39–62.

8. Ibid., 112.

9. Ibid., 158–61, 202–12.

10. Guerra y Sánchez, *Manual de historia*, 79; Torres Ramírez, *La armada de barlovento*, 202–16.

11. Guerra y Sánchez, *Manual de historia*, 80; Lyon, *The Enterprise of Florida*.

12. Arrate, *Llave del nuevo mundo*, 60–61; Guerra y Sánchez, *Manual de historia*, 80–81.

13. Ibid., 82–85

14. "Plano del puerto, bayia, y ciudad de la Havana; situada por los 23 10 de lat sept. y 29 20 de long. su 1 merido en Teneriffe, Nuevamente emmendado por D.D.D.B., año de 1730," Library of Congress, Howe Map Collection, 34; James Phelps, "A new and correct chart of the harbour of Havana on the island of Cuba with a plan of ye city &c. from an actual survey by Captain James Phelps, I Mynde, sc." (London, 1758?), Library of Congress, American Maps, v. 2, no. 52; Manuel Pérez Beato, "Plano de las operaciones del sitio y toma de la Habana por los ingleses in 1762," n.d., reprinted in A. Rodríguez, *Cinco diarios*, facing back cover; Guerra y Sánchez, *Manual de historia*, 145–46; Marrero, *Cuba*, 7:203, n. 6.

15. Arrate, *Llave del nuevo mundo*, 59; Torre, *Lo que fuimos*, 105.

16. McNeill, *Atlantic Empires of France and Spain*, 126–29; Pérez Beato, "Plano"; Marrero, *Cuba*, 7:11–20.

17. Syrett, *The Siege*, 178–79.

18. Morell de Santa Cruz, "Padrón ecclesiástico de 1754–55," 83.

19. Ibid.; Arrate, *Llave del nuevo mundo*, 103–104.

20. Arrate, *Llave del nuevo mundo*, 59; Pérez Beato, "Plano"; Knowles, "Description of the Havana," 26–27.

21. A. Rodríguez, *Cinco diarios*, 62 n. 3.

22. R. Rodríguez, *Plano topográfico*. I am indebted to Lic. Leandro S. Romero Estébañez, archaeologist of the city of Havana, for providing a copy of this map.

23. Torre, *Lo que fuimos*, 48–49.

24. R. Rodríguez, *Plano*; Villaverde, *Cecilia Valdés*.

25. R. Rodríguez, *Plano*; Sánchez Agustí, *Edificios públicos*, 66–71; Pérez Beato, *Habana antigua*, 1:85.

26. Arrate, *Llave del nuevo mundo*, 61, 177–78; A. Rodríguez, *Cinco diarios*, 38 n. 1; R. Rodríguez, *Plano*; Iglesias García, *La estructura agraria*.

27. Arrate, *Llave del nuevo mundo*, 171–75; R. Rodríguez *Plano*.

28. Arrate, *Llave del nuevo mundo,* 175–77; R. Rodríguez, *Plano;* Wright, *Cuba,* 97.

29. Pérez Beato, *Plano;* Knowles, "Description of the Havana," 29; Torre, *Lo que fuimos,* 12–13; Tylden, quoted by Karras, "La isla de Cuba," 88.

30. Knowles, "Description of the Havana," 28.

31. A. Rodríguez, *Cinco diarios,* 62 n. 3.

32. Fernández Santalices, *Las calles de la Habana intramuros,* 131.

33. Arrate, *Llave del nuevo mundo;* Knowles, "Description of the Havana," 28.

34. ANC, *Papeles,* 104–38.

35. Ibid., 41.

36. Knowles, "Description of the Havana," 27; Leandro S. Romero, archaeologist of the City of Havana, personal communication, 1993.

37. Tylden, quoted by Karras, "La isla de Cuba," 88; Morell de Santa Cruz, "Padrón ecclesiástico de 1754–55," 80.

38. Morell de Santa Cruz, "Padrón ecclesiástico de 1754–55," 80; Navarro, "Bando sobre que se destechen las Casas de Guano," 83–84. In Cuba, *guano* refers to palm leaves used for thatch: José de Rivera to Juan Ignacio de Urriza, February 16, 1786, quoted in *BAN* 53–54 (1954–55): 278; Marrero, *Cuba,* 8:224.

39. Valdés, *Historia,* 261–63; Wright, *Early History,* 20–33.

40. Arrate, *Llave del nuevo mundo,* 102; Valdés, *Historia,* 297–304.

41. McNeill, *Atlantic Empires of France and Spain,* 38; Guerra y Sánchez, *Manual de historia,* 151.

42. Sagra, *Historia económica-política;* Knight, *Slavery and the Transformation,* 16–17; Inglis, "Constructing a Tower."

43. Navarro, "Padrón General de la isla."

44. Records of the Ayuntamiento of Guanabacoa, Book Three, 1754–1764, "Narrative of the Indians who came from Florida," 7 May 1764. I thank Eugene Lyon for a copy of this document.

45. Knight, *Slavery and the Transformation,* 16; McAlister, "Social Structure," 349–70; Mörner, *Race Mixture;* Seed, "The Social Dimensions of Race," 602–4.

46. Navarro, "Padrón General de la isla."

47. AGI, SD, Legajo 1757, March 6, 1801; Torres Cuevas, *Félix Varela,* 26–33.

48. Torres Cuevas, *Félix Varela,* 33.

49. Martínez-Alier, *Marriage, Class, and Colour;* Kutzinski, *Sugar's Secrets.* The standard fictional treatment is Cirilo Villaverde's *Cecilia Valdés.*

50. AGI, PC, Legajo 87–1, copies in Stetson Collection, P. K. Yonge Library of Florida History, University of Florida, Gainesville, Fla.

51. A. Rodríguez, *Cinco diarios,* 62 n. 3.

52. Conde de Ricla to Miguel de Altarriba, May 14, 1765, in *BAN* 43 (1944): 120; Lewis, "Nueva España," 501–26; Thomas, *Cuba,* 49–53.

53. Morales's elegant signature, evidence of his literacy, graces many documents in the Library of Congress's East Florida Papers from his having served as interim

governor in 1795, during regular governor, Juan Nepomuceno de Quesada's periods of illness.

54. Riverend Brusone, *Historia económica*, 70–110.

55. Rivero Muñíz, *Tabaco*, 2:1–10; McNeill, *Atlantic Empires of France and Spain*, 156–72; Marrero, *Cuba*, 7:41–92; Riverend Brusone, *Historia económica*, 54, 94–97; Arrate, *Llave del nuevo mundo*, 150–51; Guerra y Sánchez, *Manual de historia*, 140.

56. Riverend Brusone, *Historia económica*, 60–64.

57. Nelson, "Contraband Trade," 55–67.

58. McNeill, *Atlantic Empires of France and Spain*, 117–22; Marrero, *Cuba*, 7:102–65.

59. Inglis, "The Spanish Naval Shipyard," 47–58; Ortega Pereyra, *La construcción naval;* Valdés, *Historia*, 281–89; Riverend Brusone, *Historia económica*, 65–68; Marrero, *Cuba*, 7:134–35, 8:15–22.

60. Moreno Fraginals, *El ingenio*, 1:95–102; Riverend Brusone, *Historia económica*, 108–48; Guerra y Sánchez, *Manual de historia*, 145–46; Thomas, *Cuba*, 49–52.

61. McNeill, *Atlantic Empires of France and Spain*, 156–72; Marrero, *Cuba*, 7:1–23.

62. Kuethe, *Cuba*, 70–72; Valdés, *Historia*, 275; Riverend Brusone, *Historia económica*, 141–43; Marrero, *Cuba*, 8:1–25.

63. Kuethe, *Cuba*, 70; Kuethe and Inglis, "Absolutism and Enlightened Reform," 118–43.

64. Barreto, *Contestación*.

65. Torres Ramírez, "Alejandro O'Reilly en Cuba," 1357–88; Valdés, *Historia*, 157–58.

66. Thomas, *Cuba*, 50.

67. Kuethe, "Havana in the Eighteenth Century," 23.

68. A. Rodríguez, *Cinco diarios*, 62 n. 3.

69. Arrate, *Llave del nuevo mundo*, 83–84; Marrero, *Cuba*, 8:12; Inglis, "The Spanish Naval Shipyard," 50–51.

70. Tylden, quoted by Karras, "La isla de Cuba," 92.

71. Juan de Prado, "El diario de Juan de Prado," in A. Rodríguez, *Cinco diarios*, 62 n. 3.

72. Navarro, "Bando de Buen Gobierno," 79.

73. Riverend Brusone, *Historia económica*, 140.

74. Arrate, *Llave del nuevo mundo*, 79; Marrero, *Cuba*, 8:245.

75. AGI, SD, Legajo 2197, contains the small number of licenses to emigrate to Cuba granted from 1726 through 1768.

76. Valdés, *Historia*, 174; Tylden, quoted by Karras, "La isla de Cuba," 93; Arrate, *Llave del nuevo mundo*, 79.

77. Riverend Brusone, *Historia económica*, 30.

78. Humboldt, *Ensayo político;* Berthe, "La Habana del fines," 63–86; Marrero, *Cuba*, 8:243–45; Tylden, quoted by Karras, "La isla de Cuba," 85–94; Villaverde,

Cecilia Valdés; Ribera, *Descripción;* Knowles, "Description of the Havana," 26–32; Joseph Gorham, "Diary of Major Joseph Gorham," in A. Rodríguez, *Cinco diarios,* 197–99; Fernández Santalices, *Las calles de la Habana intramuros,* 17; Pérez Beato, *Habana antigua,* 1:197.

79. Rojas-Míx, *La plaza mayor,* 131–41; Elias Durnford [1762?] in Marrero, *Cuba,* 8:facing back cover.

80. Navarro, "Bando de Buen Gobierno," 78; El Observador de la Havana, "Papel Sexto del Observador: El Relox de la Habana," *Papel Periódico de la Havana,* August 9, 1801.

81. Arrate, *Llave del nuevo mundo,* 205; Fernández Santalices, *Las calles de la Habana intramuros,* 118; Sánchez Agustí, *Edificios públicos,* 68.

82. AGI, PC, Legajo 1245, February 24, 1780; "Observaciones meteorológicas," *Papel Periódico de la Havana,* January 18, 1795.

83. Inglis, "The Spanish Naval Shipyard," 54; Marrero, *Cuba,* 8:22.

84. Wright, *Cuba,* 292–93.

85. Torre, *Lo que fuimos,* 117; El Observador, "El relox."

86. Marqués de la Torre, "Apuntes sobre las principales providencias y operaciones durante mi mando en la isla de Cuba dedse el día 18 de noviembre de 1771 hasta el de la fecha en que lo he entregado á mi sucesor el señor D. Diego Joseph Navarro," June 11, 1777, Box 3, Folder 2, Domingo del Monte Collection, Manuscript Div., Library of Congress, Washington, D.C.

87. *Papel Periódico de la Havana,* December 12, 1790.

88. Navarro, "Bando de Buen Gobierno," 83–84. Virtually every governor issued a series of proclamations upon his arrival in Cuba. In addition to the Marqúes de la Torre's proclamation (see n. 86 above), see AGI, Cuba, Legajo 1153, June 28, 1776, and for Bernardo de Gálvez, see AGI, Cuba, Legajo 1368–A, 1782.

89. Navarro, "Bando de Buen Gobierno," 78; Torre, *Lo que fuimos,* 117; Fernández Santalices, *Las calles de la Habana intramuros,* 25; Tylden, quoted by Karras, "La isla de Cuba," 92.

90. Arrate, *Llave del nuevo mundo,* 179–80; Valdés, *Historia,* 345–49.

91. Fernández Santalices, *Las calles de la Habana intramuros,* 118; Marrero, *Cuba,* 8:190

92. R. Rodríguez, *Plano topográfico.*

93. Fernández Santalices, *Las calles de la Habana intramuros,* 15.

94. Torre, *Lo que fuimos,* 64, 96 n. 1; Valdés, *Historia,* 342–43.

95. Valdés, *Historia,* 208; Arrate, *Llave del nuevo mundo,* 83–84.

96. Fernández Santalices, *Las calles de la Habana,* 21; Navarro, "Bando de Buen Gobierno," 76–77; Marrero, *Cuba,* 8:157–61.

97. The composite sketch of the woman's life comes from several sources: AGS, GM, Legajo 7257, Expediente (Cuaderno) 15, "Servicios de oficiales, sarxentos, y cadetes a la Infantería de la Havana arreglados hasta fin de Junio de 1769," folio 90; Oglesby, "Spain's Havana Squadron," 473–88; Kuethe, "Havana in the Eighteenth Century," 18; Sánchez-Albornoz, *The Population of Latin America,* 164–67.

98. Navarro, "Bando de Buen Gobierno," 75; Tylden, quoted by Karras, "La isla de Cuba," 88.

99. ANC, Realengos, Legajo 25, no. 3, 1779; Legajo 32, no. 9, 1791; Legajo 43, no. 16, 1803; Lavrin, "In Search of the Colonial Woman," 29–36; Lavrin, "Women in Spanish American Colonial Society," 325–26.

100. Navarro, "Bando de Buen Gobierno," 76.

101. Arrate, Llave del nuevo mundo, 177.

102. R. Rodríguez, Plano topográfico; Pérez Beato, Habana antigua, 1:156.

103. Torre, Lo que fuimos, 103 n. 1.

104. R. Rodríguez, Plano; Torre, Lo que fuimos, 117.

105. Leandro S. Romero, archaeologist of the city of Havana, personal communication, 1993.

106. R. Rodríguez, Plano.

107. Fernández Santalices, Las calles de la Habana intramuros, 22; Torre, Lo que fuimos, 117–120.

108. Arrate, Llave del nuevo mundo, 77.

109. Ibid., 78; Torre, Lo que fuimos, 13; Marrero, Cuba, 8:7.

110. AGI, Cuba, Legajo 1097, November 9, 1768.

111. Thomas, Cuba, 15; García Rodríguez, "Presencia Jesuita."

112. Navarro, "Bando de Buen Gobierno," 77.

113. Torre, "Apuntes sobre los principales providencias."

114. Ibid., 74–76; El Observador, "El relox."

115. Sánchez-Albornoz, The Population of Latin America, 128.

116. Navarro, "Bando de Buen Gobierno," 77.

117. Ibid., 79.

118. Papel Periódico de la Havana, November 7, November 14, 1790, February 3, April 17, 1791

119. Torre, Lo que fuimos, 122; Larry Jensen, Children of Colonial Despotism, 1–24, 137–39.

120. Valdés, Historia, 165–68.

121. Torre, Lo que fuimos, 117 n. l. On the streets of modern-day Havana, even in times of dire economic hardship, people flock to the push-carts of the granizado vendors to buy small cups of "snow" at ten centavos a cup.

122. AGI, PC, November 16, 1773.

123. José de la Luz y Caballero, quoted in José M. Hernández, "Félix Varela: El Primer Cubano," introduction to Varela, El Habanero, ix.

124. AGI, PC, Legajo 1153, September 19, September 30, 1776.

125. AGI, SD, Legajo 2551, July 29, 1786; AGS, GM, Legajo 7233, Expediente 2, May 26, 1791.

Chapter 3. Good for Farmers but Not for Soldiers

1. Lynch, Bourbon Spain, 318–19; Kuethe, Cuba, 78–112; Guerra y Sánchez, Manual de historia, 175–76.

2. McAlister, *"Fuero Militar"*; Archer, *The Army in Bourbon Mexico;* Kuethe, *Military Reform;* Kuethe, *Cuba;* Campbell, *Military and Society;* Phelan, *The People and the King;* Fisher, Kuethe, and McFarlane, *Reform and Insurrection.*

3. Domínguez, *Insurrection or Loyalty.*

4. Kuethe, *Cuba,* 174.

5. Haring, *Spanish Empire,* 114–15; Hoffman, *The Spanish Crown,* 20–62, 71–108, 122–74, 176–77, 214–15; Gascón, "The Military of Santo Domingo," 431–52.

6. Arrate, *Llave del nuevo mundo;* Valdés, *Historia;* Torre, *Lo que fuimos,* 167–70; Hart, *The Siege of Havana;* ANC, *Papeles;* A. Rodríguez, *Cinco diarios;* Syrett, *The Siege;* Parcero Torre, *La pérdida.*

7. Guerra y Sánchez, *Manual de historia,* 177.

8. Torre, *Lo que fuimos,* 42–45, 101–2.

9. ANC, Correspondencia del Capitán General, Legajo 11: 48, 1761–76; Legajo 23: 6, 1764–67; AGI, SD, Legajo 1223, July 30, August 27, 1775, photocopy in the Levi Marrero Collection, Special Collections, Florida International University, Miami, Fla.

10. Thomas, *Cuba,* 6–7; Guerra y Sánchez, *Manual de historia,* 169–75; Kuethe, *Cuba,* 18.

11. Hart, *The Siege of Havana;* ANC, *Papeles;* A. Rodríguez, *Cinco diarios;* Syrett, *The Siege;* Parcero Torre, *La pérdida.*

12. Guerra y Sánchez, *Manual de historia,* 178; Torre, *Lo que fuimos,* 104, 108; Valdés, *Historia,* 155–56.

13. Tribunal de Cuentas, "Sobre la compra y pago de terrenos y solares extramuros de esta ciudad," ANC, Expediente 1334, Libro 6, Foxas 224, 1773. Also in *BAN* 10 (May-June 1911): 130–31.

14. Guerra y Sánchez, *Manual de historia,* 178; Valdés, *Historia,* 155–56.

15. Valdés, *Historia,* 164.

16. Ibid., 286–89; Inglis, "The Spanish Naval Shipyard," 53–54; Marrero, *Cuba,* 7:134–35, 8:15–22; Ortega Pereyra, *La construcción naval;* Riverend Brusone, *Historia económica,* 65–68.

17. Kuethe, "Havana in the Eighteenth Century," 24.

18. Marichal and Souto Mantecón, "Silver and Situados," 604; Kuethe, "Guns, Subsidies, and Commercial Privilege," 130; TePaske, "La política española," 79–82; Le Riverend, *Historia económica,* 143–44. From 1780 through 1784, fully three-quarters of the money remitted to Spain from the Mexican treasury (33,346,972 pesos of 46,666,505 remitted) stayed in Havana. "Relación de valores y distribución de la real Hacienda de Nueva España en en quinquenio de 1780 a 1784," Box 6, Folder 4, Del Monte Collection.

19. Moreno Fraginals, "Sugar."

20. Marchena Fernández, *Oficiales y soldados,* 78–83; Kuethe, *Cuba,* 37–45.

21. Marchena Fernandez, *Oficiales y soldados,* 78–81, 337.

22. Ibid., 271–78.

23. Ibid., 82.

24. Kuethe, *Cuba*, 37–45; McAlister, "*Fuero Militar*," 6–11, 45–51.

25. Domínguez, *Insurrection or Loyalty*, 79–80; Klein, *Slavery in the Americas*, 211–24; Marchena Fernández, *Oficiales y soldados*, 79.

26. Marchena Fernández, *Oficiales y soldados*, 79.

27. Ibid., 81.

28. AGI, SD, Legajo 1140, February 21, March 9, 1784, July 1, 1785.

29. Ocerín, *Indice*, 1:ix–xxvi.

30. Marchena Fernández, *Oficiales y soldados*, 275.

31. Kuethe, *Cuba*, 127.

32. Marchena Fernández, *Oficiales y soldados*, 275–77.

33. Ibid., 277.

34. Torres Ramírez, "Alejandro O'Reilly," 1372; Parcero Torre, *La pérdida*, 176–82.

35. "Documents Relative to the Siege of Havana, 1762," Box 5, Folder 1, Del Monte Collection; Delgado, "El Conde de Ricla," 88; A. Rodríguez, *Cinco diarios*, 238.

36. Torres Ramírez, "Alejandro O'Reilly," 1362–64; Alejandro O'Reilly to Julián de Arriaga, April 12, 1764, AGI, SD, Legajo 1509, photocopy in Levi Marrero Collection and printed in Marrero, *Cuba*, 8:262–67; Delgado, "El Conde de Ricla," 117–21.

37. "Documents Relative to the Siege"; Kuethe, *Cuba*, 22–23; Delgado, "El Conde de Ricla," 69–75; A. Rodríguez, *Cinco diarios*, 70–120, 241, 254–55.

38. "Findings of the Court of Inquiry," Box 5, Folder 2, January 30–February 8, 1765, Del Monte Collection.

39. Kuethe, *Cuba*, 22–23; Delgado, "El Conde de Ricla," 69–75; A. Rodríguez, *Cinco diarios*, 241, 254–55.

40. A. Rodríguez, *Cinco diarios*, 235.

41. Torres Ramírez "Alejandro O'Reilly," 1368–71.

42. AGI, SD, Legajo 1141, February 17, June 19, 1787, October 6, 1781; Marrero, *Cuba*, 7:187; McNeill, *Atlantic Empires of France and Spain*, 196–201; Nelson, "Contraband Trade," 55–67.

43. Torres Ramírez, "Alejandro O'Reilly," 1368–71; Delgado, "El Conde de Ricla," 99–106.

44. ANC, Correspondencia del Capitán-General, Legajo 25: 190, June 5, 1766; A. Rodríguez, *Cinco diarios*, 241.

45. Kuethe, *Cuba*, 22–23; Delgado, "El Conde de Ricla," 69–75; A. Rodríguez, *Cinco diarios*, 70–120, 254–55.

46. Torres Ramírez, "Alejandro O'Reilly," 1368–71.

47. Ibid.; AGI, SD, Legajo 2585, May 8, 1770; AGS, GM, Legajo 7259, Expediente 15, December 31, 1765, passim; *Calendario manual*, 114.

48. McAlister, "*Fuero Militar*."

49. Delgado, "El Conde de Ricla," 103.

50. Ibid., 87; Torres Ramírez, "Alejandro O'Reilly," 1370.

51. Kuethe, *Cuba*, 35.

52. Torres Ramírez, "Alejandro O'Reilly," 1374.

53. AGI, SD, Legajo 2585, May 8, 1770; "Nota de los sujetos . . . para poblar la Nueva Florida en Jurisdicción de Matansas," April 24, 1764, ANC, Realengos, Legajo 67: 3; Delgado, "El Conde de Ricla," 103.

54. Wright, *Early History*, 62, 82, 94; Guerra y Sánchez, *Manual de historia*, 86–87; Piño-Santos, *Historia de Cuba*, 31–35; Corbitt, "*Mercedes* and *Realengos*," 269–74.

55. Johnson, "'La Guerra,'" 181–209.

56. AGI, PC, Legajo 1153, December 29, 1772.

57. Ibid., November 1, 1773.

58. AGS, GM, Legajo 6842, Expediente 89, March 30, 1789.

59. Chandler, *Social Assistance*.

60. O'Reilly to Arriaga, April 12, 1764, AGI, SD, Legajo 1509; Delgado, "El Conde de Ricla," 126.

61. AGI, PC, Legajo 1168, March 6, June 6, 1772.

62. AGI, SD, Legajo 1509, April 12, 1764; Delgado, "El Conde de Ricla," 124–25; Torres Ramírez, "Alejandro O'Reilly," 1367.

63. AGI, PC, Legajo 1269, October 5, 1779, citing the original establishment of the system of capitanes del partido by the Conde de Ricla in 1764.

64. AGI, SD, Legajo 1509, April 12, 1764; Delgado, "El Conde de Ricla," 124–25; Torres Ramírez, "Alejandro O'Reilly," 1367.

65. Wright, *Early History*, 62, 82, 94; Guerra y Sánchez, *Manual de historia*, 86–87; Corbitt, "*Mercedes* and *Realengos*," 269–74.

66. Corbitt, "Spanish Relief Policy," 67–82; Gold, "Settlement of East Florida Spaniards," 216–31.

67. "Nota de los sujetos"; Corbitt, "Spanish Relief Policy," 69–70; Gold, "Settlement of East Florida Spaniards," 221; AGI, SD, Legajo 2585, May 8, 1770.

68. Johnson, "Casualties of Peace"; Johnson, "Honor Is Life," 235–88. See also AGI, PC, Legajo 1090, August 28, 1766; AGI, PC, Legajo 548, reprinted in Carr, *Censos*, 73–92.

69. AGI, SD, Legajo 1135, September 6, 1766, photocopy in Levi Marrero Collection.

70. Ibid.

71. Patterson, "Military Organization"; Alston, *Soldier and Society*, 39–52.

72. AGI, SD, Legajo 1596, passim.

73. Morell de Santa Cruz, "Padrón ecclesiástico de 1754–55," 75–93; Navarro, "Padrón General de la isla."

74. Corbitt, "*Mercedes* and *Realengos*," 263–69. The awarding of land in circular grants was a characteristic of Cuba's land system. Cuban land grants were classified as *hatos* (cattle ranches), *corrales* (hog ranches), *potreros* (horse farms), *estancias* or *huertas* (gardens, usually for produce), *vegas* (tobacco farms), or *ingenios* (sugar plantations).

75. Navarro, "Padrón General de la isla"; McNeill, *Atlantic Empires of France and Spain*, 126–29; Humboldt, *Ensayo político*, 103–107. No contemporary approximation exists to determine the interior dimensions of the city or the *barrios*

extramuros to determine population density. Therefore, the area was extrapolated using measurements provided in Torre, *Lo que fuimos,* 84–86; Gabriel de Torres, "El Horcón (1758)," *Planos de ciudades iberoamericanas y filipinas existentes en el Archivo de Indias,* 2 vol. (Madrid), 1:78; and Corbitt, "*Mercedes* and *Realengos,*" 266.

76. AGI, PC, Legajo 1269, October 5, 1779.

77. Johnson, "'La Guerra,'" 203–207.

78. "Fechas en que comienzen los libros parroquiales," n.d., Typescript copy, Archivo de S. M. I. Catedral de la Habana, Havana, Cuba.

79. AGI, PC, Legajo 1155, January 17, 1775.

80. AGI, Mapas y planos, Santo Domingo, 501, 503, 1786.

81. Box 2, June 26, 1799, February 28, 1800, Del Monte Collection.

82. Box 3, Folder 3, 1805, Del Monte Collection; Marrero, *Cuba,* 13:250–55.

83. Navarro, "Padrón General de la isla"; McNeill, *Atlantic Empires of France and Spain,* 126–29; Humboldt, *Ensayo político,* 103–7; Inglis, "Constructing a Tower."

84. Iglesias García, *La estructura agrária.*

85. Marqués de la Torre, "Relación," June 12, 1777, Box 3, Folder 2, Del Monte Collection; Moreno Fraginals, *El ingenio,* 1:95–102.

86. AGI, PC, Legajo 1472, October 10, 1791.

87. Ibid., October 5, 1792.

88. AGI, PC, Legajo 1471, October 15, 1792[?].

89. AGI, PC, Legajo 1472, November 24, 1790; Joseph Fernández y Sotolongo, "Plano que representa la jurisdiccion de el partido de Río Blanco," n.d., AGI, Mapas y Planos, Santo Domingo, 357. Although the document is undated, it is known that Fernández y Sotolongo was the captain del partido in the 1790s.

90. Moreno Fraginals, *El ingenio,* 1:56–60.

91. AGI, PC, Legajo 1090, May 5, 1770.

92. Ibid., May 15, 1771; Legajo 1090 for 1771 and 1772, Legajo 1195 for 1773.

93. AGI, PC, Legajo 1471, October 15, 1792.

94. AGI, Ultramar 171, August 22, 1774, relates that the town held 302 residents and the district 2,038 inhabitants. In comparison, "Noticia de los vecinos que comprende el Partido de los Güines," March 20, 1786, AGI, PC, Legajo 1407, identifies over 3,000 persons in the town alone.

95. AGI, PC, Legajo 1471, October 15, 1792.

96. AGI, PC, Legajo 1195, November 22, 1771, April 4, 1772.

97. AGI, PC, Legajo 1201, February 25, 1771.

98. AGI, Correos, Legajo 257–B, May 10, 1777.

99. AGI, Correos, Legajo 258–A, August 12, 1779.

100. AGI, PC, Legajo 1259, July 20, 1777, for Trinidad and April 25, 1778, for St. Spiritus; Legajo 1260, May 8, 1779, for St. Spiritus and June 22, 1779, for Trinidad.

101. AGI, PC, Legajo 1300, February 13, 1781.

102. AGI, PC, Legajo 1201, February 25, 1771.

103. AGI, PC, Legajo 1195, June [?], 1776, for Güines; Legajo 1259, October 29,

1777, for St. Spiritus. For de la Torre's fight to get Cuban wax imported into Mexico, see Box 3, Folder 2, Del Monte Collection.

104. AGI, Ultramar, Legajo 83, January 25, 1777. Raffelín continued his military service uninterrupted: AGS, GM, Legajo 7259, Expediente 13, December 31, 1786.

105. Box 3, Folder 3, Del Monte Collection.

106. Sánchez-Albornóz, *The Population of Latin America*, 164–67; *Calendario manual*, 142; *Papel Periódico de la Havana*, January 3, 1796. McNeill, *Atlantic Empires of France and Spain*, 41, describes the city as a "clearinghouse for contagion, uniting the disease pools of Europe, Africa, and the Americas."

107. López-Valdés, "Hacia una periodización," 13–14, 29; Moreno Fraginals, *El ingenio*, 1:47–52.

108. AGI, SD, Legajos 2197–2200, 1726–1800.

109. Kuethe, "Havana in the Eighteenth Century," 22–23.

110. ANC, Asuntos Políticos, Legajo 2: 11, May 9, 1776; *Calendario manual*, 114; Delgado, "El Conde de Ricla," 99.

111. Kuethe, *Cuba*, 36–37, 95–96.

112. Luis Huet, "Plano que demuestra el acantonamiento en barracones del este . . . ," June 1, 1780, AGI, Mapas y Planos, Santo Domingo, 462.

113. AGI, SD, Legajo 2082, August 11, 1779; Kuethe, "Havana in the Eighteenth Century," 22–23; Marchena Fernández, *Oficiales y soldados*, 338.

114. Beerman, "Arturo O'Neill," 31.

115. Inglis, "The Spanish Naval Shipyard," 53–54.

116. Kuethe, *Cuba*, 15 n. 39, 126, 129. See also Marchena Fernández, "St. Augustine's Military Society," 43–71.

117. Kuethe, "Havana in the Eighteenth Century," 13–39.

118. Riverend Brusone, *Historia económica*, 142–43; Sánchez Ramírez, "Notas," 472 n. 12.

119. Marrero, *Cuba*, 7:19–27.

120. *Calendario manual*, 44.

121. Ibid., 78–80.

122. Ibid., 100–105; Arrate, *Llave del nuevo mundo*, 122; Guerra y Sánchez, *Manual de historia*, 176–80.

123. *Calendario manual*, 62–63, 129–30.

124. Ibid., 46, 50–54.

125. Geggus, *Slavery, War and Revolution*, 275–85, 347–72; Moreno Fraginals and Moreno Masó, *Guerra, migración y muerte*.

126. AGI, PC, Legajo 1154, November 4, 1772.

127. Navarro, "Padrón General de la isla."

128. Marrero, *Cuba*, 8:147–48.

129. For example, two unnamed servants arrived with José Antonio Gelabert in 1734, AGI, Contratacción, Legajo 5481, no. 2, ramo 7, May 1, 1731; Anton Arnau arrived with the family of Ventura Buceta, AGI, Contratacción, Legajo 5520, no. 2, ramo 10, April 6, 1775; and Miguel Agüero Campuzano arrived with the family of

Manuel Eligio de la Puente in 1779, AGI, Contratacción, Legajo 5542, no. 4, ramo 38, May 19, 1779.

130. Kuethe, *Cuba*, 38–40.

131. Ibid.; ANC, Asuntos Políticos, Legajo 2: 11, May 9, 1776.

132. AGI, PC, Legajo 1086, folio 1, 1766; Kuethe, *Cuba*, 47; Torres Ramírez, "Alejandro O'Reilly," 1367.

133. AGI, SD, Legajo 1256, May 19, 1780.

134. Domínguez, *Insurrection or Loyalty*, 74–81.

135. ANC, Asuntos Políticos, Legajo 2: 11, May 9, 1776.

136. Navarro, "Padrón General de la isla"; ANC, Asuntos Políticos, Legajo 2: 11, May 9, 1776.

137. ANC, Asuntos Políticos, Legajo 2: 11, May 9, 1776.

138. Domínguez, *Insurrection or Loyalty*, 76.

139. Lavrin, "In Search of the Colonial Woman," 29–36, "Women in Spanish American Colonial Society," 325–26.

140. Navarro, "Bando de Buen Gobierno," 103–4; ANC, Asuntos Políticos, Legajo 2: 11, May 9, 1776; José Escoto Collection, box 1, no. 20, Houghton Library.

141. Kuethe, *Cuba*, 37–41; Torres Ramírez, "Alejandro O'Reilly," 1375.

142. Navarro, "Padrón General de la isla"; ANC, Asuntos Políticos, Legajo 2: 11, May 9, 1776

143. Kuethe, *Cuba*, 46–48; McAlister, "*Fuero Militar*," 6–11, 45–51.

144. Kuethe, *Cuba*, 46–48; McAlister, "*Fuero Militar*," 6–11, 45–51.

145. "Estado de la fuerza y su complejo de los cuerpos de infantería y cavallería asi veterana como milicias que existen en esta plaza y sus imediaciones . . . ," AGI, SD, Legajo 2082, August 11, 1779. The same population figures for the white male population were utilized in the calculations above.

146. Andreski, *Military Organization and Society*, 33–74.

147. Navarro, "Padrón General de la isla"; ANC, Asuntos Políticos, Legajo 2: 11, May 9, 1776.

148. ANC, Asuntos Políticos, Legajo 2: 11, May 9, 1776; Kuethe, *Cuba*, 46–48.

149. AGI, PC, Legajo 1259, March 29, 1781.

150. *Calendario manual*, 116–22.

151. Pagden, *Lords*, 29–62.

152. AGS, GM, Legajo 7259, Expediente 15, December 31, 1765.

153. Marchena Fernández, *Oficiales y soldados*, 33, 81–82; Kuethe, *Cuba*, 142.

154. Valdés, *História*, 208.

155. AGI, PC, Legajo 1472, October 15, 1791; Pérez Beato, *Habana antigua*, 1:229; Marrero, *Cuba*, 8:81; Torres Ramírez, "Alejandro O'Reilly," 1379. Río Blanco was the site of a hospital for King's slaves and prisoners.

156. Torres Ramírez, "Alejandro O'Reilly," 1379.

157. Guerra y Sánchez, *Manual de história*, 178; Valdés, *História*, 155–56.

158. ANC, Realengos, Extramuros, Legajo 73: 33, 1793. See also Marchena Fernández, *Oficiales y soldados*, 335–36.

159. Kuethe, *Cuba*, 46–48; McAlister, "*Fuero Militar*," 6–11, 45–51.

160. Kuethe, *Cuba*, 46–48.

161. Kuethe, *Cuba*, 37–51, 74–75.

162. AGI, PC, Legajo 1071, December 14, December 16, December 18, 1770.

163. AGI, SD, Legajo 1481, September 1, 1791, quoting the earlier agreement.

164. AGI, PC, Legajo 1071, December 14, December 16, December 18, 1770.

165. Klein, *Slavery in the Americas*, 212–27; Deschamps Chapeaux, *El negro en la economía habanera*, 59–86; Kuethe, *Cuba*, 74–75.

166. AGI, PC, Legajo 1357, September 26, 1783; Klein, *Slavery in the Americas*, 224.

167. AGI, PC, Legajo 1357, September 26, 1783.

168. ANC, Escribanía de Guerra, ANC Guerra 1779–85, March 6, 1780; Escribanía de Guerra, 1788–97, November 29, 1794.

169. AGI, PC, Legajo 1357, September 26, 1783.

170. ANC, Escribanía de Guerra, 1788–97, November 29, 1794.

171. Julián de Arriaga to the Conde de Ricla, "Sobre la libertad de los negros esclavos que se distinguieron durante el sitio de la Habana por los ingleses en 1762," *BAN* 16 (1915): 211.

172. ANC, Escribanía de Gobierno, August 29, 1766.

173. ANC, Escribanía de Guerra, December 11, 1795.

174. ANC, Escribanía de Gobierno, March 30, 1767.

175. ANC, Escribanía de Guerra, written July 15, 1788, probated late October 1796.

176. AGS, GM, Legajo 6913, Expediente 9, November 2, 1781, February 6, 1782. Most died of disease rather than wounds.

177. AGI, PC, Legajo 1371, December 27, 1784, January 15, 1785.

178. *Papel Periódico de la Havana*, November 15, 1792, December 20, 1792, October 2, 1794.

179. Ibid., September 14, 1794.

180. AGI, Ultramar, Legajo 120, November 22, 1792.

181. Ibid.; McAlister, "*Fuero Militar*," 6–11, 45–51.

182. Kuethe, *Cuba*, 174.

183. Torres Ramírez, *Alejandro O'Reilly en las Indias*, 55–183; Saavedra, *Los decenios*, 58–59; Rodríguez Casado, *La política marroquí de Carlos III*, 237; Lynch, *Bourbon Spain*, 307.

184. AGI, Ultramar 171, August 22, 1774; "Noticia de los vezinos que comprende el partido de Jesús del Monte que como Cap^n doy al Señor Govr y Capitán General con arreglo a su orden de 2 de Marzo de 1786," AGI, SD, Legajo 1407.

Chapter 4. Honor Is Life

1. Johnson, "'La Guerra,'" 181–209.

2. Pérez Beato, *Habana antigua*, 1:406–7.

3. AGI, PC, Legajo 1246, folios 1–50, 1777; Legajo 1344, folios 100–55, 1784; Vicente de Garciny to Marqués de la Torre, May 16, 1777, in *BAN* 16 (1915): 212.

4. See March 7, 1778, and January 5, 1782, Libro 7, 1771–94, Matrimonios de Españoles, SMI.

5. SMI, Libro 6, 1754–71, January 7, 1758; Libro 7, 1771–94, January 13, 1773, May 31, 1791, Matrimonios de Españoles.

6. Pérez Beato, *Habana antigua*, 1:406.

7. Corbitt, "The Administrative System in the Floridas, Part 1," 41–47, and "The Administrative System in the Floridas, Part 2," 57–67.

8. Kuethe, *Cuba*, 47.

9. AGI, PC, Legajo 1077, October 21, 1768; Legajo 1093, November 14, 1768; Legajo 1142, November 6, 1775, are but a fraction of the examples.

10. Kuethe, *Cuba*, 42–43.

11. Delgado, "El Conde de Ricla," 128–32; Torres Ramírez, "Alejandro O'Reilly," 1367.

12. Kuethe, *Cuba*, 47; *Calendario manual*, 105.

13. AGS, GM, Legajo 7257, Expediente 15, June 30, 1769, folio 40; AGI, Contratacción, 5508, no. 1, ramo 2, August 29, 1765; Parcero Torre, *La pérdida*.

14. AGS, GM, Legajo 7257, Expediente 15, June 30, 1769, folio 24.

15. Ibid., folio 55. See also AGS, GM, Legajo 6932, Expediente 1, August 26, 1789; Legajo 6923, Expediente 41, May 1, 1792; Legajo 6858, Expediente 56, September 4, 1797.

16. AGI, SD, Legajo 2585, May 8, 1770; AGS, GM, Legajo 7259, Expediente 15, December 31, 1765, folios 5, 8, 25, 33, 34, 48, and 49.

17. AGS, GM, Legajo 7259, Expediente 15, December 31, 1765, folios 5, 8, 25, 33, 34, 48, and 49.

18. Ibid., folios 1, 3, 5, 53.

19. Ibid., folios 2, 4, 6, 8, 9, 11, 12, 16, 17; *Calendario manual*, 105–15.

20. *Calendario manual*, 105–15; AGS, GM, Legajo 7259, Expediente 15, December 31, 1765, folios 17–26, 28–29, 32–34; *Calendario manual*, 107–8.

21. AGS, GM, Legajo 7259, Expediente 15, December 31, 1765, folios 35–51, 55, 58, 59, 114–38; *Calendario manual*, 107–8.

22. AGS, GM, Legajo 7259, Expediente 15, December 31, 1765, folios 3, 25, 39.

23. AGI, PC, Legajo 1134, September 6, 1765; Legajo 1136, March 15, 1769.

24. AGS, GM, Legajo 7259, Expediente 15, December 31, 1765, folio 53.

25. AGS, GM, Legajo 7259, Expediente 15, December 31, 1765, folio 3.

26. AGI, PC, Legajo 1248, March 13, April 17, 1780, Legajo 1300, March 22, 1781.

27. Juan Ignacio de Urriza to Vicente de Zéspedes, EFP, reel 19, bundle 54b6, June 9, 1784.

28. ANC, Asuntos Políticos, Legajo 2: 11, May 9, 1776.

29. AGS, GM, Legajo 7259, Expediente 15, December 31, 1765, folio 5; AGI, PC, Legajo 1153, December 16, 1771.

30. AGS, GM, Legajo 7259, Expediente 15, December 31, 1765, folio 55; AGI, PC, Legajos 1313, folios 1–16, 1779, Legajo 1349, Expediente 6, folios 1–27, 1785; Urriza to Zéspedes, EFP, reel 19, bundle 456, June 9, 1784.

31. AGS, GM, Legajo 7259, Expediente 15, December 31, 1765, folio 48; Legajo 6843, Expediente 4, 1789, Legajo 6880, Expediente 60, 1789; AGI, PC, Legajo 1248, March 13, 1780.

32. AGS, GM, Legajo 7259, Expediente 15, December 31, 1765, folios 11, 29, 41, 58; AGI, PC, Legajo 1144, folios 1–50, Legajo 1230, 1777, Legajo 1254, 1777–81.

33. AGS, GM, Legajo 7259, Expediente 15, December 31, 1765, folio 116; AGI, PC, Legajo 1315, folios 1–4, 1784; ANC, Escribanía de Guerra, July 30, 1796.

34. AGI, PC, Legajo 1080, folios 1–33, 1766, Legajo 1072, folios 1–60, 1767.

35. AGI, SD, Legajo 1137, February 15, 1771.

36. AGI, PC, Legajo 1074, February 6, February 10, 1769.

37. Ibid., Legajo 1155, March 8, 1774, May 23, 1775.

38. Ibid., Legajo 1140, February 20, 1782.

39. Ibid., Legajo 1136, September 11, 1779

40. Juan Ignacio Urriza to Vicente de Zéspedes, EFP, reel 19, bundle 54B5, June 9, 1784.

41. *Reglamento del pie, servicio, gobierno y disciplina de la noble compañía de cadetes de la Havana, aprobado por S.M. y mandada su observancia por R.O., expedida en Sn Ildefonso a 24 de octubre de 1764* (Havana: 1765), in Colección Cubana, Biblioteca Nacional José Martí, Havana. See also Marchena Fernández, *Oficiales y soldados*, 75.

42. AGS, GM, Legajo 7259, Expediente 15, December 31, 1765, folios 114–38, Legajo 7281, December 31, 1792, folio 73.

43. Ibid., Legajo 7259, Expediente 15, December 31, 1765, folios 129–33.

44. Torres Ramírez, "Alejandro O'Reilly," 1380–86.

45. *Reglamento del pie*; AGS, GM, Legajo 7259, Expediente 15, December 31, 1765, folios 114–38; Legajo 6873, Expediente 3, 1794; Legajo 7216, Expediente 33, 1796; Legajo 6877, Expediente 49, 1798; Legajo 6880, Expediente 25, 1786.

46. AGS, GM, Legajo 7259, Expediente 15, December 31, 1765, folios 4–19, 35–51, 60–65.

47. AGI, SD, Legajo 1155, March 8, 1774.

48. AGS, GM, Legajo 7261, Expediente 11, December 31, 1788, folio 104; Legajo 6878, Expediente 20, 1799; Legajo 7224, Expediente 12, June 23, 1790.

49. Ibid., Legajo 7259, Expediente 15, December 31, 1765, folio 33; Legajo 6880, Expediente 21, January 25, 1789; Legajo 6846, Expediente 48, October 4, 1791.

50. AGI, SD, Legajo 1134, February 21, 1761.

51. AGI, Estado, Legajo 18, Numero 9:1, February 23, 1795.

52. AGS, GM, Legajo 7259, Expediente 15, December 31, 1765, folio 8; Legajo 6840, Expediente 86, May 8, 1788.

53. AGI, SD, Legajo 2585, May 8, 1770.

54. AGI, PC, Legajo 1080, folios 1–33, 1766, Legajo 1169, folios 316–50, 1772; AGS, GM, Legajo 6869, Expediente 14.

55. AGI, PC, Legajo 1379, Expediente 2, 1785.

56. AGS, GM, Legajo 7281, Expediente 11, December 31, 1792, folio 90.

57. Marchena Fernández, *Oficiales y soldados*, 335–36.

58. ANC, Escribanía de Guerra, November 23, 1782; "Documents relative to the siege of Havana, 1762," Box 5, Folder 1, Del Monte Collection.

59. AGS, GM, Legajo 7259, Expediente 15, December 31, 1765, folio 2.

60. AGS, GM, Legajo 6859, Expediente 56, September 4, 1797.

61. *Papel Periódico de la Havana*, August 25, 1791.

62. Ibid., February 23, 1792; AGI, PC, Legajo 1156, March 6, 1777.

63. AGS, GM, Legajo 7260, Expediente 3, December 31, 1788, folio 11.

64. Ibid., Legajo 7281, Expediente 11, December 31, 1792, folio 91; *Calendario manual*, 107.

65. AGS, GM, Legajo 7281, Expediente 10, December 31, 1792, folio 1.

66. AGI, Estado, Legajo 18, Numero 9: 1, February 23, 1795; AGI, SD, Legajo 1777–A. See also Sevilla Soler, *Santo Domingo*, 377–94.

67. AGS, GM, Legajo 6869, Expediente 9, April 26, 1788.

68. *Calendario manual*, 108.

69. For Pedro José Salcedo, ANC, Correspondencia del Capitán General, Legajo 30A: 190, May 17, 1771; Urriza to Zéspedes, EFP, reel 19, bundle 54B6, June 9, 1784, and Inspection Report: Third Batallion of Cuba, EFP, reel 31, bundle 84F7, November 1, 1793; and for light infantry lieutenant Pedro Caxne, AGS, GM, Cuba, Legajo 7259, Expediente 1, December 31, 1788, folio 3, and his brother-in-law Pablo Catafal, folio 8; Urriza to Zéspedes, EFP, reel 19, bundle 54b6, June 9, 1784.

70. For Juan de Cotilla, A. Rodríguez, *Cinco diarios*, 237, AGI, PC, Legajo 2585, May 8, 1770, Pérez Beato, *Habana antigua*, 1:130. For Luis Huet, AGI, PC, Legajo 1154, April 23, 1774, Legajo 1153, July 15, 1774, and Legajo 1344, folios 1–65, 1784–85. For Mariano de la Roque, AGI, PC, Legajo 1154, December 10, 1773; Legajo 1371, February 13, 1785; Urriza to Zéspedes, EFP, reel 19, bundle 54b6, June 9, 1784; Mariano de la Rocque [Roque], "Plano de la ciudad de San Agustín, 25 de abril de 1788," and "Descripción del plano de la ciudad de San Agustín de la Florida del año 1788," typescript copy in the P. K. Yonge Library of Florida History, Assessor's Report, East Florida Papers, reel 146, bundle 320, [1791].

71. For Garcini, March 7, 1778, Libro 7, Matrimonios de Españoles, SMI; AGI, PC, Legajo 1247, November 12, 1780; *Papel Periódico de la Havana*, September 29, 1791; *Calendario manual*, 108. For Risel, May 16, 1767, Libro 6, Matrimonios de Españoles, SMI; AGI, PC, Legajo 1248, July 23, 1779; *Papel Periódico de la Havana*, September 29, 1791; *Calendario manual*, 107. For Morales, ANC, Correspondencia del Capitán General, Legajo 30A: 190, March 2, 1771; Inspection Report: Third Batallion of Cuba, EFP, reel 31, bundle 84F7, April 9, 1794; *Calendario manual*, 107.

72. For Francisco de Porras from the Regiment of Savoy to the Havana Battalion of Pardos, AGI, PC, Legajo 1154, October 19, 1773; Bernardo Carillo from Santiago de Cuba to Havana, AGI, PC, Legajo 1155, October 13, 1775; Diego González Barrera, who was in the Regiment of Nueva España but who transferred to that of New Orleans, AGI, PC, Legajo 1757, June 20, 1799; *Papel Periódico de la Havana*, November 13, 1796.

73. Burkholder, "Council of the Indies," 406.

74. Marrero, *Cuba*, 13:30.

75. For Gerónimo de Hita y Salazar, AGI, PC, Legajo 1153, November 29, 1771; for Juan Manuel de Ximínez, AGS, GM, Legajo 6850, Expediente 45, April 11, 1793.

76. AGS, GM, Legajo 6852, Expediente 64, Companía de Infantería Ligera de la Havana, 1794.

77. AGS, GM, Legajo 6850, Expediente 45, January 26, 1792.

78. ANC, Realengos, Extramuros, Legajo 67: 3, 1793; Johnson, "'La Guerra,'" 181–209.

79. AGI, PC, Legajo 1153, June 6, June 28, 1776.

80. AGI, PC, Legajo 1153, April 21, 1773.

81. Box 3, Folder 2, June 12, 1777, Del Monte Collection.

82. AGI, PC, Legajo 1154, April 11, 1774.

83. *Papel Periódico de la Havana*, April 3, 1791

84. Ibid., August 19, October 13, 1791; *Calendario Manual*, 49, 53.

85. *Papel Periódico de la Havana*, July 10, 1795.

86. *Calendario manual*, 50–54.

87. *Papel Periódico de la Havana*, November 10, 1790.

88. AGI, PC, Legajo 1153, September 15, 1776.

89. Marchena Fernández, *Oficiales y soldados*, 266.

90. AGI, PC, Legajo 1153, February 3, 1777.

91. AGI, PC, Legajo 412–A, 1793–95, "Certificación de las Familias de Florida."

92. AGS, GM, Legajo 6850, Expediente 45, April 11, 1793.

93. AGI, PC, Legajo 1073, May 3, 1768.

94. AGI, PC, Legajo 1154, December 21, 1772.

95. AGI, PC, Legajo 1154, May 21, June 5, June 20, July 18, 1772, among many examples.

96. AGI, PC, Legajo 1153, May 14, 1776.

97. AGI, PC, Legajo 1168, November 1, 1771.

98. AGI, PC, Legajo 1155, February 1, 1775.

99. AGI, PC, Legajo 1371, Revista de la Tropa, January 1, 1785.

100. Ibid.

101. Ibid., April 20, 1785.

102. AGI, PC, Legajo 1153, March 20, 1777.

103. Ibid., April 11, 1777.

104. Deschamps Chapeaux, *El negro en la economía habanera*, 89–165; Klein, *Slavery in the Americas*, 143–47, 194–209.

105. AGI, SD, Legajo 1481, May 7, 1791.

106. Ibid., July 5, 1791.

107. ANC, Escribanía de Gobierno, July 21, 1777.

108. ANC, Escribanía de Guerra, December 6, 1796.

109. *Papel Periódico de la Havana*, December 25, 1794.

110. AGI, PC, Legajo 1153, March 29, 1776, Legajo 1154, January 15, 1772.

111. AGI, PC, Legajo 1260, June 28, 1780.

112. AGI, PC, Legajo 1154, August 24, 1774.

113. AGI, PC, Legajo 1153, March 20, 1776; Legajo 1154, June 19, 1772.

114. AGI, PC, Legajo 1371, January 30, 1785.

115. AGI, PC, Legajo 1247, March 18, 1778. See also Klein, *Slavery in the Americas,* 208–209 n. 27.

116. AGI, PC, Legajo 1153, May 18, 1773.

117. AGI, PC, Legajo 1472, May 23, 1791.

118. AGI, PC, Legajo 1165, September 25, 1775.

119. AGI, PC, Legajo 1470, November 3, 1795.

120. Ibid., October 29, 1790.

121. Ibid., November 3, 1795

122. AGI, SD, Legajo 2585, May 8, 1770; Iglesia Santo Angel Custodio, Libro 4B, Junio 1770–Marzo 1794, Registro de Matrimonios de Españoles, July 27, 1781.

123. *Papel Periódico de la Havana,* September 30, 1792.

124. Ibid., July 23, 1773.

125. Iglesia Nuestra Señora de la Asunción, Guanabacoa, Libro 2, Entierros de Blancos, 1763–74, May 7, 1764.

126. AGI, SD, Legajo 2585, May 8, 1770; AGI, PC, Legajo 412–A, 1793–95, "Certificación de las Familias de Florida"; Iglesia Espíritu Santo, Libro 5, Junio de 1772–Noviembre de 1783, Matrimonios de Españoles, November 8, 1775 and Libro 6, Diciembre de 1783–Noviembre de 1795, Matrimonios de Españoles, March 26, 1784.

127. AGI, PC, Legajo 412–A, 1793–95, "Certificación de las Familias de Florida."

128. Ibid.

129. SMI, Libro 7, 1771–94, Matrimonios de Españoles, November 1, 1767.

130. Ibid., November 1, 1767; AGI, PC, Legajo 412–A, 1793–95, "Certificación de las Familias de Florida"; Iglesia Espíritu Santo, Libro 5, Junio de 1772–Noviembre de 1783, Matrimonios de Españoles, May 9, 1781.

131. Iglesia Espíritu Santo, Libro 4, Matrimonios de Españoles, November 1760–June 1772, May 15, 1766, Libro 5,Matrimonios de Españoles, June 1772–November 1783, August 9, 1176, March 29, 1777; AGI, PC, Legajo 412–A, 1793–95, "Certificación de las Familias de Florida."

132. Navarro, "Bando de Buen Gobierno," 103–104.

133. *Papel Periódico de la Havana,* December 23, 1792.

134. Moreno Fraginals, *El ingenio,* 1:58.

135. ANC, Realengos, Extramuros, Legajo 27: 5, 1784–85.

136. ANC, Escribanía de Gobierno, February 13, 1778; Escribanía de Guerra, May 31, June 14, 1783.

137. AGI, PC, Legajo 1470, April 1, 1796.

138. AGI, Ultramar, Legajo 83, January 25, 1777; AGS, GM, Legajo 7259, Expediente 13, December 31, 1786; García Rodríguez, "Presencia Jesuita," 139.

139. ANC, Escribanía de Guerra, (date illegible) October, 1780.

140. ANC, Escribanía de Gobierno, February 11, 1767.

141. ANC, Escribanía de Guerra, June 6, 1797.

142. *Papel Periódico de la Havana,* June 15, 1795.

143. AGS, GM, Legajo 7259, Expediente 15, December 31, 1765, folio 35, Legajo 6913, Expedientes 9, 16, February 6, 1782; Iglesia Santo Angel Custodio, Libro 3B, Febrero 1742–Mayo 1770, Registro de Matrimonios de Españoles, January 12, 1755; ANC, Escribanía de Guerra, November 23, 1782.

144. AGS, GM, Legajo 6913, Expedientes 9, 12, February 6, 1782.

145. A popular phrase in Cuba even today is *"llega y pon,"* (come and put [yourself]), which refers to the migration to Havana from the countryside. It also comes with the inference that the arrival will become part of the suburban masses in the shantytowns surrounding the city.

146. Kuethe, *Cuba,* 47.

147. Juan Bautista Valliant, AGI, Estado, Legajo 14, Numero 104: 1, March 20, 1793.

148. AGS, GM, Legajo 7281, Expediente 11, December 31, 1792, folios 43, 61, 95, 106; Cummins, *Spanish Observers,* 115–67; Kuethe, *Cuba,* 90–94.

149. Lynch, *Bourbon Spain,* 294, describes Aranda as "a toothless, deaf, and squinting little man, his nose stained with snuff, rough-spoken but mostly taciturn." See also Rodríguez Casado, *La política y los políticos,* 215, 234–39; Ferrer del Río, *Historia del reinado,* 4:103–9.

150. Rodríguez Casado, *La política marroquí de Carlos III,* 236; Ferrer del Río, *Historia del reinado,* 4:110.

151. Saavedra, *Los decenios,* 82.

152. Ferrer del Río, *Historia del reinado,* 4:117; Rodríguez Casado, *La política marroquí de Carlos III,* 237.

153. Rodríguez Casado, *La política marroquí de Carlos III,* 238–42; Saavedra, *Los decenios,* 81, 86, 92; Ferrer del Río, *Historia de reinado,* 4:119–25. The term "flower of Spanish youth" is used throughout contemporary accounts. See Box 4, Folder 8, Del Monte Collection.

154. A bound collection of verses critical of O'Reilly, "Barios papeles que salieron contra Dn Alejandro O'rrelli sobre la Toma de Argel en el año 1775," is located in Box 4, Folder 8, Del Monte Collection. Among the many quartillas and décimas are the following:

O'rrelli debe entender,
que para un golpe de mano,
no es lo mismo el Africano,
que el culo de su mujer.

A el culo de su mujer,
un solo zapato basta,
pero a el otro ni una asta,
y por eso echo a correr.

A correr no hay tal es falso,
y lo afirmo y los hare ver,

or que un cojo, ciego, y sordo,
ni corre, ni oye, ni ve.

No corre, no fue ranchero,
o oy manda a quien mando a el,
no be lo que ha de mandar,
no oye quien le quiere bien.

Orrelli es un gran soldado,
Oreilli es gran capitan,
con todos estos citados,
Orrelli se debe aorcar.

155. Lynch, *Bourbon Spain*, 294.

156. Box 4, Folder 8, Del Monte Collection, contains the following:

Mintio la gazeta el martes,
minito el suplimento mas,
mienten los dos generales,
por toda la enternidad.
Mienten las cartas y impresas,
contra Dios y la verdad,
por que ninguna concuerda,
con su misma original.
El grande Oreilly en la suya,
culpa la oficialdad,
en la copia celebra,
pero no es por caridad.

Pretende tapar la boca,
a los que pueden gritar,
y decir al soberano,
un hierro tan general. . . .

157. Saavedra, *Los decenios*, 97–99.

158. The passage reads: "Que para cubrir su dolores ha imputado a los muertos desobedencia, que nunca pensaron, ni cometieron." Box 4, Folder 8, Del Monte Collection.

159. Torres Ramírez, *Alejandro O'Reilly en las Indias*, 10–11; Saavedra, *Los decenios*, 94–95; Ferrer del Río, *Historia del reinado*, 4:138; Kuethe, *Cuba*, 94–95; Lynch, *Bourbon Spain*, 294.

160. Kuethe, *Cuba*, 95; Lynch, *Bourbon Spain*, 293–98.

161. Lynch, *Bourbon Spain*, 295.

162. Calcagno, *Diccionario*, 172; Rodríguez Casado, *La política marroquí de Carlos III*, 274–82.

163. Morales Padrón, *Journal*, xvi–xxiv.

164. Saavedra, *Los decenios*, 90

165. Kuethe, *Cuba*, 57.

166. Thomas, *Cuba*, 1499–1507; and SMI, Libro 6, 1754–71, Matrimonios de Españoles, January 20, 1766, and December 22, 1765.

167. AGS, GM, Legajo 7259, Expediente 2, December 31, 1788.

168. Marrero, *Cuba*, 13:56.

169. AGS, GM, Legajo 6877, Expediente 48, June 12, 1796; AGI, Contratacción 5542, no. 4, ramo 38, April 30, May 19, 1779.

170. AGS, GM, Legajo 7259, Expediente 2, December 31, 1788.

171. AGS, GM, Legajo 7248, Expediente 2, March 9, 1784.

172. Ibid., May 8, 1784.

173. Ibid., May 19, May 26, 1784.

174. AGS, GM, Legajo 7259, Expediente 2, December 31, 1788.

175. Marchena Fernández, *Oficiales y soldados*, 81.

Chapter 5. Díme con Quien Andas

1. Libro 7, 1771–94: 369, Matrimonios de Españoles, SMI; Nieto y Cortadellas, *Dignidades nobilarias*, 181–82.

2. Woodward, *Tribute*, xxvi.

3. Ibid., xx.

4. Priestly, *José de Gálvez;* Lynch, *Bourbon Spain*, 253–54.

5. Lynch, *Bourbon Spain*, 253–54, 295–96.

6. Morales Padrón, *Journal*, xxii.

7. Ibid., xxii–xxiii.

8. Ibid., 363–64; Saavedra, *Los decenios*, 219–25.

9. Rodríguez Casado, *La política marroquí de Carlos III*, 274–79, 291–93. Antonio's presence as commandant of Puerto Real must have been particularly galling to Alejandro O'Reilly, who was captain general of Andalusia directly across the Straits of Gibraltar from North Africa, and to his brother-in-law, Luis de Las Casas, who was inspector of the troops along the Mediterranean coast.

10. Caughey, *Bernardo de Gálvez*, remains the seminal work.

11. In addition to Caughey, *Bernardo de Gálvez*, and Woodward, *Tribute*, xvii–xxvii, see Reparáz, *Yo Solo;* Gálvez, *"Yo Solo";* Coker and Rea, *Anglo-Spanish Confrontation;* Baker and Bissler Haas, "Gálvez's Combat Diary," 176–99; Haarman, "The Spanish Conquest," 107–34; Haarman, "The Siege of Pensacola," 193–99; Murphy, "The Irish Brigade," 216–25; Weddle, *Changing Tides*, 113, 286. Unlike most of the works on this subject, which are laudatory, Weddle is critical of Bernardo de Gálvez and the nepotistic practices of the age.

12. AGS, GM, Legajo 6912, Expediente 1, January 10, 1780.

13. Corbitt, "The Administrative System in the Floridas, Part 1," 42.

14. *Real Cédula.*

15. Rojas y Rocha, *Poema épico;* Corbitt, "The Administrative System in the Floridas, Part 1," 43.

16. Morales Padrón, *Journal*, 144–74.

17. Saavedra, *Los decenios*, 230–79, 287–89.

18. Ibid., 84, 90, 136–37.

19. Ibid., 76; Beerman, "José de Ezpeleta," 97–118; Medina Rojas, *José de Ezpeleta*.

20. Baker and Bissler Haas, "Gálvez's Combat Diary," 176.

21. Beerman, "Arturo O'Neill," 29–41, 30.

22. Armona, *Noticias privadas*, 30.

23. AGS, GM, Legajo 7259, Expediente 2, December 1788; Armona, *Noticias privadas*, 30–31; Weddle, *Changing Tides*, 113–18.

24. Weddle, *Changing Tides*, 154–61.

25. AGI, SD, August 27, 1773, January 11, February 1, 1774; Cummins, *Spanish Observers*, 99–105.

26. AGI, PC, Legajo 1160, October 21, October 24, 1774, March 9, 1775.

27. AGI, SD, Legajo 2082, December 22, 1779; AGI, PC, Legajo 1242, March 31, April 6, 1778, April 6, 1779; Legajo 1300, March 2, May 23, 1781.

28. AGI, PC, Legajo 1371, March 22, 1785; AGI, SD, Legajo 1140, November 23, 1782; Archivo Histórico Nacional de España, Diversos 44, Documento 76, 1777; Cummins, *Spanish Observers*, 105–67, 162.

29. AGI, PC, Legajo 1248, September 24, 1778, September 20, 1779.

30. AGS, GM, Legajo 7259, Expediente 2, 1788.

31. Woodward, *Tribute*, xxvi.

32. Beerman, "'Yo Solo,'" 174–84.

33. Ibid., 182–83; Saavedra, *Los decenios*, 227–28.

34. Corbitt, "The Administrative System in the Floridas, Part 2," 64–65.

35. Woodward, *Tribute*, xxvi.

36. Holmes, "Juan de la Villebeuvre," 387–99.

37. Navarro, "Padrón General de la isla."

38. Fuente García, "Los matrimonios," 507–28.

39. AGI, SD, Legajo 1137, September 20, 1775; Legajo 1139, December 17, 1781; and Legajo 1140, September 18, 1782; Villaverde, *Cecilia Valdés*; Borah, "Marriage and Legitimacy," 948–1008; Martínez-Alier, *Marriage, Class, and Colour*; Kutzinski, *Sugar's Secrets*; Socolow, "Acceptable Partners," 210–51; Twinam, "Honor, Sexuality, and Illegitimacy," 118–55; Szuchman, "A Challenge to the Patriarchs," 141–64.

40. Borah, "Marriage and Legitimacy," 948–1008; Ripodas Ardanáz, *El matrimonio en Indias*; Lavrin, "Women in Spanish American Colonial Society," 325–26.

41. Konetzke, "La prohibición," 105–20.

42. Ocerín, *Indice*, 1:678–79.

43. TePaske, *The Governorship of Spanish Florida*, 68.

44. Torres Ramírez, "Alejandro O'Reilly," 1357–88; Valdés, *Historia*.

45. *Reglamento para las milicias de la Isla de Cuba*, and *Reglamento del Monte Pío de viudas, huérfanos, y madres de oficialés militares, 1761, y Real Declaración de 17 de junio de 1773 del mismo reglamento para el gobierno y regímen del Monte*, Colección Cubana, Biblioteca Nacional José Martí, Havana, Cuba.

46. Domingo Cabello to Vicente de Zéspedes, EFP, reel 1, bundle 12, October 6, 1789.

47. Archer, *The Army in Bourbon Mexico*, 206–9; Holmes, *Do It! Don't Do It!*

48. ANC, Correspondencia del Capitán General, Legajo 20: 18, December 26, 1765, relayed by Julián de Arriaga, December 16, 1766; Domingo Cabello to Vicente de Zéspedes, EFP, reel 1, bundle 13, October 8, 1789; Socolow, *Bureaucrats*, 193–96.

49. Konetzke, *Colección*, 3:401, 406–13, 438–42; Lavrin, "Women in Spanish American Colonial Society," 325; Martínez-Alier, *Marriage, Class, and Colour*, 11–19; Socolow, "Acceptable Partners," 210–13.

50. ANC, Correspondencia del Capitán General, Legajo 5: 122, 1752; Marrero, *Cuba*, 13:39.

51. ANC, Correspondencia del Capitán General, Legajo 7: 192, 1754.

52. Ibid., Legajo 7: 220, 1756.

53. AGI, SD, Legajo 1596, 1754–70.

54. AGS, GM, Legajo 6880, Expediente 30, 1786; Legajo 6870, Expediente 18, 1789.

55. ANC, Correspondencia del Capitán General, 1754–70, Legajo 25: 183, December 31, 1765; AGS, GM, Legajo 7257, Expediente 15, June 30, 1769, folio 90.

56. ANC, Correspondencia del Capitán General, Legajo 25: 183, December 31, 1765.

57. Ibid., Legajo 26: 9, June 17, 1764.

58. Ibid., Legajo 26: 62, 1770; AGS, GM, Legajo 7257, Expediente 15, June 31, 1769, folios 9, 120.

59. AGI, SD, Legajo 1465, 1777.

60. ANC, Correspondencia del Capitán General, Legajo 25: 190, 1766.

61. Domingo Cabello to Vicente de Zéspedes, EFP, reel 1, bundle 13, October 6, October 8, 1789.

62. ANC, Escribanía de Guerra, July 9, 1782.

63. Ibid., March 13, 1780; AGI, PC, Legajo 1153, June 17, 1773.

64. ANC, Escribanía de Guerra, Pedro Castillo, mortgage on several city lots, May 22, 1777, for 3,250 pesos; Ursula de Avero, mortgage on a house in Havana, valued at 3,640 pesos, December 12, 1782; Antonio Betancourt, mortgage on 1⅔ caballerías of land valued at 5,000 pesos, June 14, 1783.

65. Ibid., May 28, 1788.

66. Ibid., March 23, 1781.

67. Ibid., Antonio Fernández for niece María Blanco, June 25, 1782; María Isabel Jaime for her granddaughter, January 1783 (specific date illegible).

68. For example, Francisco Xavier Sandoval, lieutenant of the Infantry of Nueva España, for Petrona Gaona, ANC, Escribanía de Guerra, January 14, 1794, "por el amor que la tengo." See also ANC, Escribanía de Guerra, José Pérez for María Dolores Hernández, August 16, 1796.

69. AGS, GM, Legajo 7223, Expediente 44, February 4, 1789.

70. ANC, Correspondencia del Capitán General, Legajo 7: 176, 1755; ANC, Escribanía de Guerra, date illegible, August 1785.

71. ANC, Escribanía de Guerra, April 26, 1781.

72. Ibid., October 9, 1782. Cf., Nazarri, *The Disappearance of the Dowry;* Lavrin and Couturier, "Dowries and Wills," 280–304.

73. ANC, Escribanía de Gobierno, July 19, 1777 for Miralles; Cummins, *Spanish Observers,* 115–67.

74. ANC, Escribanía de Gobierno, August 7, 1777.

75. ANC, Escribanía de Guerra, December 16, 1782.

76. AGI, PC, Legajo 1757, February 12, 1801.

77. Domingo Cabello to Vicente de Zéspedes, EFP, reel 1, bundle 13, October 6, October 8, 1789.

78. ANC, Escribanía de Guerra, June 5, 1788.

79. Manuel Fernández Biendicho and María Rafaela Rodríguez, Marriage Licenses, EFP, reel 132, bundle 298r9, January 13, 1785.

80. AGI, PC, Legajo 1757, May 7, 1799.

81. ANC, SD, Matrimonios, passim.

82. Ibid., 1776–79.

83. Ibid., Legajo 17: 2, 1776; Legajo 37: 3, 1777.

84. Ibid., Legajo 48: 11, 1797.

85. AGI, SD, Legajo 1466, November 9, 1779.

86. ANC, SD, Legajo 120: 4, 1785–86.

87. AGI, SD, Legajo 1473, December 5, 1788.

88. Ibid., March 1, 1788.

89. ANC, SD, Legajo 27: 2, 1785.

90. Ibid., Legajo 26: 6, 1786.

91. Ibid., Legajo 101: 8, 1781.

92. AGI, SD, Legajo 1616, September 1(?), 1787.

93. In a related study I have found that of 230 total marriages in Spanish Florida from 1784 to 1803, less than 1 percent of the couples (2/230 = 0.0086 percent) were unsuccessful in their choice of a marriage partner. Johnson, "Marriage and Community Construction," 1–13. These findings are similar to those of Socolow, "Acceptable Partners," 219–23, and Robert McCaa, "Calidad, Clase, and Marriage in Colonial Mexico," 490–91, for the eighteenth century; and Martínez-Alier, *Marriage, Class, and Colour,* 31, and Szuchman, "A Challenge to the Patriarchs," 148, for the nineteenth century.

94. There were four primary churches in Havana from 1758 to 1800: S. M. I. Catedral (formerly the Parroquia Mayor), Iglesia Santo Angel Custodio, Iglesia Santo Cristo del Buen Viaje, and Iglesia Espíritu Santo. Marriage entries for the white population (españoles) were collected from all four whenever possible, depending upon the condition of the documents. This figure is based upon an analysis of marriages that occurred between 1763—and the clear shift toward more rigid enforcement—and 1800. The books are as follows:

1. SMI, Libro 6, 1754–71, Libro 7, 1771–94, Libro 8, 1794–1812.
2. Iglesia Santo Angel Custodio, Libro 3B, February 1742–May 1770, Libro 4B, June 1770–March 1794.
3. Iglesia Santo Cristo del Buen Viaje, Libro 4, 1748–70, Libro 5, 1770–179, Libro 6, 1788–1800.
4. Iglesia Espíritu Santo, Libro 4, November 1760–June 1772, Libro 5, June 1772–November 1783, Libro 6, December 1783–November 1795.

95. Mariano de Almansa and María de Miranda, June 2, 1786, Felicitas de Almansa and Juan de Entralgo, March 30, 1797, EFP, reel 132, bundle 298r9.

96. See note 94 above.

97. Ibid., for years 1763–1800.

98. Ibid.

99. Ibid.

100. Kuethe, *Cuba*, 22–23; Delgado, "El Conde de Ricla," 69–75; Juan de Prado, "El diario de Juan de Prado," in A. Rodríguez, *Cinco diarios*, 254–55, 70–120.

101. See note 94 above.

102. Knight, "Origins of Wealth," 231–53.

103. Kuethe, *Cuba*, 244–49.

104. SMI, Libro 6, 1754–71, Libro 7, 1771–94.

105. AGS, GM, Legajo 7257, Expediente 15, June 30, 1769, folio 52; AGI, SD, Legajo 2585, May 8, 1770. I am grateful to Eugene Lyon and Jane Landers for sharing this document with me.

106. AGS, GM, Legajo 7257, Expediente 15, June 30, 1769, folio 3; SMI, Libro 6, 1754–71, Index.

107. AGS, GM, Legajo 7257, Expediente 15, June 30, 1769, folio 5.

108. Ibid., folio 47.

109. Ibid., folio 23; SMI, Libro 6, 1754–71, July 16, 1767.

110. AGS, GM, Legajo 7257, Expediente 15, June 30, 1769, folios 12, 43; SMI, Libro 7, 1771–94, March 25, 1773, May 2, 1776.

111. AGS, GM, Legajo 7257, Expediente 15, June 30, 1769, folio 53; SMI, Libro 6, 1754–71, October 17, 1766.

112. AGS, GM, Legajo 7281, Expediente 10, December 31, 1792, folio 2; SMI, Libro 7, 1771–94, May 21, 1773.

113. SMI, Libro 7, 1771–94, October 5, 1773.

114. Iglesia Santo Cristo del Buen Viaje, Libro 4, 1748–70, August 9, 1764.

115. SMI, Libro 7, 1771–94, February 24, 1782, June 17, 1782.

116. AGI, Contratacción 5489, no. 2, ramo 1, November 1, 1747; AGS, GM, Legajo 7257, Expediente 15, June 30, 1769, folio 18; Legajo 6852, Expediente 79, April 17, 1793.

117. SMI, Libro 7, 1771–94, February 24, 1782, June 17, 1782.

118. Ibid., February 13, 1773, February 16, 1776.

119. Iglesia Santo Angel Custodio, Libro 3B, February 1742–May 1770, August 2, 1767.

120. Ibid., May 6, 1767; SMI, Libro 7, 1771–94, November 3, 1781.

121. Iglesia Santo Angel Custodio, Libro 4B, June 1770–March 1794, June 29, 1782; Iglesia Santo Cristo del Buen Viaje, Libro 6, 1788–1800, November 10, 1783; Iglesia Espíritu Santo, Libro 5, June 1772–November 1783, October 24, 1774.

122. Iglesia Santo Angel Custodio, Libro 3B, February 1742–May 1770, Libro 4B, June 1770–March 1794.

123. See note 94 above.

124. SMI, Libro 7, 1771–94, January 5, 1782.

125. Ibid., April 15, 1788, November 6, 1789, March 5, 1790, among many examples.

126. Iglesia Santo Cristo del Buen Viaje, Libro 5, 1770–88, January 31, 1780.

127. Quoted in Szuchman, "A Challenge to the Patriarchs," 146.

128. Chandler, *Social Assistance;* Socolow, *Bureaucrats,* 185–91; Archer, *The Army in Bourbon Mexico,* 206–209. For the limosna de Florida, see ANC, Fondo de las Floridas, Legajo 14: 93, October 30, 1789.

129. AGI, SD, Legajo 2585, May 8, 1770, Legajo 1877, March 21, 1789; AGI, PC, Legajo 412–A, September 1, 1795; ANC, Fondo de las Floridas, Legajo 14: 93, October 30, 1789. These lists do not include the innumerable individual requests from widows, orphans, and mothers for royal assistance scattered throughout Cuban, Spanish, and Florida archives.

130. AGI, PC, Legajo 1154, August 14, 1772; October 31, 1774.

131. Ibid., April 25, 1775.

132. AGS, GM, Legajo 7223, Expediente 44, October 25, 1789.

133. Ibid., Legajo 7221, Expediente 29, September 13, 1787.

134. Ibid., Legajo 7224, Expediente 39, October 16, 1790.

135. Ibid., Legajo 7231, Expediente 71, August 18, 1798; "Primer memorial presentado por [Juan Manuel] de Viniegra al Rey . . . , July 17, 1772, Box 5, Folder 5, Del Monte Collection; AGI, PC, Legajo 1774–B, "Causa contra Matias de Armona y Juan Lleonart." I thank David Geggus for sharing with me this information on the proceeding against Armona and others.

136. AGS, GM, Legajo 7221, Expediente 31, December 20, 1787. Her husband died April 12, 1760.

137. AGI, PC, Legajo 1300, March 22, 1781.

138. AGS, GM, Legajo 6916, April 3, 1791, June 1, 1788.

139. Ibid., Legajo 6913, February 6, 1782.

140. AGI, PC, Legajo 1154, June 18, 1774.

141. Ibid., Legajo 1152, July 21, 1774.

142. ANC, Escribanía de Guerra, December 30, 1779, March 27, 1782, February 20, 1783.

143. Arrom, *Women of Mexico City,* 26.

144. Ulrich, *Good Wives,* 35–50.

145. Lavrin, "In Search of the Colonial Woman," 24–34.

146. EFP, Escrituras, reel 170, bundle 369, October 7, 1786.

147. ANC, Escribanía de Guerra, June 30, 1794.

148. Ibid., November 23, 1782.

149. EFP, Escrituras, reel 170, bundle 369, July 6, 1794.

150. ANC, Escribanía de Guerra, September 23, 1784.

151. Ibid., May 31, 1783.

152. ANC, Escribanía de Gobierno, March 31, 1767.

153. AGI, PC, Legajo 1165, December 30, 1776.

154. ANC, Escribanía de Guerra, Spetember 20, 1793.

155. AGI, SD, Legajo 1463, June 28, 1774.

156. Lynch, *Bourbon Spain,* 337.

157. Ayuntamiento de Havana to José de Gálvez, February 16, 1782, Box 4, Folder 1, Del Monte Collection.

Chapter 6. There Is No Subordination in These People

The epigraph for this chapter comes from Laura, *Parte tercera.*

1. *Elogio funebre que en las exequias que a Nuestro Catolico Monarca, el Senor Don Carlos III Hizo la muy noble y leal Ciudad de Sn Juan de Jaruco, sita en la isla de Cuba el 29 de Marzo de 1789 Dixo el P. Mro. F. Vicente Ferrer de Acosta . . .,* AGI, IG, Legajo 1608, March 29, 1789.

2. Ayuntamiento de Havana to José de Gálvez, February 16, 1782, Box 4, Folder 1, Del Monte Collection.

3. *Elogio funebre.*

4. Kuethe, *Cuba,* 132–33; Kuethe, "Havana in the Eighteenth Century," 13–39; Kuethe and Inglis, "Absolutism and Enlightened Reform," 109; Guerra y Sánchez, *Manual de historia,* 202; Moreno Fraginals, *El ingenio,* 1:66–67; Riverend Brusone, *Historia económica,* 144; Thomas, *Cuba,* 68–71; Knight, "Origins of Wealth," 231–53; Ringrose, *Spain, Europe, and the "Spanish miracle,"* 106–13.

5. Salvucci, "Anglo American Merchants," 127–33; Lewis, "Anglo American Entrepreneurs," 112–126; Lewis, "Nueva España," 501–26; Nichols, "Trade Relations," 289–313; Johnson, "Rise and Fall," 54–75.

6. Fisher, Kuethe, and McFarlane, *Reform and Insurrection;* Campbell, *Military and Society;* Phelan, *The People and the King;* McAlister, *"Fuero Militar";* Archer, *The Army in Bourbon Mexico;* Kuethe, *Cuba;* Kuethe, *Military Reform;* Florescano, *Precios de maíz.*

7. *Elogio funebre.*

8. Lynch, *Bourbon Spain,* 376–81; Ringrose, *Spain, Europe, and the "Spanish miracle,"* 112–19.

9. Barbier, "The Culmination of the Bourbon Reforms," 52.

10. Burkholder, "Council of the Indies," 404–23.

11. Lynch, *Bourbon Spain,* 380–81.

12. Barbier and Klein, "Revolutionary Wars," 315–39.

13. Lynch, *Bourbon Spain*, 382.

14. Lynch, *Bourbon Spain*, 375–421, describes Godoy as an "instant statesman," 382. See also Ringrose, *Spain, Europe, and the "Spanish miracle,"* 319; Barbier, "The Culmination of the Bourbon Reforms," 51–68; Kuethe, *Cuba*, 139–41. Kuethe describes Charles IV as "a man unable to manage even his own household," 140.

15. Lynch, *Bourbon Spain*, 388–95, 403–8.

16. Sevilla Soler, *Santo Domingo*, 377–94; Geggus, *Slavery, War, and Revolution*.

17. Lynch, *Bourbon Spain*, 376–77.

18. Box 6, Folder 1, 1775, Del Monte Collection; Torres Ramirez, *Alejandro O'Reilly en las Indias*, 10–11.

19. AGI, PC, Legajo 1154, April 23, 1774.

20. Thomas, *Cuba*, 72–73; Moreno Fraginals, *El ingenio*, 1:58–59; Calcagno, *Diccionario*, 171–74; González-Ripoll Navarro, "Voces de gobierno," 149–62.

21. González-Ripoll Navarro, "Voces de gobierno," 150; Calcagno, *Diccionario*, 173.

22. "Contribución a la historia," 35–48.

23. AGI, SD, Legajo 1476–B, March 13, 1787; Alvarez Cuartero, "Las Sociedades Económicas," 36–39; Thomas, *Cuba*, 72–73; Riverend Brusone, *Historia económica*, 261–64.

24. Misas Jiménez, "La Real Sociedad," 75–77.

25. Thomas, *Cuba*, 72–73; Riverend Brusone, *Historia económica*, 265; Guerra y Sánchez, *Manual de historia*, 1:202; Aimes, *A History of Slavery in Cuba*.

26. Moreno Fraginals, *El ingenio*, 1:39–50; Tornero Tinajero, *Crecimiento*; Ortiz, *Los negros esclavos*.

27. González-Ripoll Navarro, "Voces de gobierno," 152.

28. Fisher, *Commercial Relations*, 49, 65; Ringrose, *Spain, Europe, and the "Spanish miracle,"* 106–13; Barbier and Klein, "Revolutionary Wars," 315–39.

29. AGI, Ultramar, Legajo 120, 1789–94. See also Arango y Parreño, *Obras*; Pierson, "Francisco de Arango y Parreño," 451–78; Paquette, *Sugar Is Made with Blood*, 83–86; Moreno Fraginals, *El ingenio*, 1:51–80, 100–133.

30. The original document utilized for this research is in AGI, Ultramar, Legajo 120. Printed versions usually utilize the last or most polished version, submitted in 1792, and differ from the original in several aspects.

31. Arango y Parreño, *Obras*, 1:53–161.

32. AGI, Ultramar, Legajo 120, 1789–93.

33. Ibid., November 21, 1791.

34. Ibid., February 20, 1792.

35. On October 7, 1792, the *Papel Periódico de la Havana* reprinted an article originally appearing in the *Mercurio de España* (Madrid) that referred to the "catastrophe" in St. Domingue.

36. AGI, Ultramar, Legajo 120, November 22, 1792.

37. AGI, Estado, Legajo 16, Numero 5, November 10, 1794, Legajo 16, Numero 4, August 31, 1793.

38. AGI, PC, Legajo 1471, March 1, 1791.

39. Ibid., July 12, 1791.

40. Ibid., July 1, 1792.

41. The full text in AGI, Ultramar, Legajo 120, reads: "De los negros ahora, no hay que temer porque son pocos, hay buena guarnicion y estan mejor tratados que los del Guarico. Y desde ahora deben mirarse con cuidado las Milicias de Negros y Mulatos Libertos, establicimiento peligroso que no hai en ninguna otra colonia. Unos hombres acostumbrados al trabajo frugalidad y subordinacion son mui buenos soldados y convendrian al principio para la seguridad exterior. Pero ya bastaran para esto los blancos y no debe arriesgarse la tranquilidad interior. En qualquier conmocion serian terribles los dos batallones armados y aun mucho mas los veteranos licenciados ya y retirados a los campos. Porque aunque estos sea libres, al fin son negros y tanto menos en fiar quanto todos ellos, libres y esclavos, viven disgustados por su abastimiento entre nosotros."

42. Ibid., May 10, 1793.

43. Ibid., August 16, 1793. The four men were the Marqués del Real Socorro, Félix Texada, Francisco de Saavedra, and Bernardo de Yriarte.

44. Ibid., 1794.

45. Humboldt, *Ensayo político*, 102; Johnson, "'La Guerra,'" 181–209.

46. From Jesús María on July 15, 1790, and from Guanajay on July 16, 1790, AGI, PC, Legajo 1471.

47. *Papel Periódico de la Havana*, October 24, 1790.

48. Ibid., December 12, 1790.

49. *Ibid.*

50. AGI, PC, Legajo 1471, January 30, 1791.

51. Ibid., Legajo 1472, December 26, 1790.

52. Ibid., Legajo 1471, January 30, 1791.

53. Ibid., Legajo 1472, February 2, 1791.

54. Ibid., April 15, 1791.

55. AGI, PC, Legajo 1460, May 6, 1791.

56. Ibid., June 25, 1791, from Guanabacoa; Legajo 1470, June 22, 1791, from Prensa and Puentes Grandes, June 25, 1791, from Calvario; Legajo 1472, July 5, 1791, from Luyanó.

57. AGI, PC, Legajo 1154, November 11, 1772; Biblioteca Nacional de España, Miscellaneous Manuscripts, August 29, 1780; AGI, SD, Legajo 2609, August 24, 1780; AGI, PC, Legajo 1097, October-November 1768; Johnson, "Mercantilism Meets Mother Nature: Climate, Colonialism, Conflict, and Change in the Late Eighteenth-Century Caribbean," book manuscript in progress.

58. AGI, PC, Legajo 1472, June 27, 1791.

59. Ibid., June 28, 1791.

60. Ibid., June 28, July 5, 1791.

61. AGI, PC, Legajo 1471, October 1, 1791, Legajo 1472, March 27, 1792.

62. Ibid., Legajo 1471, October 1, 1791.

63. Ibid., Legajo 1460, August 12, 1791.

64. Ibid., September 3, 1791.

65. *Papel Periódico de la Havana,* September 25, 1791; AGI, PC, Legajo 1471, October 1, 1791

66. *Papel Periódico de la Havana,* September 25, 1791.

67. AGI, PC, Legajo 1460, November 9, 1791.

68. "Plano, elevación, y vista en perspectiva rigorosa del puente Blanco de Ricabal arruniado en el año de 1791," AGI, Mapas y Planos, Santo Domingo, 561; "Plano, pérfiles y elevación de un puente," AGI, Mapas y Planos, Santo Domingo, 562.

69. AGI, PC, Legajo 1460, November 9, 1791.

70. Ibid., Legajo 1471, August 2, 1791.

71. Ibid., January 6, 1791.

72. AGI, PC, Legajo 1460, February 18, 1792.

73. Ibid., Legajo 1471, May 7, 1792.

74. Ibid., Legajo 1470, May 31, 1791.

75. Ibid.

76. AGI, PC, Legajo 1470, June 11, 1792.

77. Ibid., June 20, 1792.

78. Ibid., April 28, 1792.

79. AGI, PC, Legajo 1472, November 6, 1792.

80. Ibid., January 21, 1793.

81. AGI, PC, Legajo 1471, May 22, 1791.

82. The censuses are missing from their respective legajos, AGI, PC, Legajos 1472 and 1471, suggesting that these captains too did not take the required enumeration.

83. *Papel Periódico de la Havana,* May 20, 1792.

84. González-Ripoll Navarro, "Voces de gobierno," 156–59.

85. ANC, Escribanía de Guerra, August (day illegible), 1785.

86. AGI, PC, Legajo 1460, November 8, 1792.

87. Ibid., Legajo 1472, October 19, 1792.

88. Ibid., October 2, 1792.

89. Ibid., June 6, 1793.

90. AGI, PC, Legajo 1471, November 22, 1792.

91. Ibid., Legajo 1460, November 21,1792.

92. Ibid., Legajo 1472, May 23, 1793.

93. Ibid., Legajo 1460, March 31, 1793.

94. Ibid., June 10, 1793.

95. AGI, SD, Legajo 1484, July 25, 1792.

96. AGI, PC, Legajo 1460, May 6, 1795.

97. Ibid., February 27, 1794.

98. AGI, PC, Legajo 1471, February 19, 1795; Legajo 1472, August 12, 1794, November 9, November 22, 1795, and March 9, 1796. See also *Papel Periódico de le Havana,* June 10, 1794; González-Ripoll Navarro, "Voces de gobierno," 153.

99. Laura, *Parte tercera.*

100. AGI, PC, Legajo 1472, April 6, 1794.

101. Ibid., Legajo 1471, May 12, May 23, 1794.

102. Ibid., Legajo 1458, September 20, 1794.

103. Ibid., Legajo 1471, January 12, 1794.

104. Ibid., April 24, 1794.

105. AGI, PC, Legajo 1472, July 26, 1794.

106. Ibid., August 9, 1794.

107. AGI, PC, Legajo 1470, December 17, 1792.

108. Ibid., May 31, 1792; Legajo 1470, September 19, 1794; Legajo 1472, November 19, 1794, and October 7, 1796; Legajo 1471, September 2, 1796.

109. AGI, PC, Legajo 1470, May 31, June 11, June 20, 1792.

110. AGI, PC, Legajo 1470, lists the following total number of inhabitants of Seiba del Agua for the years 1790–96: 1790: 2,937; 1791: 2,963; 1792: 3,048; 1793: data missing; 1794: 3,065; 1795: 668; 1796: 676.

111. AGI, PC, Legajo 1471, for Jesús del Monte's figures: 1790: 2,449; 1791 and 1792: data missing; 1793: 5,077; 1794: 4,757; 1795: 6,607; 1796: 3,237.

112. AGI, PC, Legajo 1471, July 31, 1794.

113. Ibid., Legajo 1472, November 2, 1793.

114. Ibid., June 21, 1794.

115. Ibid., September 4, 1794.

116. AGI, PC, Legajo 1471, October 28, 1794.

117. Ibid., Legajo 1472, July 27, 1793.

118. Ibid., June 25, 1796, July 23, 1796, enclosing the original dated July 29, 1789, approved by Domingo Cabello.

119. Ibid., September 7, 1796.

120. Ibid., October 18, 1796.

121. Ibid., October 25, 1796.

122. Ibid., October 26, 1796.

123. Gaspar and Geggus, *A Turbulent Time.*

124. AGI, Estado, Legajo 14, Numero 98, Expediente 3, November 12, 1794.

125. Ibid.

126. AGI, Estado, Legajo 14, Numero 99, Expediente 2, November 25, 1795.

127. Ibid., Numero 98, Expediente 3, November 12, 1794.

128. Ibid., Numero 99, Expediente 2, November 25, 1795

129. AGI, PC, Legajo 1471, April 11, 1795.

130. Ibid., Legajo 1472, April 15, 1795.

131. Ibid., Legajo 1460, June 30, 1795.

132. Ibid., Legajo 1471, June 26, 95.

133. Ibid., Legajo 1472, December 15, 1795.

134. Ibid., Legajo 1471, April 11, 1795.

135. Ibid., June 26, 1795.

136. AGI, PC, Legajo 1472, April 15, 1794.

137. Ibid., January 12, 1795.

138. Ibid., January 23, 1795.

139. Ibid., January 22, 1795.

140. AGI, PC, Legajo 1470, October 15, 1795.

141. Ibid., August (day illegible), 1794.

142. Ibid., February 5, 1795.

143. Ibid., February 5, 1795.

144. Ibid., February 3, 1795.

145. Scott, *Weapons of the Weak;* Colburn, *Everyday Forms of Peasant Resistance;* Stern, "New Approaches," 3–25.

146. Laura, *Parte tercera.*

Chapter 7. A Tyrant without Equal

1. "Relación de los meritos de Francisco Eligio de la Puente," AGI, IG, Legajo 145, Numero 79, 1733.

2. Corbitt, "Spanish Relief Policy," 67–82; Gold, "Settlement of East Florida Spaniards," 216–31.

3. AGI, SD, August 27, 1773, January 11, February 1, 1774; Cummins, *Spanish Observers,* 99–105.

4. Archivo Histórico Nacional de España, Diversos 44, Documento 76, 1777; Cummins, *Spanish Observers,* 105–67.

5. AGI, PC, Legajo 1371, March 22, 1785; AGI, SD, Legajo 1140, November 23, 1782; Cummins, *Spanish Observers,* 162.

6. AGS, GM, Legajo 6877, Expediente 48, September 28, 1792.

7. SMI, Libro 7, 1771–94, Matrimonios de Españoles, August 31, 1781.

8. AGS, GM, Legajo 6850, Expediente 45, January 26, 1792.

9. Ibid., Legajo 6877, Expediente 48, September 28, 1792.

10. Kuethe, *Cuba,* 140.

11. Ibid., 144–55.

12. AGI, PC, Legajo 1144, September 9, 1774.

13. Ibid., Legajo 1269, March 7, 1778.

14. Ibid., Legajo 1254, October 21, 1777, February 18, March 30, 1780.

15. Ibid., Legajo 1166, November 19, 1772.

16. Kuethe, *Cuba,* 163.

17. Ibid., 163–64.

18. Ibid., 166.

19. AGI, PC, Legajo 1470, February 22, 1794.

20. Ibid., Legajo 1471, November 10, 1791.

21. Ibid., Legajo 1460, March 4, 1791.

22. Kuethe, *Cuba,* 164.

23. Laura, *Parte tercera.*

24. AGI, Estado, Legajo 14, Numero 61:1, October 1, 1794.

25. AGS, GM, Legajo 6850, Expediente 45, October 19, 1790.

26. Corbitt, "Spanish Relief Policy," 74–75.

27. Ibid., 75.

28. AGI, SD, Legajo 1877, March 29, 1789.

29. "Certificación de las Familias de Florida," AGI, PC, Legajo 412–A, 1793–95.

30. Ibid., September 1, 1794.

31. Ibid., May 9, September 1, September 9, 1794.

32. Ibid., September 11, September 20, 1794.

33. Ibid., September 11, 1794.

34. AGS, GM, Legajo 7222, Expediente 55, March 2, 1788.

35. Ibid., Legajo 7225, Expediente 15, July 1, 1792.

36. Ibid., Legajo 7222, Expediente 26, October 8, 1788

37. Ibid., Legajo 6850, Expediente 45, October 19, 1790.

38. Ibid., Legajo 6849, Expediente 52, November 27, 1792.

39. AGI, SD, Legajo 1473, December 30(?), 1788.

40. Ibid.

41. AGS, GM, Legajo 6866, Expediente 15, December 31, 1791.

42. Ibid., Legajo 6848, Expediente 59, April 21, 1792.

43. AGI, PC, Legajo 1371, February 23, 1785.

44. Ibid., Legajo 1371, February 23, 1785.

45. Ibid., Legajo 1165, December 18, 1772.

46. Corbitt, "The Administrative System in the Floridas, Part 1," 45.

47. AGI, Estado, Legajo 14, Numero 104: 2, December 13, 1796.

48. AGI, PC, Legajo 1248, September 24, 1778, September 20, 1779, January 17, 1781.

49. Bacardí y Moreau, *Crónicas*, 1:248.

50. Ibid., 1:259.

51. AGI, Estado, Legajo 9, Numero 28: 2, September 20, 1791.

52. Arango y Parreño, *Obras*, 1:90–93.

53. AGI, PC, Legajo 1460, September 14, 1791; August 21, 1793; November 15, 1796.

54. AGI, Estado, Legajo 9, Numero 28: 2, September 20, 1791.

55. Ibid., November 25, 1791.

56. AGI, Estado, Legajo 9, Numero 28: 10, May 1, 1793.

57. Sevilla Soler, *Santo Domingo*, 377–89.

58. Ibid., 377–94.

59. "Copia del primer memorial presentado por [Juan Manuel] de Viniegra al Rey . . ." July 17, 1772, Box 5, Folder 5, Del Monte Collection.

60. AGI, SD, Legajo 1141, October 9, 1786, June 6, 1787; Legajo 1144, September 17, 1792; Legajo 1481, February 28, 1791; AGS, GM, Legajo 7231, Expediente 71, August 18, 1798. See also "Plazas perdidas con Juan Lleonart," AGS, Legajo 7161, Expedientes 12, 13, 15 (1794–95).

61. "Plazas perdidas con Juan Lleonart," AGS, Legajo 7161, Expedientes 12, 13, 15 (1794–95).

62. Ibid. See also AGI, PC, Legajo 1774–B, 1796, passim.

63. ANC, Escribanía de Guerra, 12 March 1793 for Antonio de Castro Palomino; 16 March 1793 for Francisco de Sotolongo; and 20 November 1793 for Francisco Xavier Sandoval.

64. Ibid., 2 March 1793 for Alonzo García Caxares and 23 December 1794 for Francisco de Oñoro.

65. AGS, GM, Legajo 6854, Expediente 2, 31 December 1794.

66. Sevilla Soler, *Santo Domingo*, 394.

67. AGI, Estado, Legajo 14, Expediente 87, February 16, 1794. Joaquín García erroneously listed Petit Tomás and Juan Francisco as "ingleses." See also Pezuela, *Historia*, 3:248–49.

68. Sevilla Soler, *Santo Domingo*, 394; Landers, "Rebellion and Royalism," 161–64.

69. AGS, GM, Legajo 6876, Expediente 54, 28 November 1796.

70. Sevilla Soler, *Santo Domingo*, 393.

71. AGS, GM, Legajo 6877, Expediente 49, September 9, 1797.

72. AGI, Estado, Legajo 14, Numero 98:1, Numero 98:2, November 12, 1794.

73. *Papel Periódico de la Havana*, November 24, 1794.

74. Luis de Las Casas, "Bando sobre el real decreto el 16 de febrero de 1795 indultando a los profugos del ejército," Biblioteca Nacional José Martí, Colección Cubana, also quoted in González-Ripoll Navarro, "Voces de gobierno," 155.

75. AGS, GM, Legajo 6876, Expediente 54, November 30, 1796.

76. Laura, *Parte tercera.*

77. AGI, Estado, Legajo 18, Numero 9:1, February 20, 1795.

78. Joaquín García to Juan Bautista Valliant, March 16, 1794, Biblioteca Nacional de España, Manuscritos, Documentos Varios de Cuba.

79. AGI, Estado, Legajo 14, Numero 44, October 30, 1793.

80. García to Valliant. March 16, 1794.

81. Box 6, Folder 1, 1775, Del Monte Collection.

82. AGI, PC, Legajo 1774–B, 1796, passim.

83. Pezuela, *Historia*, 248–49, 255–56.

84. AGI, Estado, Legajo 18, Numero 9:1, February 23, 1795.

85. AGS, GM, Legajo 6876, Expediente 54, December 2, 1796.

86. Ibid., Legajo 7233, Expediente 2, May 26, 1791.

87. For du Bouchet, see AGS, GM, Legajo 6849, Expediente 52, November 27, 1792; for Aldana, see AGS, GM, Legajo 6932, Expediente 1, August 26, 1789, Legajo 6914, Expediente 32, October 30, 1787.

88. AGS, GM, Legajo 7248, Expediente 2, May 26, 1784, Legajo 7153, Expediente 15, June 12, 1797.

89. ANC, Escribanía de Guerra, November 5, 1795.

90. AGI, Estado, Legajo 5A, Numero 53: 2, March 30, 1795, Numero 53: 10, April 15, 1795.

91. AGI, Estado, Legajo 9, Numero 28: 10, May 1, 1793; Legajo 14, Numero 44: 1, October 30, 1793, Numero 104:1, 1797, Numero 104: 2, December 13, 1796; Corbitt, "The Administrative System in the Floridas, Part 1," 44.

92. González-Ripoll Navarro, "Voces de gobierno," 161.

93. AGI, Estado, Legajo 5A, Numero 53: 22, n.d.

94. Ibid., Numero 53: 21, May 2, 1795; Bacardí, *Crónicas,* 275.

95. Ibid., 276.

96. AGI, PC, Legajo 1438, March 9, 1795.

97. Ibid., March 15–August 6, 1795.

98. AGI, SD, Legajo 2551, July 29, 1786; AGS, GM, Legajo 7233, Expediente 2, May 26, 1791.

99. EFP, reel 18, bundle 47H4, July 13, 1793.

100. AGS, GM, Legajo 6876, Expediente 54, November 30, 1796; Torres Cuevas, *Félix Varela,* 36–37.

101. AGI, PC, Legajo 1438, March 9, April 27, April 30, 1795.

102. Ibid., Legajo 1154, September 19, 1776, for de la Torre; AGS, GM, Legajo 6918, Expediente 16, July 13, 1795.

103. AGS, GM, Legajo 6918, Expediente 16, July 13, 1795.

104. AGI, PC, Legajo 1436, November 13, 1794.

105. AGS, GM, Legajo 6918, Expediente 16, July 13, 1795.

106. Laura, *Parte tercera.*

107. Ibid.

108. EFP, reel 124, bundle 287, May 18, 1796.

109. AGI, Estado, Legajo 5A, Numero 53: 16, n.d.

110. Ibid., Numero 53: 22, n.d.

111 Ibid., Numero 53: 16, n.d.

112. ANC, Asuntos Políticos, Legajo 5: 6, July 14, July 17, July 23, 1795; also in *BAN* 40 (January–December 1941): 59–62.

113. Laura, *Parte tercera.*

114. AGI, Estado, Legajo 17, Numero 18:1, January 18, 1795.

115. Kuethe, *Cuba,* 144–55.

116. Bacardí, *Crónicas,* 276–77.

117. AGI, Estado, Legajo 14, Numero 61: 1, October 1, 1794.

118. Ibid., Legajo 16, Numero 16, October 20, 1796.

119. Laura, *Parte tercera.*

Chapter 8. An Ungrateful People

1. *Papel Periódico de la Havana,* October 7, 1792. For an analysis of the anomalous lack of slave rebellions, see Geggus, "Slave Resistance in the Spanish Caribbean," 131–55. The original documentation for the Puerto Príncipe "uprising" is in AGI, Estado, Legajo 5A, Numero 15, August 14, August 18, 1795.

2. Laura, *Parte tercera;* Jensen, *Children of Colonial Despotism.*

3. Laura, *Parte tercera.*

4. Ibid.

5. Ibid. The text reads, "Y como al mismo tiempo contiene una apologia de mi persona y conducta, relativamente a la parte que he tenido en la execución de algunas disposiciones de V. E. en impugnación de innumerables papeles con que han procurado mancillar mi buen nombre las muchas gentes que viven resentidas de la pureza e integridad con que me he conducido."

6. Ibid.

7. Ibid.

8. Guerra y Sánchez, *Manual de historia,* 207–8.

9. Nieto y Cortadellas, *Dignidades nobilarias,* 496–99, 520–21; Kuethe, *Cuba,* 152–54; Marrero, *Cuba,* 13:254.

10. Kuethe, *Cuba,* 152–54; Moreno Fraginals, *El ingenio,* 1:58, 100–101; Marrero, *Cuba,* 13:254–57.

11. Kuethe, *Cuba,* 154; Marrero, *Cuba,* 13:251–54, 260.

12. Marrero, *Cuba,* 13:262 note x. The comment was appropriated by Jacobo de la Pezuela, who wrote of the "bad impression such monstrous prerogatives gave to the people." Pezuela, *Historia,* 3:289–90.

13. Kuethe, *Cuba,* 153; Marrero, *Cuba,* 13:251.

14. Nieto y Cortadellas, *Dignidades nobiliarias,* 495–99.

15. Jacinto Barreto, Conde de Casa Barreto, to Joaquín Beltrán de Santa Cruz, Conde de Jaruco, April 28, 1789, in Barreto, *Contestación,* 25.

16. AGS, GM, Legajo 6877, Expediente 48, January 3, 1798; Expediente 49, September 9, 1797.

17. AGS, GM, Legajo 6866, Expediente 15, January 4, 1798.

18. Ibid., Legajo 6874, Expediente 10, September 3, 1795.

19. "Testimonio . . . de Pedro Benet," ANC, Asuntos Políticos, Legajo 7, May 1799 (also in *BAN* 40 [January-December 1941]: 90), for Cabello; AGS, GM, Legajo 6919, Expediente 8, February 27, 1797, for Quesada.

20. AGI, PC, Legajo 1460, November 26, 1796.

21. AGS, GM, Legajo 7231, Expediente 71, August 18, 1798; ANC, Escribanía de Guerra, June 6, 1797; AGI, PC, Legajo 156–A, June 20, 1805.

22. AGI, Estado, Legajo 18, Numero 9:1, February 23, 1795; AGS, GM, Legajo 7161, Expediente 15, August 6, 1794, Legajo 6866, Expediente 9, December 31, 1799.

23. AGI, Estado, Legajo 11B, Numero 40, 1797.

24. AGS, GM, Legajo 6919, Expediente 8, February 27, 1797.

25. Ibid., Legajo 6918, Expediente 16, July 13, 1795.

26. EFP, Reel 67, Bundle 160D13; November (day illegible), 1801.

27. AGS, GM, Legajo 7153, Expediente 15, June 12, 1797.

28. Torres Cuevas's contention that Varela's family was of the petit bourgeoisie seems unfounded. Torres Cuevas, *Félix Varela,* 285.

29. José Francisco Lemus, quoted in Marrero, *Cuba*, 13:92, and in Varela y Morales, *El habanero*, xvii.

30. Torres Cuevas, *Félix Varela*, 37.

31. Morales y Morales, *Iniciadores*, 1:33–36; Ponte Domínguez, *La junta de la Habana*, 37–47; Riverend Brusone, *Historia económica*, 210–13, 219–21; Johnson, "Rise and Fall," 54–75.

32. Morales y Morales, *Iniciadores*, 1:33; Ponte Domínguez, *La junta de la Habana*, 28–33, 43, 61–66; Kuethe, *Cuba*, 154–62.

33. Morales y Morales, *Iniciadores*, 1:33; Ponte Domínguez, *La junta de la Habana*, 51–60, 63–72, 92–96.

34. Kuethe, *Cuba*, 155–62.

35. Ibid., 154; Marrero, *Cuba*, 13:261.

36. Barreto, *Contestación*.

37. Marrero, *Cuba*, 13:39.

38. AGI, SD, Legajo 1135, May 25, 1767, Legajo 1138, September 18, 1776.

39. Barreto, *Contestación*.

40. AGI, SD, Legajo 1480, July 2, 1791.

41. Ibid., Legajo 1487, June 23, 1795.

42. AGI, Estado, Legajo 8: Numero 14, August 7, 1796; Ponte Domínguez, *La junta de la Habana*, 52–53.

43. Barreto, *Contestación*.

44. Rivero Muñíz, *Tabaco*, 2:201–5; Ponte Domínguez, *La Junta de la Habana*, 67.

45. Rivero Múñiz, *Tabaco*, 2:201–5; Guerra y Sánchez, *Manual de historia*, 205.

46. "Documentos para la historia económica y social de Cuba," *BAN* 53–54 (1953–54): 280–83.

47. Ibid., 283–84.

48. Rivero Múñiz, *Tabaco*, 2:201–205.

49. Moreno Fraginals, *El ingenio*, 58.

50. Ponte Domínguez, *La junta de la Habana*, 67.

51. Ibid., 43; Kuethe, *Cuba*, 157–58.

52. Pezuela, *Historia*, 3:381.

53. Ibid., 3:384–95; Ponte Domínguez, *La junta de la Habana*, 51–52; Kuethe, *Cuba*, 160.

54. Pezuela, *Historia*, 3:384–85.

55. Santa Cruz y Mallén, *Historia de Familias Cubanas*, 3:219.

56. Nieto y Cortadellas, *Dignidades nobilarias*, 310.

57. AGI, SD, Legajo 1466, February 29, 1780.

58. Nieto y Cortadellas, *Dignidades nobilarias*, 144–45.

59. Ibid., 578–79.

60. Pezuela, *Historia*, 3:381; Kuethe, *Cuba*, 160.

61. Kuethe, *Cuba*, 161.

62. Marqués de Someruelos, *Proclama: Habitantes de la Isla de Cuba. Hijos*

Dignos de la Generosa Nación Española, July 17, 1808; *Nobilisimos Habitantes de la Ciudad de Cuba*, December 14, 1808, Despatches of United States Consuls in Havana, Microfilm, Roll T-20, National Archives and Records Administration, Washington D.C.

63. *Gazeta Diaria*, June 17, 1812, reprinted in Zaragosa, *Las insurrecciones en Cuba*, 2:713–15; Pezuela, *Historia*, 3:395–97, maintains that "la solo voz del Brigadier Montalvo" ("the lone voice of Brigadier Montalvo") was necessary to bring quiet back to the city.

64. Pezuela, *Historia*, 3:397.

65. Ponte Domínguez, *La junta de la Habana*, 89–96.

66. Villaverde, *Cecilia Valdés*, 99.

67. Knight, *Slave Society in Cuba*.

68. Publications such as Louis Du Broca's *Vida de J. J. Dessalines Gefe de los Negros de Santo Domingo, con notas muy circunstancias sobre el origen, caracter y atrocidades de los principales gefes de aquellos rebeldes desde el principio de la insurrección en 1791*, traducida del Francés por D.M.G.C. (Mexico: 1806), fed Creoles' fears.

69. Varela y Morales, *El habanero*; Torres Cuevas, *Félix Varela*; García, *Bibliografía*.

70. Paquette, *Sugar Is Made with Blood*, 169–71, 219, is the most comprehensive analysis of Sentmanat's involvement in Cuba to date.

71. Ibid., 169–71, 219, 247, 261.

72. Iglesia Santo Cristo del Buen Viaje, Libro 5, 1770–88, Matrimonios de Españoles, February 22, 1785.

73. *Papel Periódico de la Havana*, July 21, 1794. Sentmanat was among the first to join, superseding such better-known members as Bernabé Martínez de Pinillos, Andrés de Jauregui, Tomás Romay, and Pedro Pablo O'Reilly, all supporters of the junta of 1808. The importance of one's rank in the society is evident in that the names are presented "en orden de su antigüedad" ("in the order of their seniority").

74. Pezuela, *Historia*, 3:309.

75. "Declaración de D. Alonso Benigño Muñoz," in Barreto, *Contestación*, 18.

76. Academia de Ciencias de Cuba, *Perfil histórico*, 106–16; Nieto y Cortadellas, *Dignidades nobilarias*, 110–11.

77. Villaverde, *Cecilia Valdés*, 99. See also Paquette, *Sugar Is Made with Blood*, 113, and its endnote, 302; and Méndez Rodenas, *Gender and Nationalism in Colonial Cuba*.

78. See, for example, the testaments of Bernardo Josef Carillo de Albornóz, March 13, 1780; Francisco de Alcazár, May 24, 1784; and Tomás García, July 3, 1794, all ANC, Escribanía de Guerra.

79. Pezuela, *Diccionario* and *Historia*, and Sagra, *Historia económica-política*, are among the best-known examples.

80. Paquette, *Sugar Is Made With Blood*, 171; Torres Cuevas, *Félix Varela*, 277, 323.

81. Mendéz Rodenas, *Gender and Nationalism in Colonial Cuba*, 144–48; Paquette, *Sugar Is Made with Blood*, 86–89.

82. Del Monte Collection, Library of Congress, Manuscript Division, Washington, D.C., passim; Fé Iglesias García, personal communication to author.

83. Laura, *Parte tercera*, for 1790, and Varela, *El habanero*, after 1825.

84. See the many examples in Varela, *El habanero*, especially concerning the inability of the island to unite in opposition to Spain's arbitrary government, 75–83, 105–9, 161–67.

Chapter 9. La Voz Sagrada del Pueblo

1. AGI, PC, Legajo 1460, May 6, 1795.

2. AGI, Estado, Legajo 5A, Numero 53: 16, n.d.

3. Klein, *Slavery in the Americas*, 150.

4. Villaverde, *Cecilia Valdés*; Martínez-Alier, *Marriage, Class, and Colour*; Deschamps Chapeaux, *El negro en la economía habanera*; Klein, *Slavery in the Americas*, 194–227; Kuethe, *Cuba*, 123–26; Paquette, *Sugar Is Made with Blood*, 251; Kutzinski, *Sugar's Secrets*.

5. Szeminski, "Why Kill the Spaniard?," 166–67.

6. Ibarra, *Ideología mambisa*.

References

Manuscript Sources

Archivo General de Indias, Seville, Spain

Audiencia de Santo Domingo
Contratacción
Correos
Estado
Indiferente General
Mapas y Planos
Papeles Procedentes de Cuba
Ultramar

Archivo General de Simancas, Simancas, Spain

Archivo Histórico Nacional de España Diversos
Secretaría de Guerra Moderna

Biblioteca Nacional de España, Madrid, Spain

Manuscript Collection

Archivo Nacional de Cuba, Havana, Cuba

Asuntos Políticos
Audiencia de Santo Domingo
Correspondencia del Capitán General
Escribanía de Gobierno
Escribanía de Guerra
Fondo de las Floridas
Gobierno General
Realengos, Extramuros

Biblioteca Nacional de Cuba José Martí, Havana, Cuba

Colección Cubana
Colección Vidal Morales y Morales
Mapas y Planos
Papel Periódico de la Havana

Archivo del Arzobispo de la Habana, Havana, Cuba

Correspondencia del Obispo de la Habana, 1788–98

Archivos Parroquiales

Iglesia Espíritu Santo, Havana, Cuba
Iglesia Nuestra Señora de la Asunción, Guanabacoa, Cuba
Iglesia Santo Angel Custodio, Havana, Cuba
Iglesia Santo Cristo del Buen Viaje, Havana, Cuba
S. M. I. Catedral de la Habana, Havana, Cuba

City Council of Guanabacoa, Guanabacoa, Cuba

Records of the City Council of Guanabacoa, Book 3, 1754–64

Houghton Library, Harvard University, Cambridge, Massachusetts

José Escoto Collection

Library of Congress, Washington, D.C.

Manuscript Division:
        Cuba Miscellany
        Domingo del Monte Collection
        East Florida Papers
Map Collection
Rare Books and Pamphlets

National Archives and Records Administration, Washington, D.C.

Despatches of United States Consuls in Havana

Diocese of St. Augustine Catholic Center, Jacksonville, Florida

Cathedral Parish Records, 1784–1821

P. K. Yonge Library Special Collections, University of Florida, Gainesville, Florida

East Florida Papers (microfilm)
Latin American Collection
Papeles de Cuba (microfilm)
Rare Book Collection
Stetson Collection (microfilm and typescripts)

Florida International University, Miami, Florida
Levi Marrero Collection

Printed Primary Sources

Archivo General de Indias. *Colección de documentos inéditos para la historia de hispano-américa.* 15 vols. Madrid: Compañía Ibero-Americana de Publicaciones, 1927–32.

Archivo Nacional de Cuba. "Documentos para la historia económica y social de Cuba." *Boletín del Archivo Nacional de Cuba,* 53–54 (1953–1954): 264–85.

———. *Papeles sobre la toma de la Habana por los ingleses en 1762.* Havana: Archivo Nacional de Cuba, 1948.

Arriaga, Julián. "Sobre la libertad de los negros esclavos que se distinguieron durante el sitio de la Habana por los ingleses en 1762." *Boletín del Archivo Nacional de Cuba* 16 (1915): 211.

Cabello, Manuel. "Testimonio . . . de Pedro Benet" (May 1799). *Boletín del Archivo Nacional de Cuba* 40 (January-December 1941): 90.

Funes de Villapando, Ambrosio, Conde de Ricla, to Miguel de Altarriba, May 14, 1765. *Boletín del Archivo Nacional de Cuba* 43 (1944): 120.

Gálvez, Bernardo de. *"Yo Solo": The Battle Journal of Bernardo de Gálvez during the American Revolution.* Introduction by Eric Beerman. New Orleans: Polyanthos, 1978.

Garciny, Vicente de, to Marqués de la Torre, May 16, 1777. *Boletín del Archivo Nacional de Cuba* 16 (1915): 212.

Knowles, Charles. "Description of the Havana, 1761–1762." *Boletín del Archivo Nacional de Cuba* 37–38 (1941): 26–27.

Navarro, Diego José. "Bando de Buen Gobierno." *Boletín del Archivo Nacional de Cuba* 28 (1949): 79.

———. "Bando sobre que se destechen las Casas de Guano, o Yaguas qe. estén dentro de la Ciudad." *Boletín del Archivo Nacional de Cuba* 28 (1929): 83–84.

———. "Estracto del padrón general de havitantes de la isla de Cuba." *Revista de la Biblioteca Nacional José Martí* 29 (September-December 1987): 25.

———. "Padrón General de la isla de Cuba formado a consecuencia de Real Orden de 1o. de noviembre de 1776." *Revista de la Biblioteca Nacional José Martí* 29 (September-December 1987): 17–24.

O'Reilly, Alejandro, to Julián de Arriaga, April 12, 1764. Archivo General de Indias, Santo Domingo, Legajo 1509. Also in Levi Marrero, *Cuba, Economía y sociedad,* 14 vols. 8:262–67 (Madrid: Playor, SA, 1972–1988).

Rodriguez, Rafael. *Plano topográfico, histórico, y estadístico de la ciudad y puerto de la Habana.* Havana: Real Sociedad Patriótica, 1841.

Tribunal de Cuentas de Cuba. "Sobre la compra y pago de terrenos y solares extramuros de esta Ciudad." Archivo Nacional de Cuba, Expediente 1334, Libro

6, Foxas 224, 1773. Also in *Boletín del Archivo Nacional de Cuba* 10 (May-June 1911): 129–59.

Secondary Sources

Academia de Ciencias de Cuba. *La esclavitud en Cuba.* Havana: Editorial Académica, 1986.

———. *Perfil histórico de las letras cubanas desde los orígines hasta 1898.* Havana: Editorial Letras Cubanas, 1983.

Acosta, Antonio, and Juan Marchena Fernandez, eds. *La influencia de España en el Caribe, la Florida, y la Luisiana, 1500–1800.* Madrid: Instituto de Cooperación Iberoamericana, 1983.

Aimes, Hubert H. S. *A History of Slavery in Cuba, 1511–1868.* New York: G. P. Putnam's Sons, 1907.

Aiton, Arthur S. "Spanish Colonial Reorganization under the Family Compact." *Hispanic American Historical Review* 12 (August 1932): 269–80.

Alston, Richard. *Soldier and Society in Roman Egypt: A Social History.* London: Routledge, 1995.

Altman, Ida. *Emigrants and Society: Extremadura and Spanish America in the Sixteenth Century.* Berkeley: University of California Press, 1989.

Altman, Ida, and James Horn, eds. *To Make America: European Emigration in the Early Modern Period.* Berkeley: University of California Press, 1991.

Alvarez Cuartero, Izaskun. "Las Sociedades Económicas de Amigos del País en Cuba (1787–1832): Una Aportación al Pensamiento Ilustrado." In *Cuba: la perla de las Antillas: Actas de las I Jornadas sobre "Cuba y su Historia,"* ed. Consuelo Naranjo Orovio y Tomás Mallo González, 34–43. Madrid: Editorial Doce Calles, S.I., 1994.

Andreski, Stanislas. *Military Organization and Society.* Berkeley: University of California Press, 1968.

Arango y Parreño, Francisco de. *Obras.* 2 vols. Havana: Dirección de Cultura, Ministerio de Educacción, 1952.

Archer, Christon. *The Army in Bourbon Mexico, 1760–1810.* Albuquerque: University of New Mexico Press, 1977.

Armona, José Antonio de. *Noticias privadas de casa útiles para mis hijos (Recuerdos del Madrid de Carlos III).* Edición, introducción, y notas de Joaquín Alvarez Barrientos, Emilio Palacios Fernández, y María del Carmen Sánchez García. Madrid: Ayuntamiento de Madrid, 1988.

Arnade, Charles W. "The Avero Story: An Early St. Augustine Family with Many Daughters and Many Houses." *Florida Historical Quarterly* 40 (July 1961): 3–32.

Arrate, José Martín Félix de. *Llave del nuevo mundo: antemural de las indias occidentales.* 4th ed. Havana: Comisión Nacional Cubana de UNESCO, 1964.

Arrom, Silvia Marina. *The Women of Mexico City, 1790–1857.* Stanford: Stanford University Press, 1985.

Bacardí y Moreau, Emilio, comp. *Crónicas de Santiago de Cuba*. Ed. Amalia Bacardí Cape. 10 vols. Madrid: Gráficas Breogán, 1924.

Baker, Maury, and Margaret Bissler Haas, eds. "Bernardo de Gálvez's Combat Diary for the Battle of Pensacola 1781." *Florida Historical Quarterly* 56 (October 1977): 176–99.

Balmori, Diana A., Stuart Voss, and Miles Wortmann. *Notable Family Networks in Latin America*. Chicago: University of Chicago Press, 1984.

Barbier, Jacques A. "The Culmination of the Bourbon Reforms, 1787–1792." *Hispanic American Historical Review* 57 (February 1977): 51–68.

———. *Reform and Politics in Bourbon Chile, 1755–1796*. Ottawa: University of Ottawa Press, 1980.

Barbier, Jacques A., and Herbert S. Klein. "Revolutionary Wars and Public Finances: The Madrid Treasury, 1784–1807." *Journal of Economic History* 41 (June 1981): 315–39.

Barbier, Jacques A., and Allan J. Kuethe, eds. *The North American Role in the Spanish Imperial Economy, 1764–1819*. Manchester, England: Manchester University Press, 1984.

Barreto, José Francisco. *Contestación al impreso del Sr. Conde de O'Reilly*. Havana: Imprenta de D. Pedro Nolasco Palmer, 1812. Copy in Rare Book Room Collection, Special Collections, University of Florida, Gainesville, Fla.

Beerman, Eric. "Arturo O'Neill: First Governor of West Florida during the Second Spanish Period." *Florida Historical Quarterly* 60 (July 1981): 29–41.

———. "José de Ezpeleta." *Revista de Historia Militar* 21 (1977): 97–118.

———. "'Yo Solo' Not Solo: Juan Antonio de Riaño." *Florida Historical Quarterly* 58 (October 1979): 174–84.

Berthe, Jean-Pierre. "La Habana del fines del siglo XVII vista por un italiano, Gemelli Careri." *Revista de la Biblioteca Nacional José Martí* (May-August 1971): 63–86.

Bitlloch, Eduardo. "Trabajo, inmigración y colonización en Cuba, 1789–1847." *Siglo XIX* 3 (July-December 1988): 109–43.

Borah, Woodrow W. "Marriage and Legitimacy in Mexican Culture: Mexico and California." *California Law Review* 54 (May 1966): 948–1008.

Bourde, Guy. "Fuentes y métodos de la historia demográfica en Cuba, siglo XVIII y XIX." Trans. Aurelio Cortes. *Revista de la Biblioteca Nacional José Martí* 16 (1974): 21–68.

Burkholder, Mark A. "The Council of the Indies in the Late Eighteenth Century: A New Perspective." *Hispanic American Historical Review* 56 (August 1976): 404–23.

Burkholder, Mark A., and David S. Chandler. *From Impotence to Authority: The Spanish Crown and the American Audiencias, 1687–1810*. Columbia, Mo.: University of Missouri Press, 1977.

Calcagno, Francisco de. *Diccionario biográfico Cubano*. Facsimile ed. Miami: Ediciones Cubanas, 1996.

Calendario manual y guía de forasteros de la Isla de Cuba para el año 1795. Havana: Imprenta de la Capitanía General, 1795; facsimile ed., Miami: Ediciones Cubanas, 1990.

Campbell, Leon G. *The Military and Society in Colonial Peru, 1750–1810.* Philadelphia: American Philosophical Society, 1978.

———. "Recent Research on Andean Peasant Revolts, 1750–1820." *Latin American Research Review* 14 (January 1979): 3–49.

Carr, Peter. *Censos, padrones, y matrículas de la población de Cuba, Siglos 16, 17 & 18.* San Luis Obispo, Ca.: Cuban Index, 1993.

Castillo Meléndez, Francisco. "Población y defensa de la isla de Cuba, 1650–1700." *Anuario de estudios americanos* 44 (1987): 1–87.

Caughey, John Walton. *Bernardo de Gálvez in Louisiana, 1776–1783.* Berkeley: University of California Press, 1934.

Cepero Bonilla, Raúl. *Azúcar y abolición.* Havana: Editorial Cenit, 1948; reprint ed., Barcelona: Editorial Crítica, 1976.

Chance, John R. *Race and Class in Colonial Oaxaca.* Stanford: Stanford University Press, 1978.

Chance, John R., and William B. Taylor. "Estate and Class in a Colonial City: Oaxaca in 1792." *Comparative Studies in Society and History* 19 (1977): 486–87.

Chandler, D. S. *Social Assistance and Bureaucratic Politics: The Montepíos of Colonial Mexico, 1767–1821.* Albuquerque: University of New Mexico Press, 1991.

Chatelain, Verne E. *The Defenses of Spanish Florida to 1763.* Washington, D.C.: Carnegie Institution of Washington, 1941.

Coker, William S., and Robert R. Rea, eds. *Anglo-Spanish Confrontation on the Gulf Coast during the American Revolution.* Pensacola: Gulf Coast History and Humanities Conference, 1982.

Colburn, Forrest, ed. *Everyday Forms of Peasant Resistance.* Armonk, N.Y.: M. E. Sharpe, 1989.

"Contribución a la historia de la prensa periódica." *Boletín del Archivo Nacional* 32 (January-December 1933): 35–48.

Cook, N. David. *Born to Die: Disease and New World Conquest.* Cambridge: Cambridge University Press, 1997.

Cook, Sherburne F., and Woodrow Borah. *Essays in Population History: Mexico and the Caribbean.* 3 vols. Berkeley: University of California Press, 1971–79.

Corbett, Theodore G. "Migration to a Spanish Imperial Frontier in the Seventeenth and Eighteenth Centuries: St. Augustine." *Hispanic American Historical Review* 54 (August 1974): 415–16.

Corbitt, Duvon Clough. "The Administrative System in the Floridas, 1783–1821, Part 1." *Tequesta* 1 (1942): 41–62.

———. "The Administrative System in the Floridas, 1783–1821, Part 2." *Tequesta* 2 (1943): 57–67.

———. "Immigration in Cuba." *Hispanic American Historical Review* 22 (1944): 280–97.

————. "*Mercedes* and *Realengos:* A Survey of the Public Land System in Cuba." *Hispanic American Historical Review* 19 (August 1939): 269–74.

————. "Spanish Relief Policy and the East Florida Refugees of 1763." *Florida Historical Quarterly* 27 (July 1948): 67–82.

Cummins, Light Townsend. *Spanish Observers and the American Revolution, 1775–1783.* Baton Rouge: Louisiana State University Press, 1991.

Dana, Richard H. *To Cuba and Back: A Vacation Voyage.* Boston, 1859; reprint ed., Carbondale: Southern Illinois University Press, 1966.

Deagan, Kathleen. *Spanish St. Augustine, 1700–1763: The Archaeology of a Colonial Creole Community.* New York: Academic Press, 1983.

Deive, Carlos Esteban. *Las emigraciones Dominicanas a Cuba, 1795–1808.* Santo Domingo, Dominican Republic: Fundación Cultural Dominicana, 1989.

Delgado, Jaime. "El Conde de Ricla, capitán general de Cuba." *Revista de historia de américa* 55–56 (1963): 41–138.

Deschamps Chapeaux, Pedro. *El negro en la economía habanera del siglo XIX.* Havana: Insitituto Cubano del Libro, 1971.

Domínguez, Jorge I. *Insurrection or Loyalty: The Breakdown of the Spanish American Empire.* Cambridge, Mass.: Harvard University Press, 1980.

Du Broca, Louis. *Vida de J. J. Dessalines Gefe de los Negros de Santo Domingo, con notas muy circunstancias sobre el origen, caracter y atrocidades de los principales gefes de aquellos rebeldes desde el principio de la insurreccion en 1791.* Traducida del Francés por D.M.G.C. Mexico City: Oficina de D. Mariano de Zúñiga y Ontiveros, 1806. Copy in Latin American Pamphlets, Rare Book Room, Library of Congress, Washington, D.C.

Enciclopedia de Cuba, vol. 7: *Municipios: Pinar del Río, La Habana, Matanzas.* San Juan: Enciclopedia y Clásicos Cubanos, 1973.

Farriss, Nancy M. *Crown and Clergy in Colonial Mexico, 1759–1821.* London: University of London, Athelone Press, 1968.

Fernández Santalices, Manuel. *Las calles de la Habana intramuros: arte, historia y tradiciones en las calles y plazas de la Habana vieja.* Miami: Saeta Ediciones, 1985.

Ferrer, Ada. *Insurgent Cuba: Race, Nation, and Revolution, 1868–1898.* Chapel Hill: University of North Carolina Press, 1999.

Ferrer del Río, Antonio. *Historia del reinado de Carlos III en españa.* 4 vols. Madrid: Imprenta de las Señores Matuti y Compagni, 1856; facsimile ed., Madrid: Comunidad de Madrid Consejería de Cultura, 1988.

Fisher, John R. *Commercial Relations between Spain and Spanish America in the Era of Free Trade.* Liverpool, England: Center for Latin American Studies, University of Liverpool, 1985.

————. *Government and Society in Colonial Peru: The Intendant System, 1784–1814.* London: University of London, Athelone Press, 1970.

————. "Imperial 'Free Trade' and the Hispanic Economy." *Journal of Latin American Studies* 13 (May 1981): 21–56.

Fisher, John R., Allan J. Kuethe, and Anthony McFarlane, eds. *Reform and Insurrection in Bourbon New Granada and Peru.* Baton Rouge: Louisiana State University Press, 1990.

Florescano, Enrique. *Precios de maíz y crisis agrícola en México (1708–1810).* 2nd. ed. Mexico City: Ediciones Era, 1986.

Fuente García, Alejandro de la. "Los matrimonios de esclavos en La Habana, 1585–1645." *Ibero-Amerikanisches Archiv* 16 (1990): 507–28.

García, Enildo A., ed. *Bibliografía de Félix Varela Morales, 1788–1853.* New York: Senda Nueva de Ediciones, 1991.

García Rodríguez, Mercedes. "Presencia Jesuita en la economía de Cuba: Siglo XVIII." Ph.D. diss., University of Havana, 1999.

Gascón, Margarita. "The Military of Santo Domingo, 1720–1764." *Hispanic American Historical Review* 73 (August 1993): 431–52.

Gaspar, David Barry, and David Patrick Geggus, eds. *A Turbulent Time: The French Revolution and the Greater Caribbean.* Bloomington: Indiana University Press, 1997.

Gavira, Carmen. "La configuración del espacio colonial en Cuba (Estudio del sistema urbano en los siglos XVII y XVIII)." *Revista de la Biblioteca Nacional José Martí* 24 (January-August 1982): 63–95.

Gay-Calbó, Enrique. *Arango y Parreño: Ensayo de interpretación de la realidad económica de Cuba.* Havana: Imprenta Molina y Cía, 1938.

———. *El ideario politico de Varela.* Havana: Biblioteca Municipal de La Habana, 1936.

———. *El padre Varela en las cortes españolas de 1822–23.* Havana: Imprenta y Papelería de Rambla, Bouza y Ca., 1937.

Geggus, David Patrick. "The Enigma of Jamaica in the 1790s: New Light on the Causation of Slave Rebellions." *William and Mary Quarterly* (3rd. ser.) 44 (April 1987): 274–99.

———. "Slave Resistance in the Spanish Caribbean in the Mid-1790s." In *A Turbulent Time: The French Revolution and the Greater Caribbean,* ed. David Barry Gaspar and David Patrick Geggus, 131–55. Bloomington: Indiana University Press, 1997.

———. *Slavery, War and Revolution: The British Occupation of St. Domingue, 1793–1798.* Oxford: Oxford University Press, 1982.

Gold, Robert L. "Politics and Property During the Transfer of Florida from Spanish to English Rule, 1763–1764." *Florida Historical Quarterly* 42 (July 1963): 16–34.

———. "The Settlement of East Florida Spaniards in Cuba, 1763–1766." *Florida Historical Quarterly* 42 (January 1964): 216–31.

Gomis Blanco, Alberto. "Las ciencias naturales en la expedición del Conde de Mopox a Cuba." In *La ciencia española en ultramar: Actas de las I Jornadas sobre "España y las expediciones científicas en América i Filipinas,"* coord. by Alejandro R. Díez Torre, Tomás Mallo, Daniel Pacheco, and Angeles Alonso Flecha, 308–19. Madrid: Doce Calles, 1991.

González-Ripoll Navarro, María Dolores. "Voces de gobierno: Los bandos del capitán-general Luis de las Casas, 1790–1796." In *Cuba: la perla de las Antillas: Actas de las I Jornadas sobre "Cuba y su Historia,"* ed. Consuelo Naranjo Orovio y Tomás Mallo González, 149–62. Madrid: Ediciones Doce Calles, S.I., 1994.

Greene, Jack P. *Pursuits of Happiness: The Social Development of Early Modern British Colonies and the Formation of American Culture.* Chapel Hill: University of North Carolina Press, 1988.

Guanche Perez, Jesús, Renate Fernández Artigas, and Gertrudis Mitjans. "Los libros bautismales de blancos o de españoles del archivo parroquial del Santo Cristo del Buen Viaje en la Habana vieja (1702–1898)." In *Memorias del 5to Simposio de la cultura,* Ciudad de la Habana, 74–102. Havana: Dirección Provincial de Cultura, 1987.

Guerra y Sánchez, Ramiro. *Azúcar y población en las Antillas.* Havana: 1944; reprint ed., Havana: Editorial de Ciencias Sociales del Instituto Cubano del Libro, 1970.

———. *Manual de historia de Cuba: (Económica, social y política).* 2d ed. Havana: Consejo Nacional de Cultura, 1962.

Gutiérrez, Ramón. *When Jesus Came the Corn Mother Went Away: Marriage, Sexuality, and Power in New Mexico, 1500–1846.* Albuquerque: University of New Mexico Press, 1991.

Haarman, Albert W. "The Siege of Pensacola: An Order of Battle." *Florida Historical Quarterly* 44 (January 1966): 193–99.

———. "The Spanish Conquest of British West Florida, 1779–1781." *Florida Historical Quarterly* 39 (October 1960): 107–34.

Hahn, John H. *Mission to the Calusa.* Gainesville: University of Florida Press, 1991.

Haring, Clarence. *The Buccaneers in the West Indies in the Seventeenth Century.* New York: E. P. Dutton, 1910.

———. *The Spanish Empire in America.* Reprint ed., New York: Harcourt Brace, 1963.

Hart, Francis Russell. *The Siege of Havana, 1762.* Boston: Houghton Mifflin, 1931.

Henige, David. "On the Contact Population of Hispaniola: History as Higher Mathematics." *Hispanic American Historical Review* 58 (May 1978): 217–37.

Historical Records Survey. *Spanish Land Grants in Florida: Briefed Translations.* 5 vols. Tallahassee: State Library Board, 1940–41.

Hoffman, Paul E. *The Spanish Crown and the Defense of the Caribbean, 1535–1568: Precedent, Patrimonialism, and Royal Parsimony.* Baton Rouge: Louisiana State University Press, 1980.

Holmes, Jack D. L. *Do It! Don't Do It!: Spanish Laws on Sex and Marriage.* Pensacola: Periwinkle Press, 1982.

———. "Juan de la Villebeuvre and Spanish Indian Policy in West Florida, 1784–1797." *Florida Historical Quarterly* 58 (April 1980): 387–99.

Humboldt, Alexander Von. *Ensayo político sobre la Isla de Cuba.* Nota preliminar por José Quintero Rodríguez y introducción por Fernando Ortiz. Reprint ed., Havana: Archivo Nacional de Cuba, 1960.

Hussey, Roland D. *The Caracas Company, 1728–1784.* Cambridge, England: Cambridge University Press, 1934.

Ibarra, Jorge. *Ideología mambisa.* Havana: Instituto Cubano del Libro, 1972.

Iglesias García, Fé. "La estructura agrária en el occidente de Cuba 1700–1750." Manuscript in preparation; in possession of author.

Inglis, G. Douglas. "Constructing a Tower: The Marqués de la Torre Census of 1774." Manuscript in preparation; in possession of author.

———. "Historical Demography of Cuba, 1700–1763." Ph.D. diss., Texas Christian University, 1980.

———. "The Spanish Naval Shipyard at Havana in the Eighteenth Century." In *New Aspects of Naval History,* 47–58. Baltimore: U.S. Naval Printing Office, 1985.

Instituto de Estudios de Administración Local. *Planos de ciudades iberoamericanas y filipinas existentes en el Archivo de Indias.* Madrid: Consejo Superior de Investigaciones Científicos, 1981.

Jensen, Larry R. *Children of Colonial Despotism: Press, Politics, and Culture in Colonial Cuba, 1790–1840.* Tampa: University of South Florida Press, 1988.

Johnson, Sherry. "Casualties of Peace: Tracing the Historic Roots of the Cuban Diaspora, 1763–1800." *Colonial Latin American Historical Review,* forthcoming.

———. "Honor Is Life: Military Reform and the Transformation of Cuba, 1754–1796." Ph.D. diss., University of Florida, 1995.

———. "'La Guerra Contra los Habitantes de los Arrabales': Changing Patterns of Land Use and Land Tenancy in and around Havana, 1763–1800." *Hispanic American Historical Review* 77 (May 1997): 181–209.

———. "Marriage and Community Construction in St. Augustine, 1784–1804." In *Florida's Heritage of Diversity: Essays in Honor of Samuel Proctor,* ed. Mark D. Greenberg, William Warren Rogers, and Canter Brown Jr., 1–13. Tallahassee: Sentry Press, 1997.

———. "The Rise and Fall of Creole Participation in the Cuban Slave Trade, 1789–1796." *Cuban Studies/Estudios Cubanos* 30 (2000): 54–75.

———. "The Spanish St. Augustine Community, 1784–1795: A Reevaluation." *Florida Historical Quarterly* 68 (July 1989): 27–54.

Karras, Bill J. "La isla de Cuba en el siglo XIX vista por los extranjeros: La Habana en 1814–15 según Sir Jonh [sic] Maxwell Tylden." Trans. Celso Morán. *Revista de la Biblioteca Nacional José Martí* 13 (May-August 1972): 81–94.

Kinsbruner, Jay. "Caste and Capitalism in the Caribbean: Residential Patterns and House Ownership among the Free People of Color of San Juan, 1830–46." *Hispanic American Historical Review* 70 (August 1990): 433–52.

Kiple, Kenneth. *Blacks in Colonial Cuba, 1774–1889.* Gainesville: University Presses of Florida, 1976.

Klein, Herbert S. *African Slavery in Latin America and the Caribbean.* Oxford: Oxford University Press, 1986.

―――. "The Colored Militia of Cuba, 1568–1868." *Caribbean Studies* 6 (July 1966): 17–27.

―――. *Slavery in the Americas: A Comparative Study of Virginia and Cuba.* Chicago: University of Chicago Press, 1967; reprint ed., Chicago: Ivan R. Dee, 1989.

Knight, Franklin W. "Origins of Wealth and the Sugar Revolution in Cuba, 1750–1850." *Hispanic American Historical Review* 57 (May 1977): 231–53.

―――. *Slave Society in Cuba during the Nineteenth Century.* Madison: University of Wisconsin Press, 1970.

―――. *Slavery and the Transformation of Society in Cuba, 1511–1760: From Settler Society to Slave Society.* Mona, Jamaica: University of the West Indies, 1988.

Knight, Franklin W., and Peggy K. Liss, eds. *Atlantic Port Cities: Economy, Culture, and Society in the Atlantic World, 1650–1850.* Knoxville: University of Tennessee Press, 1991.

Konetzke, Richard. "La prohibición de casarse los oidores o sus hijos é hijas con naturales del distrito de la Audiencia." In *Homenaje a Don José María de la Peña y Cámara,* 105–20. Madrid: Ediciones J. Porrua Turanzas, 1969.

―――, ed. *Colección de documentos para la historia de la formación social de Hispanoamérica, 1493–1810.* 3 vols. Madrid: Consejo Superior de Investigaciones Científicos, 1953–62.

Kuethe, Allan J. *Cuba, 1753–1815: Crown, Military, and Society.* Knoxville: University of Tennessee Press, 1986.

―――. "The Development of the Cuban Military as a Sociopolitical Elite, 1763–83." *Hispanic American Historical Review* 61 (November 1981): 695–704.

―――. "Guns, Subsidies, and Commercial Privilege: Some Historical Factors in the Emergence of the Cuban National Character, 1763–1815." *Cuban Studies/Estudios Cubanos* 16 (1985): 123–38.

―――. "Havana in the Eighteenth Century." In *Atlantic Port Cities: Economy, Culture, and Society in the Atlantic World, 1650–1850,* ed. Franklin W. Knight and Peggy K. Liss, 13–39. Knoxville: University of Tennessee Press, 1991.

―――. "Los Llorones Cubanos: The Socio-Military Basis of Commercial Privilege in the American Trade under Charles IV." In *The North American Role in the Spanish Imperial Economy, 1764–1819,* ed. Jacques A. Barbier and Allan J. Kuethe, 134–55. Manchester, England: Manchester University Press, 1984.

―――. *Military Reform and Society in New Granada, 1773–1808.* Gainesville: University of Florida Press, 1978.

Kuethe, Allan J., and G. Douglas Inglis. "Absolutism and Enlightened Reform: Charles III, the Establishment of the *Alcabala,* and Commercial Reorganization in Cuba." *Past and Present* 109 (November 1985): 118–43.

Kutzinski, Vera. *Sugar's Secrets: Race and the Erotics of Cuban Nationalism.* Charlottesville: University Press of Virginia, 1993.

Kuznesof, Elizabeth Anne. "The Construction of Gender in Colonial Latin America." *Colonial Latin American Research Review* 1 (1992): 253–70.

Lampros, Peter J. "Merchant-Planter Cooperation and Conflict: The Havana Consulado, 1794–1832." Ph.D. diss., Tulane University, 1980.

Landers, Jane G. *African American Life in Spanish Florida*. Urbana: University of Illinois Press, 1999.

———. "An Eighteenth-Century Community in Exile: The Floridanos in Cuba." Paper presented at the Conference on Latin American History, Washington, D.C., December 28, 1992.

———. "Rebellion and Royalism in Spanish Florida: The French Revolution on Spain's Northern Frontier." In *A Turbulent Time: The French Revolution and the Greater Caribbean*, ed. David Barry Gaspar and David Patrick Geggus, 156–77. Bloomington: Indiana University Press, 1997.

———. "Spanish Sanctuary: Fugitives in Florida." *Florida Historical Quarterly* 42 (January 1984): 296–312.

Laura, Miseno de [Pablo Estévez]. *Parte tercera de las revoluciones periódicas de la Havana escribíala Miseno de Laura*. Havana: Imprenta de la Capitanía General, 1796. Copy in Latin American Pamphlets, Rare Book Room, Library of Congress, Washington, D.C.

Lavrin, Asunción. "In Search of the Colonial Woman in Mexico: The Seventeenth and Eighteenth Centuries." In *Latin American Women: Historical Perspectives*, ed. Asunción Lavrin, 23–61. Westport, Conn.: Greenwood Press, 1978.

———. "Women in Spanish American Colonial Society." In *The Cambridge History of Latin America*, vol. 2. *Colonial Latin America*, ed. Leslie Bethell, 321–55. Cambridge, England: Cambridge University Press, 1984.

———, ed. *Sexuality and Marriage in Colonial Latin America*. Lincoln: University of Nebraska Press, 1989.

Lavrin, Asunción, and Edith Couturier. "Dowries and Wills: A View of Women's Socioeconomic Role in Colonial Guadalajara and Puebla, 1640–1790." *Hispanic American Historical Review* 59 (February 1979): 280–304.

Lebróc, Reynerio. *Cuba, iglesia y sociedad, 1830–1860*. Madrid: n.p., 1976.

Levine, Daniel H. "Constructing Culture and Power," in *Constructing Culture and Power in Latin America*, ed. Daniel H. Levine. 1–25. Ann Arbor: University of Michigan Press, 1993.

Lewis, James A. "Anglo American Entrepreneurs in Havana: The Background and Significance of the Expulsion of 1784–1785." In *The North American Role in the Spanish Imperial Economy, 1764–1819*, ed. Jacques A. Barbier and Allan J. Kuethe, 112–126. Manchester, England: Manchester University Press, 1984.

———. "Nueva España y los esfuerzos para abastecer la Habana, 1779–1783." *Anuario de estudios americanos* 33 (1977): 501–26.

Liss, Peggy K. *Atlantic Empires: The Network of Trade and Revolution, 1713–1826*. Baltimore: Johns Hopkins University Press, 1983.

Lockey, Joseph Byrne. *East Florida, 1783–1785: A File of Documents Assembled, and*

Many of Them Translated. Ed. with a foreword by John Walton Caughey. Berkeley: University of California Press, 1949.

———. "The St. Augustine Census of 1786, Translated from the Spanish with an Introduction and Notes." *Florida Historical Quarterly* 18 (July 1939): 11–31.

Lockhart, James, and Enrique Otte. *Letters and People of the Spanish Indies.* New York: Cambridge University Press, 1976.

Lockhart, James, and Stuart B. Schwartz. *Early Latin America: A History of Colonial Spanish America and Brazil.* Cambridge, England: Cambridge University Press, 1983.

Lombardi, John V. *People and Places in Colonial Venezuela.* Bloomington: Indiana University Press, 1976.

López-Valdés, Rafael. "Hacía una periodización de la historia de la esclavitud en Cuba." In *La esclavitud en Cuba,* 13–29. Havana: Editorial Académica, 1986.

Lynch, John. *Bourbon Spain, 1700–1808.* Oxford: Basil Blackwell, 1989.

———. *The Spanish American Revolutions.* New York: Norton, 1973.

———. *Spanish Colonial Administration, 1782–1810: The Intendant System in the Viceroyalty of Río de la Plata.* New York: Norton, 1959.

Lyon, Eugene. *The Enterprise of Florida: Pedro Menéndez de Avilés and the Spanish Conquest of 1565–1568.* Gainesville: University of Florida Press, 1976.

Marchena Fernández, Juan. *Oficiales y soldados en el ejército de América.* Seville: Escuela de Estudios Hispanoamericanos, 1983.

———. "St. Augustine's Military Society." Translated by Luis Rafael Arana. *El Escribano, The St. Augustine Journal of History* 14 (1985): 43–71.

Marichal, Carlos, and Matilde Souto Mantecon. "Silver and Situados: New Spain and the Financing of the Spanish Empire in the Caribbean in the Eighteenth Century." *Hispanic American Historical Review* 74 (November 1994): 587–603.

Marrero y Artiles, Levi. *Cuba: Economía y sociedad.* 14 vols. Madrid: Playor S.A., 1972–88.

Martínez-Alier, Verena. *Marriage, Class, and Colour in Nineteenth-Century Cuba: Attitudes and Sexual Values in a Slave Society.* Cambridge, England: Cambridge University Press, 1974; reprint ed., Ann Arbor: University of Michigan Press, 1992.

McAlister, Lyle N. *The "Fuero Militar" in New Spain, 1764–1800.* Gainesville: University of Florida Press, 1957.

———. "Social Structure and Social Change in New Spain." *Hispanic American Historical Review* 43 (August 1966): 349–70.

McCaa, Robert. "*Calidad, Clase,* and Marriage in Colonial Mexico: The Case of Parral." *Hispanic American Historical Review* 64 (August 1984): 477–501.

McCadden, Joseph, and Helen M. McCadden. *Félix Varela: Torch Bearer from Cuba.* 2nd. ed. San Juan: Ramallo Bros. for the Félix Varela Foundation, 1984.

McNeill, John Robert. *Atlantic Empires of France and Spain: Louisbourg and Havana, 1700–1763.* Chapel Hill: University of North Carolina Press, 1985.

Medina Rojas, Francisco de Borja. *José de Ezpeleta: Gobernador de Mobila.* Seville: Escuela de Estudios Hispanoamericanos, 1980.

Méndez Rodenas, Adriana. *Gender and Nationalism in Colonial Cuba: The Travels of Santa Cruz y Montalvo, Condesa de Merlin.* Nashville: Vanderbilt University Press, 1998.

Mestre, Raul. *Arango y Parreño: El estadista sin estado.* Havana: Secretaría de Educacción, Dirección de Cultura, 1937.

Misas Jiménez, Rolando E. "La Real Sociedad Patriótica de la Habana y las Investigaciones Científicas Aplicadas a la Agricultura (Esfuerzos de Institucionalización: 1793–1864)." In *Cuba: la perla de las Antillas: Actas de las I Jornadas sobre "Cuba y su Historia,"* ed. Consuelo Naranjo Orovio y Tomás Mallo González, 74–89. Madrid: Editorial Doce Calles, S.I., 1994.

Morales Alvárez, Juan M. *Los extranjeros con carta de naturaleza de las indias, durante la segunda mitad del siglo XVIII.* Caracas: Biblioteca da la Academia Nacional de la Historia, 1980.

Morales Padrón, Francisco, ed. *The Journal of Don Francisco Saavedra de Sangronis, 1780–1783.* Trans. Aileen Moore Topping. Gainesville: University of Florida Press, 1989.

Morales y Morales, Vidal. *Iniciadores y primeros mártires de la revolución cubana.* 2 vols. Havana: Consejo Nacional de Cultura, 1963.

Morell de Santa Cruz, Agustín. "Padrón ecclesiástico de 1754–55." In "La configuración del espacio colonial en Cuba (Estudio del sistema urbano en los siglos XVII y XVIII)," by Carmen Gavira. *Revista de la Biblioteca Nacional José Martí* 24 (January-August 1982): 63–95.

Moreno Fraginals, Manuel. *El ingenio: complejo económico social cubano del azúcar.* 3 vols. 2nd ed. Havana: Instituto Cubano del Libro, 1978.

———. "Sugar in the Twentieth Century in Cuba." Paper presented in the Center for Latin American Studies, University of Florida, Gainesville, Fla., August 26, 1994.

Moreno Fraginals, Manuel, and José Moreno Masó. *Guerra, migración, y muerte: El ejército español como vía migratoria.* Barcelona: Ediciones Jucar, 1993.

Mörner, Magnus. *Race Mixture in the History of Latin America.* Boston: Little, Brown, 1967.

Mowat, Charles Loch. *East Florida as a British Province.* Berkeley: University of California Press, 1943; reprint ed., Gainesville: University of Florida Press, 1964.

Murphy, W. S. "The Irish Brigade of Spain at the Capture of Pensacola, 1781." *Florida Historical Quarterly* 38 (January 1960): 216–25.

Murray, David R. *Odious Commerce: Britain, Spain, and the Abolition of the Cuban Slave Trade.* Cambridge, England: Cambridge University Press, 1980.

Nazarri, Muriel. *The Disappearance of the Dowry: Women, Family, and Change in São Paulo, Brazil, 1600–1900*. Stanford: Stanford University Press, 1991.

Nelson, George H. "Contraband Trade under the Asiento." *American Historical Review* 51 (1956): 55–67.

Nichols, Roy F. "Trade Relations and the Establishment of the United States Consulates in Spanish America." *Hispanic American Historical Review* 13 (August 1933): 289–313.

Nieto y Cortadellas, Rafael. *Dignidades nobilarias en Cuba*. Madrid: Ediciones Cultura Hispanica, 1954.

Ocerín, Enrique, de. *Indice de los expedientes matrimoniales de militares y marinos que se conservan en el archivo militar (de Segovia) (1761–1865)*. 2 vols. Madrid: Consejo Superior de Investigaciones Científicas, 1959.

Oglesby, J. C. M. "Spain's Havana Squadron and the Balance of Power in the Caribbean, 1740–1748," *Hispanic American Historical Review* 49 (August 1969): 473–88.

Ortega Pereyra, Ovidio. *La construcción naval en la Habana bajo la dominación colonial española*. Havana: Academia de Ciencias de Cuba, 1986.

Ortiz, Fernando. *Los negros esclavos*. Havana: Editorial de Ciencias Sociales, 1975.

Pagden, Anthony. *Lords of All the World: Ideologies of Empire of Spain, Britain, and France, 1500–c. 1800*. New Haven: Yale University Press, 1995.

Paquette, Robert L. *Sugar Is Made with Blood: The Conspiracy of La Escalera and the Conflict between Empires over Slavery in Cuba*. Middletown, Conn.: Wesleyan University Press, 1988.

Parcero Torre, Celia María. *La pérdida de La Habana y las reformas Borbónicas en Cuba, 1760–1773*. Madrid: Consejo de Castilla y León, 1998.

Parry, J. H. *The Spanish Seaborne Empire*. New York: Alfred Knopf, 1966.

Patterson, John. "Military Organization and Social Change in the Later Roman Republic." In *War and Society in the Roman World*, ed. John Rich and Graham Shipley. London: Routledge, 1993.

Pérez, Lisandro. "Iron Mining and Socio-Demographic Change in Eastern Cuba, 1884–1940." *Journal of Latin American Studies* 14 (November 1982): 379–98.

Pérez Beato, Manuel. *Habana antigua: apuntes históricos*. 2 vols. Havana: Seoane, Fernandez, y Compañía, Impresores, 1936.

Pérez de la Riva, Juan. "Presentación de un censo ignorado: El padrón general de 1778." *Revista de la Biblioteca Nacional José Martí* 29 (September-December 1987): 1–16.

Pérez-Stable, Marifeli. *The Cuban Revolution: Origins, Course, and Legacy*. Oxford: Oxford University Press, 1993.

Pezuela, Jacobo de la. *Diccionario geográfico estadístico, histórico de la isla de Cuba*. 4 vols. Madrid: Imprenta del Establecimiento de Mellado, 1863–66.

———. *Historia de la isla de Cuba*. 4 vols. Madrid: Carlos Bailly-Bailliere, 1878.

Phelan, John Leddy. *The People and the King: The Comunero Revolution in Colombia, 1781.* Madison: University of Wisconsin Press, 1978.

Pierson, Jr., William Whatley. "Francisco de Arango y Parreño." *Hispanic American Historical Review* 16 (November 1936): 451–78.

Piño-Santos, Oscar. *Historia de Cuba: Aspectos fundamentales.* Havana: Consejo Nacional de Universidades, 1964.

Ponte Domínguez, Francisco J. *La junta de la Habana en 1808 (Antecedentes para la historia de la autonomía colonial en Cuba).* Havana: Editorial Guerrero, 1947.

Priestly, Herbert Ingram. *José de Gálvez, Visitor General of New Spain, 1765–1771.* Berkeley: University of California Press, 1916.

Raynal, Abbé. *A Philosophical and Political History of the Settlements and Trade of the Europeans in the East and West Indies.* 3d ed. Translated from the French by J. Justamond. London: n.p., 1777.

Real Cédula de S. M. en que se erigen por ahora las provincias de la Luysiana, Panzacola, y Movila, y demás que poseían los Yngleses con el nombre de Florida Occidental, en Govierno, y Capitanía General independiente. . . . Santa Fé de Bogotá: Don Antonio Espinosa de los Monteros, 1782. Copy in Latin American Pamphlets, Rare Book Room, Library of Congress, Washington, D.C.

Reparáz, Carmen de. *Yo Solo: Bernardo de Gálvez y la toma de Panzacola en 1781.* Madrid: Serba, 1986.

Ribera, Nicolás José de. *Descripción de la Isla de Cuba y algunas consideraciones sobre su población y comercios.* Havana, 1767; reprint ed., Havana: Ministerio del Cultura de Cuba, 1973.

Ringrose, David. *Spain, Europe, and the "Spanish miracle," 1700–1900.* Cambridge, England: Cambridge University Press, 1996.

Ripodas Ardanáz, Daisy. *El matrimonio en Indias: Realidad judicial y regulación social.* Buenos Aires: Conicet, 1977.

Riverend Brusone, Julio le. *Historia económica de Cuba.* Havana: Ministerio de Educación, 1974.

Rivero Muñíz, José. *Tabaco: su historia en Cuba.* 2 vols. Havana: Instituto de Historia, Academia de Ciencias de la República de Cuba, 1964–65.

Robinson, David J. "Migration in Eighteenth-Century Mexico: Case Studies from Michoacán." *Journal of Historical Geography* 15 (January 1989): 55–68.

Robinson, David J., ed. *Social Fabric and Spatial Structure in Colonial Latin America.* Ann Arbor: University of Michigan Press, 1979.

Rodríguez, Amalia A., ed. *Cinco diarios del sitio de la Habana.* Havana: Archivo Nacional de Cuba, 1963.

Rodríguez Casado, Vicente. "El ejército y la marina en el reinado de Carlos III." *Boletín del Instituto Riva Agüero* [Lima] 3 (1959): 129–56.

———. *La política marroquí de Carlos III.* Madrid: Consejo Superior de Investigaciones Científicas, 1945.

————. *La política y los politicos del reinado de Carlos III.* Madrid: Ediciones Rialp, S.A., 1962.

Rojas-Míx, Miguel. *La plaza mayor: El urbanismo, instrumento del dominio colonial.* Barcelona: Muchnik Editores, 1978.

Rojas y Rocha, Francisco de. *Poema épico de la rendición de Panzacola y conquista de la Florida Oriental por el Excmo Señor Conde de Gálvez.* Mexico City: Oficina de D. Mariano de Zúñiga y Ontiveros, 1785. Copy in Latin American Pamphlets, Rare Book Room, Library of Congress, Washington, D.C.

Rosa Corzo, Gabino de la. *Los cimarrones de Cuba.* Havana: Ediciones de Ciencias Sociales, 1988.

————. "Los palenques en Cuba: Elementos para su reconstrucción histórica." *La esclavitud en Cuba,* 85–99. Havana: Academía de Ciencias de Cuba, 1986.

Rutman, Darrett B. "Assessing the Little Communities of North America." *William and Mary Quarterly* (3rd. ser.) 43 (April 1986): 163–78.

Rutman, Darrett B., and Anita H. Rutman. *A Place in Time: Middlesex County Virginia, 1650–1750.* New York: W. W. Norton, 1984.

Saavedra, Francisco de. *Los Decenios: Autobiografía de un Sevillano de la Ilustración.* Transcripción, introducción y notas por Francisco Morales Padrón. Seville: Ayuntamiento de Sevilla, 1995.

Sagra, Ramón de la. *Historia económico-política y estadística de la isla de Cuba.* Havana: Imprenta de las Viudas de Arazoza y Soler, 1841.

Salvucci, Linda K. "Anglo American Merchants and Strategems for Success in Spanish Imperial Markets, 1783–1807." In *The North American Role in the Spanish Imperial Economy, 1764–1819,* ed. Jacques A. Barbier and Allan J. Kuethe, 127–33. Manchester, England: Manchester University Press, 1984.

————. "Supply, Demand, and the Making of a Market: Philadelphia and Havana at the Beginning of the Nineteenth Century." In *Atlantic Port Cities: Economy, Culture, and Society in the Atlantic World, 1650–1850,* ed. Franklin W. Knight and Peggy Liss, 40–57. Knoxville: University of Tennessee Press, 1991.

Sánchez Agusti, María. *Edificios públicos de la Habana en el siglo XVIII.* Valladolid, Spain: University of Valladolid, 1984.

Sánchez-Albornóz, Nicolás. *The Population of Latin America.* Berkeley: University of California Press, 1974.

Sánchez Ramírez, Antonio. "Notas sobre la Real Hacienda de Cuba." *Anuario de estudios americanos* 34 (1977): 465–83.

Santa Cruz y Mallén, Francisco Xavier de. *Historia de Familias Cubanas.* 9 vols. Havana: Editorial Hércules, 1940–50, 1986–89.

Scott, James C. *Weapons of the Weak: Everyday Forms of Peasant Resistance.* New Haven: Yale University Press, 1985.

Seed, Patricia. "The Social Dimensions of Race: Mexico City, 1753." *Hispanic American Historical Review* 62 (November 1982): 569–606.

————. *To Love, Honor, and Obey in Colonial Mexico: Conflicts over Marriage Choice, 1574–1821.* Stanford: Stanford University Press, 1988.

Sevilla Soler, María Rosario. *Santo Domingo: Tierra de la frontera (1750–1800).* Seville: Escuela de Estudios Hispano-Americanos, 1980.

Siebert, Wilbur H. "The Departure of the Spaniards and Other Groups from East Florida." *Florida Historical Quarterly* 19 (October 1940): 145–54.

———."How the Spaniards Evacuated Pensacola in 1763." *Florida Historical Quarterly* 11 (October 1932): 11–29.

Socolow, Susan M. "Acceptable Partners: Marriage Choice in Colonial Argentina, 1778–1810." In *Sexuality and Marriage in Colonial Latin America,* ed. Asunción Lavrin, 210–51. Lincoln: University of Nebraska Press, 1989.

———. *The Bureaucrats of Buenos Aires, 1769–1810: Amor al Real Servicio.* Durham: Duke University Press, 1987.

Stern, Steve J. "Even More Solitary." *American Historical Review* 93 (October 1988): 996–1007.

———. "Feudalism, Capitalism, and the World-System in the Perspective of Latin America and the Caribbean." *American Historical Review* 93 (October 1988): 929–73.

———. "New Approaches to the Study of Peasant Rebellion and Consciousness: Implications of the Andean Experience." In *Resistance, Rebellion, and Consciousness in the Andean Peasant World, 18th to 20th Centuries,* ed. Steve J. Stern, 3–25. Madison: University of Wisconsin Press, 1987.

———, ed. *Resistance, Rebellion, and Consciousness in the Andean Peasant World, Eighteenth to Twentieth Centuries.* Madison: University of Wisconsin Press, 1987.

Stoner, K. Lynn. "Directions in Latin American Women's History, 1977–1985." *Latin American Research Review* 22 (January 1987): 101–34.

Syrett, David, ed. *The Siege and Capture of Havana, 1762.* London: Navy Records Society, 1970.

Szeminski, Jan. "Why Kill the Spaniard? New Perspectives on Andean Insurrectionary Ideology in the Eighteenth Century." In *Resistance, Rebellion, and Consciousness in the Andean Peasant World, 18th to 20th Centuries,* ed. Steve J. Stern, 166–92. Madison: University of Wisconsin Press, 1987.

Szuchman, Mark D. "A Challenge to the Patriarchs: Love Among the Youth in Nineteenth-Century Argentina." In *The Middle Period in Latin America: Values and Attitudes in the 17th to 19th Centuries,* ed. Mark D. Szuchman, 141–64. Boulder, Colo.: Lynne Rienner, 1989.

TePaske, John Jay. "La política española en el Caribe durante los siglos XVII y XVIII." In *La influencia de España en el Caribe, la Florída, y la Luisiana, 1500–1800,* ed. Antonio Acosta and Juan Marchena Fernández, 61–87. Madrid: Instituto de Cooperación Iberoamericana, 1983.

———. *The Governorship of Spanish Florida, 1700–1763.* Durham: Duke University Press, 1963.

Thomas, Hugh. *Cuba: Or, the Pursuit of Freedom.* New York: Harper and Row, 1971.

Tornero Tinajero, Pablo. "Comercio colonial y proyección de la población: la emigración catalana a Cuba en la epoca del crecimiento azucarera, 1790–1817." *Boletín Americanista* 31 (1989–90): 235–64.

———. *Crecimiento económico y transformaciones sociales: esclavos, hacendados y comerciantes en la Cuba colonial, 1760–1840.* Madrid: Ministerio de Trabajo y Seguridad Social, 1996.

———. "Emigración, población, y esclavitud en Cuba, 1765–1817." *Anuario de estudios americanos* 44 (1986): 229–80.

———. *Relaciones de dependencia entre Florida y Estados Unidos, 1783–1820.* Madrid: Ministerio de Asuntos Exteriores, 1979.

———. "Sociedad y Población en San Agustín de la Florida." *Anuario de estudios americanos* 35 (1981): 233–63.

Torre, José María de la. *Lo que fuimos y lo que somos, o la Habana antigua y moderna.* Havana: 1857; facsimile ed., Santo Domingo, D.R.: Ediciones Históricos Cubanos, 1986.

Torres Cuevas, Eduardo. *Félix Varela: los origines de la ciencia y con-ciencia cubanas.* Havana: Editorial de Ciencias Sociales, 1995.

Torres Ramírez, Bibiano. "Alejandro O'Reilly en Cuba." *Anuario de estudios americanos* 24 (1967): 1357–88.

———. *Alejandro O'Reilly en las Indias.* Seville: Escuela de Estudios Americanos, 1969.

———. *La armada de barlovento.* Seville: Escuela de Estudios Americanos, 1981.

Twinam, Ann. "Honor, Sexuality, and Illegitimacy in Colonial Spanish America." In *Sexuality and Marriage in Colonial Latin America*, ed. Asunción Lavrin, 118–55. Lincoln: University of Nebraska Press, 1989.

———. *Public Lives, Private Secrets: Gender, Honor, Sexuality, and Illegitimacy in Colonial Spanish America.* Stanford: Stanford University Press, 1999.

Ulrich, Laurel Thatcher. *Good Wives: Image and Reality in the Lives of Women in Northern New England, 1650–1750.* New York: Oxford University Press, 1982.

Valdés, Antonio José. *Historia de la isla de Cuba y en especial de la Habana.* Havana: Oficina de la Cena, 1813; facsimile ed., Havana: Comisión Nacional Cubana de UNESCO, 1964.

Varela y Morales, Félix. *El habanero: Papel político, científico y literario.* With an introduction by José M. Hernández. Miami: Ediciones Universal, 1997.

Venegas Fornaris, Carlos. *Dos etapas de colonización expansión urbana.* Havana: Editora Política, 1979.

Villaverde, Cirilo. *Cecilia Valdés, o la loma del Angel (novela de costumbres cubanas).* Havana: Biblioteca Básica de Cultura, 1977.

Walker, Geoffrey J. *Spanish Politics and Imperial Trade, 1700–1789.* Bloomington: Indiana University Press, 1979.

Wallerstein, Immanuel. "Comments on Stern's 'Critical Tests.'" *American Historical Review* 93 (October 1988): 973–96.

————. *The Modern World System II: Mercantilism and the Consolidation of the European World Economy.* New York: Academic Press, 1980.

Weddle, Robert S. *Changing Tides: Twilight and Dawn in the Spanish Sea, 1763–1803.* College Station: Texas A&M University Press, 1995.

Woodward, Ralph Lee, Jr., ed. and trans. *Tribute to Don Bernardo de Gálvez.* Baton Rouge: Historic New Orleans Collection, 1979.

Wright, Irene A. *Cuba.* New York: Macmillan, 1905.

————. *The Early History of Cuba, 1492–1586.* New York: Macmillan, 1916.

Zaragosa, Justo. *Las insurrecciones en Cuba. Apuntes para la historia política de esta isla en el presente siglo.* 2 vols. Madrid: Carlos Bailly-Bailliere, 1872.

Index

Sherry Johnson is associate professor of Latin American history and Cuban studies at Florida International University in Miami. She is author of articles on Cuban history and is book review co-editor of *Cuban Studies/ Estudios Cubanos.*